T0210825

Lecture Notes in Computer Science 12157

More information about this series at http://www.springer.com/series/7409

Mohamed Jmaiel · Mounir Mokhtari ·
Bessam Abdulrazak · Hamdi Aloulou ·
Slim Kallel (Eds.)

The Impact of Digital Technologies on Public Health in Developed and Developing Countries

18th International Conference, ICOST 2020
Hammamet, Tunisia, June 24–26, 2020
Proceedings

 Springer

Editors
Mohamed Jmaiel
Digital Research Centre of Sfax
Sfax, Tunisia

Mounir Mokhtari
Institut Mines-Télécom, CNRS
Paris, France

Bessam Abdulrazak
Université de Sherbrooke
Sherbrooke, QC, Canada

Hamdi Aloulou
Digital Research Centre of Sfax
Sfax, Tunisia

Slim Kallel
University of Sfax
Sfax, Tunisia

ISSN 0302-9743   ISSN 1611-3349   (electronic)
Lecture Notes in Computer Science
ISBN 978-3-030-51516-4   ISBN 978-3-030-51517-1   (eBook)
https://doi.org/10.1007/978-3-030-51517-1

LNCS Sublibrary: SL3 – Information Systems and Applications, incl. Internet/Web, and HCI

This Springer imprint is published by the registered company Springer Nature Switzerland AG
The registered company address is: Gewerbestrasse 11, 6330 Cham, Switzerland

Preface

This year we organized the 18th ICOST conference, an event which has succeeded in bringing together a community from different continents for over a decade and a half and raised awareness about the frail and dependent people's quality of life in our societies.

After 17 very successful conferences held in France (2003, 2009, 2017), Singapore (2004, 2013, 2018), Canada (2005, 2011), Northern Ireland (2006), Japan (2007), the USA (2008, 2014, 2019), South Korea (2010), Italy (2012), Switzerland (2015), and China (2016), we decided to open the conference for the African continent and tackle the digital technologies impact on public health in developed and developing countries. This 18th edition of the International Conference on Smart Living and Public Health (ICOST 2020), was organized by the Digital Research Center (CRNS), Sfax, Tunisia, and the Institut Mines-Télécom (IMT), Paris, France, during June 24–26, 2020. The conference was intended to be hosted in Hammamet, Tunisia, but was finally hosted virtually given the COVID-19 situation faced this year. The theme of the conference was "The Digital Technologies Impact on Public Health in Developed and Developing Countries."

ICOST 2020 provided a premier venue for the presentation and discussion of research in the design, development, deployment, and evaluation of AI for health, smart urban environments, assistive technologies, chronic disease management, and coaching and health telematics systems. ICOST 2020 aimed to understand and assess the diverse and disparate impact of digital technologies on public health in developing and developed countries. ICOST 2020 brought together stakeholders from health care, public health, academia, and industry along with end users and family caregivers to explore how to utilize technologies to foster health prevention, independent living, and offer an enhanced quality of life. The ICOST 2020 conference featured a dynamic program incorporating a range of oral and poster presentations, along with panel sessions.

ICOST 2020 was proud to extend its hospitality to an international community consisting of researchers from major universities and research centers, representatives from industry, and users from 17 different countries. We would like to thank the authors for submitting their current research work and the Program Committee members for their commitment to reviewing submitted papers. The ICOST proceedings have now reached over 150,000 downloads and are in the top 25% of downloads of Springer LNCS. We are extremely thankful to our sponsors for their commitment and support to the vision and mission of ICOST.

June 2020

Mohamed Jmaiel
Mounir Mokhtari
Bessam Abdulrazak
Hamdi Aloulou
Slim Kallel

Organization

General Chair

Mohamed Jmaiel   Digital Research Center, Tunisia

Conference Co-chair

Mounir Mokhtari   Institut Mines-Télécom, France, and National
University of Singapore, Singapore

Steering Committee

Mounir Mokhtari   Institut Mines-Télécom, France, and Image
& Pervasive Access Lab, Singapore
Sumi Helal   Lancaster University, UK
Bessam Abdulrazak   AmI Lab, University of Sherbrooke, Canada
Hamdi Aloulou   University of Monastir, Digital Research Center,
Tunisia, and Institut Mines-Télécom, France
Mohamed Jmaiel   Digital Research Center, Tunisia
Jose Pagan   New York University, New York Academy
of Medicine, USA
Maria Fernanda Cabrera   University Politecnica de Madrid, Spain

Scientific Advisory Board

Daqing Zhang   Institut Mines-Télécom, Télécom SudParis, France
Hisato Kobayashi   Hosei University, Japan
Jongbae Kim   Yonsei University, South Korea
Christian Roux   Institut Mines-Télécom, France
Dong Jin Song   National University of Singapore, Singapore,
and Griffith University, Australia
Sungyoung Lee   Kyung Hee University, South Korea
Timo Jämsä   EAMBES, University of Oulu, Finland
Daby Sow   IBM Research AI, USA

Program Committee

Chairs

Bessam Abdulrazak	AmI Lab, University of Sherbrooke, Canada
Hamdi Aloulou	University of Monastir, Digital Research Center, Tunisia, and Institut Mines-Télécom, France

Members

Afef Mdhaffar	University of Sfax, Tunisia
Aitor Almeida	University of Deusto, Spain
Bassem Bouaziz	University of Sfax, Tunisia
Belkacem Chikhaoui	University of Quebec, Canada
Boussada Rihab	University of Manouba, Tunisia
Charles Gouin-Vallerand	University of Quebec, Canada
David Menga	EDF R&D, France
Diane Cook	Washington State University, USA
Eric Campo	CNRS, LAAS, France
Franco Mercalli	MultiMed Engineers SRLS, Italy
Fulvio Mastrogiovanni	University of Genoa, Italy
Hisato Kobayashi	Hosei University, Japan
Hongbo Ni	Northwestern Polytechnical University, China
Houssem Aloulou	University of Sfax, Tunisia
Ibrahim Sadek	Institut Mines-Télécom, Image and Pervasive Access Laboratory (IPAL), France
Iyad Abuhadrous	Palestine Technical College, Palestine
Jeffrey Soar	University of Southern Queensland, Australia
Laurent Billonnet	University of Limoges, France
Ludovic Saint-Bauzel	UPMC, France
Lyes Khoukhi	University of Technology of Troyes, France
Manfred Wojciechowski	University of Applied Sciences Dusseldorf, Germany
Meriem Zerkouk	University of Sciences and Technology of Oran, Algeria
Nadine Vigouroux	Institut de Recherche en Informatique de Toulouse, France
Neila Mezghani	University of Quebec, Canada
Salim Hima	ESME, France
Sergio Copelli	MultiMed Engineers SRLS, Italy
Sha Zhao	University of Hangzhou, China
Shafiq Rehman	University of Engineering and Technology, Pakistan
Silvia de Los Rios Perez	University of Madrid, Spain
Slim Kallel	University of Sfax, Tunisia
Sofia Ben Jebara	University of Carthage, COSIM Research Lab, Tunisia
Stefanos Kollias	University of Lincoln, UK
Timo Jamsa	Research Unit of Medical Imaging, Physics and Technology (MIPT), University of Oulu, Finland

Vladimir Urosevic	Belit, Serbia
Wael Sellami	University of Sfax, Tunisia
Yves Demazeau	CNRS, France
Zuraimi Sultan	Berkeley Education Alliance for Research in Singapore (BEARS), Singapore

Organizing Committee

Chair

Slim Kallel   University of Sfax, Tunisia

Members

Afef Mdhaffar	University of Sfax, Tunisia
Hamdi Aloulou	Digital Research Center, Tunisia, and Institut Mines-Télécom, France
Ismael Bouassida Rodriguez	University of Sfax, Tunisia
Wael Sellami	University of Sfax, Tunisia

Sponsors

Digital Research Center, Tunisia
Research Laboratory on Development and Control of Distributed Application, Tunisia
National Engineering School of Sfax, Tunisia
Association of Computer Science and Mathematics, Tunisia
Institut Mines-Télécom, France
University of Sherbrooke, Canada

Contents

Behavior and Activity Monitoring

Wellbeing Technology

Short Contributions: IoT and AI Solutions for E-Health

Short Contributions: Biomedical and Health Informatics

Short Contributions: Wellbeing Technology

IoT and AI Solutions for E-Health

Alzheimer's Disease Early Detection Using a Low Cost Three-Dimensional Densenet-121 Architecture

Braulio Solano-Rojas[✉], Ricardo Villalón-Fonseca[✉], and Gabriela Marín-Raventós[✉]

CITIC - ECCI, Universidad de Costa Rica, San José, Costa Rica
{braulio.solano,ricardo.villalon,gabriela.marin}@ucr.ac.cr

Abstract. The objective of this work is to detect Alzheimer's disease using Magnetic Resonance Imaging. For this, we use a three-dimensional densenet-121 architecture. With the use of only freely available tools, we obtain good results: a deep neural network showing metrics of 87% accuracy, 87% sensitivity (micro-average), 88% specificity (micro-average), and 92% AUROC (micro-average) for the task of classifying five different classes (disease stages). The use of tools available for free means that this work can be replicated in developing countries.

Keywords: Alzheimer · Deep learning · MRI · Computer-aided detection · Computer-aided diagnosis

1 Introduction

Alzheimer's Disease (AD) is the most common form of dementia among older adults [17]. It is a neurodegenerative disease without a cure. Its early detection is crucial because it allows those people who are going to be affected to prepare for future changes [17]. For example, some medications delay the disease. Also, their relatives can prepare and train for the care that will be necessary [17].

Early detection is not easy. One of the difficulties is the performance of people working at the clinic. People making a diagnosis are affected by several factors such as fatigue, stress, distractions, and inherent cognitive biases to specific conditions of the disease. When radiologists see a medical image, such as a magnetic resonance imaging (MRI), biased reasoning about the conditions of the disease will result in the loss of the opportunity to detect it. Graber et al. [7] found that about 74% of diagnostic errors are attributed to cognitive factors. Lee et al. [14] state that approximately 75% of all medical errors made were due to diagnostic errors by radiologists. A high workload, stress, fatigue, cognitive bias, and an inadequate system are part of the causal factors. Medical errors contrast with the fact that recently artificial intelligence, in particular, deep artificial

Supported by CITIC and ECCI, Universidad de Costa Rica.

M. Jmaiel et al. (Eds.): ICOST 2020, LNCS 12157, pp. 3–15, 2020.
https://doi.org/10.1007/978-3-030-51517-1_1

neural networks (DNNs) have shown superhuman abilities in the detection of diseases in medical computer vision, as in the work of Rajpurkar [18]. We can design DNNs to integrate them into computer-aided diagnosis protocols for the detection of many priority diseases. One of these possible diseases is AD.

Currently, there is a body of images of healthy patients and patients with AD that is available through the database Alzheimer Disease Neuroimaging Initiative (ADNI)[1]. ADNI launched in 2003 as a public and private initiative. The leadership belongs to the researcher Michael W. Weiner. The main objective of ADNI has been to test whether medical images, other biomarkers, and clinical and neuropsychological evaluation can be combined to measure the progress of AD. The early detection of AD employing software would allow us to strengthen and improve medical protocols by providing what we call Computer-Aided Diagnosis (CAD).

As we commented, DNNs have become increasingly important and useful in recent years. One kind of these type of neural network is Convolutional Neural Networks (CNN). CNNs are inspired by the biological visual cortex and are used in areas as diverse as smart surveillance and monitoring, health and medicine, sports and recreation, robotics, drones, and self-driving cars [12].

This work consists of measuring the accuracy of the detection of Alzheimer's disease of a three-dimensional CNN architecture, specifically a densenet-121, trained using the ADNI MRI images. We also have a low-cost economic objective. We aim to provide a technological artifact that has the potential of being used in the public health and wellbeing of citizens all over the world, in particular, for developing countries that have difficulties in accessing specialized hardware platforms for computation.

Before presenting the results of developing a low-cost densenet for Alzheimer's disease detection, we first provide in Sect. 2 some background definitions to support our work. In Sect. 3 we describe previous work with more detail. Then in the next section, we provide the methodology used to realize this work. We present in Sect. 5 the results of the design chose. Finally, we analyze those results with concluding remarks and future work in Sect. 6.

2   Background

We start with a short review of medical vocabulary used to provide a context for our research. First, we introduce different clinical stages of disease that we want to classify, and later, we describe two types of medical imaging used in the detection and diagnosis of AD.

2.1   Clinical Disease Stages

There are different stages before the clinical diagnosis of AD. These are cognitively normal, significant memory concern, and mild cognitive impairment.

---

[1] http://adni.loni.usc.edu.

Cognitive Normal (CN). CN patients are the control subjects in the ADNI study. They have healthy aging. They show no signs of depression, mild cognitive impairment, or dementia [1].

Significant Memory Concern (SMC). SMC is a self-report significant memory concern from the patient, quantified by using the Cognitive Change Index and the Clinical Dementia Rating (CDR) of zero. Subjective memory concerns are correlated with a higher likelihood of progression, thereby minimizing the stratification of risk among normal controls and addressing the gap between healthy elderly controls and mild cognitive impairment. However, SMC patients score within the normal range for cognition [1].

Mild Cognitive Impairment (MCI). MCI participants have reported a subjective memory concern either autonomously or via an informant or clinician. However, daily living activities are mainly preserved, there are no significant levels of impairment in other cognitive domains, and no signs of dementia exist. Levels of MCI (early or late) are determined using the Wechsler Memory Scale Logical Memory II [1].

Alzheimer's Disease. AD is the most common cause of dementia, a general term for memory loss and other cognitive abilities severe enough to interfere with daily life. It is a progressive disease, where dementia symptoms gradually worsen over several years. Individuals lose the ability to carry on a conversation and respond to their environment. Current medications cannot stop the disease from progressing, they can temporarily slow the worsening of dementia symptoms and improve quality of life for those with AD and their caregivers [17].

Since we aim to assess if those stages, including AD, are detected on medical imaging, particularly on Magnetic Resonance Imaging, we continue describing two medical imaging techniques.

2.2   Medical Imaging

Medical imaging is the process and technique of creating visual representations of the inner of a human body for clinical analysis and medical intervention. We introduce two types of medical imaging. We are especially interested in the input of Magnetic Resonance Imaging (MRI) on DNN. Moreover, we also mention Positron Emission Tomography (PET) because it is sometimes an input that accompanies MRI. We follow describing what MRI and PET are.

Magnetic Resonance Imaging. MRI is a non-invasive imaging technology that produces three-dimensional detailed anatomical images without the use of radiation that damages human tissues. It is often used for disease detection and diagnosis and treatment monitoring. It is based on sophisticated technology that excites and detects the change in the direction of the rotational axis of protons found in the water that makes up living tissues [15].

Positron Emission Tomography. PET scans use radiopharmaceuticals to create three-dimensional images. These types of scans produce small particles called positrons. A positron is a particle with roughly the same mass as an electron but oppositely charged. Positrons react with electrons in the body, and when these two particles combine, they annihilate each other. This annihilation produces a small amount of energy in the form of two photons that shoot off in opposite directions. The detectors in the PET scanner measure these photons and use this information to create images of internal organs [16].

3   Previous Work

Our literature review assesses how much progress has been made and what can be contributed in the detection of AD using deep learning, in particular with Convolutional Neural Networks (CNN). We only focus on AD however detection of another neurodegenerative disease using DNNs has been investigated [13,19].

We used IEEE[2] as the source for Artificial Neural Networks because, according to Journal Rankings[3] on the category of Artificial Intelligence, IEEE is the first on both SJR and H-Index sortings. We used the search engines Duck Duck Go, and Google Scholar to find illustrative publications.

We used the search string "deep AND learning AND alzheimer AND mri" in order to assess the use of convolutional deep learning in our application of interest. We ran the query mentioned from 2016 to the present (in 2019) since we are searching about recent advancements in neural networks. We retrieved from IEEE Digital Library 81 records with this query, including conferences, journals, and early access articles.

We screened by title, and if the title was too ambiguous by abstract. We searched for the application of convolutional deep learning and we obtained 32 articles. Notably, we searched for literature that included the design of convolutional deep learning artifacts for computer vision to detect AD in MRI and other modalities. Besides, the literature was restricted to supervised learning. For example, we did not include convolutional autoencoders alone.

For the articles we deemed appropriate, we developed a data extraction spreadsheet to serve for analysis where we collected the following information about each publication: (1) year of the paper, (2) architecture of the neural network, (3) if the MRI images were processed, (5) the modalities (number of inputs), (6) the number of classes used, and the metrics of (7) accuracy, (8) sensitivity, (9) specificity, and finally (9) the Area Under the curve Receiver Operating Characteristics (AUROC).

In this literature review, with our data extraction spreadsheet, we find a severe problem. Almost 50% of papers report accuracy but do not report sensitivity, specificity or AUROC. Accuracy alone can be misleading. A classifier can report a high accuracy and yet have a low capacity of true prediction. We also conclude that the studies are too diverse to allow a meaningful comparison.

---

[2] https://ieeexplore.ieee.org/.

[3] https://www.scimagojr.com/.

It seems that there is a race to obtain greater accuracy, although this metric is misleading. In addition, multiclass classification is avoided. Most studies implement one-vs-one classifiers, thus achieving higher accuracy values. When the number of classes increases the accuracy tends to decrease. In fact, we did not find any article with multiclass classification with more than four classes. Nor did we find many articles that used the densenet architecture. Only three papers used densenets, of which two [6,9] are three-dimensional but with shallow densenets and one [11] uses deep densenets but two-dimensional. Finally, the quantitative analysis of the collected items does not generate a great contribution due to these defects. However, in the review of the articles, we find articles of remarkable quality as [2]. We also consider that some of the papers collected are not repeatable.

In contrast to existing studies, we seek to create a multiclass neural network using only tools available for free. Besides, we do not give greater importance to accuracy over other metrics and analysis. Finally, we want our process to be repeatable, and we report it complete along with all the parameters used, as explained in the next sections.

4 Methodology

In this section, we describe how we collect data using the ADNI study and how we preprocess these data. Then, we present the development carried out and how we produced, using the Google Collaboratory tool, an Alzheimer's prediction model to fulfill the objective of measuring the accuracy of the detection of Alzheimer's disease using a three-dimensional Densenet-121.

4.1 Data Acquisition

In this work, we used the data from ADNI. We used their beta advanced search functionality with the following criteria. In Projects, we checked ADNI. In Research Group, we checked MCI, EMCI, AD, SMC, and CN. In Modality, we checked MRI. We only chose MRI and did not add PET because of economic restrictions. PET requires radiopharmaceuticals, as mentioned. It is more usual to find MRI in contexts of economic limitations. Continuing with search options, in Image Description, we used MPRAGE. In Acquisition Plane, we used SAGITTAL, and finally, in Weighting, we used T1. The rest of the search fields were left with their default values. With those parameters, we obtained 5556 magnetic resonance images with the following distribution: 1520 Cognitive Normal (CN), 186 Significant Memory Concern (SMC), 1222 Early Mild Cognitive Impairment (EMCI), 1274 Mild Cognitive Impairment (MCI), 636 Late Mild Cognitive Impairment, and 718 Alzheimer's Disease.

The images obtained from ADNI are in Digital Imaging and Communication On Medicine (DICOM) format. The files are in a zipped archive of 55.5 GB, and the uncompressed files measure 138 GB. We reduce that size with data preprocessing, and we explain how and why in the next section.

4.2   Data Preprocessing

MRI image data are groups of images. Every image is a slice, and the group of slices shapes the MRI. Every image or slice is a matrix of pixels. Each slice has an associated spatial thickness because they represent reality. Also, every pixel in every slice has a spacing, that is the space they represent. Thus, the data is volumetric or, in other words, rectangular cuboids. Taking that into consideration, we do the following transformations to the data. First, we convert all volumetric pixels (voxels) to a spacing of $1 \times 1 \times 1$ mm. This conversion may add or delete slices, or slice pixels. After that, we convert every slice to 256×256 pixels as follows. Some slices are not square. If they are not, we fill in with black pixels. After they are square, if they are not 256×256, we convert them to that size using interpolation. Concerning the size, we also make the cuboids have 256 slices using interpolation. The result is $256 \times 256 \times 256$ cubes. From these cubes, to keep "see" only the brain as would a human do, we make a cut from slice 40 to slice 214, from row 50 to row 199, and from column 40 to column 239. With that cut, we discard borders full of black pixels and conserve the inner cuboids that have useful information (the brain). Since we made all the MRI the same size, we assume that the cut keeps the brain and we do not have to apply techniques like image segmentation (cutting the brain using pattern recognition). From those cut cuboids, we use only half of the slices and half of the rows and columns of every slice by eliminating one in between for all. The latter reduces the size of the images and the dimensionality of the problem considerably. Last, we normalize the images pixel values to an interval of -1.0 to 1.0.

Data preprocessing can be done both online or beforehand. We implemented both. However, to maintain a low-cost objective, we use a script to apply the preprocessing previously to the task of neural network training, and we load the MRI data already transformed. The previous transformation may be done on a desktop or laptop computer. Although it will take hours, it is not a task that will take more than a day on current commodity hardware.

After data preprocessing the images occupy only 13.5 GB, we have reduced the size of the images slightly more than ten times. This reduction is beneficial to minimize neural network training time and storage needs of our development explained in the next section.

4.3   Our Development

We chose to use a convolutional DNN of densenet-BC architecture because of our objective to use the least resources possible. This kind of architecture has an excellent performance with fewer parameters to train [10]. We based our development on the implementation of Hara et al. [8]. We used their densenet implementation for the densenet-121 architecture. This implementation, in turn, is based on the two-dimensional implementation available in the Pytorch code. The implementation of Hara et al., however, is not generic. It was made for video and incorporates the variables *sample_size* and *sample_duration* that have to do with the size and duration of video samples. We eliminated that and made the implementation general. It works with all kinds of cuboids. Also, we added a channels parameter because the implementation always considered 3 channels (usually red, green and blue colors), but the magnetic resonance images are monochromatic.

Using this implementation we configure the training process of the neural network with the following parameters.

Training	We use 75% of the data obtained from ADNI as the training dataset. The data is obtained randomly from the complete data set
Batch size	For the phase of training, we use a batch size of 5 MRI based on experimental results by [2]
Testing	The testing dataset is the remaining 25% of the data
Channels	We send a parameter of 1 to the constructor of the neural network because the images are monochromatic
Classes	Initially, we sent a parameter of 6 to the constructor of the neural network. However, we decided to eliminate the SMC class because it is a subjective class. We consider it training noise. Finally, we use a parameter of 5 classes to classify
Dropout	We use a dropout rate of 0.7 based on observations by [2]. This prevents overfitting
Loss	We use a cross-entropy loss function. It is useful in classification problems that are not binary and, in our case, we have 5 or 6 classes
Optimizer	We use stochastic gradient descent (SGD). This popular optimizer is useful in the case of unbalanced data, which is our case
Learning	In the SGD optimizer, we use a learning rate parameter of 0.1 and a drop in the learning rate in the sixty epoch of 0.1. The latter reduces the learning rate to 0.01 in that epoch
Momentum	Since the SGD optimizer with momentum usually finds flatter local minima, we use a typical momentum of 0.9
Epochs	Since we use the Google Collaboratory platform, we set the maximum number of epochs to 80. It was not possible to exceed above 90 epochs to reach 100 epochs because the platform disconnects us before achieving it

With that parameters, we pushed the limits of the Google Colaboratory platform to produce a state-of-the-art DNN. Although other authors claim that the free-of-charge resources of Google Colaboratory "are far from enough to solve demanding real-world problems and are not scalable" [3], we use it as the platform that provides us Graphics Processing Unit (GPU) computation. This decision has limitations and implications. As explained in [3], there only 12 h of free use of the GPU backend. We have even noticed less sometimes, approximately 10 h. After that time, Google Colaboratory disconnects and deletes the virtual machine provided. If the user reconnects, the new machine supplied only offers 3 h of GPU backend. After that, it is not possible to connect to a backend with GPU for a determined number of hours. These limitations imply that the training and testing have to be done in one run before the first 12 h end. There are other implications to the restrictions. For instance, it is customary to test or validate neural networks during training; thus the loss and accuracy of the neural networks can be analyzed at each epoch. However, to reduce computation time, testing or validation of the trained DNN is only done at the end. We chose this because a validation cycle of 25% of the data takes approximately 2 or 3 min. In 30 epochs, that would take 1 h or more. This trade-off is not severe, we can save intermediate neural networks states and study them after finishing the training. However, this choice also implies that techniques like early stopping can not be employed. There are also disk size limitations.

   Taking all the limitations into account and with the mentioned configuration parameters of our development, we obtained the results that we discuss in the next section.

5   Results and Discussion

The first finding of this work is the characterization of the significant memory concern class as a noisy class for training. This problem may be due to the fact that the class is subjective and is possibly composed of at least two classes: those who will develop the disease and those who will not. Also, those who will develop it may have different levels of progression, being, in turn, a class composed of different classes. Another reason for the class to be problematic is its size. It is the smallest cohort and by far. This makes it difficult to classify during training. In the Fig. 1, we show how this class is not classified after 50 training epochs. As seen, the column of the predicted SMC class is full of zeros. It is also notable that the other classes already have a good level of correct classification. We decided to remove this class from the data set. This reduced the total data set from 5556 MRI to 5370 MRI.

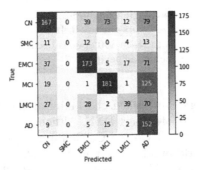

Fig. 1. Confusion matrix with the SMC class at 50 epoch

After eliminating the SMC class and training for 80 epochs, we obtain a neural network with good classification metrics of the five remaining classes.

The results can be seen in Figs. 2a and 2b. In Fig. 2a, the confusion matrix, we can see how most values are kept diagonally. There are a certain amount of incorrect predictions. However, there is an interesting, unexpected feature. These incorrect predictions are mostly pessimistic; that is, there are more errors above the diagonal that under it, and this means that the classifier is making errors that put the prediction on upper disease stages. This is clearly in favor of patients because, in terms of diagnosis of diseases, a false positive is better than a false negative. Figure 2b shows the quality of our classifier for each class and all classes together. As the area under each curve approaches the value 1.0, greater diagnostic ability of the classifier is demonstrated. It is clear that, although our classifier is not perfect, it is a good one.

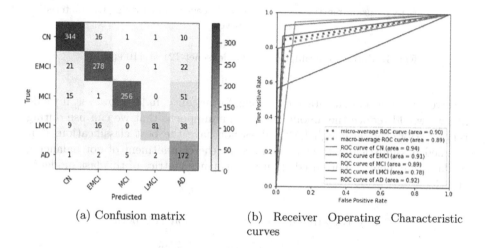

(a) Confusion matrix

(b) Receiver Operating Characteristic curves

Fig. 2. Metrics of evaluation of the densenet-121 at 80 epochs

Although we obtained an already good predictive model, we wanted to improve it using the same tools we already used. However, because we use Google Colaboratory, we could not repeat the process of training and add a significative number of epochs. Therefore, we saved the model at 80 epochs. Then, after waiting 12 h because of the Google Colaboratory restrictions, we restarted the process of training again from the 80th epoch and pushed it to 110 final epochs. The predictive performance of this new model can be seen in Figs. 3a and 3b.

This new confusion matrix (Fig. 3a) and ROC curve plot (Fig. 3b) show that it is possible to improve the prediction model even under the restrictions of free-of-charge resources like Google Colaboratory. We may notice that as we improve all classes, the Late Mild Cognitive Impairment class gets worse in the prediction. That is, we approach a local minima solution that improves the classes in general but moves away from the correct prediction of the LMCI class. We believe that this effect is due to the lack of balance in the data. LMCI is the class with the least amount of data after we removed Significant Memory Concern. This can

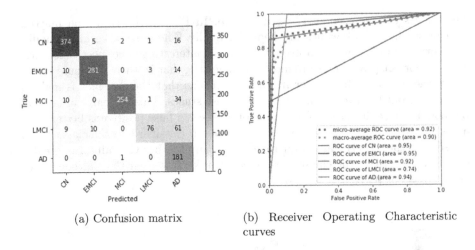

(a) Confusion matrix

(b) Receiver Operating Characteristic curves

Fig. 3. Metrics of evaluation of the densenet-121 at 110 epochs

be solved with data augmentation as done, for instance, in [4]. However, if we do this, we would reduce the amount of maximum epochs that we can use during training. However, although LMCI does not have the best classification, it is classified pessimistically, then we can accept the commitment of not balancing the data. We include more prediction performance metrics of this last model in Table 1.

Table 1. Metrics of the obtained DNN at 110 epochs

	specificity (precision)	sensitivity (recall)	f1-score	support
Cognitive Normal (CN)	93%	94%	93%	398
Early MCI (EMCI)	95%	91%	93%	308
Mild Cognitive Impairment (MCI)	99%	85%	91%	299
Late MCI (LMCI)	94%	49%	64%	156
Alzheimer's Disease (AD)	59%	99%	74%	182
Macro average	88%	84%	83%	1343
Weighted average	90%	87%	87%	1343

Accuracy	84%
Micro specificity (precision)	84%
Micro sensitivity (recall)	81%

As we can see in Table 1, the worst figures are the specificity of Alzheimer's Disease and the sensitivity of Late Mild Cognitive Impairment. We could also include the sensitivity of Mild Cognitive Impairment in the bad numbers, although the percentage of recall is not poor. The poor specificity of Alzheimer's is acceptable because it reaches almost 100% sensitivity or recall. The number is bad because other classes are classified as AD, but in a context of pattern recognition that always has risks and costs, it is in favor because it is pessimistic and in medicine that can reduce risk and future costs. In the same manner, the bad number of LMCI is also acceptable because the class is mostly classified as AD. Therefore, considering the economic restrictions, the final figures of 84% accuracy, 84% specificity (micro) and 81% sensitivity (micro) are acceptable. We chose to report final micro-average figures instead of macro-average because in a multi-class classification setup, micro-average is preferable when there is a class imbalance. However, as it can be noticed the macro average and the weighted average are better.

6   Conclusions and Future Work

The use of free-of-charge resources limited this study. With this restriction, we explored a low-cost way to generate a deep artificial neural network that shows good performance metrics. We demonstrate that the model can still be improved. This prediction model can be useful in developing countries if user interface and interpretation are added and it has the potential of being used in remote medicine contexts.

In the future, we want to create a user interface for the diagnosis of AD. We can do this based on the implementation of Chester [5], a computerized chest X-ray disease prediction system that is delivered on the web. With the recent creation of tools such as ONNX and TensorFlow.js, PyTorch-trained models can be converted to work in the browser and compute using WebGL [5]. This interface would have not only prediction but also interpretation or explanation through relevance maps or heat maps.

Last, to contribute to reproducibility and transparency in academic work, we provide the source code of our DNN at https://github.com/bsolano/Alzheimer-ResNets.

References

1. Alzheimer's Disease Neuroimaging Initiative: Study Design (2017). http://adni.loni.usc.edu/study-design/
2. Bäckström, K., Nazari, M., Gu, I.Y., Jakola, A.S.: An efficient 3D deep convolutional network for Alzheimer's disease diagnosis using MR images. In: 2018 IEEE 15th International Symposium on Biomedical Imaging (ISBI 2018), pp. 149–153, April 2018. https://doi.org/10.1109/ISBI.2018.8363543
3. Carneiro, T., Medeiros Da NóBrega, R.V., Nepomuceno, T., Bian, G., De Albuquerque, V.H.C., Filho, P.P.R.: Performance analysis of Google colaboratory as a tool for accelerating deep learning applications. IEEE Access 6, 61677–61685 (2018). https://doi.org/10.1109/ACCESS.2018.2874767
4. Cheng, D., Liu, M.: CNNs based multi-modality classification for AD diagnosis. In: 2017 10th International Congress on Image and Signal Processing, BioMedical Engineering and Informatics (CISP-BMEI), pp. 1–5, October 2017. https://doi.org/10.1109/CISP-BMEI.2017.8302281

5. Cohen, J.P., Bertin, P., Frappier, V.: Chester: A Web Delivered Locally Computed Chest X-Ray Disease Prediction System. arXiv:1901.11210 (2019)
6. Cui, R., Liu, M.: Hippocampus analysis by combination of 3-D DenseNet and shapes for Alzheimer's disease diagnosis. IEEE J. Biomed. Health Inform. **23**(5), 2099–2107 (2019). https://doi.org/10.1109/JBHI.2018.2882392
7. Graber, M., Franklin, N.: Diagnostic error in internal medicine. Arch. Intern. Med. **165** (2005). https://doi.org/10.1001/archinte.165.13.1493
8. Hara, K., Kataoka, H., Satoh, Y.: Can spatiotemporal 3D CNNs retrace the history of 2D CNNs and ImageNet? In: Proceedings of the IEEE Conference on Computer Vision and Pattern Recognition (CVPR), pp. 6546–6555 (2018)
9. He, G., Ping, A., Wang, X., Zhu, Y.: Alzheimer's disease diagnosis model based on three-dimensional full convolutional DenseNet. In: 2019 10th International Conference on Information Technology in Medicine and Education (ITME), pp. 13–17, August 2019. https://doi.org/10.1109/ITME.2019.00014
10. Huang, G., Liu, Z., Van Der Maaten, L., Weinberger, K.Q.: Densely connected convolutional networks. In: 2017 IEEE Conference on Computer Vision and Pattern Recognition (CVPR), Honolulu, HI, pp. 2261–2269 (2017). https://doi.org/10.1109/CVPR.2017.243
11. Jabason, E., Ahmad, M.O., Swamy, M.N.S.: Classification of Alzheimer's disease from MRI data using an ensemble of hybrid deep convolutional neural networks. In: 2019 IEEE 62nd International Midwest Symposium on Circuits and Systems (MWSCAS), pp. 481–484, August 2019. https://doi.org/10.1109/MWSCAS.2019.8884939
12. Khan, S., Rahmani, H., Shah, S., Bennamoun, M.: A Guide to Convolutional Neural Networks for Computer Vision. Synthesis Lectures on Computer Vision, No. 1. Morgan & Claypool Publishers (2018). https://doi.org/10.2200/S00822ED1V01Y201712COV015
13. Kollias, D., Tagaris, A., Stafylopatis, A., Kollias, S., Tagaris, G.: Deep neural architectures for prediction in healthcare. Complex Intell. Syst. **4**(2), 119–131 (2017). https://doi.org/10.1007/s40747-017-0064-6
14. Lee, C.S., Nagy, P.G., Weaver, S.J., Newman-Toker, D.E.: Cognitive and system factors contributing to diagnostic errors in radiology. Am. J. Roentgenol. **201**(3), 611–617 (2013). https://doi.org/10.2214/AJR.12.10375
15. National Institute of Biomedical Imaging and Bioengineering: Magnetic Resonance Imaging (MRI). https://www.nibib.nih.gov/science-education/science-topics/magnetic-resonance-imaging-mri
16. National Institute of Biomedical Imaging and Bioengineering: Nuclear Medicine. https://www.nibib.nih.gov/science-education/science-topics/nuclear-medicine#pid-1001
17. National Institute on Aging: Alzheimer's Disease Fact Sheet. https://www.nia.nih.gov/health/alzheimers-disease-fact-sheet. Accessed 13 May 2018
18. Rajpurkar, P., et al.: CheXNet: radiologist-level pneumonia detection on chest X-rays with deep learning. CoRR abs/1711.05225 (2017). http://arxiv.org/abs/1711.05225
19. Tagaris, A., Kollias, D., Stafylopatis, A., Tagaris, G., Kollias, S.: Machine learning for neurodegenerative disorder diagnosis — survey of practices and launch of benchmark dataset. Int. J. Artif. Intell. Tools **27**(03), 1850011 (2018). https://doi.org/10.1142/S0218213018500112

Self-adaptive Early Warning Scoring System for Smart Hospital

Imen Ben Ida[1(✉)], Moez Balti[1,2], Sondès Chabaane[3],
and Abderrazak Jemai[1,4]

[1] Electronic Systems and Communications Networks Laboratory (SERCOM),
Polytechnic School of Tunisia, Carthage University, Tunis, Tunisia
Imen.benida@gmail.com
[2] IsetCom, Carthage University, Tunis, Tunisia
[3] CNRS UMR 8201 - LAMIH - Laboratory of Automatic Mechanics
and Industrial and Human Informatics, Hauts-de-France Polytechnic University,
59313 Valenciennes, France
[4] INSAT, Carthage University, Tunis, Tunisia

Abstract. With the advent of the Internet of Things (IoT), various interconnected objects can be used to improve the collection and the process of vital signs with partially or fully automatized methods in smart hospital environment. The vital signs data are used to evaluate patient health status using heuristic approaches, such as the early warning scoring (EWS) approach. Several applications have been proposed based on the early warning scores approach to improve the recognition of patients at risk of deterioration. However, there is a lack of efficient tools that enable a personalized monitoring depending on the patient situations. This paper explores the publish-subscribe pattern to provide a self-adaptive early warning score system in smart hospital context. We propose an adaptive configuration of the vital sings monitoring process depending on the patient health status variation and the medical staff decisions.

Keywords: Computing for healthcare · Early warning scoring system · Internet of Things · Smart hospital

1 Introduction

The smart hospital (SH) is adding the intelligence to traditional hospital system to improve the quality of healthcare services. It is based on the effective use of technology and it covers all the resources and the locations with the patient information. A principal functionality in a smart hospital is the automated and continuous control of the patients during the hospitalization by measuring their vital signs. These observations are important for preventing health deterioration, reducing costs and hospitalization time, and potentially minimizing morbidity and mortality [1]. Several medical approaches are used to evaluate the collected vital sings data. A prevalent example is the Early warning scoring (EWS) approach which has been in use for several years as a tool to predict the risk level of patients [2]. It was proposed for the first time as a paper-based method that need periodical checkups to assign a score based on patient's vital

M. Jmaiel et al. (Eds.): ICOST 2020, LNCS 12157, pp. 16–27, 2020.
https://doi.org/10.1007/978-3-030-51517-1_2

signs (i.e., heart rate, respiration rate, body temperature, blood pressure). The score of each medical sign depends on the non-respect of a predefined normal interval. The summation of all scores reflects the global patients risk level [2].

By exploring the Internet of Things technologies, the vital signs control solutions are automated based on various medical devices and sensors. Smart medical devices constitute the core part of the smart hospital environment. Their main purpose is to gather vital signs data or other patient physiological conditions. These automated systems reduce the errors of the manual Early Warning Score systems [3] and facilitate the nurses' functions such as constantly gathering and storing the vital signs records.

The emergence of the Internet of Things, the electronic records and the computerized transaction systems have improved the efficiency and effectiveness of EWS systems.

In spite of such advantages using IoT, there are currently two important challenges of early warning scores systems and they need to be considered. The first issue is how to ensure a personalized monitoring of patients' vital signs depending on their situations and the medical experts' requirements especially in case of controlling an important number of patients.

The second issue is the need of timely response of medical staff in case of problem detection.

Our work is motivated by the challenges described above and its main objective is a self-adaptative Early Warning Scoring system that supports the change of the patient control frequency depending on his situation.

This paper is organized as follows: In Sect. 2 we describe the vital signs evaluation with the early warning score systems and we present some related works. Our proposed solution is detailed in Sect. 3. The Implementation and the evaluation are presented and discussed in Sect. 4. The Sect. 5 presents the concluding remarks and future work.

2 Background and Related Works

Early warning systems, also known as 'track-and-trigger' (T&T) systems, consist of evaluating vital sings using scores to recognize patients at risk of deterioration. Since 85% of severe adverse events (SAE) are preceded by abnormal vital signs, the vital signs monitoring based on EWS approach have evolved as a means of alerting health professionals to patient clinical decline [4].

In smart hospitals, particularly in intensive care units, the Early Warning Score (EWS) is a prevalent tool, by which patient's vital signs are periodically recorded and the emergency level is interpreted [3]. To this end, a score (0 for a perfect condition and 3 for the worst condition) is allocated to each vital sign according to its value and the predefined limits. The summation of the obtained scores indicates the degree of health deterioration of the patient (the higher the EWS, the worse the patient's health condition).

Physiological parameter	Score						
	3	2	1	0	1	2	3
Respiration rate (per minute)	≤8		9–11	12–20		21–24	≥25
SpO$_2$ Scale 1 (%)	≤91	92–93	94–95	≥96			
SpO$_2$ Scale 2 (%)	≤83	84–85	86–87	88–92 ≥93 on air	93–94 on oxygen	95–96 on oxygen	≥97 on oxygen
Air or oxygen?		Oxygen		Air			
Systolic blood pressure (mmHg)	≤90	91–100	101–110	111–219			≥220
Pulse (per minute)	≤40		41–50	51–90	91–110	111–130	≥131
Consciousness				Alert			CVPU
Temperature (°C)	≤35.0		35.1–36.0	36.1–38.0	38.1–39.0	≥39.1	

Fig. 1. The NEWS2 scores chart.

2.1 National Early Warning Scoring (NEWS)2 Approach

NEWS2 chart illustrated in Fig. 1 is a revised version of NEWS chart. The NEWS was created to standardize the process of recording, scoring and responding to changes in routinely measured physiological parameters in acutely ill patients. It was developed to improve the detection of clinical deterioration in patients with acute illness. In [5] NEWS was evaluated against a range of outcomes that are of major importance to patients and staff. It demonstrates a good ability to discriminate patients at risk of the combined outcome of cardiac arrest, unanticipated ICU admission or death within 24 h, which provides ample opportunity for an appropriate clinical intervention to change patient outcome [6].

NEWS2 could be made safer for patients with hypercapnic respiratory failure by having two scoring systems for (saturation pulse oxygen) SpO2:

- The existing SpO2 scoring system (Scale 1) that would apply to the majority of patients.
- A dedicated SpO2 scoring system for patients with hypercapnia respiratory failure (Scale 2). This illness means that the patient doesn't have enough oxygen in his blood and his desired oxygen saturations are set at a lower level (88–92%). The NEWS scoring system is adjusted accordingly.

2.2   Early Warning Score Systems Requirements

Early warning score systems are used to improve the process of recording, scoring and responding to changes in measured vital signs of patients. The following paragraphs present the principal requirements of EWS systems to ensure an efficient detection and response to clinical deterioration:

- Personalization

The patient vital sings data are the key of successful medical decisions. Each patient requires a personalized control depending on his situation [7]. For example a patient with a disease that causes hyperthermia, the temperature is a critical data which must be visualized with more precision; every second. While other non-critical parameters can be calculated only every hour for example.

- Medical staff engagement

The early warning scores systems are highly user-dependent and depend on the appropriate response and actions of the Medical Emergency Teams [4].

- Need for expert's decision

The warning scores cannot replace specialist's decision and the importance on knowing individual patients, they cannot also replace the background to the observations that are recorded [2].

NEWS correlated poorly with the patient's clinical status within the first 24 h post-operatively [2].

2.3   Related Works

In [8], authors present a solution which takes benefits from the concept of Edge computing and fog computing in the context of IoT based Early Warning Scores systems. The solution provides high level services in a Geo-distributed fashion at the edge of the network. The proof of concept is demonstrated with smart e-Health Gateway called UT-GATE implemented for an IoT-based remote health monitoring system. The demonstration includes the data flow processes from data acquisition at sensor nodes to the cloud and the end-users. However, the data has a static interval of acquisition which is defined at the development stage. As a result, the solution does not give the possibility of personalization. The smart e-Health Gateway proposed in [9] provides local storage to perform real-time local data processing and mining. When a patient's vital signal is processed, reliable IoT systems are provided to facilitate fault-tolerant healthcare services. Zhang et al. proposes in [10] a patient-centric cyber-physical system named Health-CPS aiming to ensure convenient Healthcare service. The Health-CPS depends on Cloud computing and data analytics to handle the big data related issues of different healthcare applications. The system is composed of several layers such as data collection layer, data management layer and data-oriented service layer. The system collects data in a unified standard. It supports distributed storage and parallel processing.

The authors present in [11] a low-cost health monitoring system that provides continuous remote monitoring of the ECG and automatic analysis and notification. The system consists of energy-efficient sensor nodes and a fog layer that take full advantage of IoT. The sensor nodes collect and wirelessly transmit ECG, respiration rate, and body temperature to a smart gateway which can be accessed by appropriate care-givers. In addition, the system can represent the collected data in useful ways, perform automatic decision making and provide many advanced services such as real-time notifications for immediate attention.

All the previous proposed solutions require different technology skills to modify or to scale out an existing system in a hospital context. The devices list is predefined at the conception level with fixed parameters of configuration. Added to that, the frequency of collecting and saving data are defined by the developers at the level of implementation without the possibility of modification after the deployment in a real case. As a result of this static configuration, a device collect data with the same parameters defined from the first step of development and it cannot be reused for personalized cases.

However, patient data are different from other collected data in IoT environments as it depends on the no stable situation of the patient health. For example, the frequency of the collected respiration data with a sensor depends on the patient illness. In some cases, an interval of 1 h is sufficient but in other cases 1 min is needed. If the storage operation of data is unique, an important unnecessary information will take place in the memory and demand useless process. In this paper, we propose a health-care system that makes it easy to personalize the vital signs monitoring of a particular patient depending on his health condition.

3   The Proposed Solution

Our proposed solution supports a patient-driven process by giving the possibility to adjust the parameters of vital signs monitoring to a specific health condition or treatment. The following paragraphs describe the solution architecture and the supported communication model.

3.1   Publish-Subscribe Communication Model

Our solution uses the publish/subscribe pattern for the data exchange between the different architecture layers. Publish-subscribe messaging systems support data-centric communication and have been widely used in IoT systems. With the publish-subscribe pattern, the exchange of messages between clients is ensured using a broker that manages topics and sub-topics. A publisher on a given topic can send messages to other clients acting as subscribers to the topic without the need to know about the existence of the receiving clients [5].

To organize the topics and sub-topics in both gateway and server brokers, we define four categories of data:

- Sensed data: The collection of time-series data sensed by the medical devices.

- EWS score data: The corresponding score of each sensed data depending on the NEWS2 specification illustrated in Fig. 1.
- Configuration data: The definition of the gateway parameters by the medical staff. For example, the frequency of saving the collected data.

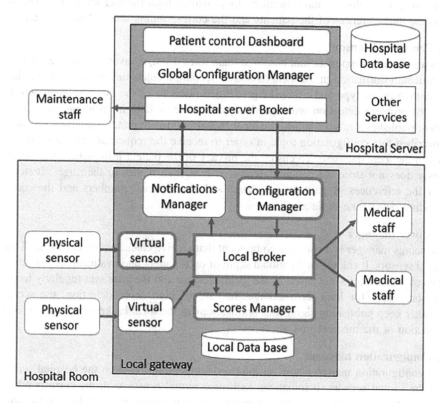

Fig. 2. The solution architecture.

3.2   Gateway Layer Components

We propose the use of a gateway as an edge layer to put the computing at the proximity of data sources. In each hospital room, a smart gateway is used to collect the vital signs of the patients. The main components of the proposed gateway illustrated in Fig. 2 are:

a) Local broker

The Broker server acts as an intermediary for messages sent between the publishers and the subscribers for a specific topic. It routes the messages based on topic rather than the IP address. When a message is sent by the publish client to the broker server, all the subscribe clients interested on the related topic of the message will receive the publication.

Medical devices are considered as data publishers. A topic is the device name and for each device, a subscriber is created to listen to the published data and save it in a local database with the required parameters. The main component of the gateway is an embedded configuration service that provides medical staff with the ability to log into and configure the data process behavior depending on patients' situations. Medical staff can configure publishers and subscribers by providing information such as the ID of the devices, the references of the patients and the corresponding dates of hospitalization.

b) The virtual sensor

It is a software component that has three main roles. First, it saves the received data as significant information in the local database. Second, it calculates the score of the data depending on its type and using the predefined intervals of the NEWS2 approach. In case of problem detection with the calculated score or data interruption, the virtual sensor publishes a notification to the local broker. Added to that, each virtual sensor is subscribed to a configuration topic in order to receive the requested interval of saving data in the local database. To ensure the privacy of the patient information, the virtual sensor does not store the patients' details such as their names or their ages. It stores only the references of patients associated with the devices' numbers and the corresponding range time of data collection.

c) Scores manager

The scores manager is a software component that receive calculated scores from all the virtual sensors. It calculates the global score of each patient and evaluates its risk level. The calculated scores are saved in the local database and they are sent regularly to the hospital server for long term storage. In case of high score detection, the scores manager keep publishing significant notifications to the local broker until it receives a validation of the medical staff intervention.

d) Configuration manager

The configuration manager is in an intermediate position between the hospital server and the virtual sensors. It initializes each new virtual sensor with the corresponding configuration. The configuration manager of each gateway is considered as a subscriber to the corresponding configuration topic defined at the Hospital server.

3.3 Methods

The main objective of our solution is to provide intelligent methods of patient control. Two types of configuration are supported by the configuration manager:

- Devices configuration

The medical staff can submit a configuration request using a web interface, the server broker publish the received request as a configuration message to the concerned gateway. If the request is about adding a new device, a new virtual sensor is created after validation. In case that the medical staff choose to modify some parameters of an existing device, the corresponding virtual sensor checks the different inserted parameters: device identifier, patient reference and the time range of saving data and save the new configuration. The separation of the virtual sensors as independent subscribers ensures that the modification or the elimination of a device does not affect the whole system.

- Data management configuration

Added to the devices configuration possibility, our system integrates an automation algorithm for the calibration of the data storage and the score calculation frequency.

For each score level, the maximum value is defined as score level limit. The configuration manager reads frequently the calculated score of each vital sign from the local database and compare it with the corresponding predefined limits.

If it captures successive abnormal values, the frequency of the collection of this data is automatically increased to be able to monitor the data concerned with more precision. The new frequency value is saved in the local database and published as a message to the corresponding virtual sensor.

When the measurements become more stable and less than the predefined limits, the administrator can decide to change this frequency.

The values of required frequencies are defined depending on the medical experts' requirements (Fig. 3).

The self-adaptivity process is illustrated in the following algorithm:

Algorithm 1 Self-adaptivity algorithm

Inputs: (SC) NEWS2 calculated score, (Freq) Corresponding frequency, (VST) Virtual Sensor Topic
    Variables: (Score0Limit, Score1Limit) NEWS2 scores limits
    Output: NewFreq (new data collection frequency).
      0: begin
    1: If ((Freq == FreqLevel1) and (SC ==0)) then
    2:     Score0Limit= GetScoreLimit (VST, 0)
    3:     If (verifEgalityOfLast2Values (VST, SC, Score0Limit)
     4:       == false) then
    5:       NewFreq = FreqLevel2
    6:    End if
    7: Else if ((Freq == 1min) and ((SC == 1) or (SC == 2))) then
    8:     Score1Limit = GetScoreLimit (VST, 1)
    9:     If (verifEgalityOfLast3Values(VST, SC, Score1Limit)
     10:    == false) then
    11:      NewFreq = FreqLevel3
     12: End if
     13: End if
     14: Publish (VST, NewFreq)
     15: end

Fig. 3. Self-adaptative configuration algorithm.

4 Implementation and Evaluation

4.1 Materials

The Gateway is a Raspberry Pi 3 which is a small size board with 1 GB of Ram and 1.2 GHz processor [12]. As an Operating System for the gateway, we use Raspbian the pre-compiled Debian OS which is especially optimized for the Raspberry Pi.

We install the InfluxDB database which is an open-source Time Series Database written in Go. At its core is a custom-built storage engine called the Time-Structured Merge (TSM) Tree, which is optimized for time-series data. InfluxDB supports SQL-like query languages named InfluxQL and has the advantage of easy scale-out. It provides support for mathematical and statistical functions across time ranges, also it is developed for custom monitoring, metrics collection and real-time analytics [13].

We use the mosquito implementation as a messages' broker and Node JS clients as subscribers [14].

The messages exchange is ensured by MQ Telemetry Transport (MQTT) protocol [15]. MQTT protocol is a lightweight application layer protocol designed for resource-constrained devices. It runs over TCP/IP, or over other network protocols that provide ordered, lossless and bidirectional connections. It uses the publish/subscribe messaging system combined with the concept of topics to provide one-to-many message distribution. The headers of MQTT messages are small and the connection set up does not require a synchronous handshake which could support a range of 10 to 100 messages per second.

MQTT applies topic-based filtering of messages with a topic being part of each published message. The broker uses the topics to determine whether a subscribing client should receive the message or not. Clients can subscribe to as many topics as they are interested in.

4.2 Evaluation and Results

The evaluation of the presented solution was done from a resource use point of view to analyze whether the self-adaptative algorithm would result in a better performance parameter. The parameters that were taken into account were memory use for stored data and the CPU use of the gateway.

To prove the benefits of the customized use of the gateway, we consider a scenario of controlling the temperature data of one patient with two different scenarios. The first is called fixed case, it is the standard case in which the data are collected with a unique interval of time. In the second case, the interval of data collection changes depending on the patient's score calculation.

In Fig. 4, we illustrate a result of the self-adaptivity configuration. We support 3 levels of data storage frequency depending on the corresponding score. The green signal presents the temperature measurements of a patient. The frequency of saving the sensed data changes when successful augmentation of temperature value is detected. The second signal which does not respect the self-adaptative algorithm contains unnecessary information for the first seven hour and before the increase of patient's temperature.

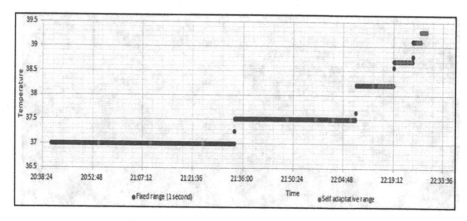

Fig. 4. Self-adaptative configuration example.

We simulate 5 devices that send temperature values using the MQTT protocol. Two scenarios were made for this simulation. The first is to use a temperature interval equal to 1 s for the 5 devices. The second is to vary the sending intervals for each device (10 min, 5 min, 1 h, 30 min, 10 s).

The evaluation results reflected in Fig. 5 and Fig. 6 are obtained using chronograf software which is an administrative tool for InfluxData deployments [16]. It shows that the use of a single data processing strategy in a fixed and non-custom way can result in an unnecessary use of gateway processor and memory which obviously affects performance and the time reaction specially in emergency cases.

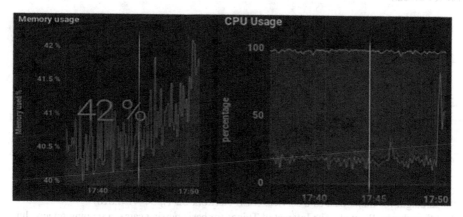

Fig. 5. Evaluation of the fixed scenario

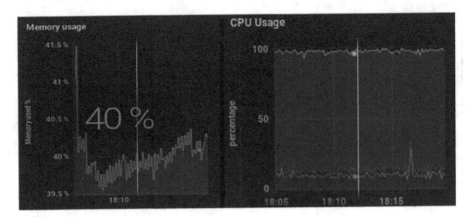

Fig. 6. Evaluation of the self-configuration scenario

5 Conclusion and Future Work

In this paper, we proposed a self-adaptative early warning scores system that respect a risk evaluation approach named NEWS2. It provides a manual and self-adaptative configuration of the vital signs monitoring process depending on the patient health status variation and the medical staff decisions. We aim in our future work to use ontologies for more interpretation of collected data.

References

1. Costa, C., Pasluosta, F., Eskofier, B., Silva, D., Righi, R.: Internet of health things: toward intelligent vital signs monitoring in hospital wards. J. Artif. Intell. Med. **89**, 61–69 (2018)
2. Downey, C.L., Tahir, W., Randell, R., Brown, J.M., Jayne, D.G.: Strengths and limitations of early warning scores: a systematic review and narrative synthesis. Int. J. Nurs. Stud. **76**, 106–119 (2017)
3. Anzanpour, A., Rahmani, A.-M., Liljeberg, P., Tenhunen, H.: Context-aware early warning system for in-home healthcare using internet-of-things. In: Mandler, B., et al. (eds.) IoT360 2015. LNICST, vol. 169, pp. 517–522. Springer, Cham (2016). https://doi.org/10.1007/978-3-319-47063-4_56
4. National Early Warning Score (NEWS) 2 (2019) https://www.rcplondon.ac.uk/projects/outputs/national-early-warning-score-news-2
5. Du, B., Huang, R., Xie, Z., Ma, J., Lv, W.: KID model-driven things-edge-cloud computing paradigm for traffic data as a service. IEEE Network **32**(1), 34–41 (2018)
6. Mieronkoski, R., et al.: The Internet of Things for basic nursing care—a scoping review. Int. J. Nursing Stud. **69**, 78–90 (2017)
7. Razzaque, M.A., Milojevic-Jevric, M., Palade, A., Clarke, S.: Middleware for internet of things: a survey. IEEE Internet Things J. **3**(1), 70–95 (2016)
8. Rahmani, A.M., et al.: Exploiting smart e-Health gateways at the edge of healthcare Internet-of-Things: a fog computing approach Future Gener. Comput. Syst. **78**(2), 641–658 (2018)
9. Farahani, B., et al.: Towards fog-driven IoT eHealth: Promises and challenges of IoT in medicine and healthcare. Future Gener. Comput. Syst. **78**(2), 659–676 (2018)

10. Zhang, Y., Qiu, M., Tsai, C.W., Hassan, M.M., Alamri, A.: Health-CPS: healthcare cyber-physical system assisted by cloud and Big Data. IEEE Syst. J. **11**, 88–95 (2017)
11. Gia, N.T., et al.: Low-cost fog-assisted health-care IoT system with energy-efficient sensor nodes. In: 13th International Wireless Communications and Mobile Computing Conference (IWCMC), Valencia, pp. 1765–1770 (2017)
12. Richardson, M., Wallace, S.: Getting Started with Raspberry PI. O'Reilly Media, Inc., Sebastopol (2012)
13. Rudolf, C.: SQL, noSQL or newSQL–comparison and applicability for Smart Spaces. Network Architectures and Services (2017)
14. Light, R.A.: Mosquitto: server and client implementation of the MQTT protocol. J. Open Source Softw. **2**(13), 265 (2017)
15. Banks, A., Gupta, R.: MQTT Version 3.1. 1, OASIS standard, vol. 29 (2014)
16. https://www.influxdata.com/time-series-platform/chronograf/

Machine Learning Based Rank Attack Detection for Smart Hospital Infrastructure

Abd Mlak Said[1]([⊠]), Aymen Yahyaoui[1,2], Faicel Yaakoubi[3],
and Takoua Abdellatif[2]

[1] Military Academy of Fondouk Jedid, Nabul, Tunisia
maliksaid@outlook.fr
[2] SERCOM Lab, Polytechnic School of Tunisia, La Marsa, Tunisia
[3] Defense Science and Technology Laboratory, Tunis, Tunisia

Abstract. In recent years, many technologies were racing to deliver the best service for human being. Emerging Internet of Things (IoT) technologies made birth to the notion of smart infrastructures such as smart grid, smart factories or smart hospitals. These infrastructures rely on interconnected smart devices collecting real-time data in order to improve existing procedures and systems capabilities. A critical issue in smart infrastructures is the information protection which may be more valuable than physical assets. Therefore, it is extremely important to detect and deter any attacks or breath to the network system for information theft. One of these attacks is the rank attack that is carried out by an intruder node in order to attract legitimate traffic to it, then steal personal data of different persons (both patients and staffs in hospitals). In this paper, we propose an anomaly based rank attack detection system against an IoT network using Support Vector Machines. As a use case, we are interested in the healthcare sector and in particular in smart hospitals which are multifaceted with many challenges such as service resilience, assets interoperability and sensitive information protection. The proposed intrusion detection system (IDS) is implemented and evaluated using Conticki Cooja simulator. Results show a high detection accuracy and low false positive rates.

Keywords: Internet of Things · Smart hospitals · Intrusion detection · Rank attack · Machine learning · RPL

1 Introduction

Nowadays, the deployment of the Internet of Things (IoT) where many objects are connected to the Internet cloud services becomes highly recommended in many applications in various sectors. A highly important concept in the IoT is Wireless Sensor Networks or WSNs where end nodes rely on sensors that can collect data from the environment to ensure tasks such as surveillance or monitoring

© The Author(s) 2020
M. Jmaiel et al. (Eds.): ICOST 2020, LNCS 12157, pp. 28–40, 2020.
https://doi.org/10.1007/978-3-030-51517-1_3

for wide areas [7]. This capability made the birth to the notion of smart infrastructures such as smart metering systems, smart grid or smart hospitals. In such infrastructures, end devices collecting data are connected to intermediate nodes that forward data in order to reach border routers using routing protocols. These end nodes are in general limited in terms of computational resources, battery and memory capacities. Also, their number is growing exponentially. Therefore, new protocols are proposed under the IoT paradigm to optimize energy consumption and computations. Two of these protocols are considered the de facto protocols for the Internet of Things (IoT): RPL (Routing Protocol for Low Power Lossy Network) and 6LoWPAN (IPv6 over Low Power Wireless Private Area Network). These protocols are designed for constrained devices in recent IoT applications. Routing is a key part of the IPv6 stack that remains to be specified for 6Low-Pan networks [6]. RPL provides a mechanism whereby multipoint-to-point traffic from devices inside the Low-Power and Lossy-Networks (LLNs) towards a central control point as well as point-to-multipoint traffic from the central control point to the device inside the LLN are supported [8,9]. RPL involves many concepts that make it a flexible protocol, but also rather complex [10]:

- DODAG (Destination Oriented Directed Acyclic Graph): a topology similar to a tree to optimize routes between sink and other nodes for both the collect and distribute data traffics. Each node within the network has an assigned rank, which increases as the teals move away from the root node. The nodes resend packets using the lowest range as the route selection criteria.
- DIS (DODAG Information Solicitation): used to solicit a DODAG information object from RPL nodes.
- DIO (DODAG Information Object): used to construct, maintain the DODAG and to periodically refresh the information of the nodes on the topology of the network.
- DAO (DODAG Advertisment Object): used by nodes to propagate destination information upward along the DODAG in order to update the information of their parents.

With the enormous number of devices that are now connected to the Internet, a new solution was proposed: 6LowPan a lightweight protocol that defines how to run IP version 6 (IPv6) over low data rate, low power, small footprint radio networks as typified by the IEEE 802.15.4 radio [11]. In smart infrastructures, the huge amount of sensitive data exchanged among these modules and throughout radio interfaces need to be protected. Therefore, detecting any network or device breach becomes a high priority challenge for researchers due to resource constraints for devices (low processing power, battery power and memory size). Rank attack is one of the most known RPL attacks where the attacker attracts other nodes to establish routes through it by advertising false rank. This way, intruders collect all the data that pass in the network [12].

For this reason, developing specific security solutions for IoT is essential to let users catch all opportunities it offers. One of defense lines designed for detecting attackers is Intrusion Detection Systems [13] (IDS). In this paper, we propose a centralized anomaly-based IDS for smart infrastructures. We chose O-SVM (One class Support Vector Machines) algorithm for its low energy consuming compared to other machine learning algorithms for Wireless sensor network (WSN) [20].

As a use case, we are interested in smart hospital infrastructures. Such hospitals have a wide range of resources that are essential to maintain their operations, patients, employees and the building itself [1,2] safety such as follow:

- Remote care assets: medical equipment for tele-monitoring and tele-diagnosis.
- Networked medical devices: wearable mobile devices (heartbeat bracelet, wireless temperature counters, glucose measuring devices...) or an equipment installed to collect health service related data.
- Networking equipment: standards equipment providing connectivity between different equipment (transmission medium, router, gateway...).
- Data: for both clinical and patient data, and staff data, which considered the most critical asset stored in huge datasets or private clouds.
- Building and facilities: the sensors are distributed in the hospital building that monitor the patient safety (temperature sensor for patient room and operation theater, gas sensor are among used sensors).

We target a common IoT architecture that can be considered for smart hospitals. In such architecture, there are mainly three type of components:

Sensing Node: composed of remote care asset, network medical device and different sensors. These sensors will send different type of data and information (patient and staff data, medical equipment status...). They are linked to microcontrollers and radio modules to transmit these data to the processing unit [3].

Edge Router: an edge router or border router is a specialized router residing at the edge or boundary of a network. This node ensures the connectivity of its network with external networks; a wide area network or the Internet. An edge router uses an external border gateway protocol, which is used extensively over the Internet to provide connectivity with remote networks. Instead of providing communication with an internal network, which the core router already manages, a gateway may provide communication with different networks and autonomous systems [4].

Interface Module and Database: this module is the terminal of the network containing all the collected data from different nodes of the network and analyze those information in order to ensure the safety of patient and improve the healthcare system.

Figure 1 [5], presents the typical IoT e-health architecture, where sensors are distributed (medical equipment,room sensors and others) and send data to the IoT gateway. In one hand, this gives the opportunity to medical supervisor to control the patient health status. In the other hand, this data will be saved into databases for more analysis.

The rest of the paper is structured as follows. Section 2 presents the related work. Section 3 presents the Rank attack scenario. Section 4 presents our proposed approach. Section 5 presents our main results and Sect. 6 concludes the paper and presents its perspectives.

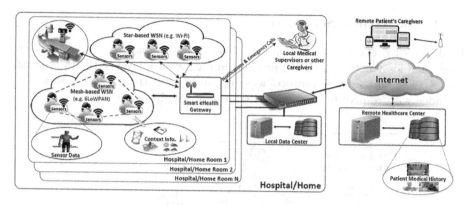

Fig. 1. Smart hospital assets.

2   Related Work

RPL protocol security especially in the healthcare domain is a crucial aspect for preserving personnel data. Nodes rank is an important parameter for an RPL network. It can be used for route optimization, loop prevention, and topology maintenance. In fact, the rank attack can decrease the network performance in terms of packet delivery rate (PDR) to almost 60% [23]. There were different proposed solutions to detect and mitigate RPL attacks such as rank authentication mechanism to avoid false announced ranks by using cryptography technique which was proposed in [24]. However, this technique is not very efficient because of its high computational cost and energy consumption. Authors in [25] propose a monitoring node (MN) based scheme but it is also not efficient because using a large network of MNs causes a communication overhead. In [26], authors propose the IDS called "SVELTE" that can only be used for detection of simple rank attack and has high false alarm rate. A host-based IDS was proposed in [27]. The IDS uses a probabilistic scheme but it is discouraged by RFC6550 for resource constrained networks. Routing Choice "RC" was proposed by Zhag et al. [28]. It is not directly related to the rank attack but it is based on false preferred parent selection. It has a high communication overhead in RPL networks. Trusted platform module (TPM) was proposed by Seeber et al. [29]. It introduces an overlay network of TPM nodes for detection of network attacks. SecureRPL (SRPL) [30] technique prevents RPL network from Rank attack, however it is characterized by a high energy consumption. Therefore, anomaly based solutions using machine learning permit a more efficient detection. Authors of [22] compared several unsupervised machine learning approaches based on local outlier factor, near neighbors, Mahalanobis distance and SVMs for intrusion detection. Their experiments showed that O-SVM is the most appropriate technique to detect selective forwarding and jamming attacks. Actually, we rely on these results in our choice of O-SVM.

3   Rank Attack Scenario

Rank attack is one of well known attacks against the routing protocol for low power and lossy networks (RPL) protocol in the network layer of the Internet of Things. The rank in RPL protocol as shown in Fig. 2 is the physical position of the node with respect to the border router and neighbor nodes [12].

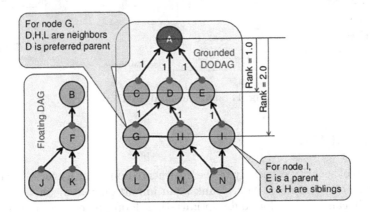

Fig. 2. The rank in IoT network.

Since our network is dynamic due to the mobility of its nodes (sensor moving with patient...), the RPL protocol periodically reformulates the DODAG. As shown in Fig. 3, an attacker may insert a malicious mote into the network to attract other nodes to establish routes through it by advertising false ranks while the reformulation of the DODAG is done [14].

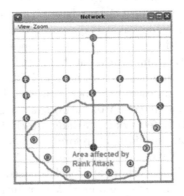

Fig. 3. Rank attack.

By default, RPL has the security mechanisms to mitigate the external attacks but it can not mitigate the internal attacks efficiently. In that case, the rank attack is considered one of dangerous attacks in dynamic IoT networks since the attacker controls an existing node (being one of the internal attack that can affect the RPL) in the DODAG or he can identify the network and insert his own malicious node and that node will act as the attack node as shown in Fig. 4.

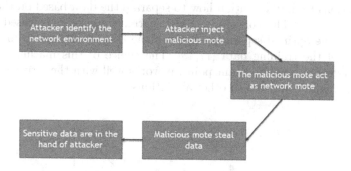

Fig. 4. The rank attack scenario.

4   Proposed Approach

The key features required for our solution are to be adaptive, lightweight, and able to learn from the past. We design an IoT IDS and we implement and evaluate it as authors did in [18, 20].

Placement Choice: one of the important decision in intrusion detection is the placement of the IDS in the network. We use a centralized approach by installing the IDS at the border router. Therefore, it can analyze all the packets that pass through it. The choice of the centralized IDS was done to avoid the placement of IDS modules in constrained devices which requires more storage and processing capabilities [15, 16]. However, theses devices have limited resources.

Detection Method Choice: An intrusion detection system (IDS) is a tool or mechanism to detect attacks against a system or a network by analyzing the activity in the network or in the system itself. Once an attack is detected an IDS may log information about it and/or report an alarm [15, 16]. Broadly speaking, we aim to choose the anomaly based detection mechanisms: it tries to detect anomalies in the system by determining the ordinary behavior and using it as baseline. Any deviations from that baseline is considered as an anomaly. This technique have the ability to detect almost any attack and adapt to new environments. We chose Support Vector Machines (SVM) as an anomaly based machine learning technique. It is a discriminating classifier formally defined by a separating hyper-lane. Given labeled training data (supervised learning), the algorithm outputs an optimal hyper-lane which categorizes new examples. In two dimensional space this hyper-lane is a line dividing a plane in two parts where each class lays in either side. It uses a mathematical function named the kernel to reformulate data. After these transformations, it defines an optimal borderline between the labels. Mainly, it does some extremely complex data transformations to find a solution how to separate the data based on the labels or outputs defined. The concept of SVM learning approach is based on the definition of the optimal separating hyper-plane (Fig. 5) [21] which maximizes the margin of the training data [17,18]. The choice of this machine learning algorithm refers to one important point, it works well with the structured data as tables of values compared to other algorithms.

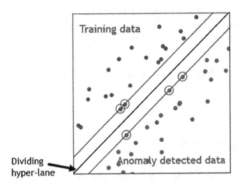

Fig. 5. SVM classification.

We implement the IDS in the smart IoT gateway shown in Fig. 1.

5 IDS Solution and Results

To investigate the effectiveness of our proposed IDS, we implement three scenarios of rank attack using Contiki-Cooja simulator [19]. We assess how our IDS module can detect them. We present next the simulation setup, evaluation metrics, and we discuss the results achieved.

5.1 Simulation Setup

Our simulation scenario consists of a total 11 motes spread across an area of 200×200 m (Simulation of area of hospital where different sensors are placed in every area to control the patient rooms). The topology is shown in Fig. 6 using four scenarios. There is one sink (mote ID:0 with green dot) and 10 senders (yellow motes from ID:1 to ID:10). Every mote sends packet to the sink at the rate of 1 packet every 1 min. We implement the centralized anomaly based IDS at the root mote or the sink and we collect and analyze network data as shown in

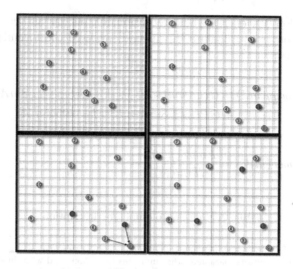

Fig. 6. Simulation topology (Color figure online)

Fig. 6. We inject malicious motes (purple colour) in a random position. Table 1 summarizes the used simulation parameters.

We run four simulation scenarios for 1 h (Fig. 6):

- scenario 1: IoT network without malicious motes.
- scenario 2: IoT network with 1 randomly placed malicious mote.
- scenario 3: IoT network with 2 randomly placed malicious motes.
- scenario 4: IoT network with 4 randomly placed malicious motes.

Table 1. Simulation parameters

Parameter	Value
Platform	Cooja Contiki 3.0
Number of nodes	10 senders, 1 sink
Topology	Star
Area	200 m
Sending rate	1 packet/minute
Simulation run time	1 h
Number of attackers	1, 2 and then 4

5.2 Evaluation Parameter

To evaluate the accuracy of the proposed IDS, we rely on the energy consumption parameter. We collect power tracking data per mote in terms of radio ON energy, radio transmission TX energy, radio reception RX energy and radio interfered INT energy. In order to calculate this metrics we used the formula [31] (Eq. 1, Table 2) as follow :

$$Energy(mJ) = (transmit * 19.5mA + listen * 21.8mA$$
$$+ CPU * 1.8mA + LPM * 0.0545mA)$$
$$* 3V/4096 * 8 \tag{1}$$
$$Power(mW) = \frac{Eneregy(mJ)}{Time(s)}$$

Table 2. Equation parameters description

Variables	Meaning
LPM	Power consumption parameter that indicates the power used when in sleep condition
CPU	Power parameter that indicates the level of node processing
Transmit	Parameter related with node communication while transmitting
Listen	Parameter related with node communication while receiving

5.3   Power Tracking per Mote for Each Simulation

We used data containing 1000 instances of consumed energy values for each node in the network. Figure 7 depicts the evolution of power tracking of each node in the four scenarios:

- scenario 1: when we have a normal behavior in the network, all the sensors show a regular energy consumption in terms of receiving (node 0) and sending (nodes from 1 to 10). We use this simulation to collect the training data for the proposed IDS.
- scenario 2, 3 and 4: for those scenarios, we have a high sending values for the malicious motes. This is explained by the fact that when a malicious mote joins the network, it asks the other motes to recreate the DODAG tree and also to send data that they have, in order to steal as much data as it can. That is why it have a high receiving values too. The other motes do not distinguish that this is a malicious mote, therefore they recreate the DODAG tree, and send their information through the malicious node. We used the first simulation scenario as dataset for our IDS, describing the normal behavior of the network. This 1 h information was enough to detect the malicious activities of the rank attack. Meanwhile, each time we add a malicious mote, the anomaly detection rate increases as shown in Fig. 8.

In each simulation of malicious mote, the proposed IDS indicates the anomaly detection ratio which increases each time while adding another malicious mote. This aims to determine the impact of the number malicious motes compared to normal behavior of the system.

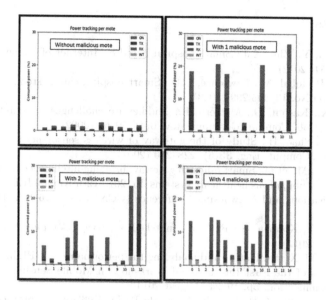

Fig. 7. Power tracking per each mote

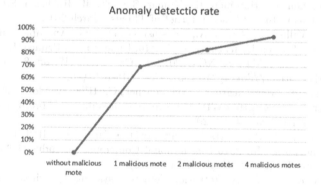

Fig. 8. Evolution of anomaly detection rate

6 Conclusion

In this paper, we propose an intrusion detection system "IDS" for smart hospital infrastructure data protection. The chosen IDS is centralized and anomaly based using a machine learning algorithm OSVM. Simulation results show the efficiency of the approach by a high detection accuracy which is more precise when the number of malicious nodes increases. As future work, we are interested in developing a machine learning based IDS for more RPL attacks detection. Furthermore, we aim to extend this solution to anomaly detection in IoT systems composed not only of WSN networks but also of cloud-based services.

References

1. Yu, L., Lu, Y., Zhu, X.J.: Smart hospital based on Internet of Things. J. Netw. **7**(10), 1654 (2012)
2. Attaluri, P., Iqbal, M., Lawrence, C.D.: Smart hospital care system. U.S. Patent Application No. 13/445,299 (2013)
3. Römer, K., Kasten, O., Mattern, F.: Middleware challenges for wireless sensor networks. Mob. Comput. Commun. Rev. **6**(4), 59–61 (2002)
4. Kuang, X., Shao, H.: Study of the gateway of wireless sensor networks. Jisuanji Gongcheng/Comput. Eng. **33**(6), 228–230 (2007)
5. Rahmani, A.M., et al.: Smart e-health gateway: bringing intelligence to internet-of-things based ubiquitous healthcare systems. In: 2015 12th Annual IEEE Consumer Communications and Networking Conference (CCNC), pp. 826–834. IEEE, January 2015
6. Gaddour, O., Koubâa, A.: RPL in a nutshell: a survey. Comput. Netw. **56**(14), 3163–3178 (2012)
7. Zhang, T., Li, X.: Evaluating and analyzing the performance of RPL in contiki. In: Proceedings of the First International Workshop on Mobile Sensing, Computing and Communication, pp. 19–24, August 2014
8. Winter, T., Thubert, P., Brandt, A., et al.: RPL: IPv6 routing protocol for low-power and lossy networks. In: RFC 6550, March 2012
9. Garcia-Morchon, O., Hummen, R., Kumar, S.S., Struik, R., Keoh, S.L.: Security Considerations in the IP-based Internet of Things, March 2012
10. Perazzo, P., Vallati, C., Arena, A., Anastasi, G., Dini, G.: An implementation and evaluation of the security features of RPL. In: Puliafito, A., Bruneo, D., Distefano, S., Longo, F. (eds.) ADHOC-NOW 2017. LNCS, vol. 10517, pp. 63–76. Springer, Cham (2017). https://doi.org/10.1007/978-3-319-67910-5_6
11. Kushalnagar, T., Montenegro, G., Schumacher, C.: IPv6 over low-power wireless personal area networks (6LoWPANs): overview, assumptions, problem statement, and goals. In: RFC, vol. 4919 (2007)
12. Rehman, A., et al.: Rank attack using objective function in RPL for low power and lossy networks. In: 2016 International Conference on Industrial Informatics and Computer Systems (CIICS). IEEE (2016)
13. Farooqi, A.H., Khan, F.A.: Intrusion detection systems for wireless sensor networks: a survey. In: Ślęzak, D., Kim, T., Chang, A.C.-C., Vasilakos, T., Li, M.C., Sakurai, K. (eds.) FGCN 2009. CCIS, vol. 56, pp. 234–241. Springer, Heidelberg (2009). https://doi.org/10.1007/978-3-642-10844-0_29
14. Wallgren, L., Raza, S., Voigt, T.: Routing attacks and countermeasures in the RPL-based Internet of Things. Int. J. Distrib. Sens. Netw. **9**(8), 794326 (2013)
15. Zarpelão, B.B., Miani, R.S., Kawakani, C.T., de Alvarenga, S.C.: A survey of intrusion detection in Internet of Things. J. Netw. Comput. Appl. **84**, 25–37 (2017)
16. Yang, K., Ren, J., Zhu, Y., Zhang, W.: Active learning for wireless IoT intrusion detection. IEEE Wirel. Commun. **25**(6), 19–25 (2018)
17. Kim, D.S., Nguyen, H.N., Park, J.S.: Genetic algorithm to improve SVM based network intrusion detection system. In: 19th International Conference on Advanced Information Networking and Applications (AINA 2005), Volume 1 (AINA papers), vol. 2, pp. 155–158. IEEE, March 2005
18. Wang, J., Hong, X., Ren, R.R., Li, T.H.: A real-time intrusion detection system based on PSO-SVM. In: Proceedings The 2009 International Workshop on Information Security and Application (IWISA 2009), p. 319. Academy Publisher (2009)

19. Bagula, B.A., Erasmus, Z.: IoT emulation with cooja. In: ICTP-IoT Workshop, March 2015

20. Yahyaoui, A., Abdellatif, T., Attia, R.: READ: reliable event and anomaly detection system in wireless sensor networks. In: 2018 IEEE 27th International Conference on Enabling Technologies: Infrastructure for Collaborative Enterprises (WET-ICE), pp. 193–198. IEEE (2018)

21. Wang, J., Chen, Q., Chen, Y.: RBF kernel based support vector machine with universal approximation and its application. In: Yin, F.-L., Wang, J., Guo, C. (eds.) ISNN 2004. LNCS, vol. 3173, pp. 512–517. Springer, Heidelberg (2004). https://doi.org/10.1007/978-3-540-28647-9_85

22. Garcia-font, V., Garrigues, C., Rifà-pous, H.: A comparative study of anomaly detection techniques for smart city wireless sensor networks. Sensors **16**(6), 868 (2016)

23. Le, A., Loo, J., Luo, Y., Lasebae, A.: The impacts of internal threats towards routing protocol for low power and lossy network performance. In: IEEE Symposium Computer and Communications (ISCC), pp 789–794 (2013)

24. Dvir, A., Holczer, T., Buttyan, L.: VeRA-version number and rank authentication in RPL. In: 2011 IEEE 8th International Conference on Mobile Ad hoc and sensor systems (MASS). IEEE (2011)

25. Anhtuan, L, et al.: Specification-based IDS for securing RPL from topology attacks. In: 2011 IFIP Wireless Days (WD), pp. 4–6. IEEE (2011)

26. Raza, S., Shahid, L.W., Voigt, T.: SVELTE: real-time intrusion detection in the Internet of Things. Ad Hoc Netw. **11**(8), 2661–2674 (2013)

27. Iuchi, K., et al.: Secure parent node selection scheme in route construction to exclude attacking nodes from RPL network. IEICE Commun. Express **4**(11), 340–345 (2015)

28. Zhang, L., Feng, G., Qin, S.: Intrusion detection system for RPL from routing choice intrusion. In: 2015 IEEE International Conference on Communication Workshop (ICCW), pp. 2652–2658. IEEE (2015)

29. Sebastian, S., et al.: Towards a trust computing architecture for RPL in cyber physical systems. In: 2013 9th International Conference on Network and service management (CNSM), pp. 134–137. IEEE (2013)

30. Glissa, G., Rachedi, A., Meddeb, A.: A secure routing protocol based on RPL for Internet of Things. In: 2016 IEEE Global Communications Conference (GLOBE-COM). IEEE (2016)

31. Hassani, A.E., Sahel, A., Badri, A.: Impact of RPL objective functions on energy consumption in Ipv6 based wireless sensor networks, June 2019

Remote Health Monitoring Systems Based on Bluetooth Low Energy (BLE) Communication Systems

Lamia Chaari Fourati[(✉)] [ID] and Sana Said

Digital Research Center of Sfax (CRNS), Laboratory of Technologies and Smart Systems (LT2S), University of Sfax, Sfax, Tunisia
lamiachaari1@gmail.com

Abstract. Nowadays, remote healthcare monitoring systems (RHMS) are attracting patients, doctors and caregivers. RHMS reduces the number of unessential hospitalizations by providing the required healthcare services for patients at home. Furthermore, continuous health monitoring using RHMS is a hopeful solution for elderly people suffering from chronic diseases. RHMS is in general three tiers architecture where the first tier uses intelligent wearable sensors to gather physiological signs. The majority of wearable sensors constructors commercialized sensing devices with Bluetooth Low Energy (BLE) communication interfaces, which lead to the development of diverse RHMS deploying BLE communication interfaces for physiological patient data gathering. In this paper, we introduce the basic concepts related to RHMS design and development. Besides that, we focus our investigation on the BLE communication protocol used in the healthcare context and its configuration to sense several physiological data. Also, we highlight the different steps enabling reading sensed data on mobile application.

Keywords: Remote health monitoring system · Bluetooth Low Energy · Healthcare services

1 Introduction

1.1 General Context

Healthcare is one of the fastest-growing business fields and an important market for most countries and healthcare services are the most needed and consumed service by elderly people in the word. Providing healthcare services for every citizen everywhere becoming possible thanks to remote healthcare monitoring systems (RHMS), which allow long-term management of health conditions, diseases prevention and detection of emergencies. RHMS is based on the deployment of Wireless Body Area Network (WBAN) using wearable and/or implantable sensors in or around the human body. The sensed physiological data are forwarded

Supported by SFAX Digital Research Center: CRNS.

M. Jmaiel et al. (Eds.): ICOST 2020, LNCS 12157, pp. 41–54, 2020.
https://doi.org/10.1007/978-3-030-51517-1_4

to collecting node known as data collector or a gateway or a coordinator (smartphone or PDA: Personal Data Assistant) which is connected to the remote server (for data processing and storage) through the internet network (via WiFi) or the cellular networks (4G or 5G) [1]. RHMS could be based on three or four tiers architectures [2]. In this work, we focus our investigation on the first tier. Therefore, different communication technologies were suggested for the data exchange between the body sensors nodes and the coordinator(the first tier). Among the most deployed communication technologies in the first tier, we can highlight the following:

IEEE 802.15.4 [3–6].

IEEE 802.15.6 [7–12].

Bluetooth Low Energy [13–15].

The IEEE 802.15.6 [7] is the dedicated standards for the communication between the sensors and the coordinator. Nowadays, sensing devices with 802.15.6 modules are not available enough for the commercial usage in the market and they are more expensive than wearable sensors with Bluetooth Low Energy (BLE) which are widely commercialized by many sensors constructors such as libelium, mindwave.... For this reason, in this paper, our investigation is related to RHMS using sensors with BLE interfaces.

1.2   Contributions and Paper Organisation

The goal of this article is to study and analyze the most significant efforts related to RHMS integrating BLE communication modules. Accordingly, this paper provides a rich bibliography in the domain that can support future reading in this emerging field and pinpoints the technical issues related to the design and development of the BLE based RHMS. Furthermore, this investigation selects and considers several pioneering studies that can act as a roadmap of this wideranging research area. Although there is a lot of research works recently proposed that focused on RHMS, to the best of our knowledge, there is no thorough study that cogitates all BLE based RHMS design and development issues. The main contributions of this paper summarized as follows:

(1) state-of-the-art analysis related to BLE based RHMS for mono and multi physiological data sensing;

(2) comprehensive study and roadmap related to the design and the development of BLE based RHMS;

(3) BLE Processing and computation issues of sensed physiological data.

The rest of this paper is organized as follows: the second section describes the basic architecture of RHMS and analyses some related works about BLE based systems for single or multiple sensors. The third section overviews the basic concepts of communication systems based on BLE. The fourth section describes BLE Processing and computation of sensed physiological data such as ECG, SpO2, EMG, HR, etc... and highlights BLE service characteristics data related to each sensor. Finally, the fifth section concludes the paper and draws our future directions.

2   BLE Based RHMS

This section illustrates and explains the general architecture of the RHMS. Then, it studies and analyzes related works focusing on RHMS that integrate BLE communication interfaces between the physiological sensors and the PDA.

2.1   RHMS Basic Architecture

Generally, RHMS can be structured into three or four tiers [2]. In the following, we highlight the basic elements related to RHMS that are based on the three tiers architecture. The first tier involves the wearable sensors attached to the human body and the gateway or the coordinator. In this paper, the selected communication technology between the sensors and the PDA is BLE. Therefore the first tier which is the WBAN is composed by wearable sensors that sense the body vital signs (e.g. body temperature, heart rate, ECG, etc.) through the sensor nodes and sent them to the smartphone via BLE communication interfaces. The second tier that includes the networking infrastructure provides the connectivity between (1) the PDA and the remote medical servers, (2) between the PDA and the cloud. The third tier includes the medical web servers for data visualisation and the cloud (private: for security issues) for the data storage and processing. Figure 1 illustrates the RHMS three tiers architecture incorporating BLE communication interfaces.

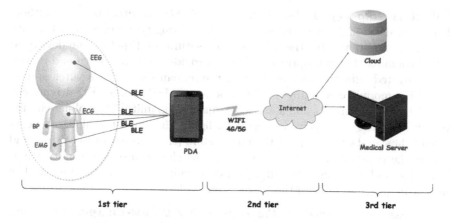

Fig. 1. Remote healthcare monitoring system integrating BLE communication interfaces.

2.2   Related Works About RHMS Using BLE

Several communication technologies could be used in the first tier (as we mentioned in the introduction). In this section, we will focus only on the RHMS related works that are based on the BLE protocol for data gathering. We classified the studied contributions into two categories. The first category corresponds to RHMS that control or sense one physiological patient data. The second category resembles the RHMS using multiple sensors to sense several physiological data.

Mono-Sensing RHMS. In this subsection, we will analyze related works about RHMS that sense and collect physiological information from a single sensor.

- *Wearable Noncontact Armband for Mobile ECG Monitoring System:* Rachim and all. [16] proposed to implement a mobile ECG monitoring system using a wearable noncontact armband ECG signal. The proposed system solved the problem of the previous healthcare heart devices which do not provide patient's information such as heartbeat, heart disease, and heart conditions. The proposed system consists of capacitive-coupled electrodes fixed in an armband which is more convenient (smaller) than systems with ECG sensors strapped to the chest. The capacitive-coupled electrodes can sense bio-signals through the clothes. According to the experimental results carried by the authors, the developed system can still function with different clothing thicknesses between the sensors and the skin and when the user carries out various daily living activities. Furthermore, the authors developed an Android application showing in real-time the evolution of the ECG signal on a graph and analyze the sensed data for first notifications making.

- *Wireless Ring-Type Pulse Oximeter with Multi-detectors:* The authors of [17] conceived and developed a wireless finger ring-type pulse oximeter with multi-detectors to monitor the blood oxygen saturation (SpO2). The developed system contains (1) three optical probes to provide the light source and receive the penetrated light that passes through the human tissue; (2) a wireless data acquisition module containing a microprocessor (MSP430), a LED driving circuit, PD amplifier circuits and a wireless transmission unit. PD amplifier circuits amplify and filter the received penetrated light. Therefore, the digitized penetrated light signal will be sent to the host system (that receive, display, store and analyze the penetrated light signal) using a wireless transmission unit including a Bluetooth v2.0 module and a printed circuit board (PCB) antenna. The monitoring program built in the host system will.

- *Wireless Scale Based on the Bluetooth 4.0 Low-Energy:* Huang and all. [18] realized a low power and smart Bluetooth scale with a sensor chip CC2540 monitored through a mobile application. The weight sensors produce deformation and change their shapes when a patient ascend on the scale this lead to a variation of the driven voltage. Therefore, these signals are amplified and transmitted to an A/D converter.

- *Muscule Activity Monitoring:* Several systems integrating EMG sensors to measure the electrical muscle activity and a BLE communication module to transmit gathered data to a mobile phone. In this context, authors in [19] designed a fabric stretch sensor embedded system for muscle activity monitoring. The strain sensor resistance varies sensitively with body movements. The designed system includes an application that shows muscle activity data and highlights the features such as muscle movement distribution. To avoid sports injuries during exercise, authors in [20] designed an EMG patch to supervise the muscle fatigue conditions during isotonic contraction. The developed system deploys two electrodes to measure the sEMG signal. A microcontroller unit in the EMG patch is used to measure in real-time the median frequency of an EMG signal. When the muscle is tired, the median frequency will shift to a low value. The sensed values are sent via BLE to a mobile phone running an APP that displays the muscle fatigue levels and the user riding information.

- Brain Activity Monitoring: Sullivan and all. [21] proposed a brain activity monitoring system using the non-invasive electroencephalogram EEG sensor that measures the neural electrical activity of the brain from the scalp surface. The developed EEG monitoring system assisted by deep learning mechanism provides information about neonatal brain health to help clinicians in neonatal EEG abnormalities diagnosing. The proposed system uses a low-cost -low-power EEG acquisition system including BLE interface for communication. Besides that, the authors developed an Android app visualizing single-channel EEG and the neonatal seizure presence. A deep convolutional neural network and an algorithm for EEG sonification used to perceive EEG morphology changes.

- Breath Rate Monitoring: Authors in [22] developed a new system to supervise in real-time the respiratory signal. The developed system includes three parts: smart belts, a display unit, and an online storage unit. A textile-based pressure fabric attached to a belt converting the stomach movement into an electrical signal that is transmitted via BLE to a remote station where it is displayed in real-time and uploaded to an online repository for future analysis. The authors tested the performance of the system when individuals performed activities like talking and walking. In [23] authors developed a system detecting sleep disorders such as respiratory flow repetitive cessations during sleep using a magnetometer sensor placed onto the body detecting millimetre night-time breathing movements by measuring the change in the magnetic vectors. The developed system includes a noninvasive wearable sensor, a wireless BLE module and a low-power microcontroller.

Table 1 gives a summary of all mono-sensing RHMS based BLE system.

Multi-sensing RHMS. This subsection analyzes related works about RHMS that sense and collect physiological informations from more than one physioligical sensor.

- Cardiovascular RHMS Using Multi-sensing: Authors in [30] designed an epidermal patch, which is called Chem-Phys that offers simultaneous real-time monitoring of a biochemical (lactate) and an electrophysiological signal (electrocardiogram) for fitness monitoring. Besides that, for monitoring the cardiovascular disease authors in [31] designed wearable devices such as ECG and heart

Table 1. Recapitulative table related to monosensing RHMS based BLE.

Ref and date	Sensors	Placement	Applications
[16] 2016	ECG	Arm	Wearable Noncontact Armband for Mobile ECG Monitoring System
[17] 2014	SpO2	Finger	Oxygenated hemoglobin in the blood
[18] 2015	Weight	Outside the body	Low power and smart Bluetooth scale for weight monitoring.
[19] 2017	Strain	Fabric stretch sensor attached to the clothes	-Muscle activaty Monitoring and body motion recognition
[20] 2019	EMG	Lower leg, the gastrocnemius muscle	Real time monitoring of muscle attached to the clothes
[21] 2018	EEG	Scalp	Brain activity Monitoring
[22] 2018	PPG	Stomach movement	Respiratory rate monitoring

rate that can be integrated into clothes or attached directly to the human body. In addition, Li Jinming and all. [26] proposed a multi-parameter cardiac remote monitoring system based on ECG, pulse rate and heart sound sensed data. This system is composed of a multi-channel physiological parameter acquisition unit, an Android terminal, a cloud server and a Bluetooth Low Energy BLE protocol for data communication. Besides that, [29] introduced heart-monitoring system evaluating the heart conditions based on sensed data from several wearable devices such as heart rate, blood pressure, body and skin temperature. The sensed patient information are transmitted to a smartphone (running an Android application) by the low energy protocol BLE and then will be visualized on the Web application. According the authors, evaluation of the developed monitoring system under expert's supervision for 40 individuals (aged between 18 and 66 years) showed that the proposed system is convenient and reliable generating warning messages to the doctor and patient under critical circumstances.

- Diabete Chronic Condition Monitoring Using Multi-sensing: Muhammad Syafrudin and all. [27] developed a healthcare monitoring system wich utilizing BLE based sensors to control the personal vital signs data such as heart rate, blood glucose, and blood pressure to support diabetic patients to manage individually their chronic condition. The BLE used in this system to transmit patient's health information from sensors to the smartphone, while to manage the sensor data by utilizing the real-time data processing, which used the Apache Kafka as a platform and MongoDB as a database for storing the patient's informations.

- A Wearable Human Healthcare Monitoring System: proposed by [19] supervising personal's information such as body temperature, heart rate, and blood oxygen saturation. The sensing node is wearable, miniaturized and based on the microchip CC2538 and Contiki OS. The sensed data are transmitted via a BLE communication interface to a mobile application. These data are stored on cloud server using the MQTT protocol and analyzed via the data

mining approaches to diagnose user's health status. In addition, authors in [28] designed a low-cost healthcare monitoring IoT-based system with the Fog layer sensing vital signs such as ECG, body temperature, and the respiration rate and contextual data (i.e. humidity and environment temperature).

- *Chronic Respiratory Monitoring Using Multi-sensing:* James and all. [22] developed BLE-based RHMS to monitor chronic respiratory disease that sense multi-parameters. The system comprises a chest patch and a wristband. The chest patch sensors corresponds to ECG, PPG, motion and acoustic signal. The wristband sensors track ozone exposure, ambient relative humidity, ambient temperature, PPG and motion. The data from each sensor is transferring by BLE communication interface to the server for storage.

3   BLE Communication Protocols

3.1   Basic Concepts

Bluetooth v4.0 known as Bluetooth Low Energy is ideal for applications requiring sporadic or periodic transfer of small amounts of data. Thus, BLE is well suited for sensors, actuators and other small devices requiring low power consumption. BLE works well with high numbers of communication nodes with limited latency requirements, very low power consumption and short connection times and wake-up. BLE aims to provide the same communication range as classic Bluetooth while consuming less power. The most significant differences between BLE and Classic Bluetooth are (1) the BLE has a lower data rate, (2) BLE use just 40 channels (37 for data and 3 for advertising) instead of 79, (3) no support for audio and (4) simplified state machines. Both BLE and Classic Bluetooth, operates in the 2.4 GHz ISM (industrial scientific and medical) frequency band, precisely BLE frequency band range from 2.402 GHz to 2.480 GHz. To minimize the overlapping with other IEEE 802.11 channels, the three advertisement channels (37, 38, and 39) centered on 2,402 GHz, 2,426 GHz and 2,480 GHz. Advertising is a process required for devices to find each other. At the link layer BLE device, function as a state machine with four states: standby, scanning (master procedure), advertising (slave procedure), initiating and connection. Furthermore, BLE operates in piconets wit a star topology. The central node is the master and all other nodes in the piconet are slaves. BLE has an architecture client/server which the client can be the Master such as smartphone, gateway, etc and the server is the peripheral such as sensors.

The connection establishement occurs after sending connection request packet which handle connection parameters (connection interval, slave latency and supervision timeout).

- *Connection interval:* corresponds to the time elapsed between two connection events. BLE devices are communicating only in connection events to save energy. So bigger interval between those events will save more energy but decrease data rate. No matter if device has data to send, it has to wait until next connection event. The interval can be set from 7.5 ms to 4 s.

- **Slave latency:** is the number of connection events, that sensor node can skip to save energy without the risk of disconnected.

- **Connection supervision timeout:** specifies the maximum time between two valid data received before a connection is lost.

The master coordinates the MAC using a TDMA scheme, determines the instants in which slaves are required to listen, and provides them with the map of data channels to be used.

3.2 BLE Protocols Stack

BLE protocol stack involves two main elements: the controller and the Host. The Controller includes the physical layer and the link layer. Both implemented on a single chip with an integrated radio interface. The Host runs on an application processor. It covers five upper layer functionalities (the Logical Link Control and Adaptation Protocol (L2CAP), the Attribute Protocol (ATT), the Generic Attribute Profile (GATT), the Security Manager Protocol (SMP) and the Generic Access Profile (GAP). The standardized Host Controller Interface (HCI) provides the exchange between the Host and the Controller. An application layer can be developed on the top of the Host.

- **L2CAP:** acts as an interface between the link layer and the Upper layer protocols (ATT, SMP and Link Layer control signaling). It multiplexes, segments, reassembles data packets and offers support quality of service management.

- **ATT:** is a client/server stateless protocol based on attributes presented by a device. Each server holds data organized in the form of attribute managed by the GATT. Universally unique identifier (UUID), a set of permissions and a value identify each attribute (see Fig. 2).

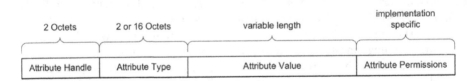

Fig. 2. Attribute representation.

- **SMP:** offers security services for protecting the information exchange between two connected peers. It allows the generation and the exchange of security keys and it hide the public Bluetooth Address if required.

- **GATT:** defines the GATT server and the GATT client and specifies the framework and operations for data transfer procedures over a BLE connection. A GATT client requests and receives data from a GATT server, whose makes the data available to the GATT client. Data is structured in sections called services that assembles related pieces of user data known as characteristics.

- **GAP:** outlines rules and concepts to standardize the low-level operation of devices. It defines how devices perform control procedures such as device discovery, security establishment and connection... to guarantee interoperability between devices from different vendors.

4 Reading Sensed Physiological Signs with BLE

The most difficult task confronted during mobile healthcare application development is sensed data reading. In this paper, we use BLE to get data from sensors and forward them to the PDA. In general, we develop an application for Android device (PDA: mobile phone) to get data from sensors. The complexity resides in the diversity of health devices (thermometer, heart-rate monitor, blood pressure monitor, scale ...), where each device has a specific profile, services, UUID, characteristics, and descriptors. Therefore, to read measured data from sensors, we need to develop a specific application for each profile. In this paper, we describe two health devices equipped with the BLE corresponding respectively to Health Thermometer and Blood Pressure Monitor.

4.1 Example of Services and Characteristics of HDP

In order to standardize the way medical data is transmitted over BLE technology, the Bluetooth Special Interest Group (SIG) released in 2008 the Health Device Profile (HDP) that utilizes the IEEE 11073-20601 Data Exchange Protocol as the transport content. Below the specification of the service and characteristic of the studied health devices which according to the SIG group.

Thermometer:
(1) Health Thermometer Service: (UUID = 0x1809; Definition: This service exposes temperature and other data from a Health Thermometer Sensor; Type = org.bluetooth.service.health-thermometer),
(2) Temperature Measurement Characteristic (UUID = 0x2A1C; Definition: This characteristic is used to send a temperature measurement; Type: org.bluetooth.characteristic.temperature measurement).

SPO2:
(1) Health PulseOximeter Service: (UUID = 0x1822; Definition: This Service exposes pulse oximetry data related to a non-invasive pulse oximetry sensor for consumer healthcare applications; Type = org.bluetooth.service.pulse-oximeter),
(2) PLX Continuous-Measurement (UUID = 0x2A5F; Definition: This characteristic is used to send a PulseOximetre measurement; Type: type = org.bluetooth.characteristic.plx-continuous-measurement).
Developers can obtains the services and characteristics of any BLE health device from the main Bluetooth webpage [24].

4.2 Steps for Reading Sensed Data on Mobile App

The development of a Mobile App able to read BLE sensed data can be resumed by the following steps:

Step 1: Declaring permission on a manifest file is required to use BLE features and to perform BLE communication toward requesting or accepting connection or reading the different measurements.

Step 2: Assigning UUID for service and characteristic as declared in the previous subsection.

Step 3: Chekinging that BLE is supported on the PDA and enable it.

Step 4: Turning On the Bluetooth and displaying dialogue box on the PDA that asking for permission from the user to turn on Bluetooth.

Step 5: Scanning and visualizing nearby BLE health devices and their addresses on the PDA.

Step 6: Connecting to a GATT server on health device to manage the connection and to send data using the connectGatt() method that requires as parameters(a Context object, autoConnect and a reference to a BluetoothGattCallback). The BluetoothGattCallback is used to deliver GATT client operations to the client (Mobile App on the PDA).

Step 7: Discovering, reading and displaying GATT services and characteristics by controlling the device activity (DeviceControlActivity).

Step 8: Reading Sensed Data(for example: temperature). Thus, we set notification or indication value on Temperature Measurement Characteristic then write to the descriptor to set the right value for characteristics. The updates from the health device on characteristics value will be posted on the next callback using onCharacteristicChanged.

Developers can get detailed description and example of codes from the main android(section Bluetoot connectivity) webpage [25].

We recapitulate the different steps required for enabling a mobile App to get sensed data from health devices in Fig. 3.

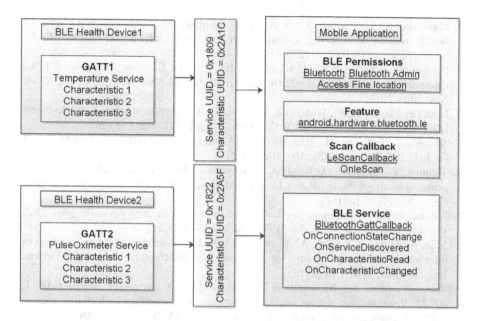

Fig. 3. Required components for android BLE communication.

5   Conclusion

In this paper, we provided a detailed study related to RHMS based on BLE communication. We notice that several RHMS based BLE was developed and tested for different physiological signs, accordingly, in this paper, we studied and highlighted different mono and multi-sensing RHMS using BLE communication interfaces for physiological signs sensing. Besides that, we overviewed BLE communication in a comprehensive way to help readers and mobile app developers to understand the basic concepts of BLE communication. Furthermore, we detailed the different steps required for enabling sensor-side control and BLE communication on an android system as the mobile platform for the health sensor's client application. We limited our investigation to sensed data reading. In an extended version of this work, we will provide a whole prototype that could be tested beyond the development environment and providing several vital signs monitoring (remote control, data visualization graphically) and decision making through the processing of sensed vital signs.

References

1. Movassaghi, S., Abolhasan, M., Lipman, J., Smith, D., Jamalipour, A.: Wireless body area networks: a survey. IEEE Commun. Surv. Tutorials **16**(3), 1658–1686 (2014)

2. Manirabona, A., Fourati, L.C.: A 4-tiers architecture for mobile WBAN based health remote monitoring system. Wireless Netw. **24**(6), 2179–2190 (2017). https://doi.org/10.1007/s11276-017-1456-7

3. Fourati, H., Khssibi, S., Val, T., Idoudi, H., Van den Bossche, A., Saidane, L.A.: Comparative study of IEEE 802.15. 4 and IEEE 802.15. 6 for WBAN-based CANet, November 2015

4. Iova, O., Theoleyre, F., Watteyne, T., Noel, T.: The love-hate relationship between IEEE 802.15. 4 and RPL. IEEE Commun. Mag. **55**(1), 188–194 (2016)

5. Ahmed, N., Rahman, H., Hussain, M.I.: A comparison of 802.11 ah and 802.15. 4 for IoT. ICT Express **2**(3), 100–102 (2016)

6. Tennina, S., Gaddour, O., Koubâa, A., Royo, F., Alves, M., Abid, M.: Z-monitor: a protocol analyzer for IEEE 802.15. 4-based low-power wireless networks. Comput. Netw. **95**, 77–96 (2016)

7. Astrin, A.: IEEE Standard for Local and metropolitan area networks part 15.6: Wireless Body Area Networks. IEEE Std 802.15. 6 (2012)

8. Mile, A., Okeyo, G., Kibe, A.: Hybrid IEEE 802.15. 6 wireless body area networks interference mitigation model for high mobility interference scenarios. Wireless Eng. Technol. **9**(02), 34 (2018)

9. Zhao, B., Lian, Y., Niknejad, A.M., Heng, C.H.: A low-power compact IEEE 802.15. 6 compatible human body communication transceiver with digital sigma-delta IIR mask shaping. IEEE J. Solid-State Circ. **54**(2), 346–357 (2018)

10. Sarkar, S., Misra, S., Bandyopadhyay, B., Chakraborty, C., Obaidat, M.S.: Performance analysis of IEEE 802.15. 6 MAC protocol under non-ideal channel conditions and saturated traffic regime. IEEE Trans. Comput. **64**(10), 2912–2925 (2015)

11. Salehi, S.A., Razzaque, M.A., Tomeo-Reyes, I., Hussain, N.: IEEE 802.15. 6 standard in wireless body area networks from a healthcare point of view. In: IEEE, 22nd Asia-Pacific Conference on Communications (APCC), pp. 523–528, August 2016

12. Liu, H., et al.: Performance assessment of IR-UWB body area network (BAN) based on IEEE 802.15. 6 standard. IEEE Antennas Wirel. Propag. Lett. **15**, 1645–1648 (2016)

13. Sherratt, R.S., Janko, B., Hui, T., Harwin, W., Diaz-Sanchez, D.: Dictionary memory based software architecture for distributed bluetooth low energy host controllers enabling high coverage in consumer residential healthcare environments. In: 2017 IEEE International Conference on Consumer Electronics (ICCE), pp. 406–407. IEEE, January 2017

14. Şişman, C., Sağir, S., Kaya, İ., Ünal, S., Baltaci, Y.: Coding and diversity gains of low power radio communications: BLE and ZigBee. In: 2018 41st International Conference on Telecommunications and Signal Processing (TSP), pp. 1–4. IEEE, July 2018

15. Santos, D.F., Gorgônio, K.C., Perkusich, A., Almeida, H.O.: A standard-based and context-aware architecture for personal healthcare smart gateways. J. Med. Syst. **40**(10), 224(2016)

16. Rachim, V.P., Chung, W.Y.: Wearable noncontact armband for mobile ECG monitoring system. IEEE Trans. Biomed. Circuits Syst. **10**(6), 1112–1118 (2016)

17. Huang, C.Y., Chan, M.C., Chen, C.Y., Lin, B.S.: Novel wearable and wireless ring-type pulse oximeter with multi-detectors. Sensors **14**(9), 17586–17599 (2014)

18. Huang, Q., Chen, K.: The implementation of wireless scale based on the Bluetooth 4.0 low-energy. In: 2015 International Industrial Informatics and Computer Engineering Conference. Atlantis Press, March 2015

19. Vu, C., Kim, J.: Muscle activity monitoring with fabric stretch sensors. Fibers Polym. **18**(10), 1931–1937 (2017). https://doi.org/10.1007/s12221-017-7042-x
20. Liu, S.H., Lin, C.B., Chen, Y., Chen, W., Huang, T.S., Hsu, C.Y.: An EMG patch for the real-time monitoring of muscle-fatigue conditions during exercise. Sensors **19**(14), 3108 (2019)
21. O'Sullivan, M., et al.: Neonatal EEG interpretation and decision support framework for mobile platforms. In: 2018 40th Annual International Conference of the IEEE Engineering in Medicine and Biology Society (EMBC), pp. 4881–4884. IEEE, July 2018
22. Mukhopadhyay, B., Sharma, O., Kar, S.: IoT based wearable knitted fabric respiratory monitoring system. In: 2018 IEEE SENSORS, pp. 1–4. IEEE, October 2018
23. Milici, S., Lázaro, A., Villarino, R., Girbau, D., Magnarosa, M.: Wireless wearable magnetometer-based sensor for sleep quality monitoring. IEEE Sens. J. **18**(5), 2145–2152 (2018)
24. Bluetooth   Homepage.   https://www.bluetooth.com/specifications/gatt/characteristics/. Accessed 09 Feb 2020
25. Android   Homepage.   https://developer.android.com/guide/topics/connectivity/bluetooth-le/. Accessed 09 Feb 2020
26. Jinming, L., Cheng, Z., Yinlong, L., Yihe, W.: Multi-parameter cardiac remote monitoring system based on Android. J. Excellence Comput. Sci. Eng. **2**(2), 18–24 (2016)
27. Alfian, G., Syafrudin, M., Ijaz, M.F., Syaekhoni, M.A., Fitriyani, N.L., Rhee, J.: A personalized healthcare monitoring system for diabetic patients by utilizing BLE-based sensors and real-time data processing. Sensors **18**(7), 2183 (2018)
28. Gia, T.N., Jiang, M., Sarker, V.K., Rahmani, A.M., Westerlund, T., Liljeberg, P., Tenhunen, H.: Low-cost fog-assisted health-care IoT system with energy-efficient sensor nodes. In: 2017 13th International Wireless Communications and Mobile Computing Conference (IWCMC), pp. 1765–1770. IEEE, June 2017
29. Kakria, P., Tripathi, N.K., Kitipawang, P.: A real-time human-health monitoring system for remote cardiac patients using smartphone and wearable sensors. Int. J. Telemed. Appl. **2015** (2015)
30. Imani, S., et al.: A wearable chemical–electrophysiological hybrid biosensing system for real-time health and fitness monitoring. Nat. Commun. **7**(1), 1–7 (2016)
31. Pigini, L., et al.: Pilot test of a new personal health system integrating environmental and wearable sensors for telemonitoring and care of elderly people at home (SMARTA project). Gerontology **63**(3), 281–286 (2017)

Modeling and Specification of Bootstrapping and Registration Design Patterns for IoT Applications

Mohamed Hadj Kacem$^{(\boxtimes)}$, Imen Tounsi, and Najeh Khalfi

ReDCAD laboratory, University of Sfax, Sfax, Tunisia
mohamed.hadjkacem@isimsf.rnu.tn, imen.tounsi@redcad.org
http://www.redcad.org/members/hadjkacemm/,
http://www.redcad.org/members/imen.tounsi/

Abstract. The architectures of software systems are becoming more complex, large, and dynamic. The design of these architectures allows architects to master building complex software systems. But, their informal description, may give rise to ambiguity, their understanding becomes more and more difficult and leads to the incorrect implementation of these software systems. There are many solutions allowing software architecture design. In this paper, we use software design patterns as a solution. This is due to their reusable software elements. Our principal objective is to propose other alternatives to the informal visual description of software architectures. In past work, we have studied Service Oriented Architectures. We used SOA design patterns with standard formal notations. This work is a continuation to the past one. We apply our approach on design patterns for the Internet of Things. We introduce a refinement-based approach for modeling IoT design patterns. It takes advantage of graphical modeling and formal method. It is organized around two main axes. The first axis is to provide modeling solutions in conformance with the UML standard language. The second axis covers the general specification of design pattern models with the Event-B method. As a result, we propose a design support tool for IoT architectures based on IoT design patterns. It allows modeling of correct-by-design software systems.

Keywords: Design patterns · UML modeling · Event-B method · Pattern modeling · Formal specification

1 Introduction

The Internet of Things (IoT) is a complex domain of application that allows objects to exist on the Internet. Creating systems in this domain is a challenge because it involves both software and hardware, sensing and actuating devices, a communication infrastructure, in addition to storage constraints. For this, a variety of IoT design patterns have been proposed in various categories to address variety of issues [7]. They propose solutions for common and recurring

© The Author(s) 2020
M. Jmaiel et al. (Eds.): ICOST 2020, LNCS 12157, pp. 55–66, 2020.
https://doi.org/10.1007/978-3-030-51517-1_5

problems to architects and designers in the IoT domain. Most of these patterns are presented visually and informally, there is no formal semantics associated with them. Hence, their meanings may be imprecise. They can lead to their misunderstanding and misuse.

To remedy this problem, we propose an approach that allows to model and specify these patterns with a formal notation that allows to reuse them correctly. Our objective is to prove the relevance of these patterns. We illustrate our approach with different pattern examples. We propose a graphical modeling of these patterns in order to describe both their structural and behavioral features. Then, we propose a generic formal specification of these patterns using the formal Event-B method. Finally, we develop a graphical editor describing our approach using the Eclipse modeling platform.

The rest of this paper is organized as follows. Section 2 focuses on the structural modeling of IoT design patterns and Sect. 3 focuses on the behavioral modeling. In Sect. 4, we present an application to a case study of our approach. Section 5 describes how to formally specify IoT design patterns with the Event-B method. In Sect. 6, we present our tool, which implements the proposed approach. Section 7 discusses related work. Section 8 concludes and gives future work directions.

2   Structural Patterns Modeling

We provide a modeling solution for describing IoT design patterns using a visual notation based on the graphical UML language in order to give readable models. We first describe a meta-model, then we present a model instance of the design pattern. The metamodel extends the component diagram of UML 2.0 (Unified Modeling Language). The use of UML is motivated by four distinct rationales: (i) It is a standard modeling language defined by OMG. (ii) It is used to describe software architectures. (iii) Component diagrams of UML allow us to represent structural features of patterns. (iv) Sequence diagrams of UML allow us to represent behavioral features of patterns.

Structural features of patterns are generally specified by the types of entities. The configuration of the entities is also described in terms of static relationships between them [16]. We model structural features of design patterns with the extended *Component* diagram. In the following, we present the proposed metamodel. An example of a corresponding model is presented and illustrated with case studies as follows.

2.1   Metamodel

The extended *Component* diagram describes, by a set of concepts, the structure of an IoT architecture. We use it to describe the architecture of IoT design patterns. More specifically, it is to define the entities that can be involved in the pattern, their types and their dependencies (connections). The metamodel presented in Fig. 1 extends the metamodel of the component diagram of UML

2.0. In this metamodel, we concentrate on two categories of design patterns; "Bootstrapping Design Patterns" and "Registration Design Patterns".

"Bootstrapping Design Patterns" allow configuring new devices. They are composed of "Medium Based Bootstrap Pattern" and "Remote Bootstrap Pattern". "Medium Based Bootstrap Pattern" allows to configure a new device on-site through a removable storage medium inserted in the device. This support contains the necessary information for configuration. "Remote Bootstrap Pattern" is a configuration pattern used in case that a device is placed far away and is difficult to reach. The configuration in this case is done by downloading configuration information from a bootstrap server.

"Registration Design Patterns" allow to register the attributes and the features of a new device on the Back-end server. The registration is used to facilitate the communication and the interrogation with other connected objects. There are many registration patterns. In this work, we present two patterns. So "Registration Design Patterns" are composed of "Automatic Client Driven Registration Pattern" and "Server Driven Model Pattern". The "Automatic Client Driven Registration Pattern" allows the device to register on the Back-end server via an API call. The "Server Driven Model Pattern" is used to create a device model that includes its description and functionality.

The basic elements of the metamodel are:

Component and Object: Entities, that make up the architecture of an IoT design pattern, can be either *Components* or *Objects*. All objects are components, but not all components are necessarily objects. An object can be connected to the internet, it can receive and send data.

Port: Entities can have *Ports* that constitute interaction points with their environment. These *Ports* are related to one or more *provided* or *required Interfaces*.

Interface: The interfaces are the points of communication that allow interaction with the environment. For an entity, there are two types of interfaces. The *Provided Interfaces* describe the services provided by the component. The *Required Interfaces* describe the required services that other components must provide for the good functioning of component. These interfaces are specified via the ports.

Connector: The communication path between Entities within an architecture is called a *Connector*. It ensures the link between a *Provided* port and a *Required* port to form a complete and coherent system.

Device: A device is an Object. It is the entry point of the physical environment, it is used to process sensor data and to control actuators.

2.2 General Pattern Model

In this section, we present two general pattern models as instances of the proposed metamodel. We have used different notations that can be used as a graphical description of the entities presented in the model. We are based on the work of Reinfurt et al. [8].

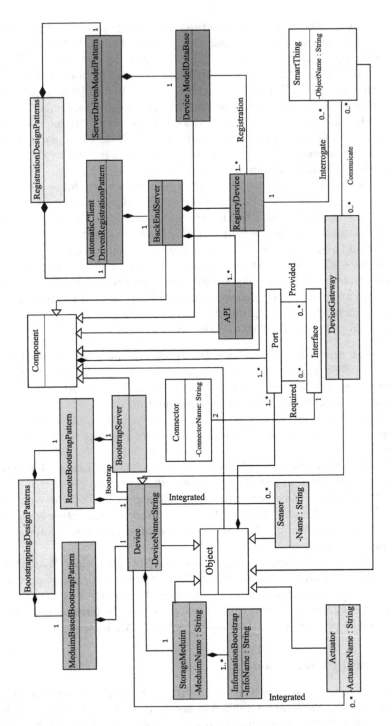

Fig. 1. Metamodel of IoT design patterns

There are two possible general models depending on the location of the device. If the device is placed locally, we use the "Medium Based Bootstrap Pattern" as a solution to configure the new device. If it is placed at a distance, we use the "Remote Bootstrap Pattern" as a solution. In Fig. 2, we represent the general pattern model of the "Medium Based Bootstrap Pattern". The solution proposed by this pattern to configure a new local device is to use an object of type *Storage Medium* containing information configuration. In Fig. 3, we represent the general pattern model of the "Remote Bootstrap Pattern". The solution proposed by this pattern to configure a new remote device is to use a component of type *BootstrapServer* allowing the upload of the configuration information using the **PushBD** connector.

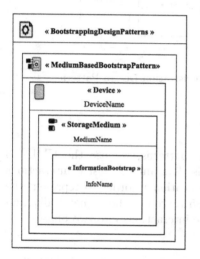

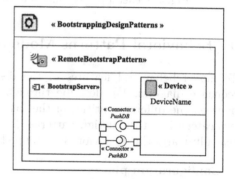

Fig. 2. General pattern model of the Medium Based Bootstrap Pattern

Fig. 3. General pattern model of the Remote Bootstrap Pattern

In Fig. 4, we represent the general pattern model of the "Registration Design Pattern". The solution proposed by this pattern to register a new device. The device is related to the *BackEndServer* with a connector named **PushDA** in order to be registered on it via an *API* call. Meta-data entered by the device are recorded in the *RegistryDevice* through the **PushAR** connector. The *RegistryDevice* component has a connector named **PushRDm** to store a device template in a database component named *Device Model DataBase* of the "Server Driven Model pattern". A device can integrate an object of type *Sensor* or an *Actuator*. All objects of the patterns have ports to communicate with others.

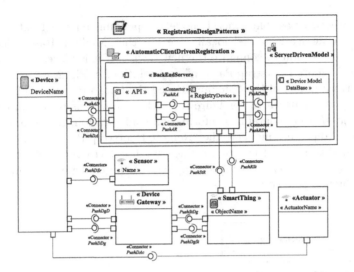

Fig. 4. General pattern model of the Registration Design Pattern

3   Behavioral Patterns Modeling

To model behavioral features of the design patterns, we use the UML 2.3 sequence diagram. We describe through this diagram successive interactions between the different entities of the IoT application in order to represent the two categories of the design patterns. Figure 5 represent the sequence diagram that illustrates this behavior. We grouped the interactions into two phases.

– **Configuration phase:**
  • **Local configuration:** In the configuration phase and at the "Medium Based Bootstrap Pattern" level, the configuration is done by cutting the storage medium configuration information (*Storage Medium*) to the device.
  • **Remote configuration:** The configuration at the "Remote Bootstrap Pattern" is done by downloading information from a *Bootstrap Server* to the device.
– **Registration phase:** In the registration phase, the device triggers a registration process on the *Back-end Server*. After the registration, the metadata provided by the device are registered in the *RegistryDevice*. Subsequently, an instance of the model of this device is stored in a *Device Model Database*.

If the device, go through the configuration and the registration phases, it becomes able to create communication links with other connected objects. The exchange of messages between them is done through a communication intermediary (*Device Gateway*). A connected object (smart thing) can interact directly with the *RegistryDevice* to retrieve information about a device if it is offline.

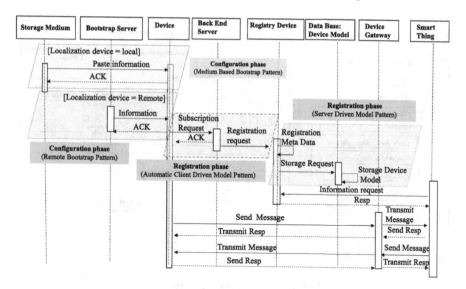

Fig. 5. Sequence diagram of the used IoT patterns

4 Case Study: Smart Home

To validate our approach, we chose to apply a case study in the IoT application domain called "Smart Home".

A smart home is usually made up of remote-controlled automated components which can be doors, windows, lamps, etc. It can include several other components that can be monitored and controlled remotely. Most of these components can be controlled by a mobile device or a computer. In our case study, we add a new device (a camera) to a smart home. This device makes it possible to control the various rooms of the house. For example, if a door or a window left open, the camera informs the user immediately through a notification sent to their smartphone. It can also send alerts when it detects unknown faces.

First, the camera is added without any information to initiate its first connection. We then apply the Meduim Based Bootstrap design pattern to have its configuration information. This information is inserted into the device through a memory card. Second, we go through the registration procedure on the main server (BackEndServer). This procedure is done through the use of the two patterns of the Registration Design Patterns category which are the automatic client driven registration pattern and the server driven model pattern which allow registering the device on the main server. Finally, the camera became able to communicate and create connection links with its communication partners. The camera communicates with the user's smartphone to notify him of what is happening in real-time.

We model this application through the use of the model shown in Fig. 6. The camera is associated with an object of type "Device", the memory card is defined as an object of type "Storage Medium" and the Smart phone is associated as

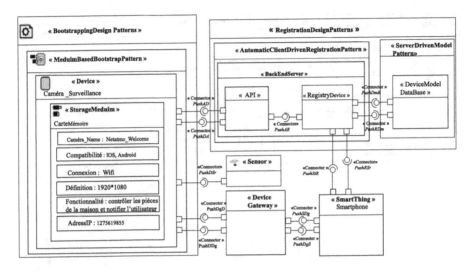

Fig. 6. Smart home case study

an object of type "SmartThing". The propagation of events between objects is done through a *DeviceGateway*.

5   Patterns Specification

UML, as semi-formal language offers several benefits to the definition of IoT design patterns, such as visual and standard notation. This graphical aspect is certainly interesting and useful to an architect, in the sense that graphic design is easy. However, the fact that UML lack a precise semantics is a serious drawback because this language did not allow checks which we must carry. So, pattern models generated at the modeling approach can be ambiguous and imprecise. In addition, during the modeling phase, the architect can easily fall into the error. This is due to the absence of a precise formal semantics of UML that do not provide rigorous tools for verification and proof. However, any error or any bad modeling of a design pattern can cause serious problems that generate bad consequences.

Thus, ensuring the reliability and the correctness of IoT design patterns is a goal that we have fixed. For this, we propose an approach to formally specify design patterns by using the formal method Event-B that is well suited to our needs and goals. Thus, each diagram graphically modeled will be accompanied by a formal semantics. This approach allows the validation of the modeling part and ensure the verification of the relevant properties of design patterns.

Event-B method is well-suited for specifying IoT design patterns: (i) The primary concept in doing formal developments in Event-B is that of a model. It is made of several components of two kinds: machines and contexts. Machines contain the dynamic parts of a model, whereas contexts contain the static parts of a model [1]. Thanks to this classification, Event-B allows the specification of structural and behavioral features of design patterns. (ii) Refinement techniques proposed by this method allow us to build patterns gradually and at different abstraction levels. (iii) Mathematical proofs allow verifying model consistency and consistency between refinement levels. (iv) The most important reason to use Event-B method is the availability of a supporting tool called the Rodin platform [2]. It is an Eclipse-based tool set that provides effective support for modeling and automated proof. The platform is open source and is further extendable with plug-ins. A range of plug-ins have already been developed including ones that support animation and model checking like the Prob plug-in [5] that we used.

Extended *Component* diagram that model structural features of design patterns are transformed to a context in the Event-B method in which we specify entities of the architecture and their relations. The *Sequence* diagram is transformed into a machine in Event-B in which we specify events made between entities of the patterns. This transformation is proposed in order to attribute formal notations to IoT design patterns for the purpose of checking their design correctness in a second step. We explicitly defined a refinement strategy to follow. This strategy is interesting because it defines the pattern development process and improves the quality of the obtained models, and therefore the success of the formal development process. We defined specification levels by using a step-wise development approach.

6   Tool Support

We developed a graphical modeling tool that implements our approach; it ensures an easy and efficient modeling way for users. With our tool, we aim to make concrete the aforementioned concepts. The architect can model the solution of the IoT design patterns using an Eclipse plug-in that we propose. The tool, in its development, is based on EMF[1] (*Eclipse Modeling Framework*) [10]. This was chosen since we use models, which are basic building units, to develop our approach (Fig. 7).

7   Related Work

Research connected to design patterns in the field of software architecture, are mainly classified into four branches of work according to their architectural style. The first is about design patterns for Object-Oriented Architectures, the second is about design patterns for Enterprise Application Integration (EAI), the third is for Service Oriented Architectures (SOA) and the fourth one is for connected object architectures.

Most of the proposed design patterns are described with a combination of a text description and a graphical representation sometimes using a proprietary notation in the aim of making them easy to understand. However,

---

[1] https://wiki.eclipse.org/Eclipse_Modeling_Framework.

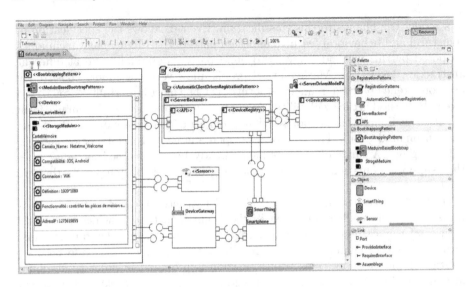

Fig. 7. The tool editor

these descriptions make patterns ambiguous and may lack details. Some work so have proposed the semi-formal representations of these patterns using modeling languages [4]. Some other works use or provide formal languages based on mathematical notation for a precise pattern specification [16]. However, these approaches require knowledge of mathematics and first order logic to use them. Some research has chosen to combine the semi-formal and formal representations of patterns. This representation ensures a better understanding and precision of patterns. Generally speaking, there is a consensus on the elements that make up and define a design pattern. However, there is no consensus on the specification of the patterns.

In past work [11,13] we focused on both the modeling, the formal specification and the composition of SOA design patterns [12,14] and established the link between them with an automatic transformation [15]. We used the SoaML language for the pattern modeling that ease the understanding of pattern models. For the pattern specification, we used the Event-B formal method in order to attribute formal notations to SOA design patterns for the purpose of checking their design correctness.

In this work, we are interested with the IoT design patterns. In this context we find several researchers who proposed a set of IoT design patterns in various categories. Eloranta et al. [3] proposed patterns for the construction of distributed control systems. Qanbari et al. [6] presented four patterns for the supply, deployment, orchestration and monitoring shipboard applications. Reinfurt et al. [7,9] have published patterns for device power supply, operation and communication modes and a number of IoT design models. All these patterns are described with a visual and informal notation. There is no formal semantics associated. There is no research work that deals with the modeling of IoT patterns. In this paper, we present the modeling of IoT design patterns proposed by Reinfurt et al. [7].

8   Conclusions

In this paper, we presented an approach that allows to model and specify connected object architecture design patterns. In particular modeling the "Bootstrapping Design Patterns" category and the "Registration Design Patterns" category. The modeling phase consists of presenting models of the design patterns in order to present a meta-model that presents an abstract view of a model of the patterns. Subsequently, we described the structural and behavioral features of the pattern. Then, we formally specified these design patterns using the formal Event-B method. Finally, we developed a plug-in under the Eclipse Modeling platform that offers a graphical editor for modeling IoT design patterns. Currently, the transition from the SoaML modeling to the formal specification is achieved manually, we are working on automating this phase by implementing transformation rules.

References

1. Abrial, J.R.: Modeling in Event-B: System and Software Engineering, 1st edn. Cambridge University Press, New York (2010)
2. Abrial, J.R., Butler, M., Hallerstede, S., Hoang, T., Mehta, F., Voisin, L.: Rodin: an open toolset for modelling and reasoning in event-B. Int. J. Softw. Tools Technol. Transf. **12**(6), 447–466 (2010)
3. Chandra, G.S.: Pattern language for IoT applications. In: PLoP Conference, USA (2016)
4. Dong, J., Alencar, P., Cowan, D.D., Sheng, Y.: Composing pattern-based components and verifying correctness. J. Syst. Softw. **80**, 1755–1769 (2007)
5. Leuschel, M., Butler, M.: ProB: a model checker for B. In: Araki, K., Gnesi, S., Mandrioli, D. (eds.) FME 2003. LNCS, vol. 2805, pp. 855–874. Springer, Heidelberg (2003). https://doi.org/10.1007/978-3-540-45236-2_46
6. Qanbari, S., et al.: IoT design patterns: computational constructs to design, build and engineer edge applications. In: 2016 IEEE First International Conference on Internet-of-Things Design and Implementation (IoTDI), pp. 277–282 (2016)
7. Reinfurt, L., Breitenbücher, U., Falkenthal, M., Leymann, F., Riegg, A.: Internet of things patterns for device bootstrapping and registration. In: Proceedings of the 22Nd European Conference on Pattern Languages of Programs, EuroPLoP 2017, pp. 15:1–15:27. ACM, New York (2017)
8. Reinfurt, L., Breitenbücher, U., Falkenthal, M., Leymann, F., Riegg, A.: Internet of things patterns for devices. In: Proceedings of the Ninth International Conferences on Pervasive Patterns and Applications (PATTERNS), pp. 117–126 (2017)
9. Reinfurt, L., Falkenthal, M., Breitenbücher, U., Leymann, F.: Applying IoT patterns to smart factory systems. Advanced Summer School on Service Oriented Computing, Summer SOC (2017)

10. Steinberg, D., Budinsky, F., Paternostro, M., Merks, E.: EMF: Eclipse Modeling Framework 2.0, 2nd edn. Addison-Wesley Professional (2009)
11. Tounsi, I., Hadj Kacem, M., Hadj Kacem, A.: An approach for modeling and formalizing SOA design patterns. In: Proceedings of the 22nd IEEE International Conference on Enabling Technologies: Infrastructure for Collaborative Enterprises, WETICE 2013, pp. 330–335. IEEE Computer Society, Hammamet, June 2013
12. Tounsi, I., Hadj Kacem, M., Hadj Kacem, A., Drira, K.: An approach for SOA design patterns composition. In: Proceedings of the IEEE 8th International Conference on Service-Oriented Computing and Applications, (SOCA 2015), pp. 219–226. IEEE Computer Society, Rome, Italy, October 2015
13. Tounsi, I., Hadj Kacem, M., Hadj Kacem, A., Drira, K.: A refinement-based approach for building valid SOA design patterns. IJCC, Int. J. Cloud Comput. **4**(1), 78–104 (2015). https://doi.org/10.1504/IJCC.2015.067705
14. Tounsi, I., Hadj Kacem, M., Hadj Kacem, A., Drira, K.: Transformation of compound SOA design patterns. In: The 8th International Conference on Ambient Systems, Networks and Technologies (ANT 2017)/The 7th International Conference on Sustainable Energy Information Technology (SEIT 2017), 16–19 May 2017, Madeira, Portugal, pp. 408–415 (2017)
15. Tounsi, I., Hrichi, Z., Hadj Kacem, M., Hadj Kacem, A., Drira, K.: Using SoaML models and Event-B specifications for modeling SOA design patterns. In: Proceedings of the 15th International Conference on Enterprise Information Systems, ICEIS 2013, Angers, France, pp. 294–301, July 2013
16. Zhu, H., Bayley, I.: Laws of pattern composition. In: Dong, J.S., Zhu, H. (eds.) ICFEM 2010. LNCS, vol. 6447, pp. 630–645. Springer, Heidelberg (2010). https://doi.org/10.1007/978-3-642-16901-4_41

Biomedical and Health Informatics

EEG-Based Hypo-vigilance Detection Using Convolutional Neural Network

Amal Boudaya[1,2]([⊠]), Bassem Bouaziz[1,2]([⊠]), Siwar Chaabene[1,2], Lotfi Chaari[3], Achraf Ammar[4], and Anita Hökelmann[4]

[1] Multimedia InfoRmation Systems and Advanced Computing Laboratory (MIRACL), University of Sfax, 3021 Sfax, Tunisia
amalboudaya71@gmail.com, Bassem.Bouaziz@isims.usf.tn,
siwarchaabene@gmail.com
[2] Digital Research Center of Sfax, B.P. 275, 3021 Sakiet Ezzit, Sfax, Tunisia
[3] University of Toulouse, IRIT-ENSEEIHT, Toulouse, France
lotfi.chaari@toulouse-inp.fr
[4] Institute of Sport Science, Otto-von-Guericke University Magdeburg,
39104 Magdeburg, Germany
ammar.achraf@ymail.com, anita.hoekelmann@ovgu.de

Abstract. Hypo-vigilance detection is becoming an important active research areas in the biomedical signal processing field. For this purpose, electroencephalogram (EEG) is one of the most common modalities in drowsiness and awakeness detection. In this context, we propose a new EEG classification method for detecting fatigue state. Our method makes use of a and awakeness detection. In this context, we propose a new EEG classification method for detecting fatigue state. Our method makes use of a Convolutional Neural Network (CNN) architecture. We define an experimental protocol using the Emotiv EPOC+ headset. After that, we evaluate our proposed method on a recorded and annotated dataset. The reported results demonstrate high detection accuracy (93%) and indicate that the proposed method is an efficient alternative for hypo-vigilance detection as compared with other methods.

Keywords: Hypo-vigilance detection · EEG · CNN

1 Introduction

Hypo-vigilance has been one of the major causes of accidents in many areas such as driving [1], aviation [2] and military sector [3]. Hence, the drowsiness problem has gained great interest from researchers. This is today a real up to date problem within the current Covid-19 [4] pandemic where medical stuff is generally overbooked. In fact, the drowsy condition is expressed predominantly by the emergence of various behavioral signs such as heaviness in terms of reaction, reflex reduction, occurrences of yawning, heaviness of the eyelids and/or the difficulty of keeping the head in the frontal position relative to the field of

M. Jmaiel et al. (Eds.): ICOST 2020, LNCS 12157, pp. 69–78, 2020.
https://doi.org/10.1007/978-3-030-51517-1_6

vision. Many studies [5–8] have been proposed to detect hypo-vigilance based on biomedical signals such as electroencephalogram (EEG), electrocardiogram (ECG), electromyogram (EMG), and electrooculogram (EOG). Given, its high temporal resolution, portability and reasonable cost, the present work focus on hypo-vigilance detection by analyzing EEG signal of various brain's functionalities using fourteen electrodes placed on the participant's scalp. On the other hand, deep learning networks offer great potential for biomedical signals analysis through the simplification of raw input signals (i.e., through various steps including feature extraction, denoising and feature selection) and the improvement of the classification results.

In this paper, we focus on the EEG signal study recorded by fourteen electrodes for hypo-vigilance detection by analyzing the various functionalities of the brain from the electrodes placed on the participant's scalp.

Various deep learning architectures [9] exist such as Convolutional Neural Network (CNN), Recurrent CNN (R-CNN), Auto-Encoder (AE), Deep Belief Network (DBN), including Long Short-Term Memory (LSTM) and Gated Recurrent Units (GRU). As in [10], the CNN architecture is the most used to biomedical signals analysis providing a high classification accuracy. Previous related work [11] proposes a hypo-vigilance detection method using CNN by facial features. This method showed a classification accuracy of 92.33%. Likewise [12], introduces an adaptive conditional representation learning system for driver drowsiness detection based on a 3D-CNN. The proposed system consists of four steps (spatio-temporal representation, data preprocessing, features combination and somnolence detection). The experimental results show a detection accuracy equal to 92.04%. In this paper, we propose a CNN hypo-vigilance detection method using EEG data in order to classify drowsiness and awakeness states. Accordingly, the proposed approach including used equipment are presented in Sect. 2. Section 3 describes the experimental results and the evaluation of the employed method. Finally, a conclusion and future work are drawn in Sect. 4.

2 Proposed Approach

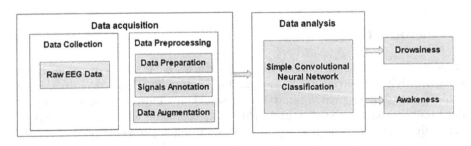

Fig. 1. Pipeline for the proposed approach.

As shown in Fig. 1, the realization of the proposed approach is suggested by two primary procedures: data acquisition and data analysis. The following subsections provide a detailed explanation of each procedure.

2.1 Data Acquisition

The EEG data acquisition procedure is made up of two main steps which are data collection and data preprocessing.

Data Collection: To collect the raw EEG data from participants, we use an Emotiv EPOC+ headset as shown in Fig. 2[a] for the data acquisition process. The key feature of this headset is a non-invasive Brain computer Interface (BCI) tool designed for the development of human brain and contextual research [13].

The Emotiv EPOC + helmet contains fourteen active electrodes with two reference electrodes (DRL and CMS), as shown in Fig. 2[b]. The electrodes are placed around the participant's head in the structures of the following zones: frontal and anterior parietal (AF3, AF4, F3, F4, F7, F8, FC5, FC6), temporal (T7, T8) and occipital-parietal (O1, O2, P7, P8).

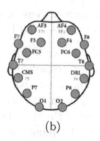

(a)   (b)

Fig. 2. (a) Emotiv EPOC+ helmet, (b) Location of the Emotiv EPOC+ helmet electrodes (10–20 International Standard).

Data Preprocessing: The specific preprocessing steps of the data revolve around the following points which are data preparation, data annotation and data augmentation.

– **Data Preparation**

During data acquisition, our raw EEG signals may be influenced by various sources of artifacts and noise such as endogenous electrical properties, specific fabrics physical structure, dipolar size variation, muscle shifts and Blinks. Hence, data processing is a preliminary step to denoising the raw signals. We suggest using an infinite impulse response (IIR) filter that manages an impulsive signal within time and frequency domains. Other sophisticated denoising approaches could be considered at the expense of higher computational complexity [14,15].

– **Signals Annotation**

To evaluate each individual's state of exhaustion, we concentrate on the brain areas that are responsible for hypo-vigilance detection. In this regard, different brain waves are targeted such as [16]:

- **Delta waves** refer to consciousness, sleep or deep sleep states. These waves were found in the temporal and occipital conditions with low frequency (less than 4 Hz) and high amplitude.
- **Theta waves** design the relaxation and hypnosis states with a range of frequency between 4 and 8 Hz. Theta waves are extracted from the temporal zone and are produced during the first phase of slow sleep or in deep relaxation state.
- **Alpha waves** refer to waking but relaxed states. These waves are captured in the posterior part, precisely the occipital region, with a frequency interval between 8 and 12 Hz and a low amplitude interval between 20 and 60 μV.
- **Beta waves** relate to alertness states. These waves are captured from the temporal and occipital lobes of the brain. They are characterized by high frequency interval of 12 to 30 Hz with a low amplitude interval of 10 to 30 μV.
- **Gamma waves** refer to hypervigilance states with a frequency interval between 30 to 80 Hz.

In the data annotation step, we only use the O1 and O2 electrodes of occipital zone which are responsible for drowsiness sensation.

As an annotation example, Fig. 3 indicates the amplitudes of the alpha and theta signals from the two O1 and O2 electrodes reported for a participant in three periods of the day. The relaxation state has been indicated by alpha waves which have a frequency interval between 8 to 12 Hz and an amplitude interval between 20 to 60 μV. The somnolence state has been indicated by theta waves which have a frequency interval between 4 to 8 Hz and an amplitude interval between 50 and 75 μV.

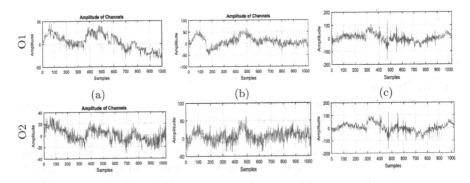

Fig. 3. The monitoring of O1 and O2 electrodes in the mornings (a), afternoons (b) and evenings (c).

– **Data augmentation**

In order to reduce overfitting and increase testing accuracy, we use the data augmentation technique [17] which consists of increasing the training set by label-retaining data transformations. The purpose procedure is to extend the data by doubling the vectors from (5850, 2) to (59053, 2) where 5850 (resp. 59053) represents the vector size and 2 represents the class number.

2.2 Data Analysis: Simple CNN Classification

The diagram of the neural network simple CNN used in our EEG drowsiness detection approach is represented in Fig. 4. The proposed simple CNN model is composed of the following six main layers:

– **The convolutional layers** allow the filter application and the features extraction characteristics of the input signals.
– **The sample-based discretization max-pooling-1D blocks** is used to sub-sample each input layer by reducing its dimensionality using a decrease in the number of the parameters to learn, there by reducing calculation costs.
– **The flatten layer** is used to flatten out multidimensional data.
– **The dropout layers** help to reduce the loss accuracy by regularizing and enhancing the overfitting of neural networks during the classification process.
– **The BatchNormalization layers** are used to scale and speed up learning of all activations. These layers normalize the previous activation layer output by subtracting the batches average and dividing it by the standard deviation to improve a neural network's stability.
– **The dense layers** allow to done a connectivity function between the next and intermediate neurons layer.

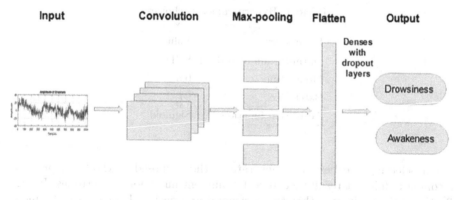

Fig. 4. The diagram of the simple CNN used in the proposed approach.

3 Experimental Evaluation

Our protocol revolves around the following axes: eight volunteers in which four women and four men aged twenty six and fifty eight with normal mental health. For each participant, we make three recordings of sixteen minutes divided over three day periods (morning, afternoon and evening). To fully understand the condition of the participants, we split the signal into windows to accurately identify these different states.

In the proposed simple CNN architecture for EEG signals classification, we use the Keras deep learning library. The different parameters as filters, kernel-size, padding, kernel-initializer, and activation of the four convolutional layers have the same values respectively 512, 32, same, normal and relu. The parameter values of the remaining layers are detailed in the following:

- the dropout layer value equal to 0.2 (respect. 0.5) is used to inactivate 20% (respect. 50%) of neurons in order to prevent overfitting.
- the Max-Pooling 1D layer is used with a filter size of 128.
- The muti-dimensional data output flatting using 1D flatten layer.
- For better classification results, two dropout layers are used. The first hidden layer takes a value of 128 neurons. Since a binary classification problem, the second layer takes a value of 1.

The choice of the optimization algorithm makes the difference between good results in minutes, hours or even days. There are various optimizers like Adam [18], SGD [19] and RMS pop optimizer [20]. In our model, we use the SGD optimizer which is more popular [21]. The method of this optimizer is simple and effective for finding optimal values in a neural network. Table 1 presents the hyperparameters choice of our model.

Table 1. Hyperparameters choices.

Parameters	Value
Optimization algorithm	SGD
Momentum	0.5
Batch size	64
Activation function	Sigmoid

For selecting the best accuracy rate of the proposed method, we propose to compare different results recorded by different numbers of electrodes. In [22, 23], the authors discover that the prefrontal and occipital cortex are the most important channels to better diagnose the hypo-vigilance state. In this regard, we choose the following recorded data:

- Recorded data by 2 electrodes (O1 and O2) electrodes from the occipital area.

- Recorded data by 4 electrodes (T7, T8, O1 and O2) from temporal and occipital areas.
- Recorded data by 7 electrodes (AF3, F7, F3, T7, O2, P8, F8) from prefrontal and occipital areas.
- Recorded data by 14 electrodes.

For the distribution of our data, we choose 70% for the train part and 30% for the test. Table 2 presents the reported testing and training accuracy respectively with two, four, seven and fourteen electrodes. After convergence the optimum number of test epochs for all the different electrodes results establish a value equal to 80. The best results are given by the recording of 2 electrodes from the occipital area. The curves of testing and training results for recorded data by O1 and O2 electrodes are represented in Fig. 5.

Table 2. Training and testing results of the different numbers of electrodes with data augmentation.

Number of electrodes	2	4	7	14
Accuracy train	98.18%	98.28%	98.99%	98.99 %
Accuracy test	93.94%	65.58%	76.43%	77.43 %

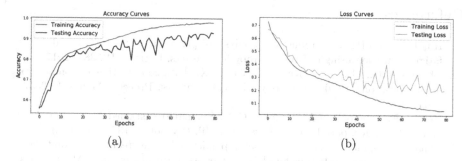

Fig. 5. (a) Accuracy graph, (b) Loss graph.

According to results obtained in Fig. 5, we note that the test accuracy increases after a certain number of epochs and the test loss decreases. To test our system's efficiency we measured the precision, recall and F1-score. Table 3 shows these different measures in our experimental configuration.

For comparison purposes, we compare the proposed method with recent drowsiness methodology [24] where the authors propose a driver hypovigilance detection using the Emotiv EPOC+ helmet. The Common Spatial Pattern (CSP) algorithm is used for optimization accuracy of Extreme Learning Machine (ELM). The reported values in Table 4 indicate that our method gives the optimum accuracy value classification.

Table 3. Accuracy, precision, recall and F1-score of our experimental configuration

Accuracy	Precision	Recall	F1 score
93.94%	87.29%	99.79%	93.12%

Table 4. Accuracy comparison with related works.

Drowsiness detection methodology	Accuracy	Classification method
R. Osmalina et al. [24]	91.67%	CSP algorithm
Proposed method	**93.94 %**	CNNs

4   Conclusion

The present work proposes a CNN based approach for Hypo-vigilance detection. In order to create a EEG dataset, we recorded raw EEG data using Epoc+ headset. The suggested system achieves an average classification accuracy to 93.94% by testing it on a real dataset of eight participants. In future work, we will focus to improve classification accuracy with large datasets. Additionally, fusion with other biomedical signals should be also considered to improve the classification accuracy.

References

1. Hu, J., Wang, P.: Noise robustness analysis of performance for EEG-based driver fatigue detection using different entropy feature sets. Entropy **19**, 385 (2017)
2. Thomas, L.C., Gast, C., Grube, R., Craig, K.: Fatigue detection in commercial flight operations: results using physiological measures. Procedia Manuf. **3**, 2357–2364 (2015)
3. Neri, D.F., Shappell, S.A., DeJohn, C.A.: Simulated sustained flight operations and performance, part 1: effects of fatigue. Mil. Psychol. **4**, 137–155 (1992)
4. Chaari, L., Golubnitschaja, O.: Covid-19 pandemic by the "real-time" monitoring: the Tunisian case and lessons for global epidemics in the context of 3PM strategies. EPMA J. (2020)
5. Sahayadhas, A., Sundaraj, K., Murugappan, M.: Electromyogram signal based hypovigilance detection. Biomed. Res. (India) **25**, 281–288 (2014)
6. Wang, F., Wang, H., Fu, R.: Real-time ECG-based detection of fatigue driving using sample entropy. Entropy **20**(3), 196 (2018)
7. Ahn, S., Nguyen, T., Jang, H., Kim, J.G., Jun, S.C.: Exploring neuro-physiological correlates of drivers' mental fatigue caused by sleep deprivation using simultaneous EEG, ECG, and fNIRS data. Front. Hum. Neurosci. **10**, 219 (2016)
8. Basri, C., et al.: Muscle fatigue detections during arm movement using EMG signal. IOP Conf. Ser. Mater. Sci. Eng. **557**, 012004 (2019)
9. Alom, M.Z., et al.: A state-of-the-art survey on deep learning theory and architectures. Electronics **8**(3), 292 (2019)

10. Kiranyaz, S., Ince, T., Abdeljaber, O., Avci, O., Gabbouj, M.: 1-D convolutional neural networks for signal processing applications. In: ICASSP, IEEE International Conference on Acoustics, Speech and Signal Processing - Proceedings, pp. 8360–8364, May 2019

11. Dwivedi, K., Biswaranjan, K., Sethi, A.: Drowsy driver detection using representation learning. In: IEEE International Advance Computing Conference, IACC, pp. 995–999, February 2014

12. Yu, J., Park, S., Lee, S., Jeon, M.: Driver drowsiness detection using condition-adaptive representation learning framework. IEEE Trans. Intell. Transp. Syst. **20**, 4206–4218 (2018)

13. Strmiska, M., Koudelkova, Z.: Analysis of performance metrics using Emotiv EPOC+. MATEC Web Conf. **210**, 4–7 (2018)

14. Laruelo, A., et al.: Hybrid sparse regularization for magnetic resonance spectroscopy. In: IEEE International Conference of Engineering in Medicine and Biology Society (EMBC), pp. 3–7, July 2013

15. Chaari, L., Tourneret, J.-Y., Chaux, C.: Sparse signal recovery using a Bernouilli generalized gaussian prior. In: European Signal Processing Conference (EUSIPCO), Nice, France, 31 August–4 September 2015 (2015)

16. Surangsrirat, D., Intarapanich, A.: Analysis of the meditation brainwave from consumer EEG device. In: IEEE SOUTHEASTCON, pp. 1–6, June 2015

17. Solé-Casals, J., et al.: A novel deep learning approach with data augmentation to classify motor imagery signals. IEEE Access **7**, 15945–15954 (2019)

18. Jung, J.J., Youn, Y.C., Camacho, D., Li, G., Lee, C.H.: Deep learning for EEG data analytics: a survey. Concurr. Comput. (2019)

19. Shaf, A., Ali, T., Farooq, W., Javaid, S., Draz, U., Yasin, S.: Two classes classification using different optimizers in convolutional neural network. In: International Multi-topic Conference (INMIC), pp. 1–6 (2018)

20. Tafsast, A., Ferroudji, K., Hadjili, M.L., Bouakaz, A., Benoudjit, N.: Automatic microemboli characterization using convolutional neural networks and radio frequency signals. In: 2018 International Conference on Communications and Electrical Engineering (ICCEE), pp. 1–4, December 2018

21. Reddy, S.V.G., Reddy, K.T., ValliKumari, V.: Optimization of deep learning using various optimizers, loss functions and dropout. Int. J. Innov. Technol. Explor. Eng

22. Nugraha, B.T., Sarno, R., Asfani, D.A., Igasaki, T., Munawar, M.N.: Classification of driver fatigue state based on EEG using Emotiv EPOC+. J. Theor. Appl. Inf. Technol. **86**, 347–359 (2016)

23. Sarno, R., Nugraha, B.T., Munawar, M.N.: Real time fatigue-driver detection from electroencephalography using Emotiv EPOC+. Int. Rev. Comput. Softw. (IRE-COS) **11**, 214 (2016)

24. Osmalina, R., Rahmatillah, A.: Drowsiness analysis using common spatial pattern and extreme learning machine based on electroencephalogram signal. J. Med. Signals Sens. **9**(2), 130–136 (2019)

Respiratory Activity Classification Based on Ballistocardiogram Analysis

Mohamed Chiheb Ben Nasr[1(✉)], Sofia Ben Jebara[1], Samuel Otis[2],
Bessam Abdulrazak[4], and Neila Mezghani[2,3]

[1] Higher School of Communication of Tunis, Carthage University, Aryanah, Tunisia
{mohamedchihab.bennaser,sofia.benjebara}@supcom.tn
[2] Laboratoire de recherche en imagerie et en orthopédie, CRCHUM,
Montreal, Canada
samuel.otis.1@ens.etsmtl.ca
[3] LICEF Institute, TELUQ University, Montreal, Canada
neila.mezghani@teluq.ca
[4] Department of Computer Science, Sherbrooke University, Sherbrooke, Canada
Bessam.Abdulrazak@usherbrooke.ca

Abstract. Ballistocardiogram signals describe the mechanical activity of the heart. It can be measured by an intelligent mattress in a totally unobtrusive way during periods of rest in bed or sitting on a chair. The BCG signals are highly vulnerable to artefacts such as noise and movement making useful information like respiratory activities difficult to extract. The purpose of this study is to investigate a classification method to distinguish between seven types of respiratory activities such as normal breathing, cough and hold breath. We propose a feature selection method based on a spectral analysis namely spectral flatness measure (SFM) and spectral centroid (SC). The classification is carried out using the nearest neighbor classifier. The proposed method is able to discriminate between the seven classes with the accuracy of 94% which shows its usefulness in context of Telemedicine.

Keywords: Ballistocardiogram · Machine learning · Biomedical signal processing · Spectral analysis

1 Introduction

The development of connected object for personalized services, especially for monitoring purposes, have significantly increased worldwide over the last few years [1]. More specifically those that deals with the monitoring of respiratory and cardiac diseases. Indeed these diseases are among the leading cause of death and disability in the world. One of these respiratory diseases is the Chronic Obstructive Pulmonary Disease COPD [2] a progressive life threatening lung disease. According to the World Health Organization [3], COPD affects more than 250 million cases globally, a staggering 3.17 million deaths per year and

© The Author(s) 2020
M. Jmaiel et al. (Eds.): ICOST 2020, LNCS 12157, pp. 79–88, 2020.
https://doi.org/10.1007/978-3-030-51517-1_7

is associated with a huge economic burden. In fact, numbers published by the Global initiative for Chronic Obstructive Lung Disease [4] shows that the direct costs of respiratory disease in the European Union are estimated to be about 6% of the total annual healthcare budget with COPD accounting for 56% (38.6 billion Euros) of the cost of respiratory disease. These numbers are further amplified by the ever-growing healthcare costs, the aging of the population and the widespread of such diseases. The monitoring of respiratory activities plays an important role in the current management of patients with acute respiratory failure [5]. As a consequence, it is recommended to have continuous monitoring of the vital signs to ensure an optimal diagnosis of a patient's state [6]. Moreover, monitoring of respiratory activity is useful for detecting respiratory disorders, such as the sleep apnea, cessation of breathing in infants, shortness of breath in patients with heart failure, and so on. Hence, it is important to monitor respiratory activities such as normal breathing, cough, hold breath expiration.

A new generation of sensor-based mattress is able to unobtrusively monitor vital signs such as the Heart rate Beat Rate (HBR) and the Respiratory Rate (RR). Indeed, this study considered an Optical Fiber based Sensor (FOS) [7] for the unobstructed monitoring of the Ballistocardiogram (BCG) signal. Due to the ejection of the blood during the systole, the body's mechanical reaction is measured hence the BCG signal. Our aim is to investigate a classification method to distinguish between several types of respiratory activities such as normal breathing, cough and hold breath using the BCG signal.

This paper is organized as follows. Section 2 is dedicated to describe the material and method. It describes the data collection, BCG signal analysis and feature extraction and classification. Section 3 provides information about the experimental results mainly feature illustration and classifier evaluation. Finally, Sect. 4 concludes the study and gives perspectives.

2 Material and Method

2.1 Data Collection

The system used for collecting data includes a small FOS mattress and a module to gather optical data coming from the mattress [8,9]. The FOS mattress was fixed on the back of a regular office chair. The raw data is sampled at 50 Hz by the module.

The BCG signals were acquired on 6 healthy participants: 3 male and 3 female aged between 21 and 32 years. The participants were asked to perform a certain experimental protocol. A part of normal breathing, other human body activities that commonly occur are introduced in this protocol. It is composed of the following steps by following activities: normal breathing (C1), cough (C2), Normal breathing after cough (C3), hold breath (C4), expiration (C5), movement (C6). We also consider a class other to regroup all other activities (C7). Figure 1 illustrates an example of the BCG signal. The different human body activities are plotted in different colors. The objective is to highlight the differences in the BCG signal according to the activity.

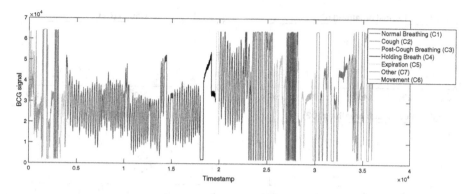

Fig. 1. Illustration of the BCG signal during the experimental protocol activities. (Color figure online)

2.2 BCG Signal Analysis

In this subsection we inspect the effect of different activities in the BCG signal. Figure 2 illustrates five different activities. In the plot illustrating Normal respiration (C1), we can easily extract both the HBR and RR, the big period corresponds to the movements of the thoracic cage. By extracting the distance between two consecutive peaks of this waveform, we can extract the RR. The small period appearing in the BCG signal represents the heart beats. The extraction of these little fluctuations results in the extraction of the HBR.

The signals corresponding to the cough (C2) and movement (C6) are very similar. Both signals attain the upper limit of the acquisition equipment which is explained by the broad peaks in the BCG signals. We believe however that these broad peaks have different explanations. The peaks in the movement signal comes from the acceleration of the subject's body and the peaks during the cough comes from the reaction of the body after coughing.

The post-cough normal breathing is corrupted and we can hardly find the peaks of the respiratory activity. The peaks are broader and that results in a lack of precision of HBR and RR.

The holding breath BCG contains only cardiac information. The periodicity is clearly noticed which was not obvious in other activities.

This analysis of the BCG signal's content motivates the use of an approach based on the characterization of the useful frames. This particular problem is complex and thus is demanding when it comes to the choice of the features with physical significance. In the next subsections, we will define the features and try to highlight the intuition behind each one of them.

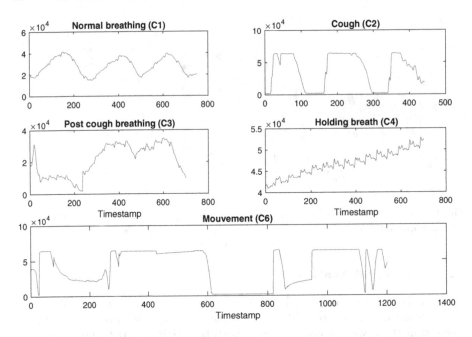

Fig. 2. Illustration of the BCG signal of the different activities of the subjects.

2.3   BCG Signal Feature Extraction

A periodic signal can be represented as a sum of sine waves and thus the Fourier transformation of this particular signal will be spiky. This statement motivated the idea of using the following two features: Spectral Flatness Measure (SFM) and Spectral Centroid (SC).

Let $x(n)$ be a BCG signal. The later is decomposed into frames of short duration. These frames should be long enough to carry information about the activity but not too long to avoid an overlap of two or more different activities. In the frequency domain, the short-term Fourier transform is calculated and its amplitude is extracted. It is denoted $|X(m,k)|$, where m is the frame index and k is the discrete frequency.

Spectral Flatness Measure (SFM): The SFM, also known as Wiener entropy, is a signal processing measure used to describe the flatness of the spectrum of the signal [10,11]. The SFM is defined as the ratio of the geometric mean and arithmetic mean of the Fourier transforms. When the spectrum is flat (white noise signal), the resulting measure is close to 1.

$$SFM(m) = \frac{\sqrt[N]{\prod_{k=1}^{N} |X(m,k)|}}{\frac{\sum_{k=1}^{N} |X(m,k)|}{N}}, \tag{1}$$

where k is the frequency bin index and N is the number of frequency bins.

Spectral Centroid (SC): The SC indicates where the center of mass of the spectrum is located.

$$SC(m) = \frac{\sum_{k=1}^{N}(|X(m,k)| * f(k))}{\sum_{k=1}^{N}|X(m,k)|}, \tag{2}$$

where $f(k)$ is the frequency in Hz of the bin k.

BCG Feature Engineering: The SFM and SC measures have been evaluated on each frame of the BCG signal. However, in order to avoid complexity that comes with it (overlap noise propagation, presence of different labels in the same frame, frames too small to be representative...), we propose to create a time-series out of the SFM and SC values in each frame.

- Signal decomposition: the original BCG signal is decomposed into frames of length 1024 with an overlap of 960 samples. Hence we used a windowing function. In this work we used a *Hamming* window with an increment of 64 samples.
- The feature vector $F(m) = [SFM(m), SC(m)]^T$ is extracted from each frame.
- Each feature of raw data $SFM = [sfm(1), sfm(2)...sfm(L)]^T$ (L is the number of frames) is transformed into a time-series (equivalent to a signal) by overlapping and adding the sfm of each frame. Note that the latter is a constant vector, whose value is sfm and whose length is the frame size.

The sfm_{signal} and sc_{signal} are then used for the purpose of classification.

2.4   Activities Classification

Respiratory activities classification has been performed using a K-nearest neighbors classifier. It is a non-parametric classification method which classifies a sample based on a plurality vote of its neighbors. The sample is assigned to the class most common among its K nearest neighbors (K is a positive integer) in terms of minimal distance. The algorithm adopted is Fine KNN which is the finest variation of KNN since it labels the new input with the same label as only one of its nearest neighbour $K = 1$. The evaluation of the algorithm as well as the classification results were conducted using k-fold cross validation with $k = 5$.

2.5   Classification Evaluation

The classification performance is evaluated in terms of true positive rate and positive predicted value.

True Positive Rate: The performance of our model will mainly be measured using the confusion matrix [12]. Specifically TPR measures the proportion of detected positives from the actual positive in other terms TPR measures how sensitive your model is to the positive class.

$$TPR^i = \frac{true\ positives}{true\ positives + false\ negatives}, \tag{3}$$

where i corresponds to the class (activity) of the subject ($i = 1..7$). The terms of the confusion matrix presented in Fig. 4 are defined as follows:

$$Conf_{tpr}(i,j) = \frac{M_{ij}}{\sum_{j=1}^{C} M_{ij}}, \tag{4}$$

where C is the number of classes, M_{ij} is the number of predictions of class i that actually belongs to class j it is usually measured by comparing the test results to the ground truth.

Positive Predictive Value: The proportion of the predictions made that are actually true and happened. PPV Highlights mostly how refined our model is and how frequent we have false alerts.

$$PPV^i = \frac{true\ positives}{true\ positives + false\ positives}. \tag{5}$$

The terms of the confusion matrix presented in Fig. 5 are defined as follows:

$$Conf_{ppv}(i,j) = \frac{M_{ij}}{\sum_{i=1}^{C} M_{ij}}, \tag{6}$$

3 Experimental Results

3.1 Feature Illustration

This section illustrates the feature analysis and interpretation by providing the means of the SFM and SC for each activity.

The BCG signal we are working with is the same displayed on Fig. 1. The mean values are given in Table 1. We note that the normal breathing mean value of the SFM is the lowest which confirms the periodicity hypothesis. The values of SFM and SC taken during the coughing portion (C2) as well as the movement portion (C6) are relatively high which further confirms the non-periodicity in the corresponding portions.

For the post-cough breathing, we notice that, unlike the portion of normal breathing, the values of the descriptors are high and close to those during the movement and coughing activities which supports our choice to isolate these portions.

The closest values of the descriptors to the ideal ones (those of the normal breathing) are the values recorded during the holding breath, this is due to the fact that the portions of holding breath are periodic and carry only the heart rhythm information.

Table 1. Mean value of SFM and SC during each activity.

Activities	SFM	SC
Normal respiration (C1)	0.02	0.807
Cough (C2)	0.1582	2.3591
Post cough breathing (C3)	0.14	1.2638
Holding breath (C4)	0.102	0.7662
Movement	0.2293	1.4844

Figure 3 show the sfm_{signal} of some activities. In the top right, the normal respiration phase is considered. The values of SFM are low as expected to be. This fact is due to the clear periodicity in that activity. The SFM of holding breath (down left plot) is pretty low and that is as well an expected result since there's the cardiac information in the holding breath activity. Both cough and movement activities (right plots) manifest big fluctuations in their respective sfm_{signal}, this is due to the absence of periodicity in these signals.

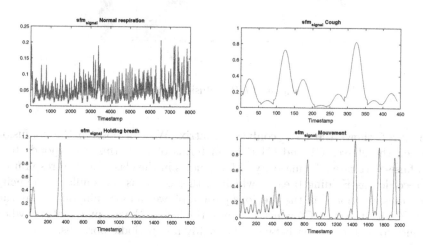

Fig. 3. Variation of sfm signal of the sample for each activity.

3.2   Classifier Evaluation

Using the sfm_{signal} and sc_{signal} we obtained a classification rate of 94%. Figure 4 shows the TPR confusion matrix. We can observe that our model performs very well overall. The TPR value appears in the diagonal of the confusion matrix. Most of the errors are detected in the class $C4$, where 31% of the latter (corresponds to the class: holding breath) is predicted as normal respiration. This result is expected since the periodicity in the holding breath portions is present due to the cardiac activity. We observe as well a high confusion between the class cough (C2) and the class movement (C6). This is due to the fact that our predictors are well equipped to detect the existence of the periodicity in the portions.

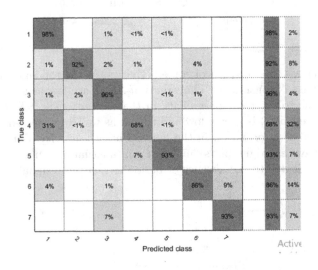

Fig. 4. TPR confusion matrix

Figure 5 shows the PPV confusion matrix. We can observe the confusion between the classes C1 and C4 (7%) in terms of PPV this corresponds to a high false-alert rate (the majority of false alerts in the class: Normal respiration are recorded as Holding breath) which further confirms the similar periodicity hypothesis mentioned in the previous paragraph we can also pinpoint an alarming 13% with the class C5 which is due to the lack of the adopted features when it comes to differentiating between the highly non-periodic portions.

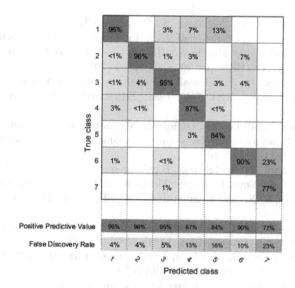

Fig. 5. *PPV* Confusion matrix

4   Conclusion

In this study we investigated the respiratory activity classification based on the BCG signal. We used a reconstructed time-series signal from the spectral flatness measure (SFM) and spectral centroid (SC) of the raw data. We obtained a classification rate of 94% which show the effectiveness of the proposed method. The supervised classification process, however, is demanding when it comes to data and computation. Treating the feature extraction process by generating a time series is a novelty which motivates the use of more sophisticated deep-learning algorithms such as the Long Short Term Memory LSTM as one of the most used Recurrent Neural Network RNN architectures in time series related problems.

References

1. Wearable Monitoring System for Chronic Cardio-Respiratory Diseases. In: 30th Annual International IEEE EMBS Conference Vancouver, British Columbia, Canada, 20–24 August 2008
2. Forum of International Respiratory Societies: The Global Impact of Respiratory Disease, 2nd edn. European Respiratory Society, Sheffield (2017)
3. Who.int. Chronic respiratory diseases (2020). https://www.who.int/health-topics/chronic-respiratory-diseases. Accessed 18 Feb 2020
4. Global strategy for the diagnosis, Management and prevention of Chronic Obstructive Pulmonary Disease 2020 report
5. Clinical review: Respiratory monitoring in the ICU - a consensus of 16. Crit Care. **16**(2), 219 (2012). https://doi.org/10.1186/cc11146. PMCID: PMC3681336PMID: 22546221

6. Liu, J., Wang, Y., Chen, Y., Yang, J., Chen, X., Cheng, J.: Tracking vital signs during sleep leveraging off-the-shelf WiFi. In: Proceedings of the 16th ACM International Symposium on Mobile Ad Hoc Networking and Computing, MobiHoc 2015, New York, NY, USA, pp. 267–276. ACM (2015)

7. Sadek, I., Biswas, J., Abdulrazak, B.: Ballistocardiogram signal processing: a review. Health Inf. Sci. Syst. **7**(1), 1–23 (2019). https://doi.org/10.1007/s13755-019-0071-7

8. Ramakrishnan, M., Rajan, G., Semenova, Y., Farrell, G.: Overview of fiber optic sensor technologies for strain/temperature sensing applications in composite materials. Sensors **16**(1), 99 (2016)

9. Otis, S., Mezghani, N., Abdulrazak, B.: Comparative Study of Heart Rate Extraction Methods for a Novel Intelligent Mattress. In: IEEE International Symposium on signal Image, Video and Communications (ISIVC), pp. 27–29, Rabat, Morocco (2018)

10. Dubnov, S.: Generalization of spectral flatness measure for non-gaussian linear processes. IEEE Sig. Process. Lett. **11**(8), 698–701 (2004)

11. Madhu, N.: Note on measures for spectral flatness. Electron. Lett. **45**, 1195–1196 (2009). https://doi.org/10.1049/el.2009.1977

12. Stehman, S.: Selecting and interpreting measures of thematic classification accuracy. Remote Sens. Environ. **62**(1), 77–89 (1997)

A Convolutional Neural Network
for Lentigo Diagnosis

Sana Zorgui[1](✉), Siwar Chaabene[1](✉), Bassem Bouaziz[1](✉), Hadj Batatia[2](✉),
and Lotfi Chaari[2](✉)

[1] MIRACL and CRNS, University of Sfax, Sfax, Tunisia
sanazorgui@gmail.com, siwarchaabene@gmail.com,
bassem.bouaziz@isims.usf.tn
[2] University of Toulouse, IRIT - INP-ENSEEIHT, Toulouse, France
{hadj.batatia,lotfi.chaari}@toulouse-inp.fr

Abstract. Using Reflectance Confocal Microscopy (RCM) for lentigo
diagnosis is today considered essential. Indeed, RCM allows fast data
acquisition with a high spatial resolution of the skin. In this paper, we
use a deep convolutional neural network (CNN) to perform RCM image
classification in order to detect lentigo. The proposed method relies on an
InceptionV3 architecture combined with data augmentation and transfer
learning. The method is validated on RCM data and shows very efficient
detection performance with more than 98% of accuracy.

Keywords: Reflectance Confocal Microscopy · Lentigo · CNN
classification · InceptionV3

1 Introduction

Reflectance Confocal Microscopy (RCM) [1] is a modality increasingly used in
medical imaging like MRI (Magnetic Resonance Imaging) [2–4] or X-ray imaging [5]. In vivo RCM technique is easy to use during the patient examination and
acquires high resolution skin images in a short time. This modality can be used
to help dermatologists diagnose different skin diseases. However, it takes a long
time for dermatologists to make full use of the possibilities of this technique for
diagnostic purposes. Our work aims to develop a new tool to automate certain
diagnostic steps required using deep learning [6]. On the other side, the lentigos
are age spots that mainly appear on the hand or on the areas most frequently
exposed to the sunlight. On the surface, they appear as a darker spot. Inside the
skin layers, it is mainly at the level of the dermis-epidermis junction that the
differences can be visible [7]. Therefore, the distinction of lentigos can be made
using the RCM images. Several deep learning architectures, especially convolutional neural network (CNN) [5,8] show great potential in medical imaging
classification. In this paper, we propose a new 3D RCM image (2D + depth)
classification method for lentigo detection. The method is based on a CNN on
InceptionV3 architecture [9].

© The Author(s) 2020
M. Jmaiel et al. (Eds.): ICOST 2020, LNCS 12157, pp. 89–99, 2020.
https://doi.org/10.1007/978-3-030-51517-1_8

Until now, little works have been proposed for lentigo/healthy classification of RCM images. In [10], the authors perform a two-dimensional wavelet decomposition. Then a generalized Gaussian distribution was applied to the wavelet coefficients in order to perform a quantitative analysis assisted by a support vector machine (SVM) to classify RCM images obtaining an accuracy of 84.4%. Another approach in [11] explores a new unsupervised Bayesian algorithm for the joint reconstruction and classification of RCM images. The resulting algorithm for healthy and lentigo classification reached an accuracy percentage of 97%. Beside, the paper [12] automatically diagnosed lentigo by using three separate feature extraction methods like Wavelets, Haralick and CNN by Transfer Learning. The healthy/lentigo classification results reached an accuracy of 76%.

The present paper is organized as follows. Section 2 presents the problem formulation of lentigo diagnosis. Section 3 detailed the proposed lentigo detection method. Section 4 presents the experiment validation of our method. Finally, conclusion and some perspectives are drawn in Sect. 5.

2   Related Work

2.1   Lentigo Detection

Lentigo is a lesion that occurs in the dermal epidermal junction between the dermis and the epidermis involving a high concentration of melanocytes in the dermal papillae walls. Most forms of lentigo are benign [13] like lentigo simplex as Fig. 1(a) and solar lentigo as Fig. 1(b). They are usually removed for cosmetic purposes. However, certain types such as lentigo maligna [14] as Fig. 1(c) may be harmful and must be removed.

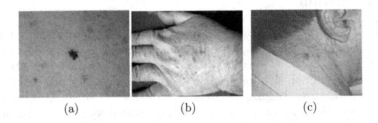

| (a) | (b) | (c) |

Fig. 1. Lentigo simplex (a), Solar lentigo (b) and Lentigo maligna (c).

Usually, lentigo is diagnosed using dermatoscopy [15]. Sadly, non-pigmented melanocytes with this modality can go completely unnoticed leading to complications in identifying the lesion contours with precision. Hispathology [16] is also used to confirm the diagnosis, but it can be inconvenient due to the fact that it is an in vitro technique involving performing a biospy from the pigmented areas. For these reasons, the RCM modality emerged to solve the problems encountered before. Therefore, this modality allows the expert to carry out a real-time 3D data acquisition and to facilitate the full observation of the biological structures in deformation over time. Due to all of these reasons, our approach is based on images acquired thanks to this modality. In [10,11], the authors propose two RCM lentigo detection methods based on the statistical and Bayesian models [17] respectively. The methods have proved complicated and hard to implement. They require manual procedures like feature selection and data preparation. To this regard, we propose here a method for RCM image classification using a CNN architecture. Indeed, CNNs have proven their capacity to efficiently solve several complex problems in medical imaging.

2.2   Convolutional Neural Networks

The CNN [8] is a deep learning architecture that is primarily used for image classification and object detection. Figure 2 displays a general CNN architecture, where one can easily identify the following layers:

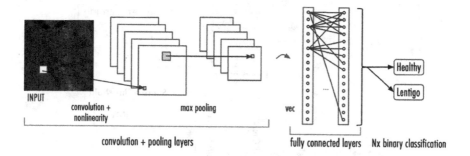

Fig. 2. The CNN architecture model.

- The convolutional layers: a key component of a CNN architecture, used for automatic feature extraction.
- The rectified linear units (ReLU): used after each convolutional layer. Each layer combines nonlinear layers and rectification layers to add nonlinearity to the system.
- The pooling layers: used for feature selection by maximum or/and average pooling.
- The fully connected layers: also known as dense layers receiving the flattened (1D) feature map. Usually, the final fully connected layer has the same number of output nodes as the class numbers.
- The Softmax function: calculates the probabilities of each target class over all possible classes. This function helps determine the target class for the given inputs.

3   Proposed Method for Lentigo Detection

The proposed method consists of classifying RCM images into healthy/lentigo classes using an InceptionV3 architecture. Our lentigo detection method combines the InceptionV3 model with other known deep learning techniques like transfer learning [18] and data augmentation [19]. Figure 3 presents the different steps used in the proposed lentigo detection method. The following subsections give detailed descriptions of each step.

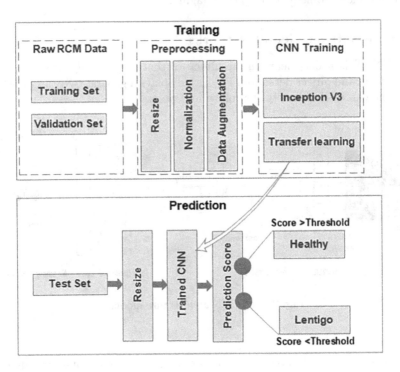

Fig. 3. Pipeline of the proposed method.

3.1   Data Preparation

The input RCM images for the training procedure combines two sets such as a 73% training set and a 14% validation set. The remaining 13% is dedicated to the prediction phase. In order to avoid overfitting, a validation set is added to our training phase because the non linear InceptionV3 model will possibly achieve 100% training accuracy and overfit.

3.2 Data Preprocessing

In the first step of the preprocessing procedure, the RCM images of the training set are resized to fit in the InceptionV3 network. A normalization step is added to help the CNN better process the input images, in order that all feature values have the same range and the system needs only one global learning rate multiplier. Afterwards, the data augmentation step is proposed to improve our classification results. This step prevents accuracy decay and overfitting. In [20] the authors demonstrate the importance of data augmentation as a regulazier in the CNN classification model.

3.3 InceptionV3 Model

The InceptionV3 model is a complex heavily engineered network that considered a major breakthrough in CNN's [9]. Before the current model, many common CNN's claimed that stacking layers after layers is the only way to increase accuracy. However, this network suggested some solutions to improve accuracy and speed without piling many layers. As shown in Fig. 4, the InceptionV3 model consists of a combination of three main modules.

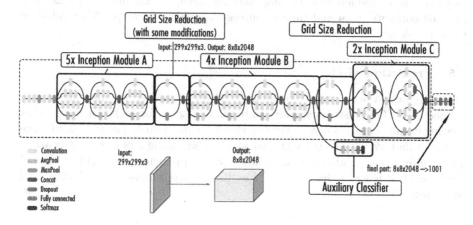

Fig. 4. Architecture of the InceptionV3 model.

The first one (Module A) uses two smaller convolution layers (3×3) to decrease the computational cost by reducing the number of parameters to improve performance. Module B divides each convolution layer of $n \times n$ size to two layers of $1 \times n$ and $n \times 1$ dimensions to have a less complex network. Finally, Module C reduces the representational bottleneck by expanding the filters in order to evade information loss. More upgrades are also proposed by the InceptionV3 network other than the smart factorization methods such as:

- RMSProp optimizer allows a faster convergence of the model thus allowing a higher learning rate.

- BatchNorm reduces the covariance shift and allows each network layer to learn a little independently of the others.
- Label Smoothing is a regularizing component applied to the loss formula to prevent overfitting.

The InceptionV3 network is 42 layers deep. Therefore, the computational cost is just around 2.5 higher than GoogLeNet's [21]. In addition, the inception modules are a novel and popular concept due to their smaller convolutions, which explains the reduction in the number of parameters. The InceptionV3 model gathers more information without impacting the computational speed thanks to its depth and the various kernel sizes used in the convolution operations.

3.4 Transfer Learning

As shown in Fig. 3, transfer learning [22] is proposed in order to ensure better performance of the model. The model needs lots of labeled images to be capable of solving complex problems. This has proved to be challenging especially when the available dataset is small. Transfer learning is a deep learning method, in which a model developed for a task is reused for a second task. This technique uses pre-trained models as a starting point for other medical imaging tasks given the vast computational and time resources required to develop CNN models on these problems.

3.5 Prediction Model

In the prediction phase, the RCM images test set are resized and provided to the trained CNN. Our system calculates a prediction score for each test image after resizing it and compares it with the threshold T equal to 0.5. The threshold value is chosen that way due to the fact that we are performing a binary classification. The classification condition is as follows: if the predicted score (PS) value of the image test is lower than T then this RCM image is classified as lentigo and conversely.

4   Experimental Validation

This section evaluates the validation of the proposed lentigo detection method on real RCM data. In our work, the dataset is provided from Lab. Pierre Fabre. In this experiment, the data include 428 RCM images which high spatial resolutions and annotation on each image into two healthy and lentigo classes. The images were acquired with a Vivascope 1500 apparatus. Each RCM image shows a field of view of $500 \times 500\,\mu m$ with 1000×1000 pixels. A selection of 45 women aged 60 years were recruited. All participants have offered their informed consent to the RCM skin test. We split these data into three main sets:

- A 314 images training set divided into two classes of 160 healthy images and 154 lentigo images.

- A validation set of 60 images, divided equally between two classes of lentigo and healthy. The validation set has been added to evaluate our training procedure. The main objective is to prevent over-fitting.
- A 54 RCM images testing set divided equally for healthy and lentigo classes.

Our classification method based on the InceptionV3 network is build using the Keras library. The InceptionV3 model is configured to accept the greyscale RCM images. As initialization, all RCM images were resized into new dimensions of 299×299 pixels and rescaled to help CNN processing. The parameter values of data augmentation step are presented in Table 1. The shear, zoom and translation ranges vary from 0 to 1. We choose the value of 0.2 for each to enrich the dataset without altering the image main features and confusing the system. The rotation range varies to $0°$ from $180°$ and a small rotation angle was proposed for the same reasons.

Table 1. Data augmentation parameters.

Parameter	value
Shear	0.2
Zoom	0.2
Rotation degree	20°
Horizontal translation	0.2
Vertical translation	0.2

Figure 5 displays the accuracy curves of the training and validation sets, as well as the training loss. The accuracy curves suggest that our system converged after 40 epochs. The system reached an accuracy value of 94% for training and 69% for validation. Hence, the reported values indicate that our system learns well without over- or under-fitting.

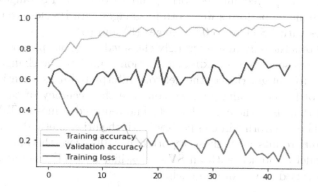

Fig. 5. Proposed method accuracy graph and loss graph for training and validation sets after each epoch.

The performance of the proposed method is indicated by the test set according to the ability to correctly diagnose the provided skin tissues. The reported values in Table 2 indicate the performance of our classification method. Therefore, 53 out of 54 images test set were correctly classified with an accuracy of **98,14%**.

Table 2. Confusion matrix.

	Lentigo	Sane
Lentigo	27/27 = 100% (TP)	1/27 = 3,7% (FN)
Sane	0/27 = 0% (FP)	26/27 = 96,3% (TN)

In Table 2, TP, TN, FP and FN represent respectively true positives, true negatives, false positives and false negatives. Based on the confusion matrix, Accuracy, Precision, Specificity, Recall and F-score values are reported in Table 3. All the mentioned measures indicate a good performance of the proposed method with values equal or very close to one.

Table 3. Quantitative evaluation of the proposed method performance.

Accuracy	$(TP + TN)/(TP + TN + FP + FN)$	0.98
Precision (P)	$TP/(TP + FP)$	1
Specificity	$TN/(FP + TN)$	1
Recall (R)	$TP/(TP + FN)$	0.96
F-score	$(2 \times P \times R)/(P + R)$	0.97

Figure 6 presents four correct classification examples of RCM images from the test set. The reported values shown with each test image indicate the prediction score (PS). The displayed images correspond to different PS ranges. We can notice that the model performs well both for images with PS close to 0 or 1, but also for images with PS close to 0.5 (images (b) and (d)).

Figure 7 shows the only image wrongly classified using our proposed method. This image shows some type of skin deformation similar to the changes the skin undergoes due to lentigo. Hence, the network interpreted it as a lentigo lesion. For the sake of further evaluation, we compare the accuracy of the test with related works that used the same dataset. The reported values in Table 4 show that our model outperforms in comparison with the other methods. Specifically, we compare our results with those reported in [10] where the authors used a Statistical model combined with an SVM classifier and [11] where the authors use an unsupervised Bayesian approach.

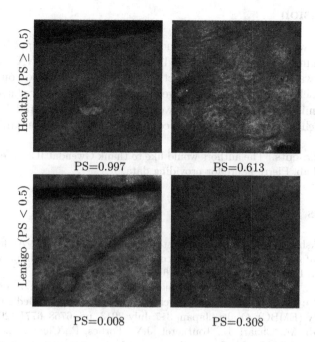

Fig. 6. Correct classification examples of RCM images for Healthy and Lentigo patients classified by the proposed method.

Fig. 7. The only false classification (PS = 0.0005).

Table 4. Comparison performance with state of the art methods.

Lentigo detection method	Accuracy
Halimi et al. 2017 [10]	84.4%
Halimi et al. 2017 [11]	97.7%
Proposed method	**98,14%**

5   Conclusion

In this paper, we proposed a new method to classify RCM images into healthy and lentigo skins. This method is based on the InceptionV3 CNN architecture. The network was trained with a dataset of 374 images and tested on 54 images of different stacks and depths. The suggested CNN method shows huge potential and very promising results. In future work, we will focus on applying the proposed approach to larger datasets and comparisons to other deep architectures.

Acknowledgements. The authors would like to thank Gwendal JOSSE et Jimmy Le Digabel from Lab. Pierre Fabre for providing data.

References

1. Rajadhyaksha, M., Grossman, M., Esterowitz, D., Webb, R.H., Anderson, R.R.: In vivo confocal scanning laser microscopy of human skin: melanin provides strong contrast. J. Invest. Dermatol. **104**, 946–952 (1995)
2. Laruelo, A., et al.: Hybrid sparse regularization for magnetic resonance spectroscopy. In: IEEE International Conference of Engineering in Medicine and Biology Society (EMBC), Osaka, Japan, 3–7 July 2013, pp. 6768–6771 (2013)
3. Albughdadi, M., Chaari, L., Tourneret, J.Y., Forbes, F., Ciuciu, P.: A Bayesian non-parametric hidden Markov random model for hemodynamic brain parcellation. Sig. Process. **135**(10223), 132–146 (2017)
4. Chaabene, S., Chaari, L., Kallel, A.: Bayesian sparse regularization for parallel MRI reconstruction using complex Bernoulli–Laplace mixture priors. SIViP **14**(3), 445–453 (2019). https://doi.org/10.1007/s11760-019-01567-5
5. Fakhfakh, M., Bouaziz, B., Gargouri, F., Chaari, L.: 1ProgNet: Covid-19 prognosis using recurrent and convolutional neural networks. IEEE Trans. Artif. Intell. (2020, submitted)
6. Geert, L., et al.: A survey on deep learning in medical image analysis. Med. Image Anal. **42**, 60–88 (2017)
7. Calzavara-Pinton, P., Longo, C., Venturini, M., Sala, R., Pellacani, G.: Reflectance confocal microscopy for in vivo skin imaging. Photochem. Photobiol. **84**, 1421–1430 (2008)
8. Yamashita, R., Nishio, M., Do, R.K.G., Togashi, K.: Convolutional neural networks: an overview and application in radiology. Insights Imaging **9**(4), 611–629 (2018). https://doi.org/10.1007/s13244-018-0639-9
9. Szegedy, C., Vanhoucke, V., Ioffe, S., Shlens, J., Wojna, Z.: Rethinking the inception architecture for computer vision. Computing Research Repository (CoRR) (2015)
10. Halimi, A., Batatia, H., Digabel, J., Josse, G., Tourneret, J.Y.: Statistical modeling and classification of reflectance confocal microscopy images. In: Computational Advances in Multi-Sensor Adaptive Processing (CAMSAP), pp. 1–5, December 2017
11. Halimi, A., Batatia, H., Digabel, J., Josse, G., Tourneret, J.Y.: An unsupervised Bayesian approach for the joint reconstruction and classification of cutaneous reflectance confocal microscopy images. In: European Signal Processing Conference EUSIPCO, pp. 241–245, August 2017

12. Cendre, R., Mansouri, A., Benezeth, Y., Marzani, F., Jean, P., Cinotti, E.: Two schemes for automated diagnosis of lentigo on confocal microscopy images. In: International Conference on Signal and Image Processing (ICSIP), pp. 143–147, July 2019
13. Ève, O.: Les produits dépigmentants: le point en 2011, p. 78, September 2011
14. Cohen, L.M.: Lentigo maligna and lentigo maligna melanoma. J. Am. Acad. Dermatol. **33**(6), 923–936 (1995)
15. Bollea-Garlatti, L.A., Galimberti, G.N., Galimberti, R.L.: Lentigo maligna: keys to dermoscopic diagnosis. Actas Dermo-Sifiliográficas (English Edition) **107**(6), 489–497 (2016)
16. Andersen, W.K., Labadie, R.R., Bhawan, J.: Histopathology of solar lentigines of the face: a quantitative study. J. Am. Acad. Dermatol. **36**(3), 444–447 (1997)
17. Chaari, L.: A Bayesian grouplet transform. SIViP **13**(5), 871–878 (2019). https://doi.org/10.1007/s11760-019-01423-6
18. Ribani, R., Marengoni, M.: A survey of transfer learning for convolutional neural networks. In: Conference on Graphics, Patterns and Images Tutorials, pp. 47–57 (2019)
19. Shorten, C., Khoshgoftaar, T.M.: A survey on image data augmentation for deep learning. J. Big Data **6**(1), 1–48 (2019). https://doi.org/10.1186/s40537-019-0197-0
20. García, A.H., König, P.: Further advantages of data augmentation on convolutional neural networks. In: Kůrková, V., Manolopoulos, Y., Hammer, B., Iliadis, L., Maglogiannis, I. (eds.) ICANN 2018. LNCS, vol. 11139, pp. 95–103. Springer, Cham (2018). https://doi.org/10.1007/978-3-030-01418-6_10
21. Szegedy, C., et al.: Going deeper with convolutions. In: IEEE Conference on Computer Vision and Pattern Recognition (CVPR), pp. 1–9, June 2015
22. Yosinski, J., Clune, J., Bengio, Y., Lipson, H.: How transferable are features in deep neural networks? Computing Research Repository (CoRR), pp. 3320–3328 (2014)

Deep Learning-Based Approach for Atrial Fibrillation Detection

Lazhar Khriji[1,2(✉)], Marwa Fradi[2], Mohsen Machhout[2],
and Abdulnasir Hossen[1]

[1] College of Engineering, Sultan Qaboos University, Muscat, Oman
{lazhar,abhossen}@squ.edu.om
[2] Faculty of Sciences of Monastir, Monastir University, Monastir, Tunisia
marwafradi32@gmail.com, machhout@yahoo.fr

Abstract. Atrial Fibrillation (AF) is a health-threatening condition, which is a violation of the heart rhythm that can lead to heart-related complications. Remarkable interest has been given to ECG signals analysis for AF detection in an early stage. In this context, we propose an artificial neural network ANN application to classify ECG signals into three classes, the first presents Normal Sinus Rhythm NSR, the second depicts abnormal signal with Atrial Fibrillation (AF) and the third shows noisy ECG signals. Accordingly, we achieve 93.1% accuracy classification results, 95.1% of sensitivity, 90.5% of specificity and 98%. Furthermore, we yield a value of zero error and a low value of cross entropy, which prove the robustness of the proposed ANN model architecture. Thus, we outperform the state of the art by achieving high accuracy classification without pre-processing step and without high level of feature extraction, and then we enable clinicians to determine automatically the class of each patient ECG signal.

Keywords: ECG-classification · AF detection · Confusion matrix · ROC · ANN · Histogram error

1 Introduction

ECG signals classification is a crucial step to determine given the importance to assign to each patient its ECG class. Indeed, heart diseases have known a big spread in the last recent years. Such as arrhythmia cardiac problems like Atrial Fibrillation (AFIB). The prevalence of arterial fibrillation (AF) is increasing during the last few years and presenting the most common health problem in many countries [1]. AF presents a very critical health issue, which affects the quality of life of persons and leading to many risks such as cardiac stroke. An analysis of AF is based on a clinical evaluation and requires electrocardiogram (ECG) documentation during the arrhythmia. During the last few years, deep learning (DL) revolutionized the medical area as the deep neural networks presented the state of the art results in many applications such as computer vision, image processing, robotics, medical imaging, etc. The high performance obtained by the deep neural network is based on the use of powerful graphic processing units (GPUs) which allowed these implementations to outperform the classic ones.

M. Jmaiel et al. (Eds.): ICOST 2020, LNCS 12157, pp. 100–113, 2020.
https://doi.org/10.1007/978-3-030-51517-1_9

Because of the outstanding development in DL, its application in medical field (using biomedical signals) is of huge interest. Accordingly, many works were developed using DL models for ECG classification. In this context, our work in this paper presents a new contribution using artificial neural network (ANN) architecture, to classify MIT-BIH dataset signal into normal and AFIB ECG signals.

The rest of this work is divided into 4 sections. Section 2 summarizes the state of the art. Section 3 presents the propounded neural network model and experimental results. Discussions and conclusion are depicted in Sects. 4 and 5, respectively.

2   State of the Art

In [2], Rahal et al. proposed a new approach for active classification of electrocardiogram ECG signals based on deep neural networks (DNN). Electrocardiogram ECG classification plays an essential role in clinical diagnosis of cardiac insufficiency. Zubair et al. in [3] proposed an ECG beat classification system based on convolutional neural network (CNN). This model is divided into two main parts, one for features extraction and the second for classification. Electrocardiogram ECG interpretation plays an important role in clinical ECG workflow. Rajpurkar et al. [4] developed a new method based on deep convolutional neural network to classify ECG signals belonging to fourteen different classes. Acharya et al. [5] did another study where they designed a novel deep CNN for ECG signals classification. Another work was proposed in [6] based on deep belief Net used for classifying heartbeats into four classes. A new method is presented in [7], which presents a new deep learning approach used for detecting atrial fibrillation in real time. In this work, authors used an end-to-end neural network combining a convolutional with a recurrent neural network (CNN, RNN) in order to extract high-level features from the input signals.

This hybrid model was trained and tested under three different datasets containing a total number of 85 classes. This model presents a particular performance by its ability of analyzing 24 h of ECG recordings in less than one second. This algorithm was tested on the three datasets in order to test its robustness and achieved the following results: 98.96% of specificity and 86.4% for sensitivity. Figure 1 presents a classic architecture of a Convolutional neural network (CNN).

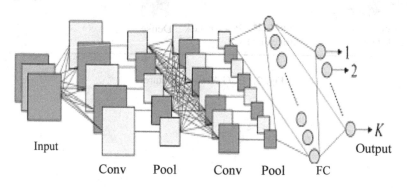

Fig. 1. A CNN classical architecture

There are many different approaches to the task of arrhythmia classification of ECG signals in terms of which method is used, which arrhythmias are classified, which data set is used, which features are extracted and whether individual beats or longer intervals are classified. For example, Rajpurkar et al. [4] uses a deep convolutional neural network trained on 30-s intervals of raw ECG signal data to classify 14 different classes, including normal sinus rhythm, noise, atrial fibrillation and atrial flutter.

Atrial fibrillation presents a very complex input data for a neural network. Deep neural networks have shown a big performance in learning non-linear input data. As deep neural network is able to learn complex pattern presenting AF in ECG signal, these techniques can widely help researchers on finding parts that are more important on the ECG to focus on during the training set. Indeed, using a CNN results accuracy overcome 95% [8, 10]. Accordingly, in [13], authors introduce a 2-channels neural network in order to address the problem of AF presence in the ECG signals. This new neural network is named "ECGNet". By using this model, authors achieved very encouraging results coming up to 99.4% as detection accuracy in MIT-BIH atrial fibrillation dataset with 5-s ECG segments. Figure 2 presents the architecture of the proposed ECGNet neural network. This DL technique has shown its ability to detect FA in a short time process. In addition, the Attention Network has achieved 99.8 of accuracy.

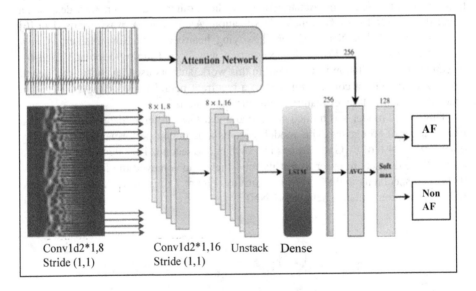

Fig. 2. ECG-Net architecture

3 Method and Results

3.1 Method

3.1.1 Dataset

The MIT-BIH dataset is known by its popularity as it has served for a long time as an interesting reference to be useful for ECG signals classification and diagnosis detection. In this context, we use three types of records from MIT-BIT dataset such as 100 samples of Normal sinus rhythm NSR, 40 samples of Atrial Fibrillation ATFIB and finally 60 samples of Noisy ECG signals. Each sample constitutes of a matrix with a size of 3600 * 1, reaching a total of 202 * 3600 for the input ECG data. Records as depicted in Table 1 recognize each type of signals. For each record, an atrial fibrillation should be classified similarly as a specialist would, the annotated parameters have been labelled by specialist for a long time.

Table 1. MIT-BIH dataset

Records	Samples	Matrix-size of samples	Annotations
100,101,105,109,112,113,114,115,116,117	100	3600 * 1	NSR
201, 202, 203, 210, 219	42	3600 * 1	AFIB
205, 223, 207	60	3600 * 1	Noisy-ECG

Each record consisted of 3600 samples, with a frequency of sampling of 1/360 s. Figures 3, 4 and 5 represent an ECG signal of record 201, 203 and 100, respectively, with 3600 samples for each record.

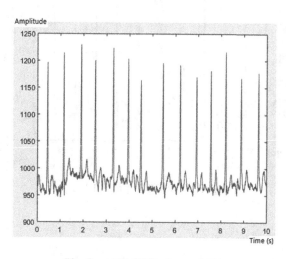

Fig. 3. AFIB ECG of record 201

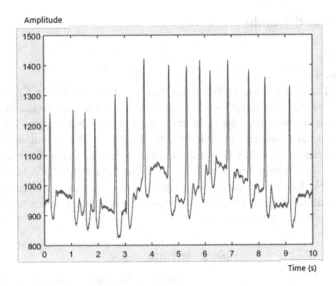

Fig. 4. AFIB ECG of record 203

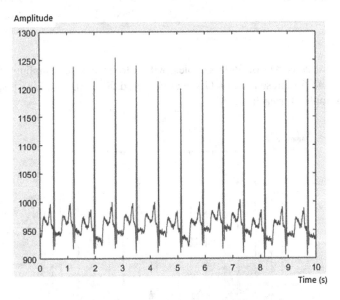

Fig. 5. SNR ECG of record 100

3.1.2 Artificial Neural Network (ANN)

The Propounded ANN Architecture

The idea of creating an artificial neural network architecture was inspired by the biological neural system [12]. Indeed, our proposed artificial neural network consists on the input layer, which contains 202 samples of ECG signals, each sample consists of a matrix sized 3600 * 1; the input dataset is a 202 samples of vectors, constituting a matrix of 3600 * 202 of ECG signals. Then, a sigmoid activation function is applied, creating a respectful numbers of parameters, which present the feature maps of the ECG signals, passing through 10 hidden layer, and 10 neurons per layer, having 100 parameters, with a sigmoid activation function as depicted by the Eq. (1). Then a softmax function, presented by the Eq. (2), is applied to classify signals into three classes the first present an AFIB signal however, the second presents a SNR signal and the third depicts noisy ECG-signals. The suggested ANN architecture is depicted in Fig. 6 and Fig. 7 (a, b and c). The latter shows the used architecture when the number of Hidden Layers (HL) is 10, 2, and 20, respectively.

$$y = \frac{1}{1 + e^{-x}} \tag{1}$$

$$Softmax(x_i) = \frac{e^{x_i}}{\sum_j e^{x_j}} \tag{2}$$

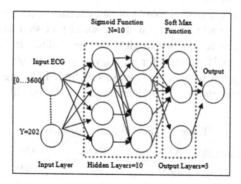

Fig. 6. Synoptic flow of the proposed ANN architecture

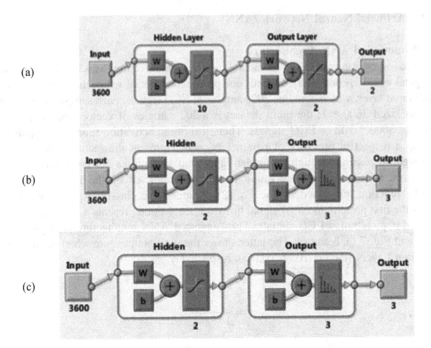

Fig. 7. ANN trained architecture: (a) ANN with HL = 10, (b) ANN with HL = 2, (c) ANN with HL = 20.

Training Data Parameters

Training parameters have a crucial role to obtain excellent accuracy. For this fact, the number of parameters should be done with the exact precision to get high accuracy, sensitivity and specificity results and to yield the best values. In fact, For ANN1, we use 10 hidden layer with 10 neurons for each layer. Thus, we obtain a number of 100 parameters, presenting the feature maps extracted from ECG signals. However, for ANN2 and ANN3, the number of hidden layers is 2 and 20 respectively. Thus,

Table 2. Training data parameters

Training parameters	ANN1	ANN2	ANN3
Iterations	1000	1000	**1000**
Activation function	Sigmoid	Sigmoid	Sigmoid
Classifier function	Soft-max	Soft-max	Soft-max
Hidden layers	**10**	**2**	**20**
Parameters numbers	100	20	200
Train-samples	142	142	142
Validation-samples	30	30	30
Test-images	30	30	30
Error-rate	0.001	0.001	0.001
Batch	3600 samples	3600 samples	3600 samples

accuracy results will be discussed in the next section. Then, more the number of iterations is increasing; more classification results are going higher. Table 2 depicts all used parameters for the ECG classification process.

3.2 ECG Classification Results

The propounded artificial neural network is presented with the confusion matrix, the histogram error, and the curve ROC and training performance results.

3.2.1 Confusion Matrix

A confusion matrix is a crucial method to determine the performance classification of a system since it divides the results into four classes such as True Positive (TP), True Negative (TN), False Positive (FP) and False Negative (FN). Accordingly, in Fig. 8, FP results are shown in the confusion matrix in the last row and the FN are depicted in the last column. It summarizes the prediction results on a classification issue. Therefore, it answers the problem of determination of the class of each signal. Indeed, it is depicted by a size of n × n associated with a classifier showing the predicted and actual classification, where n is the number of different classes. Table 1 shows a confusion matrix for n = 3. It gives us a sight not only into the errors being made by a classifier but more importantly the types of errors that are being made. The classification accuracy alone can be misleading where we have an unequal number of observations in each class or in case of having more than two classes in the dataset. Calculating a confusion matrix gives a better idea of what a classification model is getting right and what types of errors it is making. Indeed, performance results are calculated by the following equations presenting the sensitivity, the specificity and the accuracy.

$$Sensitivity\ (True\ positive\ rate) = \frac{TP}{TP + FN} \tag{3}$$

$$Specificity\ (False\ positive\ rate) = \frac{TN}{TN + FP} \tag{4}$$

$$Accuracy\ (percent\ of\ all\ samples\ correctly\ classified) = \frac{TN + TP}{TN + TP + FN + FP} \tag{5}$$

The prediction results (Fig. 8) show an accuracy of 100% for the training process, 80% for the validation process and 73.3% for the testing process. These results presented a high precision of classification, which proves the robustness of the used artificial neural network architecture. Indeed, there are no misclassified signals in the training confusion matrix. However, in the validation confusion matrix in all confusion matrix a value of 0% for misclassified signal is achieved. The green colour in the confusion matrix represents the true positive classified ECG signals; however, the red colour depicts the misclassified signals. The first class presents the atrial fibrillation

ECG signal, the second-class presents the SNR classified ECG signals. We used 142 records in the training process, where 69 records are classified as SNR signals, 28 records are classified as AFIB signals and 45 records are classified as noisy ECG signals, yielding a value of 100% of sensitivity and specificity. Moreover, for the validation stage, we used 30 records where 24 records are well-classified achieving accuracy value of 80%. Accordingly, test process achieved also a value of 73.3, where 22 records with 3600 samples for each record are well assigned to the right class, and 8 records are misclassified (3 records for the first class, 2 records for the second class and 3 records for the third class). These results are achieved due to the proposed architecture with 10 hidden layers, 10 neurons for each layer, with a sigmoid activation function and finally Softmax classifier proves its ability not seen before by the system. However, using a small number of hidden layers, the accuracy classification is with 82.6% and 87% using a high number of layers. Thus, the choice of a precision number of hidden layers for getting precise number of parameters shows its worth in the ECG-classification process.

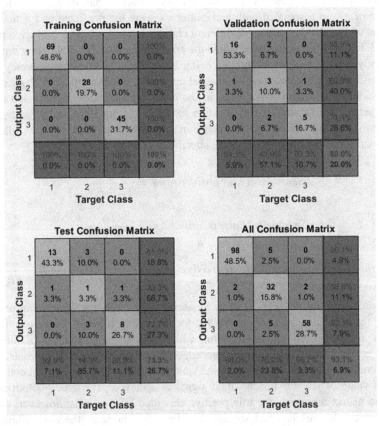

Fig. 8. Confusion Matrix: training, validation and testing results with ANN1

3.2.2 Histogram Error

The histogram error determines the rate of the existent error in classifying the signals used for training, for validation and for testing. The precision shows whether the classification is well done or not (i.e. with errors). Indeed, in our ECG signals classification results yield roughly 0.07% errors as depicted in Fig. 9 where the data fitting errors are presented within a reasonably good range close to zero.

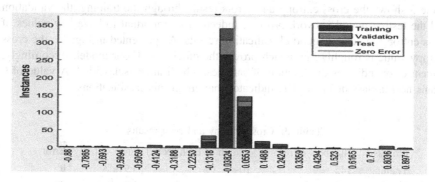

Fig. 9. Histogram error results where Errors = Targets−Outputs

3.2.3 Receiver-Operating Curve (ROC)

The ROC curve (Fig. 10) is a graphical tool allowing presenting the capacity of a test to discriminate between different classes. It plays a huge role to depict TP rate against FP

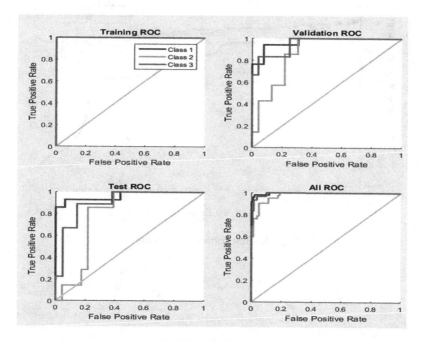

Fig. 10. ROC results

rate in medical statistics and more specifically in the field of ECG signals classification. Indeed, within our proposed ANN, we have an excellent rate of classification as seen in the ROC and a perfect prediction would yield an AUC of 0.93, presenting a value close to 1 for the training process, blue coloured in the curve. Similarly, test and validation process present high accuracy rate according to the curve.

3.2.4   Cross Entropy Results

Table 3 shows the cross entropy and errors result through the training, the validation and the testing neural network process. Indeed, it is important to have low values of cross entropy to achieve good classification results. As presented in Fig. 11, the cross entropy value is roughly low which proves the efficiency of our model. Accordingly, Percent error indicates the fraction of samples, which are misclassified. A value of 0 means no misclassifications, 100 indicates maximum misclassifications.

Table 3. Cross-entropy and error results

Process	Numbers of records	Length of each record	Cross-entropy	Error
Training	142	10-s	$5.91e^{-1}$	0
Validation	30	10-s	$1.94e^{0}$	20
Testing	30	10-s	$1.95e^{0}$	26.7

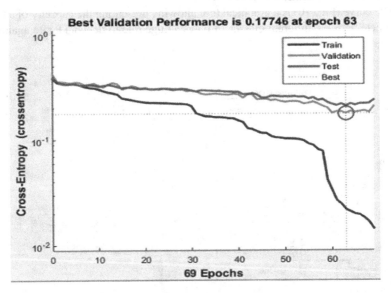

Fig. 11. Best performance results

3.2.5   Processing Time

Experimental results obtained from using the MIT-BIH Arrhythmia Database showed that the processing time efficiency of our system can be highly increased by implementing the algorithm on GPU instead of the actual CPU. By using CPU, our algorithm took 2.052 s to make the real time classification of an ECG signal. Nevertheless, further improvement can be done on this method to achieve higher accuracy with less processing time.

4   Discussions

The ANN application for ECG signals classification demonstrates greater accuracy compared to the state of the art, which proves that the ANN system is able to get more and more advanced results. Indeed, the state to have 100% of accuracy and 0% of error is hard to achieve. Despite this problem, ANN achieves high accuracy in comparison with related works. In [2], authors achieved 86% of accuracy. Accordingly, our ANN method overcomes results depicted in [2] with 7% of accuracy for ECG signals classifications. Indeed more, we are going deeper through layers, more accuracy results are better. We have achieved the top accuracy for MIT-BIH-ECG signal classification using the artificial neural network model by a value of 93.1% of accuracy where CNN comes with the third top accuracy with 92.7%. In Fact, we overcome [9], where authors proposed an Echo state neural network, with 92.7% of accuracy. Moreover, we surpass the state of the art in [11] with more than 3% of accuracy, and we have an error close to zero in histogram error detection with a low value of cross entropy, which proves the robustness of our classifier model. To conclude, the achieved results as depicted in Table 4 are comparable with the state of the art in fully automatic ECG classifiers and even outperform other ECG classifiers that follow more complex feature-selection approaches. Indeed, as presented in Table 4, we achieved encouraging results coming up to 93%, close to ECG –Net that is very complex and time consuming (it is using a huge amount of parameters and samples leading to increase the network complexity). Thus, there is no doubt to say that we succeed to better compromise between the testing accuracy and the network parameters complexity.

Table 4. Comparative study with the state of the art

Method	Best accuracy	Time process
Our work: **ANN1**	**93.1%**	**2.052 s**
CNN + FCN layers [2]	86%	–
DenseNet [11]	89.5%	–
SVM [3]	87.5%	....
Echo state networks [9]	92.7%	.....
ECG-Net [13]	**94.0%**	......

5 Conclusion

In this paper, we have achieved the top accuracy of MIT-BIH-ECG signal classification using the artificial neural network model by a value of 93.3% of test-accuracy, of sensitivity and of precision. Accordingly, the ROC shows an excellent curve of rate classification results. Accordingly, the histogram presents 0.07% error, which overcomes the state of the art without a huge number of feature extraction and without pre-processing stage. Our method is promising and can help clinicians to determine the class of each ECG patient. Indeed, for going faster, the next step will be dedicated to our application implementation on GPU and then on an FPGA.

Acknowledgment. The authors would like to thank OMANTEL and Sultan Qaboos University for their financial support, grant number "EG/SQU-OT/18/01".

References

1. Visa, S., Ramsay, B., Ralescu, A.L., Van Der Knaap, E.: Confusion matrix-based feature selection. MAICS **710**, 120–127 (2011)
2. Pyakillya, B., Kazachenko, N., Mikhailovsky, N.: Deep learning for ECG classification. In: Journal of Physics Conference Series, vol. 913, no. 1, p. 012004. IOP Publishing (2017)
3. Celin, S., Vasanth, K.: ECG signal classification using various machine learning techniques. J. Med. Syst. **42**(12), 241 (2018)
4. Rajpurkar, P., Hannun, A.Y., Haghpanahi, M., Bourn, C., Ng, A.Y.: Cardiologist-level arrhythmia detection with convolutional neural networks (2017). ArXiv e-prints,. arXiv: 1707.01836
5. Acharya, U.R., et al.: A deep convolutional neural network model to classify heartbeats. Comput. Biol. Med. **89**, 389–396 (2017)
6. Wu, Z., et al.: A novel features learning method for ECG arrhythmias using deep belief networks. In: 2016 6th International Conference on Digital Home (ICDH), pp. 192–196. IEEE (2016)
7. Andersen, R.S., Peimankar, A., Puthusserypady, S.: A deep learning approach for real-time detection of atrial fibrillation. Exp. Syst. Appl. **115**, 465–473 (2019)
8. Kachuee, M., Fazeli, S., Sarrafzadeh, M.: Ecg heartbeat classification: a deep transferable representation. In: 2018 IEEE International Conference on Healthcare Informatics (ICHI), pp. 443–444. IEEE (2018)
9. Alfaras, M., Soriano, M.C., Ortín, S.: A fast machine learning model for ECG-based heartbeat classification and arrhythmia detection. Front. Phys. **7**, 103 (2019)
10. Ji, Y., Zhang, S., Xiao, W.: Electrocardiogram classification based on faster regions with convolutional neural network. Sensors **19**(11), 2558 (2019)
11. Guo, L., Sim, G., Matuszewski, B.: Inter-patient ECG classification with convolutional and recurrent neural networks. Biocybern. Biomed. Eng. **39**(3), 868–879 (2019)

12. Bouallegue, K.: A new class of neural networks and its applications. Neurocomputing **249**, 28–47 (2017)
13. Mousavi, S., Afghah, F., Razi, A., et al.: ECGNET: learning where to attend for detection of atrial fibrillation with deep visual attention. In: 2019 IEEE EMBS International Conference on Biomedical & Health Informatics (BHI), pp. 1–8. IEEE (2019)

Unsupervised Method Based on Superpixel Segmentation for Corpus Callosum Parcellation in MRI Scans

Amal Jlassi[1(✉)], Khaoula ElBedoui[1,2], Walid Barhoumi[1,2], and Chokri Maktouf[3]

[1] Institut Supérieur d'Informatique, Research Team on Intelligent Systems in Imaging and Artificial Vision (SIIVA), LR16ES06 Laboratoire de recherche en Informatique, Modélisation et Traitement de l'Information et de la Connaissance (LIMTIC), Université de Tunis El Manar, Tunis, Tunisia
amal.jlassi1991@hotmail.com
[2] Université de Carthage, Ecole Nationale d'Ingénieurs de Carthage, Tunis, Tunisia
{khaoula.elbedoui,walid.barhoumi}@enicarthage.rnu.tn
[3] Nuclear Medicine Department, Pasteur Institute of Tunis, Tunis, Tunisia

Abstract. In this paper, we introduce an unsupervised method for the parcellation of the Corpus Callosum (CC) from MRI images. Since there are no visible landmarks within the structure that explicit its parcels, non-geometric CC parcellation is a challenging task especially that almost of proposed methods are geometric or data-based. In fact, in order to subdivide the CC from brain sagittal MRI scans, we adopt the probabilistic neural network as a clustering technique. Then, we use a cluster validity measure based on the maximum entropy (Vmep) to obtain the optimal number of classes. After that, we obtain the isolated CC that we parcel automatically using SLIC (Simple Linear Iterative Clustering) as superpixel segmentation technique. The obtained results on two challenging public datasets prove the performance of the proposed method against geometric methods from the state of the art. Indeed, as best as we know, it is the first work that investigates the validation of a CC parcellation method on ground-truth datasets using many objective metrics.

Keywords: Corpus callosum · MRI · Parcellation · Superpixel

1 Introduction

Thanks to advances in magnetic resonance imaging, neuroscientists and clinicians can study in depth the Corpus Callosum (CC) and mainly the correlation between the CC's dimensions and some neurological diseases. The CC, which is the largest white matter structure and the biggest fiber tract connecting corresponding regions of the cerebral cortex in the two cerebral hemispheres, integrates motor, sensory, and cognitive functions of the brain [1]. Anatomically,

© The Author(s) 2020
M. Jmaiel et al. (Eds.): ICOST 2020, LNCS 12157, pp. 114–125, 2020.
https://doi.org/10.1007/978-3-030-51517-1_10

more than half of the axons composing the CC are surrounded by myelin, which gives this structure its remarkable appearance in midsagittal T1-weighted MRI images. However, in many sagittal brain MRI slices, the fornix appears in the neighborhood of the CC with a similar intensity (Fig. 1) [2]. The CC is usually divided into smaller regions such as rostrum, genu, body, and splenium. This subdivision of the CC is called parcellation and it is proving to be very use-ful for an effective analysis of the CC [2,3]. In fact, the CC shape may be the cause of many neurodegenerative diseases such as epilepsy, alzheimer, autism, depression and other types of psychosis [4]. The CC analysis is also important for studying aging, gender differences and laterality [5]. Hence, various studies have evaluated shape or volume variation of the CC parcels. They revealed a cor-relation between CC's abnormalities and many diseases. For instance, [6] shows that the rate of change in CC or one of its sub-regions is more closely asso-ciated with the progression of Alzheimer's disease. Moreover, the CC parceling can be an appropriate group biomarker for an objective evaluation of treatments aimed at slowing the progression of Alzheimer [7]. Furthermore, several works have identified volume alterations of the CC and its sub-regions in subjects with Autism Spectrum Disorders (ASD). In this context, a study of the CC volume of 40 pre-schoolers, with different sex and age, suffering from ASD was made by applying the "FreeSurfer" automated parcellation software. This study demon-strated that the total volume of the CC and its sub-regions is correlated with autism severity [8]. Another study conducted on 75 participants with Parkinson Disease (PD) and 24 Healthy Control (HC) confirms that CC sub-regions abnor-malities might be the cause of Parkinson disease. Indeed, participants with PD showed an increase in the 3 anterior callosal segments compared to HC [9].

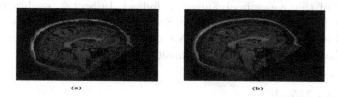

Fig. 1. Example of sagittal brain MRI slices from the OASIS dataset: (a) The input MRI. (b) Delineation of the CC, where the fornix (framed in blue) appears in the neighborhood of the CC while being of similar appearance. (Color figure online)

Generally, the CC parcellation into callosal regions allows for a precise differ-entiation of motor connectivity and the structural integrity of these tracts in the CC [10]. Thus, the CC parcellation should be so helpful to better understand inter-hemispherical callosal connectivity in patients or healthy subjects [11]. In particular, MRI takes advantage of the macroscopic geometrical arrangement of white matter bundles that it makes capable of generating good CC visualization from the sagittal plane. In any way, the parcellation of the CC stills an impor-tant task for radiologic assessment despite there are no real or visible borders to allow this subdivision. Nevertheless, the visual inspection of CC structures in MRI scans suffers from both inter- and intra-specialist variability. On the one hand, the manual CC segmentation methods require strongly visual effort, specialized training skill, and are time-consuming processes. On the other hand, several geometrical methods for the CC parcellation have been proposed such as Witelson and Hofer methods [12]. However, these methods cannot be satisfactorily validated due to the lack of qualitative parameters and reference standards. Although all these difficulties, the development of an automatic CC parcellation method is an inescapable need to ensure a reliable diagnosis. Such parcellation is so independent from the operator skills and may be extended to other brain structures parcellation. Thus, since there are no visible landmarks indicating where the CC should be subdivided, the development of a fully automatic CC parcellation method is highly challenging, even for specialists. To deal with this issue, we propose to automatically parcel the CC within MRI images. By validating it, for the first time, on large and public datasets, the proposed method records promising results. In fact, the contribution of this work is twofold:

- As best as we know, we adopt for the first time the superpixel segmentation algorithm called Simple Linear Iterative Clustering (SLIC) for the CC parcellation [13]. Despite its simplicity, SLIC has been demonstrated to be effective in various computer vision applications [14].
- The subdivision process of the proposed method is fully automatic and it is the second study that proposed a non-geometric analysis for the CC parcels, to the best of our knowledge [15]. Although it is based only on the MRI data of each analyzed subject, with no parameter adjusting, the proposed method proved quantitatively its superiority over state-of-the-art methods.

The rest of this paper is organized as follows. In Sect. 2, we briefly review existing methods for the CC parcellation. Section 3 presents the proposed method based on SLIC. Experimental results are discussed in Sect. 4. The last section concludes the paper and points some directions for future work.

2 Related Work

Few CC parcellation methods were proposed. However, most of these methods have not surmounted all the challenges encountered. In fact, the CC parcellation is a challenging task given that a normal shape of the CC might not clearly highlight all parcels, what can increase the diagnosis complexity. In addition, many internal abnormalities might include bumps which are hard to detect. Existing CC parcellation methods can be divided into two main classes: geometric methods and non-geometric ones. On the one hand, since there are no real or visible boundaries allowing the CC parcellation, several geometrical methods were presented to perform this task. Among these methods, two particular ones are widely adopted. The first was proposed by Witelson and it is based on postmortem connectivity analysis in primates and humans [16]. This method divides the CC into five regions ranging from anterior dimension to the posterior dimension. The CC subdivision is done into an anterior third, the middle of the anterior and posterior midbody, a posterior third and the posterior one-fifth. The rostrum, genu, and rostral body presenting the regions of the anterior third illustrate the prefrontal, premotor, and supplementary motor cortical areas. However, the posterior midbody is crossed by the somaesthesic and posterior parietal fiber bundles. The sub-regions of the posterior third, containing the isthmus and splenium, are allocated to temporal, parietal, and occipital cortical regions. Thus, this parcellation method, and as any geometric methods, neither reflects the real texture nor the internal organization of the CC. In addition, the CC parcellation is strongly dependent on the brain conservation process, since it is based on post-mortem data. Differently, Hofer proposed the only work based on tractography of DTI (Diffusion Tensor Imaging) by subdividing the CC into five regions from an average behavior observed via tractography in a specific population of 8 subjects [1]. As already proposed by Witelson, the geometric baseline in the midsagittal section of the CC is defining the anterior and posterior points of the structure. The first region, which represents the first sixth, contains fibers projected in the prefrontal region. The remainder of the anterior half CC illustrates the second region containing the fibers that form the motor and motor areas of the cerebral cortex. In fact, these fibers form together the largest CC region and are placed in the back section of the structure. The third region presents the posterior half minus the posterior third. It contains fibers responsible for the primary motor cortex. However, this part of the parcellation scheme is in conflict with Witelson's method. The fourth region forms third minus the posterior quarter, presenting the primary sensory fibers. The last and the fifth region represents the CC posterior quarter crossed by the parietal, temporal and visual fibers. Figure 2 shows a comparison between the geometric schemes proposed by Witelson and Hofer. We notice that geometric methods allow only to divide the CC into the same regions among all subjects without considering the human and individual brain features between different subjects. On the second hand, differently to geometric parcellation methods, Rittner proposed a data-driven method based on the Watershed technique [15]. This method is composed of four steps. The first step consists in the weighting of the fractional anisotropy. The second step performs the selection of the brain midsagittal plane, followed by the third and the last step which are the CC segmentation using the Watershed technique, and its parcellation with fixed markers. Nevertheless, this method suffers from sensitivity to parameters selection. In order to overcome its limitations, Cover extended the Rittner method with some important changes [12]. Practically, the author replaced all steps except the first step in order to lead to a more robust data-driven method. Indeed, the parcellation is improved by applying the K-means algorithm after defining the CC centerline. When comparing this method to that of Rittner, and although both are based on Watershed, it is confirmed that this method had a better generalization ability using no fixed markers to execute the Watershed transform. However, due to the lack of quantitative metrics and reference standards, these methods cannot be correctly validated.

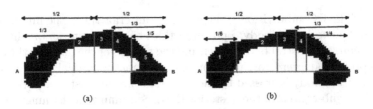

Fig. 2. CC geometric parcellation with divisions presenting the five regions (on an MRI scan from the OASIS dataset) using the method of: (a) Witelson. (b) Hofer.

3   Proposed Method

Differently to existing methods, we propose a subdivision scheme that considers only the MRI data [14]. Using the SLIC superpixel segmentation technique, the method is composed of two main steps: CC segmentation and CC parcellation. This comes from that the SLIC presents one of the most popular images over segmentations that is commonly used as supporting regions for primitives to reduce computations in various computer vision tasks.

3.1   CC Segmentation of the Midsagittal Slice

We adopt herein our previous method [17] for the automatic CC segmentation of MRI sagittal section. It includes three main steps: image preprocessing using the Anisotropic Diffusion Filtering (ADF), classification based on the unsupervised Probabilistic Neural Network (PNN) classifier, and CC isolation using a spatial filtering (Fig. 3). In fact, the first step aims to enhance the signal-to-noise ratio by eliminating unwanted parts in the background and smoothing the internal part of the region while preserving its borders. In fact, ADF allows to unblock high-frequency noise while preserving the main edges of structures [18]. Then, the classification step permits to define the target classes using K-means, before classifying them by the PNN [17]. Thereafter, the Vmep index, which is based on the maximum entropy principle as an evaluation method that is called the cluster validity, is applied in order to determine the optimal number of clusters. The optimal number of classes is obtained when the Vmep validity index reaches its maximum value. This number is adopted for the PNN classification process to obtain the final cluster map. Once the CC class is identified, the CC region will be isolated by a spatial-based filtering. Finally, we defined the CC contour by applying a follow-up algorithm on the border pixels of the CC region that are characterized by a maximum of the spatial gradient [19].

3.2   CC Parcellation

We propose a CC parcellation method based on SLIC, which is non-geometric and fully automatic superpixel segmentation technique. It works with no parameter adjusting and with no instantaneous training, leading to a more robust technique. Thus, in order to segment the CC into a set of superpixels, which refer

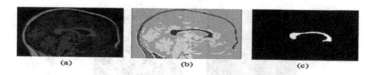

Fig. 3. CC segmentation: (a) Input sagittal MRI. (b) Cluster Map. (c) Isolated CC.

to groups of pixels that represent perceptually significant small defined regions, we adopt the SLIC technique. It is an arrangement of K-means for superpixel generation in order to be faster than existing methods, more memory efficient while improving significantly the segmentation accuracy. It allows two important directions [14]. Firstly, it reduces greatly the number of distance calculations by restricting the search space to a region corresponding to the superpixel size. Therefore, a reduction in the complexity of being linear is achieved in the pixels' number N and superpixels' number K that is independent and user-defined. In our case, N and K are equal to 256 and 200, respectively. Secondly, a combination of color and spatial proximity is reached by a weighted distance measure that allows both controls over the size and compactness of the superpixels. Thus, each slice of the input MRI image is partitioned into different size regions. In fact, the initial grid size is defined as S (1). From the geometric center, the center superpixel of each region is computed. This geometrical center of each region is recursively updated in each iteration.

$$S = \sqrt{\frac{N}{K}}. \tag{1}$$

In order to regroup the pixel, both spatial and intensity distances are used. The spatial distance between the pixels i and j is defined as follows (2):

$$S_d = \sqrt{(p_j - p_i)^2 + (q_j - q_i)^2}, \tag{2}$$

where the coordinate values of pixel i and j are represented by p and q. The Eq. 3 calculates the intensity distance.

$$I_d = \sqrt{N_j + N_i}, \tag{3}$$

where N_j and N_i represent the normalized intensity of pixel j and i, respectively. Equation 4 defines the combined distance measure C_d of spatial and intensity.

$$C_d = \sqrt{I_d^2 \cdot \left(\frac{S_d}{S}\right)^2 + e^2}, \tag{4}$$

where e denotes the compactness coefficient. In fact, larger value of e illustrates more compact segments, whereas lower value of e represents flexible boundaries. The compactness coefficient is fixed in the range of $[0, 1]$. The superpixel computation of the proposed method is shown in Fig. 4.

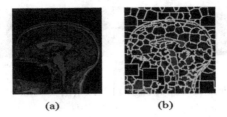

(a)   (b)

Fig. 4. SLIC-based parcellation: (a) The input MRI. (b) Result of the SLIC method.

4   Experimental Results

For the evaluation of the proposed parcellation method, we are the only study that used brain MRI scans from two public datasets. On the one hand, we used the Open Access Series of Imaging Studies (OASIS) dataset, which is freely available on www.oasis-brains.org. It is created by Washington University Alzheimer's disease Research Centre. This MRI dataset included a longitudinal collection of 416 subjects aged between 18 and 96 years, men and women, including 100 individuals with very mild to moderate Alzheimer's disease (AD). All images were acquired on the same scanner using the same sequences. Each subject was scanned on two or more visits, separated by at least one year for a total of 373 imaging sessions. Each MR image within this dataset is composed of 128 slices with a resolution of 256×256 ($1 \times 1mm$). In this work, we selected 1806 sagittal images that are qualified by a quality control according to severe artifacts. On the other hand, Autism Brain Imaging Data Exchange (ABIDE) is also investigated. In order to accelerate understanding of the neural bases of autism, the ABIDE dataset has supplied functional and structural brain imaging data collected from laboratories around the world. This dataset is composed of two large-scale collections called ABIDE-I and ABIDE-II. Each collection was collected independently across more than 24 international brain imaging laboratories. Thus, we generate a total of 2200 sagittal images with a resolution of 256×256. It is worthy noting that we have a challenging heterogeneous set of images of normal subjects and individuals with Autism and Alzheimer.

4.1   Qualitative Evaluation

For each subject, the proposed parcellation method gives an apparent variation in the positioning of the CC parcels. This is because this method is purely automatic and does not follow any atlas or any prior knowledge (Fig. 5). The geometric methods of Hofer and Witelson do not present the variation of their proportion of CC parcels and consequently, the same behavior can be observed on the results of all the subjects. Figure 5 shows that the proposed CC parcellation method is more similar to the Hofer parcellation than the Rittne one. This can be explained by the fact that Hofer subdivisions are based on the connections of the cortical fibers to find the CC parcels. The largest differences between the proposed parcellation and that of Witelson are observed in the parcels 1 and 4. In fact, according to our collaborator clinician expert, the CC shape and parcellation are well defined and the delineated CC area shows closely the five anatomical subdivisions of the CC, especially the critical ones: the rostrum and the splenium. The fornix is correctly removed from the CC area and the obtained CC parcellation shows a precise subdivision of CC into five regions within brain MRI scans, without penetrating the irrelevant neighboring structures. Note that, within the selected sample of MRI brain scans, the CC is extracted and parcelled both on female (column 1 and 3) and male (column 2 and 4) subjects. In fact, we applied the proposed method on subjects from the ABIDE dataset (column 1 and 2) as well as from the OASIS dataset (column 3 and 4).

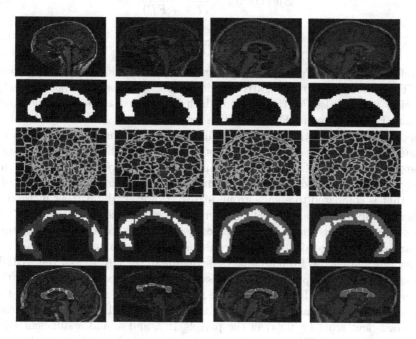

Fig. 5. Experimental results: 1st line: Input image. 2nd line: Isolated CC. 3rd line: Brain parcellation. 4th line: Proposed CC parcellation. 5th line: Ground-truth.

4.2   Quantitative Evaluation

In order to evaluate the performance of the proposed method, we used the following commonly used metrics: Dice, accuracy, sensitivity, specificity and precision.

- The Dice coefficient (5) is a statistical measure that is used for comparing the similarity of two sample sets.
- The accuracy (6) is defined as the rate of correctly classified items.
- The sensitivity (7) is the proportion of positive items correctly classified.
- The specificity (8) is the rate of negative items rightly identified.

- The precision (9) is the ratio of correctly predicted positive samples to the total predicted positive samples.

$$Dice = \frac{2 \times TP}{2 \times TP + FN + FP} \qquad (5)$$

$$Accuracy = \frac{(TP + TN)}{(TP + FN + TN + FP)} \qquad (6)$$

$$Sensitivity = \frac{TP}{(TP + FN)} \qquad (7)$$

$$Specificity = \frac{TN}{(TN + FP)} \qquad (8)$$

$$Precision = \frac{TP}{(TP + FP)} \qquad (9)$$

TP refers to the True Positive (region correctly parcelled as the concerned parcel), TN refers to the True Negative (region correctly classified as background), FP refers to the False Positive (region which is parcelled as the concerned parcel) and FN refers to the False Negative (region which is incorrectly classified as background). We notice that we produce five parcels, and for each parcel we measure the five metrics. It is worthy noting that for the first time, a very useful ground-truth for CC segmentation and parcellation within the challenging widely used OASIS and ABIDE datasets is used. Therefore, we are the only work that is compared to a such ground-truth. However, the Rittner method is evaluated only on the agreement between the results achieved by different CC parcellation methods. In fact, a professional neurologist from Pasteur Institute of Tunis and a junior doctor have been charged with manually preparing the CC regions and parcels from all images belonging to the OASIS and the ABIDE datasets. Besides, we applied post-processing in order to exclusively extract the CC area and parcels. Table 1 shows the recorded results comparatively to the ground-truth. It is clear that the Proposed Method (PM) records the higher Dice coefficient score (> 0.84) in the parcels 1, 2, and 5, and a sufficient Dice coefficient score (> 0.75) in parcels 3 and 4 comparatively to the ground-truth. Evenly, it reaches a higher accuracy, specificity and sensitivity scores with values > 0.90. The decline of the proposed method performance according to the precision metric can be explained by the cause of the ground-truth which is manually drawing and the processing applied to do the evaluation in each parcel. Furthermore, for the two datasets and for each CC parcel, the Dice coefficient was computed pairwise for the methods of the state of the art (Table 2) as it is used in the Rittner work. Therefore, the previous analyzes allow only verifying the similarity between the resulting CC parcels, or which present statistical differences between methods of the literature since this is a problem without a gold standard (Table 2). Hence, it is now possible to know the correct CC parcellation by producing ground-truth for both Witelson and Hofer methods. Since the Hofer and Witelson CC parcellation methods are based on geometric CC parcellation, their results did not vary among different subjects throughout the experimented dataset. This explains this overlap measurement obtained which would have maximum value if any of the methods was the same. The most pertinent difference between these CC parcellation methods was related to the automatic and non-geometric behavior defined by our proposed parcellation. Table 2 presents different results between methods while recording interesting similarities in some cases. The proposed CC parcellation method demonstrates to be nearby to the Hofer method, mainly on parcels 1, 2 and 3, while the Witelson method presents significant statistical difference on the parcels 4 and 5.

Table 1. Evaluation of the proposed method.

	Dice	Accuracy	Sensitivity	Specificity	Precision
Parcel 1	0.9401	0.9986	0.9992	0.9986	0.7246
Parcel 2	0.8488	0.9927	0.9935	0.9927	0.4817
Parcel 3	0.7583	0.9944	0.9959	0.9944	0.5496
Parcel 4	0.7707	0.9960	0.9972	0.9960	0.6280
Parcel 5	0.8473	0.9889	0.9845	0.9890	0.3790
Mean$\pm std$	0.8330 ± 0.050	0.9941 ± 0.003	0.9941 ± 0.001	0.9941 ± 0.013	0.5526 ± 0.363

Table 2. Dice coefficient for the two datasets (best value are in bold).

	Witelson vs PM	Hofer vs. PM	PM vs. GT	Witelson vs. GT	Hofer vs. GT
Parcel 1	0.8512	0.9100	**0.9401**	0.6125	0.7013
Parcel 2	0.6001	0.7589	**0.8488**	0.2822	0.1624
Parcel 3	**0.8845**	0.8700	0.7583	0.4760	0.47163
Parcel 4	0.5113	0.5236	**0.7707**	0.4909	0.5120
Parcel 5	0.5112	0.4958	**0.8473**	0.6868	0.8014

5   Conclusion

CC is the biggest fiber tract within the human brain that allows the communication between the two cerebral hemispheres. The CC form and sub-regions might cause some diseases. The CC parcellation from MRI images can predict future cases of diseases or progress neurological patterns in the development of different diseases. This paper presented a fully automatic non-geometric CC parcellation based on the SLIC superpixel algorithm, with no parameter adjusting and instantaneous training. Since there is no gold standard used to evaluate the existing methods, we produced for the first time a ground-truth led to evaluate quantitatively CC parcellation methods. Extensive experiments and quantitative comparisons with relevant CC parcellation methods, proved the accuracy of the proposed method on two challenging standard datasets. Indeed, the proposed method achieves higher performance values for each parcel. As future work, we aim to propose a super voxel method based on the SLIC algorithm, from not only MRI scans but also from functional magnetic resonance imaging.

References

1. Hofer, S., Frahm, J.: Topography of the human corpus callosum revisited–comprehensive fiber tractography using diffusion tensor magnetic resonance imaging. Neuroimage **32**(3), 989–994 (2006)
2. Lacerda, A., Brambilla, P., Sassi, R., Nicoletti, M.: Anatomical MRI study of corpus callosum in unipolar depression. J. Psychiatr. Res. **39**(4), 347–354 (2005)
3. Witelson, S., Goldsmith, C.: The relationship of hand preference to anatomy of the corpus callosum in men. Brain Res. **545**(1–2), 175–182 (1991)
4. El-Baz, A., Elnakib, A., Casanova, M.: Accurate automated detection of autism related corpus callosum abnormalities. J. Med. Syst. **35**(5), 929–939 (2011)
5. Johnson, S., Farnworth, T., Pinkston, J.: Corpus callosum surface area across the human adult life span: effect of age and gender. Brain Res. Bull. **35**(4), 373–377 (1994)
6. Van Schependom, J., Niemantsverdriet, E.: Callosal circularity as an early marker for Alzheimer's disease. NeuroImage Clin. **19**(1), 516–526 (2018)
7. Bachman, A., Lee, S., Sidtis, J.: Corpus callosum shape and size changes in early Alzheimer's disease: a longitudinal MRI study using the OASIS brain database. J. Alzheimers Dis. **39**(1), 71–78 (2014)
8. Giuliano, A., Saviozzi, I., Brambilla, P.: The effect of age, sex and clinical features on the volume of Corpus Callosum in pre-schoolers with Autism Spectrum Disorder: a case-control study. Eur. J. Neurosci. **47**(6), 568–578 (2018)
9. Bledsoe, I., Stebbins, G.: White matter abnormalities in the corpus callosum with cognitive impairment in Parkinson disease. Neurology **91**(24), e2244–e2255 (2018)
10. Domin, M., Lotze, M.: Parcellation of motor cortex-associated regions in the human corpus callosum on the basis of Human Connectome Project data. Brain Struct. Funct. **224**(4), 1447–1455 (2019). https://doi.org/10.1007/s00429-019-01849-1
11. Anand, C., Brandmaier, A., Arshad, M.: White-matter microstructural properties of the corpus callosum: test-retest and repositioning effects in two parcellation schemes. Brain Struct. Funct. **224**(9), 3373–3385 (2019)
12. Cover, G., Pereira, M., Bento, M.: Data-driven corpus callosum parcellation method through diffusion tensor imaging. IEEE Access **5**(1), 22421–22432 (2017)
13. Cover, G., Herrera, W., Bento, M.: Computational methods for corpus callosum segmentation on MRI: a systematic literature review. Comput. Methods Programs Biomed. **154**(1), 25–35 (2018)
14. Achanta, R., Shaji, A.: SLIC superpixels compared to state-of-the-art superpixel methods. IEEE Trans. Pattern Anal. Mach. Intell. **34**(11), 2274–2282 (2012)
15. Rittner, L., Freitas, P.: Automatic DTI-based parcellation of the corpus callosum through the watershed transform. Revista Brasileira de Engenharia Biomedica **30**(2), 132–143 (2014)
16. Witelson, S.: Hand and sex differences in the isthmus and genu of the human corpus callosum: a postmortem morphological study. Brain **112**(3), 799–835 (1989)
17. Jlassi, A., ElBedoui, K., Barhoumi, W., Maktouf, C.H.: Unsupervised method based on probabilistic neural network for the segmentation of corpus callosum in MRI scans. the 14th International Joint Conference on Computer Vision, Imaging and Computer Graphics Theory and Applications, no. 4, pp. 790–798 (2019)

18. Baâzaoui, A., Berrabah, M., Barhoumi, W., Zagrouba, E.: Multimodal registration of PET/MR brain images based on adaptive mutual information. In: Blanc-Talon, J., Distante, C., Philips, W., Popescu, D., Scheunders, P. (eds.) ACIVS 2016. LNCS, vol. 10016, pp. 361–372. Springer, Cham (2016). https://doi.org/10.1007/978-3-319-48680-2_32
19. Barhoumi, W., Zagrouba, E.: Boundaries detection based on polygonal approximation by genetic algorithms. Frontiers Artif. Intell. Appl., 1529–1533 (2002)

Behavior and Activity Monitoring

Using Learning Techniques to Observe Elderly's Behavior Changes over Time in Smart Home

Dorsaf Zekri[1,2(✉)], Thierry Delot[1(✉)], Mikael Desertot[1(✉)],
Sylvain Lecomte[1(✉)], and Marie Thilliez[1(✉)]

[1] Université Polytechnique Hauts-de-France, LAMIH UMR CNRS 8201,
Hauts-de-France, France
{Dorsaf.Zekri2,Thierry.Delot,Mikael.Desertot,Sylvain.Lecomte,
Marie.Thilliez}@uphf.fr
[2] ReDCAD Laboratory, University of Sfax, B.P. 1173 Sfax, Tunisia

Abstract. Smart environments and technology used for elder care, increases independent living time and cuts long-term care costs. A key requirement for these systems consists in detecting and informing about abnormal behavior in users'routines. In this paper, our objective is to automatically observe the elderly behavior over time and detect anomalies that may occur on the long term. Therefore, we propose a learning method to formalize a normal behavior pattern for each elderly people related to his Activities of Daily Living (ADL). We also adopt a temporal similarity score between activities that allows to detect behavior changes over time. In change behavior period we focus on each activity to detect anomalies. A use case with real datasets are promising.

Keywords: Behavior change observation · Elderly people · Smart home · Activities of Daily Living

1 Introduction

With the growing elderly population, research in elderly living and well-being has been aimed toward medical analysis and supporting independent living of elderly people. Elderly people are often disabled by several interacting problems, such as loss of function and social and environmental factors. All these factors, separately or together, determine the elderly person's level of independence and influence his/her quality of life.

In this context, most researchers aim to improve the living of elderly people with medical issues, such as diabetes and cognitive disabilities, by analyzing the behavior of residents within sensor-based environments. The progress of technology (wearable sensors, smart phones and other mobile devices, wireless communications, etc.) enables the development of effective solutions to help older people to live independently in their homes.

M. Jmaiel et al. (Eds.): ICOST 2020, LNCS 12157, pp. 129–141, 2020.
https://doi.org/10.1007/978-3-030-51517-1_11

The smart home concept includes homes equipped with simple environmental sensors and more complex systems including audio, video and biometric systems. The raw information captured by the sensors can obviously not be shared as such with the medical staff or used directly to detect changes in behavior automatically. On the contrary, extracted knowledge could be used to enrich the information displayed to the medical staff and improve the precision of early detections. There is evidence that opportunistic home surveillance prevents in some cases hospitalization.

In this paper, we focus on the problem of learning from smart home sensor data describing elderly's activities. Our objective in this work is to propose an approach to identify periods of time when behavior changes occur and detect anomalies in this period (e.g., the elderly sleep less and less every month). Our contributions in this paper can be summarized as follows.

1. We model a behavior pattern using training dataset, defined as the user's usual activities in his/her daily routine.
2. We calculate a daily score by comparing activity patterns. This daily score variation provides a global vision of the behavior of the elderly person over a period of time.
3. We detect anomalies related to every activity in the period of behavioral deviation.

The rest of this paper is organized as follows. In Sect. 2, we discuss related works. In Sect. 3 we present our approach. In Sect. 4 we report the experimentation of our proposal on real datasets. In Sect. 5 we present our conclusions and some research directions.

2   Related Works

With the use of smart homes, the daily activities and behavioral patterns of residents can now be monitored through sensors embedded within various areas in the home. This allows elderly people to be more independent while providing assistance to their family and caregivers. In this section, we describe some research works regarding the analysis of behavior and health monitoring for elderly people in the smart home context.

Works in [1] use anomaly detections on wearable sensors to provide an intelligent living environment for elderly residents. The detection of anomalies is based on several parameters: location, time, duration, type of activity and transitions between activities. The experiments provided consist in a semi-supervised learning approach.

[2] and [3] study elderly residents diagnosed with dementia living independently in real home environments. They applied respectively neural networks and clustering algorithms to predict sensor activity. When an error is detected, timely audio or visual prompts are sent to the dementia patients.

Gjoreski et al. [4] have proposed a system to monitor users' daily activity by combining accelerometers with an electrocardiogram (ECG) sensor. Measured acceleration data can thus be analyzed in conjunction with the ECG signals to detect anomalies in the user's behavior and heart-related problems.

Another detection strategy was proposed by Sprint et al. [5]. First, sensor data are labeled to correspond to activity "to sleep". Features are then extracted and used as inputs to change detection algorithms such as RuLSIF, virtual classifier, and sw-PCAR to detect and analyze behavior changes that accompany health events. If the change is significant, change analysis is performed to explain the source of change. Use cases studied in this context concern older adults who experienced major health events, including cancer treatment and insomnia.

Anomaly detection systems for detecting abnormal behavior has been surveyed and reviewed in [6–8] implicitly rely of representation of the human activity in a spatiotemporal context highlighting various techniques/methods (classification, clustering, nearest neighbor, statistical).

Previous works describe existing research regarding the analysis of behavior and health monitoring from a smart home. A set of these works [1,4] only use wearable sensors to monitor vital signs. Works in [2,3,5–8] consider home sensors to monitor daily activities but do not analyze all activities of the elderly person at the same time. For example, [5] studied the behavior change related to sleeping only. All the solutions mentioned previously have been developed to quickly detect and react as soon as possible when a sudden behavior change occurs, especially "the fall" of the monitored person. Our objective in this work is, not only to detect sudden changes, but also to analyze the possible evolution of the behavior over a long period of time.

3 Our Approach

The overall objective of this study is to analyze the daily behavior of elderly people in their apartment through ambient sensors. In the following, we introduce our model to characterize the normal behavior pattern for elderly people. This normal behavior pattern can then be used to detect behavior changes over time by comparing the current behavioral data of an elderly with her/his usual behavior pattern.

3.1 Activities and Daily Behavior Pattern

Activities of Daily Living (ADLs) is a term used by healthcare professionals to refer to the basic self-care tasks an individual does on a day-to-day basis. These fundamental activities are crucial for maintaining independence. They are used by health professionals as a way of measuring an individual's functional status, especially for elderly people.

The importance of this issue has led to the development of numerous solutions that can monitor activities (e.g., [9]). Basic ADLs are self-care activities routinely performed which include, but are not limited to seven activities: sleeping, getting dressed, eating (three times per day), going to the toilet, hygiene activities (to take shower and/or bathing) and going outside.

Our notion of activity comprises two key criteria used also in [10] that are at the basis of our verification process:

1. Location: the specific place where an activity occurs, for example, "eating" takes place in the kitchen.
2. Time: the duration and occurring time of an activity. The user may perform a same activity at different times (e.g., going to the toilet) but some activities only occur at specific times of the day (e.g., eating breakfast). The start time and duration of each activity instance may be logged by the user, or better detected by an activity recognition system based on in-home sensors.

Let $A = \{a_1; a_2; ...; a_4\}$ the set of activities labels. An activity pattern represents when and where an activity usually occurs. It is defined as a tuple:

$$P_a = (a_i, S_a(t), D_a(t))$$

where:

- $a_i \in A$ is an activity label
- $S_a(t)$ is a time interval representing the usual start time of activity a_i
- $D_a(t)$ is a time interval representing the usual duration of activity a_i

The daily behavior pattern involves several activity patterns. It defines order constraints on them and introduces eventual temporal delays. The daily behavior pattern describes how the user performs her/his activities at different times and models links between them. The daily behavior pattern is represented by a sequence of usual activities. It can be built from data derived from sensors in a smart home.

$$B = (P_{a1}, P_{a2}, P_{a3}) \text{ Where } P_{ai} \text{ is an activity pattern}$$

For each day of the week D_i we built a behavior pattern B_i which is a set of segments P_{ai}, where each segment P_{ai} is a sequence of tuples $a_i, S_a(t), D_a(t)$ related to each activity. In this pattern we consider three activities: "sleeping", "eating", "taking a shower", which occur at specific times of the day. "Going to the toilet" may occur at many times during the day. It will be studied separately as we will see later.

3.2 Normal Behavior Pattern for the Elderly

The first step of any behavior anomaly detection system is to characterize the normal behavior, also called *routine behavior* or *regular behavior*, based on training data to model regularities in every individual activity. The normal behavior consists of the list of activities that a resident performs in her/his house, with time of the day and the duration. Thus, it captures the repetitive daily routines and deviations from the normal behavior may indicate changes of lifestyle or loss of capacity.

To build the routine behavior model, we follow the following steps:

1. We first use training data collected during the previous period which was treated as a baseline behavior period. We then follow an unsupervised learning approach: clustering to find point anomalies. To address this, we cluster instances of each activity based on start time and duration without considering the day of the week. For clustering, we use the DBSCAN algorithm [11] which is a density based clustering algorithm. The major advantage of DBSCAN, compared with other clustering algorithms like K-means, is that we do not need to specify how many clusters should be identified. After clustering, DBSCAN marks each point as belonging to a cluster or as noise(anomaly).
2. We eliminate point anomaly and we calculate the average start time and duration for each activity in training data.

The activity "going to the toilets" that occurs several times a day is treated separately. There are usually regular schedules for this activity. It is not essential to be very precise on the realization time of this activity. We then choose to study its frequency rather than the occurring time. Using the same training data to model regularities in the three studied activities, we calculate the frequency, per n hours, of the activity "going to the toilets".

3.3 Elderly's Behavior Change Detection

Once computed, the normal behavior pattern can be used to detect anomalies by comparing the current behavioral data of an elderly with her/his normal behavior pattern. The basic idea of our behavioral deviation detection system is to estimate the similarity between both patterns using a score. We therefore consider three criteria for the activities: the time, duration and chronological order of the activities in the sequence.

Behavior Modeling Using a Daily Activity Score: Intuitively, a particular activity is similar to a pattern if its start time, duration and location are similar to the ones defined by the pattern. The similarity of the time and duration for each activity is estimated by a score.

The similarity score of an activity a in a day d is calculated by the formula (1). It is given as a percentage and represents the temporal intersection of the normal behavior pattern and one observed day pattern, for the same activity. We note that S_{ad} is the start time of activity a_d, D_{ad} is the duration of activity a_d and $E_{ad} = S_{ad} + D_{ad}$ is the end time of activity a_d

$$Similarity\ score = \frac{(\inf(E_{an}, E_{ad}), \sup(S_{an}, S_{ad})) * 100}{D_{an}} \qquad (1)$$

The similarity score for one day is the average of similarity scores for all activities occurring in this day.

The duration score is calculated by the formula (2). It is a percentage of the duration of an activity in an observed day compared to the duration of the same activity in the normal behavior pattern.

$$Duration\ score = \frac{D_{ad} * 100}{D_{an}} \tag{2}$$

The duration score for one day is the average of duration scores for all activities occurring on this day. The duration score can exceed 100% if the duration of an activity at the observed day is greater than the expected duration in the normal behavior pattern. This simply means that the elderly takes longer to achieve the activity which may be caused by a loss of autonomy if this is observed regularly.

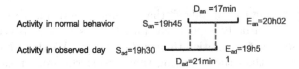

Fig. 1. Illustration of the similarity and duration scores for the activity "eating lunch"

In the example presented in Fig. 1, the similarity score is 35.29%. It represents the temporal intersection for the activity "to eat lunch" in one observed day pattern compared to the same activity in the normal behavior pattern. The duration score (80.95% in our example) is the percentage of the duration of the activity "to eat lunch" in an observed day compared to the duration of the same activity in the normal behavior pattern.

The variation of these scores over time, represents the evolution of the elderly's life pace. These scores thus give us an indication of the variation with an elderly's usual behavior for a particular activity. A large decrease in these scores over a long period (from a few days to a few weeks) may be an initial signal of decline and should generate a notification to the caregivers or the family members.

For regular activities, occurring several times a day, we compare the frequency between a routine day and an observed day. By simply plotting the daily score along time, it is possible to identify certain days with unusual activities (i.e., with lower scores), or trends of evolution that indicate deviations from the previous activity routine.

A subsequent work detailed in Sect. 3.3 consists in studying in details the activities related to the behavior change period to discover the deviation cause(s).

Anomaly Detection in Behavior Change Period: In this section, we investigate the accuracy of anomaly detection: per day and per hour of the day, in the behavior change period. Activities in this period has been mapped and compared with normal life pattern.

In the domain of at-home activities, anomalies can be classified as point, collective and contextual anomalies. The *point anomaly* [12–14] considers each activity independently and decides whether it is normal or not with respect to the normal behavior. The *collective anomaly* [15] considers groups of activity instances together to determine whether the group is normal or not. The *contextual anomaly* [16,17] considers activities under a particular context (e.g., day of week, person under medication, etc.). In our work, we focus on detecting *point anomaly* (i.e., missing activity or activity with an unusually long/short duration).

For the activity "going to the toilet" which occurs several times per day, we model and compare frequencies between a routine day and the observed day in the behavior change period. A frequency is provided by the normal behavior pattern. This will be illustrated in the following section.

4 Use Case

In this section, we present in 4.1 the dataset used as use case. We detail in 4.2 the learning steps for building the normal behavior pattern. By plotting the daily score along time in 4.3, we exhibit the period when the score changes over time and then identify daily anomalous activities found in the behavior change period.

4.1 Dataset

The dataset used for our analysis is provided by Washington State University's CASAS program[1] [18]. CASAS (Center for Advanced Studies in Adaptive Systems) aims to provide aid to residents using smart home technology. They therefore collect and use real-time data from sensors to analyze and monitor residents'health and behavior to improve future smart home living.

We use one public data set (named HH120) [18] which was used in other works like [19]. It includes one unique subject, covering a total of 63 days. All data used in this paper was handled in an anonymized way. The set of activities includes "sleeping", "eating meals", "taking a shower", "going outside" and "going to the toilet". The data sets do not provide any medical information. For training the normal behavior model, we use the first month while the rest of the available data is used to test the effectiveness of our proposals.

4.2 Learning for Building the Normal Behavior Pattern

For building the normal behavior pattern from the training data set, we follow the different learning steps presented in the Sect. 3.2. We then apply the

---

[1] http://casas.wsu.edu/.

DBSCAN algorithm on the training dataset for clustering and eliminate activities out of the identified clusters and marked as noise. DBSCAN has two parameters; one is *min_pts* which is the minimum number of points in a cluster, and the other is *Eps* which is the maximum distance between two data points for them to be considered in the same cluster. While learning, data out of *Eps* would be considered out of clusters so marked anomalous. Trained results are depicted in Fig. 2.

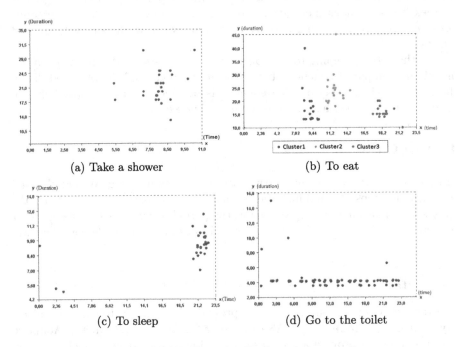

(a) Take a shower

(b) To eat

(c) To sleep

(d) Go to the toilet

Fig. 2. DBSCAN Clustering for detecting anomalies

Figure 2(b) illustrate 3 clusters which represent 3 daily meals. The elderly person is habituated to have her breakfast at 9:44 AM for maximum 25 min. Figure 2(b) shows that this person can have her breakfast for 40 min which is abnormal behavior depicted by the point outside the middle cluster.

We then eliminate point anomalies and calculate, for every activity in the training data set representing one month of collected data, the average start time and average duration. Figure 3 illustrates the daily behavioral model thus generated using the previous learning step.

4.3   Behavior Change Period and Anomalous Activities

In the first stage of our experiments, we computed the daily scores introduced in Sect. 3.3. By plotting scores, we can observe the behavior evolution day by

Fig. 3. Normal behavior pattern

day to follow the evolution of elderly's life pace. Thus, it is possible to identify trends in the daily evolution scores as shown in Fig. 4 where we can observe a decrease compared to the previous routine activity.

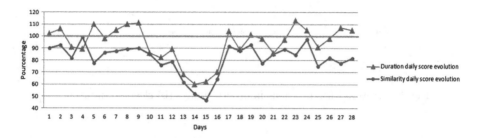

Fig. 4. Daily scores evolution

In the second stage of our experiment, we focus on the deviation period (days with decreasing/increasing scores) to detect point anomalies due to a missing activity or activities with unusually long/short durations. To do this, we plot in Figs. 5 and 6 duration and start time respectively for 3 activities (to sleep, to eat (breakfast, lunch, dinner) and take a shower). In these figures, the average start time and the average duration in normal behavior pattern are represented for each activity by an horizontal line.

At days 13 and 14, Figs. 5 and 6 reveal unusual sleep times, shorter than usual, as well as later times to go to bed (2:00 AM and 4:00 AM). The results also indicate that day 15 is a day with unusual activity because the elderly skipped a lunch. At the same day, the elderly performs more times than usual the activity "taking a shower" and "sleeping". During these 3 days we detect 2 types of anomaly: point anomaly due to missing activity and activities in unusually long/short durations.

As mentioned previously, the activity "going to the toilet" that occurs several times a day is treated separately. As for the other activities, anomalies related to duration are eliminated using DBSCAN as illustrated in Fig. 2. To analyze the elderly's behavior, we focus both on the frequency per 2 h and the duration. Figure 7 shows that both these parameters increase in the deviation period compared to the normal behavior (represented with the horizontal line).

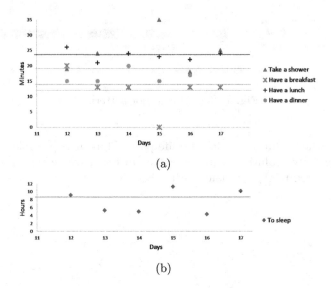

Fig. 5. (a) Activities durations in observed days (b) sleeping duration

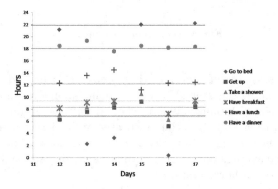

Fig. 6. Activities start time in observed days

All these anomalies may be a signal of sickness (urinary tract infection, gastrointestinal problem, etc.) so our system may send an alert message to inform remote caregivers.

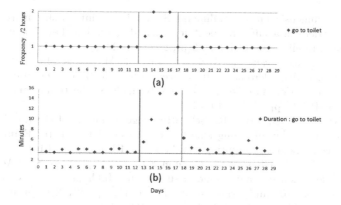

Fig. 7. (a) Frequency "go to the toilet" (b) Duration "go to the toilet"

5   Conclusion

In this article, we presented our research work to detect behavioral changes in the elderly's usual behavior. Our solution relies on the construction of a behavior model. Thanks to this scheme and based on the detection of anomalies, we are able to detect changes in the elderly behavior, not only sudden changes such as a fall or a temporary illness, but also changes over time. For example, the elderly sleep less and less every month, which can be worrying and cause many problems. In the future, we would like to integrate other activities into our model, such as "going outside", which are an important aspect for characterizing the elderly's health. This information should also be coupled with contextual elements such as weather conditions. Other information on health conditions can also be used to refine our detection of behavioral changes. Finally, when our system detects changes in behavior, it must make a decision on the appropriate solution: for example, if it is a sudden and persistent change, it may be an emergency solution and if it is a degradation of the subject's daily routine, a visit from the caregiver would be necessary. It is difficult to make the "best" decision so we plan at this point to talk to healthcare professionals to configure our decision support system.

Acknowledgements. This work has been sponsored by the ELSAT2020 project co-financed by the European Union with the European Regional Development Fund, the French state and the Hauts de France Region Council.

References

1. Zhu, C., Sheng, W., Liu, M.: Wearable sensor-based behavioral anomaly detection in smart assisted living systems. IEEE Trans. Autom. Sci. Eng. **12**(4), 1225–1234 (2015)
2. Ord, F.J., de Toledo, P., Sanchis, A.: Sensor-based bayesian detection of anomalous living patterns in a home setting. Pers. Ubiquit. Comput. **19**, 259–270 (2015)

3. Lotfi, A., Langensiepen, C., Mahmoud, S.M., Akhlaghinia, M.J.: Smart homes for the elderly dementia sufferers: identification and prediction of abnormal behaviour. J. Ambient Intell. Hum. Comput. **3**(3), 205–218 (2012)
4. Gjoreski, H., Rashkovska, A., Kozina, S., Lustrek, M., Gams, M.: Telehealth using ECG sensor and accelerometer. In: Proceedings of the 37th International Convention on Information and Communication Technology, Electronics and Microelectronics (MIPRO), pp. 270–274 (2014)
5. Sprint, G., Cook, D., Fritz, R.: Schmitter-Edgecombe, M.: Detecting health and behavior change by analyzing smart home sensor data. In: IEEE International Conference on Smart Computing (SMARTCOMP), pp. 1–3 (2016)
6. Bakar, U.A.B.U.A., Ghavyat, H., Hasanm, S.F., Mukhopadhyay, S.C.: Activity and anomaly detection in smart home: a survey. In: Mukhopadhyay, S.C. (ed.) Next Generation Sensors and Systems. SSMI, vol. 16, pp. 191–220. Springer, Cham (2016). https://doi.org/10.1007/978-3-319-21671-3_9
7. Dhiman, C., Vishwakarma, D.K.: A review of state-of-the-art techniques for abnormal human activity recognition. Eng. Appl. Artif. Intell. **77**, 21–45 (2019)
8. Essghaier F., Delcroix V., Marcal de Oliveira K., Puisieux F., Gaxatte C., Pudlo P.: Towards a fall prevention system design by using ontology. Francophone Days of Knowledge Engineering (IC) (2019)
9. Hossain, M.A.: Perspectives of human factors in designing elderly monitoring system. Comput. Hum. Behav. **63–68**, 33 (2014)
10. Kaddachi, F., et al.: Technological approach for behavior change detection toward better adaptation of services for elderly people. In: HEALTHINF, pp. 96–105 (2017)
11. Ester, M., Kriegel, H., Sander, J., Xu, X.: A density-based algorithm for discovering clusters in large spatial databases with noise. In: Proceedings of the Second International Conference on Knowledge Discovery and Data Mining, KDD 1996, pp. 226–231 (1996)
12. Riboni, D., Bettini, C., Civitares, G., Janjua, Z.H.: SmartFABER: recognizing fine-grained abnormal behaviors for early detection of mild cognitive impairment. Artif. Intell. Med. **67**, 57–64 (2016)
13. Janjua, Z.H., Riboni, D., Bettini, C.: Towards automatic induction of abnormal behavioral patterns for recognizing mild cognitive impairment. In: Proceedings of the 31st Annual ACM Symposium on Applied Computing, SAC 2016, pp 143–148 (2016)
14. Riboni, D., Bettini, C., Civitarese, G., Janjua, Z.H., Helaoui, R.: Fine-grained recognition of abnormal behaviors for early detection of mild cognitive impairment. In: IEEE International Conference on Pervasive Computing and Communications (PerCom), pp. 149–154 (2015)
15. Anderson, D.T., Ros, M., Keller, J.M., Cuellar, M.P., Popescu, M., Delgado, M.: Similarity measure for anomaly detection and comparing human behaviors. Int. J. Intell. Syst. **27**(8), 733–756 (2012)
16. Hoque, E., Dickerson, R.F., Preum, S.M., Hanson, M., Barth, A., Stankovic, J.A.: Holmes: a comprehensive anomaly detection system for daily in-home activities. In: International Conference on Distributed Computing in Sensor Systems, Fortaleza, pp. 40–51 (2015)
17. Hayes, M.A., Capretz, M.A.M.: Contextual anomaly detection framework for big sensor data. J. Big Data **2**(1), 1–22 (2015). https://doi.org/10.1186/s40537-014-0011-y

18. Cook, D.J., Crandall, A.S., Thomas, B.L., Krishnan, N.C.: CASAS : a smart home in a box. IEEE Comput. **46**(7), 62–69 (2013)
19. Lago, P., Jimz-Guar, C., Roncancio, C.: Contextualized behavior patterns for change reasoning in ambient assisted living: a formal model. Exp. Syst. **34**(2), e12163 (2017)

Personalized and Contextualized Persuasion System for Older Adults' Physical Activity Promoting

Houssem Aloulou[1($\boxtimes$)], Hamdi Aloulou[2($\boxtimes$)], Bessam Abdulrazak[3($\boxtimes$)], and Ahmed Hadj Kacem[1($\boxtimes$)]

[1] ReDCAD, University of Sfax, Sfax, Tunisia
Houssem.aloulou@gmail.com,
ahmed.hadjkacem@fsegs.usf.tn
[2] ReDCAD, Digital Research Centre of Sfax, Sfax, Tunisia
hamdi.aloulou@redcad.tn
[3] University of Sherbrooke, Quebec, Canada
Bessam.Abdulrazak@usherbrooke.ca

Abstract. Aging often involves a significant change in roles and social positions. The greatest health risk for seniors is the adoption of a sedentary lifestyle that causes isolation, depression, and many diseases. However, convincing an older adult to regularly do physical activities is not generally a simple mission.

This paper proposes a personalized and contextualized persuasion system to promote physical activities for older adults. In fact, our approach considers the personal and health profile of the older adult. It also considers different context parameters (context-awareness). This intelligence is guaranteed thanks to the use of the semantic modeling and reasoning, which from different types of information would be able to decide the best moment to trigger notifications from our persuasive system to the participating older adults.

Keywords: Persuasion strategy · Captology · Physical activities · Older adults · Context-awareness · Semantic modeling · Semantic reasoning · Pervasive technology

1 Introduction

Nowadays, information technology has a growing influence around the world and brings new opportunities to solve many of society's problems. One of the most irritating problem is the sedentary lifestyle of older adults. In fact, the lack of physical activities accelerates the transition of people to the age of dependency.

The best way to thwart the sedentary lifestyle among the older adults is to promote physical activities [1]. Generally, older adult trend to limit their physical activities as they often consider them difficult to do. Hence, they must be motivated to change their behavior. Motivation is a set of dynamic factors that guide the action of a person toward a given purpose, which determine his behavior and cause him to behave in a given way or modify his actual behavior [1].

© The Author(s) 2020
M. Jmaiel et al. (Eds.): ICOST 2020, LNCS 12157, pp. 142–154, 2020.
https://doi.org/10.1007/978-3-030-51517-1_12

There exist several behaviors change techniques which use persuasion methods to convince subjects to change behaviors. These techniques are inspired by social and cognitive psychology and models associated with them.

We have based our methodology on the output of these technics' analysis. We have also taken into consideration the older adults' profiles and contextual information to increase the probability of success of our persuasion technique. Persuasion technics, profiles and contextual information were modeled and realized using the semantic modeling while persuasion strategies were guaranteed using the semantic reasoning.

Following, Sect. 2 presents a detailed state of the art of behavior change persuasion theories and existing systems for promoting physical activities. Section 3 expound our proposed persuasion technique. In Sect. 4, we introduce the used architecture. Then in Sect. 5, we present our first prototype. To validate our persuasive approach and decision-making platform, we propose a first textbook case. Finally, we conclude this article.

2 State of the Art

2.1 Behavior Change Persuasion Theories

There are several theories that presents methods that aim to persuade people to change their behavior. Bandura presented a comprehensive theory of human motivation and action called the "Social Cognitive Theory" as an extension of his theory of social learning [2, 3]. In this theory, people are not motivated by internal forces, but by external factors. He emphasizes reciprocal causation through the interplay of cognitive (personal) factors, behavioral factors, and environmental factors. These prominent factors are guided by several variables that intervene in the process of behavior change: self-efficacy, outcome expectations, self-control, reinforcements, emotional coping, and observational learning.

Fogg has identified many principles of persuasion that new technologies can use to influence the behavior of their users. He called this concept the "Captology" (Computers As Persuasive Technology) [4]. He described it as the region where technology and persuasion overlap. For him, behavior change must be voluntary and by conviction. Fogg has also emphasized computer efficacity to persuade users to change behavior through a functional triad. He asserted that, from a user's point of view, there is three fundamental roles that a computer can play: as tool, as social actor and as media. Each role of the triad is divided into several strategies. For a computer system to be persuasive, it must apply all or most of these strategies.

Additionally, Fogg also demonstrated in his behavior model FBM [5] that 3 conditions must converge at the same time for a behavior to be realized: sufficient "motivation" and "capacity" to do the requested behavior and a well-chosen moment to "trigger" the behavior (physical location, emotions, availability, proximity, etc.) when the person is most open to persuasion (Kairos factor) and thanks to the availability and portability of mobile devices (convenience factor).

For the motivation, Fogg created a framework with three basic motivators formed by tuples in [5]: Sensation (Pleasure/Pain), Anticipation (Hope/Fear) and Belonging (Social acceptance/Social rejection).

Oinas-Kukkonen et al. were inspired by Fogg's works when proposing the process of "Persuasive System Design" (PSD) [6] that aims to facilitate design and evaluation of persuasive system. The framework is based on seven (7) hypotheses to understand the problems of persuasive systems. The context of persuasion is then analyzed by designers to have a deepening understanding of changes using three (3) major elements: Intention, Event and Strategy. Outcomes are then used to design system's qualities by meeting several criteria: primary tasks support, dialogue, credibility, and social support.

Later, Oinas-Kukkonen presented the "Behavior Change Support Systems" (BCSS) as an extension of the PSD process [7]. BCSS uses persuasive technology which allows to create, reinforce, and change behaviors. It is based on a design matrix to determine the nature of the behavior change. Rows of the matrix contain types of outcome (formation, altering or reinforcing) and columns contain types of changes (complying, behavior, or attitude).

To help designers in matching target behaviors with solutions for achieving them, Fogg and Hreha proposed the "behavior Wizard" based on the "behavior Grid" [8]. The latter consists of three (3) rows to present the duration of the target behavior and five (5) columns to present the nature of the target behavior. The intersection of a row and a column presents a behavior changing strategy.

Tracking behaviors change of a person involves following the steps of changing actions from the current unwanted behavior to the requested or desired behavior. In this research, we will apply the most important elements of behavior change theories to motivate seniors to adopt a healthy lifestyle. The biggest challenge remaining now is how to adapt the persuasion to the complexity and versatility of every older adult to maximize persuasive effectiveness.

2.2 Existing Systems for Promoting Physical Activity

There are several systems that apply persuasive technology in different domains like health care, leisure, e-commerce, education, etc. Many of these applications were created to promote physical activities. In [9], authors identified 64 apps to promote physical activity among adults. They rated them based on the taxonomy of behavior change techniques. For instance, in [10] research was to understand motivators of changing behavior and sharing results on tweeter by the users of RunKeeper App. It takes the theory of planned behavior as a starting point for their conceptual model. There model consider the influence of altruism, reputation building, community identification, social norms, getting feedback and information sharing. Strava [11] is a persuasive app created for runners and cyclists to track adults activities and offer analysis on their performance. It aims on encouraging running and cycling by competitive motivation when activities are done in group, and challenges when exercising alone. When a participant success the challenge, he earns a "badge" for their "trophy case." Endomondo [12] is a mobile app that tracks physical activity by monitoring duration, distance and speed. Il motivates users by providing audio feedback, pep talks from friends and user's friends' activities and statistics. Flowie is an application that target older adults [13]. In Flowie, the performance of a senior, collected with a pedometer, is translated by the expression of a small animated flower in a touch-screen photo frame. Ubifit Garden [14] and Fish'n'steps [15] are two other applications that use persuasive technology to support healthy behavior via pedometer. Ubifit Garden uses a floral garden wallpaper, in a mobile application, that flourish and blooms as the person performs activities. Move2Play [16] and Healthopia [17] are mobile applications that promote a healthier lifestyle and motivates to participate in regular physical activity using wearable and mobile sensors. Many of the existing systems lack context-awareness when proposing physical activities. They also don't consider the profile of the person and his health state. There is also no flexibility when asking a person to do behavior nor customization.

3 Methodology: Personalization and Customization of the Behavior Change Strategy

We argue that targeting better motivation of senior and successful change of their behavior requires that a persuasion technique that take into consideration, in addition to the Captology elements, several factors in relation with the older adult's life such as his health state, his environment, his preferred activities and his tendencies. Therefore, a pre-persuasion step is required to form the senior's profile. The user profile is composed of a personal profile (demographic data, preferred activities and hobbies, social relationships, etc.) and a health profile (physical and mental state). We mainly used the Health Utilities Index Mark 3 (HUI3) [18], a generic health profiles and preference-based systems for measuring health status, reporting health-related quality of life, and producing utility scores, to model the health profile.

The user profile (personal and health) is then used as an entry to our persuasive strategy in conjunction with contextual information to help increase the likelihood of behavioral change success. Our persuasion strategy inspired from Fogg's functional triad and Fogg Behavior Model (FBM) uses the received element to convince older adults to adopt a healthy lifestyle and to avoid sedentary. Our approach is presented in Fig. 1 below.

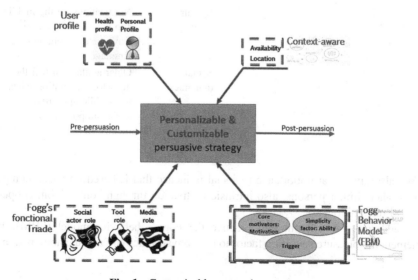

Fig. 1. Customizable persuasion strategy

In our persuasion strategy, we took advantage of Fogg's functional triad and FBM model to promote physical activity of older adults. The following Table 1 presents each element of Fogg's functional triad and how it is considered in our system.

Table 1. Adopted behavior change theory

Role	Implementation	Strategy	Examples
Tool	Provide a mobile app that act as a persuasion tool to convince the older adult to change his behavior	Reduction	Simplify the complexity of activities: giving the difficulty of cleaning the house for an older person, we break this activity down into several sub-activities
		Suggestion	Take into consideration the condition of the user when choosing behavior to change: needs, interests, personality, context of use, environment, proximity, availability and adaptability
		Self-monitoring	The older adult receives information on his performance through the mobile app
Media simulation	The mobile app displays sensitive videos showing dangers of a sedentary lifestyle.		
Social actor	The mobile app will act as a social actor	Physical attractiveness	An attractive GUI with several features to attract the user
		Encouraging language	Notifications on the mobile app have to include positive waves and encouraging language
		Social dynamics	Older adults will feel the need for recognition when the mobile app provides social support and serves them well

We also give great importance to social influence that is based on social comparison to other similar persons, also intrinsic motivation through competition, cooperation, and recognition.

In addition, we will put into practice the Fogg's behavior model (FBM). We implement the pleasure sensation factor to do a physical activity and the anticipation of hope for a healthy aging. Also, all the 6 factors for maximal ability (time, money, physical effort, brain cycles, social deviance, and non-routine) are considered in our reasoning and persuasion strategy.

4 Proposed Architecture

The connectivity and portability of smartphones makes possible to reach older adults at any time and place using automated notifications. All notifications and encouragement for an older adult are posted on his smartphone via a mobile app. In addition, this app enables collecting information on senior behavior and sent them instantly to a remote decision-making platform via Internet. The platform filters and processes collected data. Additionally, the reasoning of the context and profile, that is based on an onto-logical model, allow our platform to choose rationally the best persuasion strategy and to propose, at the right time and place, contextualized physical activities based on several criteria such as his personal profile, his health status, his context, his preferred activities, etc. A typical scenario would be sending a notification requesting to do a given activity only if the older adult has the physical and mental capacity to perform it (based on HUI3 utilities) and considering his context (availability and location). Figure 2 shows a simplified presentation of the architecture of our approach.

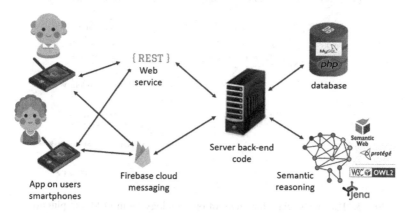

Fig. 2. Overview of the architecture using semantic reasoning

5 Active Senior's First Prototype

Our goal at this stage of the project is to develop a computer system serving as proof of concepts that we have named "Active Senior". The main objective is to validate the functioning of the first components of our system, i.e., the mobile app, the software modules of the server platform and the communication module.

The server app is connected to a database which contains the data of participants, there login information, the list of activities, to which an older adult can register, and the list of notifications received by all participants and information whether the activity has been done or not yet by corresponding person. In fact, when receiving a notification to do a behavior on mobile app, an older adult can inform the server that he accepts to do the behavior and he can inform it when the behavior is done. All information about notifications, the deadline for accepting the activity and carrying it out are stored in the database for statistics purpose.

We have defined a new ontology to be able to offer older adults contextualized activities. We have saved our ontology in OWL format which provides a rich vocabulary to add semantics and context and to allow reasoning and inference. Below in Fig. 3 parts of our ontology displayed with OWLViz[1] plugin. For lack of space, we have chosen to present only the three (3) first levels of our ontological model.

Fig. 3. Part of the class hierarchy of our ontology (with OWLViz plugin)

"Object properties" were defined to describe relationships between two instances of classes (individuals) and "data properties" were defined to describe relationships between instances of classes and their respective values (Fig. 4).

---

[1] https://github.com/protegeproject/owlviz.

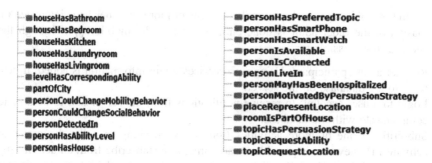

Fig. 4. Examples of defined object properties

Among created "object properties" we cite:

- "personHasPreferredTopic": allows to link the "Person" class to the "Topic" class. This will therefore make it possible to know the activities in which the older adult is interested.
- "topicHasPersuasionStrategy": allows to link a "Topic" to a "PersuasionStrategy."
- "personIsConnected" and "personIsAvailable": help to guarantee the person's context-awareness: his current location and his availability.
- "personMotivatedByPersuasionStrategy": connects each person to the persuasion strategy that most closely matches his profile, state of health and context.

Among created "data properties" we cite: "persuasionStrategyHasDescription" which allows to assign a description to a "persuasionStrategy" and "levelValue" which have a value between 1 and 6 presenting the value of an instance of the class presenting the HUI3 health indicator for a given person. One of the main benefits of building an ontology-based application is the ability to derive additional knowledge about the concepts modeled by using a reasoner. So, to make our persuasion strategy contextual and personalized, we used the "Apache Jena"[2] reasoning engine. It is an open source Semantic Web Framework for Java that supports OWL. Thereby, we defined rules so that the reasoner can decide if it would be appropriate to ask a senior to do an activity or not.

The exchanges between the server app and the mobile app are done through REST[3] (REpresentational State Transfer) web services while the notifications are guaranteed with FCM[4] (Firebase Cloud Messaging) Google protocol.

---

[2] https://jena.apache.org/.

[3] https://restfulapi.net/.

[4] https://firebase.google.com/docs/cloud-messaging.

From the mobile app, each senior chooses one or more activities he is interested in. Persuasion of the older adult is done entirely through the mobile app. Through the mobile app, it is possible to:

- Register a new participant: Using web services, login information is added, in real time, to the database on the server.
- Login to a user account: to receive notifications from the server and to be able to communicate with the database.
- Subscribe to one or more activities (topics) by checking in a list the preferred activities. However, it is possible, at any time, to unsubscribe from an activity (by unchecking it in the list). By clicking on the "Save" button, the information is sent in real time to the server and the database is then updated with the user's new choices. Then, he will no longer receive notifications to do the unchecked activity.
- Receive notifications: When it's time to do an already chosen activity, the senior receives a notification on his smartphone asking him to do it. We use the self-monitoring technique that we find in several behavior change theories [4]. Indeed, this method empowers the older adult to reach objectives set in advance. While being convinced of the usefulness of the activity to be carried out, the person will make his effort to complete it (Fig. 5).

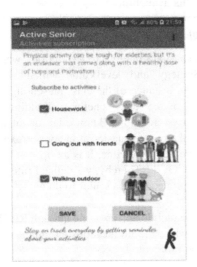

Fig. 5. Subscribing/unsubscribing to activities (topics) and receiving notifications

Our mobile application displays all notifications received by the user and which are incomplete. For each notification, it shows the date and time of its reception, the name of the activity and its description, and 2 buttons:

- Button "Accept": allows the user to acknowledge receipt and acceptance of the notification. By clicking on this button, the date and time are saved in the database.
- Button "Done": when the senior complete the requested activity, he clicks on "Done" button. The date and time are sent to the database.

Fig. 6. List of notifications received by a senior

The data of the activities carried out by an older adult are saved in the server database for statistical purposes and to periodically encourage participants whose results will experience an evolution. This will motivate seniors to maintain their effort and to try to achieve better performance (Fig. 6).

6 Validation

To do a first validation of our approach, we propose a textbook case with a limited number of participants and activities. It is an important step that allows us to test the effectiveness and efficiency of our persuasive approach and our decision-making platform before deploying it on a larger scale.

We have defined three topics (preferred activities): "housework," "walking outdoor" and "going out with friends". For each topic we have established some expressions based on Fogg's motivators such as "encouraging language", "hope anticipation" and "fear anticipation". For instance, a notification to do housework that uses a hope anticipation motivator may contains the text "A clean and organized home is a beautiful home. It eliminates the risk of developing allergies and asthma; it also reduces stress and it is extremely vital to your mental health". A fear anticipation motivator in a notification to walk outdoor can be done with the text "Sedentary lifestyle can lead to difficulties in performing the activities of daily living, there's greater risk of heart disease, diabetes and depression." An encouraging language motivator in a notification to go out with friends can be "An outing is scheduled tonight by your kind friends. It will be a good opportunity to relax, exchange stories and forget everyday worries".

We have also created the profiles of three older adults: "JohnDoe", "JohnWalker" and "JohnGoe". Each profile contains the physical and health status of the person, his concerns, his environment, his availability, and his location. "JohnDoe" is subscribed to "housework" activity, "JohnWalker" is subscribed to "walking outdoor" activity and "JohnGoe" is subscribed to "going out with friends" activity.

The ontology allows to personalize and customize the persuasive strategy according to the older adult's profile. In Fig. 7 below, we have some Individuals defined in the ontology for the participating older adults and "Property assertions" used for "JohnGoe".

Using the ontology, it is possible to generate new knowledge using inference rules. In fact, inference rules allow to decide the best moment to trigger a behavior.

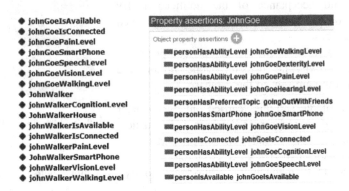

Fig. 7. Some older adults' individuals and property assertions from the ontology

Here is an example of a used rule written in Jena syntax:

```
[Rule1:
(?u pre:personHasPreferredTopic ?t)
(?t pre:topicRequestAbility ?a)
(?u pre:personHasAbilityLevel ?cl)
(?cl pre:levelHasCorrespondingAbility ?a)
(?cl pre:levelValue ?v) lessThan(?v, 3)
(?t pre:topicRequestLocation ?loc)
(?u pre:personDetectedIn ?h)(?h pre:placeRepresentLocation
?loc)
(?t pre:topicHasPersuasionStrategy ?s)
-> (?u pre:personMotivatedByPersuasionStrategy ?s)]
```

Using this rule, the person is motivated by the persuasion strategy only if the following conditions are valid:

- The older adult has a favorite topic and the topic has a persuasion strategy.
- The chosen topic requires one or more health capacities among the 8 elements of HUI3 health status (Vision, Hearing, Speech, Ambulation, Dexterity, Emotion, Cognition, Pain).
- For each state of health, the person has a level between 1 and 6. When the value is 1, it means that he has no health problems for the state of health.
- It is not possible to allow the older adult to do the activity if the value of the health level is > 3 because it could present a risk to his safety and health.
- We also check if the topic requests a location and if the person is this location.

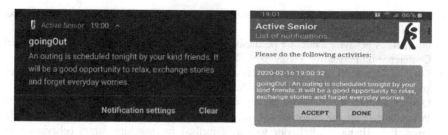

Fig. 8. Received notification by JohnGoe

Our persuasion strategy is therefore personalized in the sense that it respects abilities, habits, choices, health situation, context, etc. of the person being followed.

Figure 8 below show a notification received by JohnGoe whose profile meets the conditions of the ontology rule mentioned above.

7 Conclusion

Persuasive technologies have shown a lot of potentials to influence the behavior and attitudes of individuals. In this paper, we adopted Fogg's persuasive techniques to promote physical activity of older adults. To change the behavior of an older adult, we defined a realistic persuasion strategy which considers senior's profile, his environment and his context. To make our persuasion strategy customizable and contextualizable, we defined an ontology and used rules to deduce new knowledges in order to choose the right moment and place to request the execution of an activity. As first validation of our approach, we developed a first prototype of "Active Senior" to test the used concepts. The first results seem to be promising.

To be successful, new behavior must be maintained and preserved as several older adults may adopt the new proposed behavior for a limited period and they give up after a certain time. This can be explained by the fact that preserving a behavior or attitude requires a lot of effort, energy and time, etc.

In future work, our work will be validated with real volunteer subjects who will be asked to use the mobile app to promote their physical activities. Selection criteria will be set in order to choose subjects with different profiles (physical capacity, habits, social situation, health status, environment, etc.). This will allow us to validate the proposed solution with different profiles.

References

1. W. H. O. (WHO), World Report on Ageing and Health, Geneva (2015)
2. Bandura, A.: Social Foundations of Thought and Action. Englewood Cliffs, NJ (1986)
3. Bandura, A.: Social cognitive theory: an agentic perspective. Annu. Rev. Psychol. **52**(1), 1–26 (2001)

4. Fogg, B.J.: Persuasive technology: using computers to change what we think and do, vol. 2002, December 2002
5. Fogg, B.: A behavior model for persuasive design. In: Proceedings of the 4th International Conference on Persuasive Technology - Persuasive 2009, p. 1 (2009)
6. Oinas-Kukkonen, H., Harjumaa, M.: Persuasive systems design: key issues, process model, and system features. Commun. Assoc. Inf. Syst. **24**(1), 485–500 (2009)
7. Oinas-Kukkonen, H.: Behavior change support systems: a research model and agenda. In: Proceedings of the 5th International Conference on Persuasive Technology, pp. 4–14 (2010)
8. Fogg, B.J., Hreha, J.: Behavior wizard: a method for matching target behaviors with solutions. In: International Conference on Persuasive Technology, pp. 117–131 (2010)
9. Middelweerd, A., Mollee, J.S., van der Wal, C.N., Brug, J., Te Velde, S.J.: Apps to promote physical activity among adults: a review and content analysis. Int. J. Behav. Nutr. Phys. Act. **11**(1), 97 (2014)
10. Stragier, J., Mechant, P.: Mobile fitness apps for promoting physical activity on Twitter: the# RunKeeper case. In: Etmaal van de Communicatiewetenschap (2013)
11. West, L.R.: Strava: challenge yourself to greater heights in physical activity/cycling and running. Br. J. Sport. Med. **49**(15), 1024 (2015)
12. Endomondo. https://www.endomondo.com/. Accessed 10 Feb 2020
13. Albaina, I.M., Visser, T., Van Der Mast, C.A.P.G., Vastenburg, M.H.: Flowie: a persuasive virtual coach to motivate elderly individuals to walk. In: 2009 3rd International Conference on Pervasive Computing Technology Healthc (2009)
14. Consolvo, S., et al.: Activity sensing in the wild: a field trial of ubifit garden. In: Proceedings of the SIGCHI Conference on Human Factors in Computing Systems, pp. 1797–1806 (2008)
15. Lin, J.J., Mamykina, L., Lindtner, S., Delajoux, G., Strub, H.B.: Fish'N'Steps: encouraging physical activity with an interactive computer game. In: Proceedings of the 8th International Conference on Ubiquitous Computing, pp. 261–278 (2006)
16. Bielik, P., Tomlein, M., Krátky, P., Mitrik, Š., Barla, M., Bieliková, M.: Move2Play: an innovative approach to encouraging people to be more physically active. In: Proceedings of the 2nd ACM SIGHIT International Health Informatics Symposium, pp. 61–70 (2012)
17. Min, C., Yoo, C., Lee, Y., Song, J.: Healthopia: towards your well-being in everyday life. In: Proceedings of the 4th International Symposium on Applied Sciences in Biomedical and Communication Technologies, p. 108 (2011)
18. John Horsman, G.W.T., Furlong, W.J., Feeny, D.I.: The Health Utilities Index (HUI®): concepts, measurement properties and applications. Health Qual. Life Outcomes (2003)

Baseline Modelling and Composite Representation of Unobtrusively (IoT) Sensed Behaviour Changes Related to Urban Physical Well-Being

Vladimir Urošević[1]($\boxtimes$), Marina Andrić[1], and José A. Pagán[2]

[1] Belit d.o.o. Beograd, Trg Nikole Pašića 9, 11000 Belgrade, Serbia
vladimir.urosevic@belit.co.rs
[2] The New York Academy of Medicine, 1216 Fifth Avenue, New York
NY 10029, USA

Abstract. We present the grounding approach, deployment and preliminary validation of the elementary devised model of physical well-being in urban environments, summarizing the heterogeneous personal Big Data (on physical activity/exercise, walking, cardio-respiratory fitness, quality of sleep and related lifestyle and health habits and status, continuously collected for over a year mainly through wearable IoT devices and survey instruments in 7 global testbed cities) into 5 composite domain indicators/indexes convenient for interpretation and use in predictive public health and preventive interventions. The approach is based on systematized comprehensive domain knowledge implemented through range/threshold-based rules from institutional and study recommendations, combined with statistical methods, and will serve as a representative and performance benchmark for evolution and evaluation of more complex and advanced well-being models for the aimed predictive analytics (incorporating machine learning methods) in subsequent development underway.

Keywords: Behaviour recognition · Wearable devices · Unobtrusive sensing · Well-being · Vital health parameters · Data labelling · Composite index modelling

1 Introduction

The urban public health, well-being monitoring, and prevention are recently being transformed from reactive to a predictive and eventually long-term risk mitigating systems, through a number of research initiatives and projects, such as the ongoing PULSE Project (**P**articipative **U**rban **L**iving in **S**ustainable **E**nvironments, funded from the EU Horizon 2020 programme) focusing on the chronic metabolic and respiratory diseases (such as type 2 diabetes and asthma) affected or exacerbated by the preventable or modifiable environmental and lifestyle factors, and well-being/resilience. A major challenge in the Project is the modelling and assessment/prediction of citizen well-being from the collected and processed Big Data of unprecedented variety and from highly heterogeneous sources (health and vital activity personal data obtained

M. Jmaiel et al. (Eds.): ICOST 2020, LNCS 12157, pp. 155–167, 2020.
https://doi.org/10.1007/978-3-030-51517-1_13

through wearable devices and other sensing technologies, geo-located online surveys, open/public smart city datasets...), on individual and collective (population/cluster) levels. Overall well-being and its main domains (vitality, supportive relationships, stress levels...) are all significant factors affecting the onset and exacerbation of the stated chronic diseases which are becoming more and more widespread and progressing in urban environments, and overall resilience of citizens and urban communities is increasingly important against other pertaining global and sustainability challenges, like climate change.

The proposed and deployed elementary statistical model presented in this paper is to be the basis for interpretation and contextualization of changes to well-being, and a performance benchmark for evaluation and comparison of more complex and advanced well-being models of the aimed predictive analytics and final intelligent system (incorporating machine learning methods) in subsequent development, supporting the PULSE PHOs (Public Health Observatories established for the relevant policy making and execution in smart cities).

2   Conceptual Background and Approach

The activity and vital/health parameters data measured mostly unobtrusively by wearable devices (wristbands, smartwatches) have particular significance for behaviour analysis and change recognition in PULSE, as these are the input data streams with highest volume, acquisition "velocity", and temporal resolution/granularity of all the various data collected in the Project, and therefore practically the most (and only) suitable data comprising the sufficiently continuous and non-sparse time series over months, to properly derive or construct the behavioural patterns and analyze behaviour changes. Recent studies performed by the stated major wearable device manufacturers over billions of records of temporal measurements data [1, 2], as well as the experiences from projects like the just concluded City4Age (www.city4ageproject.eu) [3, 4], show the significance and general predictive ability of the measured main vital/health and activity parameters (walking, climbing stairs, physical activity/exercise, heart rate data, consumed calories...) for overall health and physiological/physical well-being assessment. The additional complementary socio-demographic, health, lifestyle/habits and environmental data in less frequent temporal resolution, ingested from the open/public datasets or manual "obtrusive" inputs, are combined to cross-check, adjust and improve integrity of the recognized behaviour changes derived from the main time-series data acquired through the wearable devices.

We adopt a combined knowledge- and data-driven approach in detection and characterization of relevant behaviours that denote significant variations in well-being, with multi-level hierarchical model topology and range/threshold based computational rules as basic primary formal knowledge structures, and statistical analytics as baseline (and performant) data-driven detection methods.

The complexity of human behaviours is commonly represented through multi-level hierarchical structured models, decomposed to more granular "units" like activities and action events [5, 6], with multiple variables from behavioural, physiological and environmental domains of well-being known to additionally increase complexity and dimensionality [7]. There are other contending approaches, like the monitoring and analysis of individual well-being or behavioural domain indicators or determinants independently in parallel, without hierarchical structuring and substantial synthesis into fewer higher-level composite factors or score(s) [8]. Most, including the adopted and followed approach works (like [9]), are comprehensively covered or referenced in the *Encyclopedia of Quality of Life and Well-Being Research* (Springer 2014) that summarizes recent research works related to well-being and quality of life in spanned various research and policy-making/implementation fields. Main advantages of a few composite synthetic indicators/factors over a battery of multiple separate indicators, namely:

- ability to summarize complex and multi-dimensional real-life phenomena or domains (like well-being),
- easier for interpretation and comparison among (socio-demographic, geospatial/regional...) groups or population clusters,
- more effective for comprehending overall trends, particularly when a number of the underlying indicators denote opposing-trend changes,

are of crucial significance in usage and context settings of the PULSE project, with over 60 indicators formalized in the initial knowledge-based well-being model topology from the systematization of collected data, and with

- visible set of indicators to various stakeholders (policy makers, researchers, general public) needing to be minimal without omitting important underlying information,
- and collaboration, communication and comparison of complex dimensions by various stakeholders needing to be most straightforward, facilitated and effective.

We therefore propose two complementary approaches for synthesis of the composite well-being indicators composed from underlying streamed IoT-sourced time-series data in the context of PULSE. The indicators summarize multi-dimensional aspects of citizen well-being and enable the assessment of individual and synthesized collective urban well-being over time. The notion is illustrated through analysis within the scope of four representative and characteristical key summary indicators of citizen health and fitness, derived from activity and vital/health parameters measured, as stated, using wearable sensing devices: motility, physical activity, sleep quality and cardio-respiratory health/fitness (Fig. 1).

In the first approach, daily and intra-daily underlying measurements (Table 1) are used to estimate levels of adherence to rule- and range-based recommendations matured from institutional knowledge of relevant authorities and population-significant studies in the field, accumulated for over decades in the stated four example domains of motility, physical activity, sleep quality and cardio-respiratory fitness [8, 10, 11].

The complementary data-driven statistical approach is predicated on standard scores that denote the number of standard deviations that a given measurement deviates from the sample mean. This approach allows comparison of individual scores to the corresponding norm groups stratified by common socio-demographic parameters (age, gender...), when considered conditionally independent nodes in the complete model topology. It also allows to place a score for any individual and variable with respect to alternative descriptive statistic or measure of central tendency (variable median,

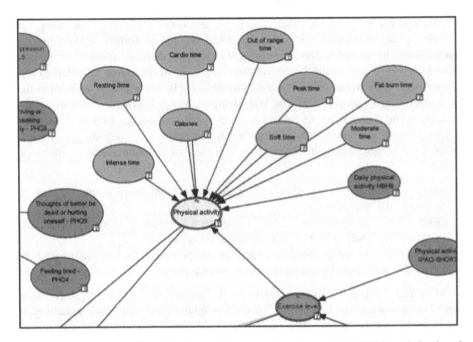

Fig. 1. Excerpt from the hierarchical network structure topology of the initial knowledge-based PULSE well-being model (*blue-coloured nodes* are variables measured by wearable sensing devices, and *magenta-coloured* are reported/input through online app. questionnaires) (Color figure online)

geometric mean, standard deviation or error), so that more accurate or optimal comparison for specific variable distribution can be made.

3   Citizen Activity and Vital/Health Parameters Data

The data are collected by several types of health and fitness wearable tracker devices manufactured by Fitbit, Garmin and ASUS, monitoring physical and walking activity, sleep and heart/cardio parameters, for over 300 recruited citizens participating in the study in 7 global testbed cities (Barcelona, Birmingham, New York, Paris, Pavia(Italy), Singapore, and Keelung/Taipei), supplied with wearable tracker devices by the Project.

Physical activity level as a single measure is mainly expressed in terms of time spent and calories burned while performing light/soft, moderate, and intense/vigorous physical activity. Walking activity is captured with walked steps, distance, speed, and climbed stairs/floors measurements. Heart rate measures capture time spent in different target heart rate zones (like peak, cardio, fat burn), resting and maximal heart rate (hr_{max}), and some still experimental measures like systolic and diastolic blood pressure, measured by the newest recently released devices such as ASUS VivoWatch BP, but not yet acquired in significant volume sufficient for analysis. The peak heart rate zone by default definition ranges from 85 to 100% of person's maximum heart rate (hr_{max}), the cardio zone ranges from 70 to 84% of hr_{max}, and the fat burn zone ranges from 50 to 69% of hr_{max}. Sleep quality/hygiene measures mainly capture time spent in defined phases of sleep. All the processed measures are listed in Table 1, collected or aggregated with a default daily periodicity, except the ones in gray-shaded rows which are acquired in higher intra-daily temporal resolution, mostly once in every 15 min or up to once in a minute, depending on the variable.

Table 1. List of variables measured by the used wearable devices, with descriptions and *units of measure* (SI base units in square brackets where applicable, like [s]-*seconds*, or [m]-*meters*)

Measured variable	Description [unit]
still_calories	amount of calories burned while being still
total_calories	total amount of calories burned (default in a day)
walk_steps	number of walked steps
walk_distance	walked distance [m]
stairs_floor_changes_up	number of floors traversed in climbing stairs up
elevation	vertical distance [m] traversed in climbing stairs
still_time	time [s] spent being still
physicalactivity_soft_time	time [s] spent performing light/"soft" physical activities like relaxed walking/strolling or standing up and moving around in the home, workplace or community
physicalactivity_moderate_time	time [s] spent performing moderate physical activities like swift walking, dancing, gardening
physicalactivity_intense_time	time [s] spent performing intense/vigorous physical activities like running, fast cycling or swimming, tennis, jumping rope
physicalactivity_calories	amount of calories burned while performing physical activities
heartrate_cardio_time	time [s] duration of the heart rate being within the defined "cardio" target range
heartrate_peak_time	time [s] duration of the heart rate being within the defined "peak" target range
heartrate_resting	resting heart rate
heartrate_avg	average heart rate
heartrate_max	maximal heart rate
sleep_time	total time [s] spent in all phases of sleep
sleep_efficiency	calculated score derived from sleep_time, sleep_asleep_time and sleep_wake_time
sleep_deep_count	number of times falling into deep sleep
sleep_deep_time	total time [s] spent in deep sleep
sleep_light_count	number of times falling into light sleep
sleep_light_time	total time [s] spent in light sleep
sleep_rem_count	number of times falling into REM sleep stage
sleep_rem_time	total time [s] spent in REM sleep stage
sleep_wake_count	number of times waking up
sleep_wake_time	total time [s] spent in waking up
sleep_awake_time	total time [s] spent awake during sleep
sleep_awake_count	number of times awakening during sleep
sleep_restless_time	total time [s] spent being restless during sleep
sleep_restless_count	number of times getting restless during sleep
sleep_asleep_time	total time [s] spent being fully asleep
sleep_asleep_count	number of times falling fully asleep

In addition to stated behavioral time-series data, an extensive set of personal socio-demographic, profile (age, gender, ethnicity, educational and marital status, employment status and occupational environment...), as well as health state, risk factors and habits, lifestyle, neighbourhood and quality of life assessment, and other relevant behavioural data are manually input/submitted on each citizen participating in the study via online forms, composed from adapted relevant survey/assessment instruments for each specific field, like Framingham, EuroQoL-5, IPAQ-SF. These data are geo-localized to the residence location of each responding citizen for the purposes of analytics of collective/community well-being, and are collected from a greater number of recruited respondents, but just in rare cases in more than one iteration over time due to the high number and scope of covered variables, and therefore suitable for a broad but mainly static "snapshot" assessment of current well-being state rather than for behaviour change model and analytics. Incorporating both these static and IoT-sensed temporal data into a fully comprehensive predictive well-being model is an ongoing task in progress throughout the end of the Project, with results to be presented in other upcoming publications.

4   Derivation of Domain/Dimension Indices

4.1   Physical Activity/Exercise

Physical activity in our first approach stated above in Sect. 2 can be discretized using several common baseline categorizations related or derived from the above mentioned relevant institutional/governmental and professional expert guidelines for the urban population groups. The example approach taken in the recent health survey of England from 2016 [12] compared well-being and mental health of adults in different socio-demographically stratified population groups by physical activity, among others. The activity level categories used in the analysis were the following:

- *Meets aerobic guidelines*: At least 150 min moderately intensive physical activity or 75 min vigorous activity per week or an equivalent combination of these
- *Asserted activity*: 60 to 149 min moderate activity or 30–74 min vigorous activity per week or an equivalent combination of these
- *Low activity*: 30 to 59 min moderate activity or 15 to 29 min vigorous activity per week or an equivalent combination of these
- *Inactive*: Less than 30 min moderate activity or less than 15 min vigorous activity per week or an equivalent combination of these,

and the corresponding linear scaled scoring function denotes "*Meets aerobic guidelines*" with a score of 4, "*Certain activity*" - 3, "*Low activity*" - 2, and "*Inactive*" with 1. This baseline scoring scale, besides sufficient granularity and robustness exhibited in referenced comprehensive studies, is also convenient for

- mapping to the defined activity level categories used as input parameters for the consensus models for prediction of risk of Type 2 Diabetes (T2D) and asthma onset and exacerbation, developed for the PULSE project [13, 17]

- quantification of longer-term and/or periodic activity level behaviours directly from categorized daily or incidental activity level values as measured and acquired from the wearable tracker devices through relevant APIs (*light/soft*, *moderate*, and *vigorous/intense* activity).

4.2 Specific Walking Activity

Similarly, the authors in [14] and [15] demonstrate the following referent threshold ranges of the number of daily walked steps to be used for classification of walking activity in healthy adults, and the corresponding scoring function linearly assigning the following 1–5 integer scores to the classification categories: *highly active* (12,500 or more steps/day) – 5, *active* (10,000–12,499 steps/day) – 4, *somewhat active* (7,500–9,999 steps/day) – 3, *lowly active* (5,000–7,499 steps/day) – 2, and *sedentary* (under 5,000 steps/day) - 1.

4.3 Cardiovascular Fitness - VO₂max

VO₂max is the metric denoting the maximum amount of oxygen that an individual can use during intense exercise. It is widely and commonly used as an indicator of cardiorespiratory fitness.

A simple generic estimate of VO₂max of an individual can be obtained using their maximum and resting heart rates in the following formula, publised in [16]:

$$VO_2 max \approx \frac{hr_{max}}{hr_{rest}} * 15.3 \, mL/(kg * min) \tag{1}$$

Where hr_{max} can be crudely estimated as $220 - age\ of\ the\ person$.

A relatively standard convenient and meaningful categorization of VO₂max for Western European and USA populations can be on a scale from 1 - *very low*, through 2 - *low*, 3 - *fair*, 4 - *moderate*, 5 - *good*, and 6 - *very good*, to maximal 7 - *elite*, depending of the individual's gender and age, with common categorization for males and females aged 6 to 75 published by Shvartz & Reibold in [11].

4.4 Quality of Sleep

Total average sleep duration in 24 h is a straightforward direct metric for assessing the quality of sleep in terms of longer-term stable behaviour across complete populations. The US National Sleep Foundation recently provided the following referent expert sleep duration recommendations (in terms of recommended (or not) threshold values for both oversleep and undersleep), categorized by precise granular age ranges [10]:

These recommendations categorize possible output sleep duration times as either *recommended*, *may be appropriate*, or *not recommended*, and the optimal *recommended* duration is 7–9 h for majority of the populations.

Table 2. Detailed US National Sleep Foundation recommended threshold values and ranges for sleep duration per age category

Category *age*	Recommended	Considered appropriate	Not recommended
Newborns *0–3 months*	14 to 17 h	11 to 13 h 18 to 19 h	Less than 11 h More than 19 h
Infants *4–11 months*	12 to 15 h	10 to 11 h 16 to 18 h	Less than 10 h More than 18 h
Toddlers *1–2 years*	11 to 14 h	9 to 10 h 15 to 16 h	Less than 9 h More than 16 h
Preschoolers *3–5 years*	10 to 13 h	8 to 9 h 14 h	Less than 8 h More than 14 h
School-aged Children *6–13 years*	9 to 11 h	7 to 8 h 12 h	Less than 7 h More than 12 h
Teenagers *14–17 years*	8 to 10 h	7 h 11 h	Less than 7 h More than 11 h
Young Adults *18–25 years*	7 to 9 h	6 h 10 to 11 h	Less than 6 h More than 11 h
Adults *26–64 years*	7 to 9 h	6 h 10 h	Less than 6 h More than 10 h
Older Adults *65 years and over*	7 to 8 h	5 to 6 h 9 h	Less than 5 h More than 9 h

Additionally, relevant recent findings like the extensive meta-analysis performed by the American Diabetes Association to assess the dose-response relationship between sleep duration and risk of type 2 diabetes [18], have concluded that the lowest type 2 diabetes risk is for the average overnight sleep duration from 7 to under 9 h per day, and that both shorter and longer sleep durations than this optimum range denote up to 1.5 times increased risk (and up to 2 times increased cardiac conditions risk shown in the related studies [21], also relevant in the Project). We therefore slightly alter the *may be appropriate* category from the otherwise adopted recommendations from Table 2 above to *mildly risky*, reflecting the importance of stated health risks in PULSE, and the effect of common or periodically repeated behaviour patterns over months or years to the exasperation of the risks. This categorization will also consequently be communicated on the data visualizations and public health/prevention interventions and campaigns deployed and administered through relevant PULSE system applications and modules (PHO Dashboards, PulsAIR gamified mobile app.) towards the citizens and urban communities, and the resulting function scores assigned to the categories are therefore: **1** for *not recommended*, **1.75** for *mildly risky*, and **2** for *recommended*, inversely proportional to the pesimistically estimated risks increase brought by shorter durations. Complex eventual relations of detailed specific measured sleep parameters to well-being will be explored by more advanced methods in other subsequent work.

4.5 The Composite Physical Well-Being Indicator

From several existing elementary statistical approaches for aggregating the underlying dimensional indices and constructing the summary composite indicator value, we consider the weighted geometric mean of the four constituting dimensional indices as most adequate and appropriate for this specific well-being problematics:

$$WB_{ph} = \sqrt[4]{I_w^{Wt_w} * I_p^{Wtp} * I_s^{Wt_s} * I_c^{Wt_c}}, \qquad (2)$$

where summary dimensional indices denoted by the scoring function values are: I_w – walking activity index, I_p – physical activity/exercise index, I_s – sleep duration index, I_c – cardio-respiratory fitness index (through VO$_2$max), and Wt_w, Wt_p, Wt_s, and Wt_c are respective weight factors, derived from expert assessments and rank data from relevant previous studies and experience, and assigned to adjust the relative importance and contribution of each of the indices to the resulting composite indicator value, per compositing methods outlined in [19] and [9], or for derivation of composite UN Human Development Index (HDI). As all 4 constituting indices are directly proportional to the resulting composite indicator (i.e. the higher the activity levels or cardio-respiratory fitness scores, the higher the well-being), and low value of either of the four is significant for decreased overall composite (although there is some correlation between the indices - e.g. decrease in cardio-respiratory fitness in most cases causes decreased activity levels as well), the geometric mean is adequate for its sensitivity to low values of each individual constituting index, and ability to combine values on completely different scales without normalization required. Initially assigned values of weight factors are 0.9 for I_w, 1 for I_p, and 1.05 for I_s and I_c, taking into account the importance of specific indices for respiratory disease and T2D risk, volatility of the collected data by now, and known overestimation of some measured variable values (like number of walked steps, VO$_2$max estimate, or recognized sessions of cycling and some other exercise types) by the predominantly used wearable devices - Fitbit Charge 2 [20]. The weight factors are set as configuration parameters in the model, so they can be changed to fine-tune the composition according to the data insights acquired over time or the results of the validation described in Sect. 5 below.

Time series of the values of the composite indicator are formed from weekly and monthly aggregations of underlying daily and intra-daily measurements into the 4 constituting index values. Method for computing those values from the measured values of variables listed in Table 1 above is as developed and introduced in [22] for synthesis of indicators and geriatric factors from the same source IoT data, based in this case on univariate normalization of relative changes (quantified in standard scores, as stated above in the "Approach" Sect. 2) of acquired Big temporal Data during the complete study period, and then multivariate weighted linear aggregation of obtained normalized indicators and descriptive statistics into higher-level composite factors, to capture weekly and monthly behavioural patterns and trends, less susceptible to influence of outliers and ocassional notably deviating values.

5   Preliminary Validation of the Composite Index and Conclusion

Validation metric is the correlation with specific corresponding summary measure(s) of current well-being, self-reported by the respondent citizens through web and mobile app. questionnaires as mentioned above. They can be summarized from two relevant subset questionnaires: 1) European Social Survey (ESS), and 2) EuroQoL-5D (EQ5) survey instrument, both standardized (with minor adaptations) and common for measuring well-being in multiple continuous and/or repeated relevant Europe-wide and national-level studies, and robust to some degree against extreme fully subjective bias.

15 statements of the ESS questionnaire broadly cover social and most of the other aspects of personal and community well-being that the respondent rates on a 5-degree Likert scale (*Strongly agree*-4, *Agree*-3, *Neither agree nor disagree*-2, *Disagree*-1, *Strongly disagree*-0), the total possible questionnaire score thus ranging from 0, denoting the lowest/worst well-being, to 60 representing the optimum.

EQ5 instrument is focused on physical and mental health status and daily life activities measured in 5 dimensions (mobility, self-care, usual activities, pain/discomfort and anxiety/depression), also self-rated on a 5-degree scale from perceived worst to best like in ESS. Last question asks for assessment of the respondent's overall health state (*hsa*) on the current day, on the scale from 0 (worst) to 100 (best imaginable), also mapped to a number ranged from 1 to 5 by the formula *1 + 4 * hsa/100* for the purpose of this evaluation. Total cumulative EQ5 score thus ranges from 6 to 30.

Figure 2 below shows the correlation scatter plot of ESS scores and composite well-being indices for 97 respondents of which 12 filled EES questionnaire twice, two filled it three times, and the rest only once during the observed period of 11 months.

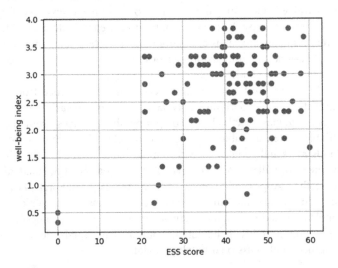

Fig. 2. Scatter plot of composite well-being index vs. cumulative ESS score values

Figure 3 shows the relationship between the composite well-being indices and the obtained EQ5 scores of 107 respondents, 3 of which filled the questionnaire three times, 20 filled it twice, and the rest once during the observed data collection period.

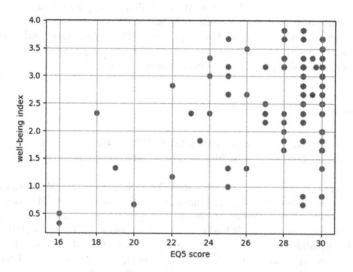

Fig. 3. Scatter plot of composite well-being index vs. cumulative EQ5 score values

The analysis reveals a medium positive correlation of 0.424 (with the p-value of approx. 3.7×10^{-7}) between our constructed composite index and cumulative EQ5 scores. The composite indicator and its constituting domain indices can therefore be considered promising for their intended purpose of basic representation of the urban physical well-being aspects modelled from a variety of heterogeneous underlying activity and health/vital parameters measured by IoT wearable devices, summarized in 4 main dimensional and one overall derived score convenient for comparisons, interpretation and presentation to the end-users, particularly in the required shortest most concise manner and form, such as through a mobile app. UI or intervention messages.

As almost half of the questions in EQ5 are very remotely or not at all related to the physical well-being aspects summarized by the composite indicator, the correlation is expected to increase when the ongoing work in incorporating social and other well-beung aspects fully in the model is completed.

Found small positive correlation of 0.287 (p-value 0.001) between the composite indicator and cumulative scores of ESS questionnaire (in which most of the questions are not related to physical well-being) additionally points to the significance of this composite indicator to the overall well-being. The work also continues on the cleaning and pre-processing the data collected on the remaining monitored citizens, incorporation of machine learning methods in the model and exploration and modelling of the influence of detailed sleep and cardiac parameters, as well as of the sensed ambiental data, on the main well-being domains.

Acknowledgment. This work has received funding from the European Union's Horizon 2020 research and innovation programme under the grant agreement No. 727816 (PULSE). The performed research studies have all been granted ethical approval from the relevant IRB authority in each PULSE pilot testbed city (Ethics Committee of the Parc de Salut Mar hospital in Barcelona, through NHS Health Research Authority IRAS (Integrated Research Application System) in Birmingham, New York Academy of Medicine IRB in New York City, etc.), resulting from comprehensive multimonthly evaluation processes. The inclusion and exclusion methods and criteria for recruiting citizens have been specified in relevant previous publications of the Project, such as in Section 2.2.1. *Participation Criteria* in [23].

References

1. https://www.businesswire.com/news/home/20180214005548/en/. Accessed Feb 2020
2. https://www.digitaltrends.com/health-fitness/fitbit-resting-heart-rate-study. Accessed Feb 2020
3. Abril-Jiménez, P., Rojo Lacal, J., de los Ríos Pérez, S., Páramo, M., Montalvá Colomer, J. B., Arredondo Waldmeyer, M.T.: Ageing-friendly cities for assessing older adults' decline: IoT-based system for continuous monitoring of frailty risks using smart city infrastructure. Aging Clin. Exp. Res. **32**(4), 663–671 (2019). https://doi.org/10.1007/s40520-019-01238-y
4. Almeida, A., Mulero, R., Rametta, P., Urošević, V., Andrić, M., Patrono, L.: A critical analysis of an IoT-aware AAL system for elderly monitoring. Future Gener. Comput. Syst. **97**, 598–619 (2019). https://doi.org/10.1016/j.future.2019.03.019
5. Díaz Rodríguez, N.: Semantic and fuzzy modelling for human behaviour recognition in smart spaces. In: Studies on the Semantic Web, vol. 23. IOS Press Amsterdam (2016)
6. Azkune, G., Almeida, A.: A scalable hybrid activity recognition approach for intelligent environments. In: Journal of LaTeX Class Files, vol. 14, no. 8 (2015)
7. Kolarz, P., Angelis, J., Krčál, A., Simmonds, P., Traag, V., Wain, M.: Comparative impact study of the European social survey (ESS) european research infrastructure consortium (ERIC). Final Report. ESS-SUSTAIN Project (H2020 funded), Technopolis Group (2017)
8. Bagnall, A., South, J., Mitchell, B., Pilkington,, G., Newton, Rob., Di Martino, S.: Systematic scoping review of indicators of community wellbeing in the UK. "What Works" Centre for Wellbeing (2017). https://doi.org/10.13140/rg.2.2.21762.17604
9. Land, K.C.: Composite index construction. In: Michalos, A.C. (eds.) Encyclopedia of Quality of Life and Well-Being Research. Springer, Dordrecht (2014). https://doi.org/10.1007/978-94-007-0753-5_3317
10. Hirshkowitz, M., Whiton, K., Albert, S.M., Alessi, C., Bruni, O., Ohayon, M.: National sleep foundation's sleep time duration recommendations: methodology and results summary. Sleep Health **1**, 40–43 (2015)
11. Shvartz, E., Reibold, R.: Aerobic fitness norms for males and females aged 6 to 75 years: a review. Aviat. Space Environ. Med. **61**(1), 3–11 (1990)
12. Morris, S., Earl, K., Neave, A.: Health survey for England 2016: well-being and mental health. NHS Digital Health and Social Care Information Centre and the UK Office for National Statistics (2017). ISBN 978-1-78734-099-2
13. Di Camillo, B., et al.: HAPT2D: high accuracy of prediction of T2D with a model combining basic and advanced data depending on availability. Eur. J. Endocrinol. **178**(4), 331–341 (2018)
14. Tudor-Locke, C., Bassett, D.: How many steps/day are enough? Sports Med. **1**, 1–8 (2004)

15. Tudor-Locke, C., Craig, C.L., Brown, W.J., Clemes, S.A., Cocker, K.D., Schmi, M.D.: How many steps/day are enough? For adults. Int. J. Behav. Nutr. Phys. Act. **8**, 79 (2011)

16. Uth, N., Sorensen, H., Overgaard, K., Pedersen, P.: Estimation of VO2max from the ratio between HRmax and HRrest - the heart rate ratio method. Eur. J. Appl. Physiol. **91**(1), 111–115 (2004). https://doi.org/10.1007/s00421-003-0988-y

17. Sambo, F., et al.: A Bayesian Network analysis of the probabilistic relations between risk factors in the predisposition to type 2 diabetes. In: Conference Proceedings IEEE Engineering Medicine Biology Society, pp. 2119–2122 (2015). https://doi.org/10.1109/embc.2015.7318807

18. Shan Z., et al.: Sleep duration and risk of type 2 diabetes: a meta-analysis of prospective studies. Diabetes Care **38**(3), 529–537 (2015). https://doi.org/10.2337/dc14-2073

19. Smith, L., Smith,, H., Case, J., Harwell, L., Summers, J., Wade, C.: Indicators and methods for constructing a US human well-being index (HWBI) for ecosystem services research. US Environmental Protection Agency, Report #EPA/600/R-12/023 (2012)

20. Freeberg, K.A., Baughman, B.R., Vickey, T., Sullivan, J.A., Sawyer, B.J.: Assessing the ability of the fitbit charge 2 to accurately predict VO2max. mHealth **5**, 39 (2019). https://doi.org/10.21037/mhealth.2019.09.07

21. Li, W., et al.: Sleep duration and risk of stroke events and stroke mortality: a systematic review and meta-analysis of prospective cohort studies. Int. J. Cardiol. **223**, 870–876 (2016). https://doi.org/10.1016/j.ijcard.2016.08.302

22. Ricevuti, G., Venturini, L., Copelli, S., Mercalli, F., Nicolardi, G.: Data driven MCI and frailty prevention: geriatric modelling in the City4Age project. In: IEEE 3rd International Forum on Research and Technologies for Society and Industry (RTSI), Modena, pp. 1–6 (2017)

23. Ottaviano, M., et al.: Empowering citizens through perceptual sensing of urban environmental and health data following a participative citizen science approach. Sensors **19**(13), 2940 (2019)

Wellbeing Technology

Automatic Daily Activity Schedule Planning for Simulating Smart House with Elderly People Living Alone

Can Jiang[1(✉)] and Akira Mita[2]

[1] Graduate School of Science and Technology, Keio University, 3-14-1 Hiyoshi, Kohoku-ku, Yokohama, Kanagawa, Japan
canjiang@keio.jp
[2] Department of System Design Engineering, Keio University, 3-14-1 Hiyoshi, Kohoku-ku, Yokohama, Kanagawa, Japan
Mita@keio.jp

Abstract. A simulation tool that supports developers to build scenarios automatically in multiple simulation platforms is proposed. As an essential part of this simulator, this study proposed an activity schedule generator to mimic the daily life of elderly people living alone. This generator outperforms existing methods of activity schedule planning in three aspects: 1) it is adaptive to the layout of a simulated smart house; 2) there is no unspecified time in the timeline of generated schedules; and 3) it generates stable, but not tedious schedules for a number of days. A real-time location data generator is proposed to convert generated schedules to simulated real-time location data of the resident, and a proposed interface converts these simulated location data to simulated records of virtual passive infrared (PIR) sensors, which can be used to optimize placement of PIR sensors in a smart house.

Keywords: Elderly people living alone · Smart home simulator · Activity of daily living · Motivation · Automatic scenario generation

1 Introduction

The elderly population is increasing worldwide. An estimated 617.1 million people are aged 65 and over in 2015, and this number is projected to increase to 1 billion in 2030, and 1.6 billion in 2050 [1]. More than 20% of men and 40% of women aged 65 and older chose an independent lifestyle in many countries [2]. Pimouguet et al. [3] indicated living alone shortened life expectancy by 0.6 years for elderly people. Elderly individuals living alone would benefit from specialized care, but a shortage in the global workforce of aged-care workers [4] has made this difficult.

Under these conditions, smart houses with a sensor network and domestic robots have been built to address the aged-care worker shortage. The sensor networks provide real-time health monitoring [5] and a means of detecting emergencies [6], while mobile domestic robots provide location-based support [7] and services [8] for residents. To ensure the effectiveness of the sensor networks and robots, real test beds were built to conduct experiments for collecting data. However, building a test bed is expensive, and

M. Jmaiel et al. (Eds.): ICOST 2020, LNCS 12157, pp. 171–183, 2020.
https://doi.org/10.1007/978-3-030-51517-1_14

simulations are necessary for smart house developers to test and verify their ideas before building a real one.

Developers typically conduct simulations using the following three steps. (1) Manually create a simulation scenario by first building a house and resident body models and defining the activity schedules and movement routes of the virtual resident or controlling the virtual resident manually. (2) Place virtual sensors, devices, or robots to record data and/or operation performances. (3) Analyze recorded data or operation performances and evaluate simulation design. As a typical simulation constructed in step (1) requires a lot of time, developers can only prepare a limited number of scenarios. Moreover, the developers may use multiple simulators for different purposes, e.g., using CST Microwave Studio to test the communication of a wireless sensor network, OpenSHS [9] to collect virtual sensor records for sensor arrangement optimization, and Stage [10] to plan the operation policies of mobile robots. When the developers use another simulator, they must repeat steps (1) even if they use the same simulation scenario.

We propose a simulation tool that provides diverse simulation scenarios and can support smart house developers to complete step (1) automatically in multiple simulation platforms [11]. This simulator consists of generators and interfaces as show in Fig. 1. The proposed generators produce diverse information such as indoor spatial attributes and resident travel patterns. This information is used to create a scenario that can run on different simulation platforms through various interfaces. We proposed a spatial attribute generator [12] and travel pattern generator [11], and used two interfaces [11] to transfer the data generated by them to models and virtual sensor records of the simulators.

As an essential part of our simulator, we propose an activity schedule generator. With generated travel patterns, these schedules are converted to simulated real-time location data, which can be used in simulations with interfaces. The rest of this paper is organized as follows. In Sect. 2, we review related work of daily activity schedule generation. Section 3 describes the methodology to generate activity schedules. Section 4 details the performance of this generator. Section 5 introduces how the generated data can be used in simulations.

2   Related Works

A number of scholars generated daily activity schedules as intermediate results to generate sensor records in a virtual smart house, which are essential for simulations.

Renoux et al. [13] generated activity schedules with a constraint-based planning method. The constraints include that the start time and duration of each activity are over reasonable intervals, and a number of activities need to be performed within certain time intervals before their corresponding activities, e.g., preparing lunch for 0 to 5 min before having lunch.

Bouchard et al. [14] generated activity schedules using behavior trees (BTs) as intermediate results to generate the simulated evolution of signal strength between RFID readers and tags. However, designing BTs is complicate, and the authors only showed an example of generating the schedule for making coffee or tea.

Alshammari et al. [9] replicated and modified schedules originally designed by humans. The methods of modification include combining two samples of original schedules and changing the start and end time of activities. The activity schedules correspond to virtual binary sensor records, thus, a large number of records are generated simultaneously. This method is simple, but generated schedules may have high similarity.

Mshali et al. [15] generated long-term activity schedules using a Markov model, and five transition matrices associated to different periods of a day were designed. The authors also proposed an adaptive and context-aware algorithm for monitoring the daily activities of elderly and dependent persons, and generated schedules were used to test the algorithm in simulations.

Lee et al. [16] generated activity schedules with a motivation-driven method. A motivation value (MV) represents the desire of a virtual agent to perform a class of activities with the agent performing an activity when its corresponding MV reaches its threshold. Motivations are classified by levels; if two MVs reach their thresholds at the same time, the agent will perform the activity that corresponds to the higher-level motivation. This method has sufficient potential for improvement if the mechanism of evolution of the MVs is designed carefully.

3 Activity Schedule Generation

3.1 Problem Statement

To build our activity schedule generator module, we need to improve upon the methods mentioned in Sect. 2 by addressing the following issues. 1) The list of activities that can be performed by a virtual resident is determined by the layout of simulated house, e.g., the resident can only watch TV if a TV is in the house. The above methods are for a determined layout with a fixed activity list. As our simulator contributes to provide diverse simulation scenarios by producing diverse layouts, we need a method that can process dynamic activity lists. 2) The above methods generate schedules whose timelines include unspecified times between the end time of an activity and the start time of the next one. Where the resident has been and what he/she has done during the unspecified time are undetermined, thus, generated sensors records did not cover entire days. 3) Most of the above methods generated schedules for one day or less, but long-term activity schedules are required for our simulation.

We developed a motivation-driven method on the basis of that presented in the reviewed study [16] to build our activity schedule generator. An MV represent a resident's desire to perform an activity sequence (AS). While performing the activity is dependent on its MV reaching its threshold in [16], in our method, the MVs are used to determine the probability distribution (P) of sampling the next AS. The evolution of the MVs is adaptive to the input indoor spatial data and resident's profile. The input data represent a layout that determines what AS can be performed, thus, this adaptive evolution mechanism addresses issue 1). The profile represents a resident's tendencies to activities, which is quantified by durations (D), periods (T) and frequencies (f) of an AS. We need to design an evolution mechanism and initialize the MVs carefully to

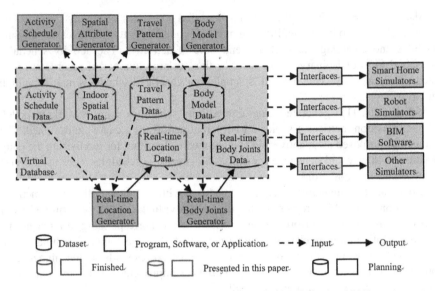

Fig. 1. General framework for building the simulation tool [11].

generate stable, but not tedious, activity schedules in the long term that will address issue 3). We can address issue 2) by taking into account more activities. The studies mentioned in Sect. 2 took into account a limited number of activities, implying that these activities occupy the entire timeline, which is unrealistic.

3.2   Model of AS, *MV*, Resident Profile, and *P*

Mapping the Relationship Between AS and *MV*. A resident performs activities on the basis of motivation, in which MVs quantify the degree of motivation. When an MV is high, the resident may perform a sequence of activities to satisfy the motivation, e.g., if the value of hunger motivation is high, he/she will cook and eat.

We determined that a resident has 13 motivations at most, which correspond to 13 MV_i-AS_i pairs: MV_1: wash and brush teeth => sleep (at night) => wash and brush teeth, MV_2: sleep (at noon), MV_3: take food => cook => take tableware => eat, MV_4: take a bath => get dressed => put clothes in wash machine, MV_5: get dressed => go out => get dressed, MV_6: go to toilet (short duration), MV_7: go to toilet (long duration), MV_8: watch TV, MV_9: read, MV_{10}: clean, MV_{11}: take clothes out of washing machine, MV_{12}: wander, and MV_{13}: relax. An AS consists of one or more activities, and activities in the AS are performed in order without lag to satisfy the corresponding motivation and decrease the corresponding MV_i. MV_i determines the possibility of performing ith AS, P_i.

AS and *MV* Are Adaptive to the Layout. The actual composition of an AS is also adaptive to the layout like the evolution of MVs. An activity in an AS will be omitted if its corresponding places are not in the layouts The mapping relationship of all activities and places is shown in Table 1, e.g., if the kitchen stove, refrigerator, and cupboard are not in the house, AS_3 will omit the procedure take food => cook => take tableware, which implies the resident eats food prepared by someone out of the house in this case. If all activities of an AS can not be performed because of the layout, its MV_i will always be 0.

Resident's Personal Profile. To keep generated schedules diverse and reasonable, parameters corresponding to the evolution of MVs should depend on the resident's profile. The profile represents a resident's tendencies to satisfy different motivations, which is determined by sampling D, T, and f of an AS performed over reasonable intervals. Di means the duration of the resident performing the ith AS in a period (T_i), e.g., D_8 means how long the resident performed the activity "watch TV" per day on average if $T_8 = 1$ day. T_i and f_i mean the period and frequency of performing the ith AS, respectively, e.g., T_{12} means how many days between two instances of the resident's wandering and f_6 means how many times the resident performed the activity "go to toilet (short duration)" per day on average, where $T_i \times f_i = 1$.

Mechanism of MVs Evolution. MVs quantify the motivations to perform activities, MV_i usually decreases when the ith AS is performed, increases when other ASs are performed, and remains unchanged in special cases. The values of D, T, and f determine the speed of the increase and decrease of MVs. The rules below show the evolution of MVs, where *Rules* 1.1) and 1.2) indicate the situations when MV_i remains unchanged, 2.1) to 2.4) show the mechanism of MVs increasing, and 3.1) to 3.4) show the mechanism of them decreasing.

Rule 1.1) MV_i is always 0 if ith AS can not be performed.
Rule 1.2) $MV_{13} = 1.02$Norm_MV in any case, where Norm_MV is a constant.

Note: MV_{13} corresponds to relax. This rule means the resident is performing the activity "relax" when all other MVs are low. Setting MV_{13} as a constant keeps MVs stable in the long term.

Rule 2.1) Ways of MVs increasing include linear and step functional increasing.
Rule 2.2) If MV_i is not fixed and $i \neq 7$ or 11, MV_i increases linearly when the ith AS is not performed. The increment is determined by Eq. (1),

$$MV_i(t + \Delta t) = \begin{cases} MV_i(t) + \omega_i\Delta t + \varepsilon, & \text{if the resident is not sleeping.} \\ MV_i(t) + 0.1\omega_i\Delta t + \varepsilon, & \text{if the resident is sleeping, } and\ i = 3 \text{ or } 6. \\ MV_i(t) + \varepsilon, & \text{if the resident is sleeping, and } i \neq 3 \text{ and } 6. \end{cases}$$

$$(1)$$

where ω_i is an increasing rate and ε is random noise.

Note: When the resident is sleeping, the increasing rates of the MVs of "eat" and "go to toilet (short duration)" decrease to 10%, rates of other MVs decrease to 0.

Table 1. Mapping relationship between activities and places.

Activity	Place
Sleep (at night)	Bed
Sleep (at noon)	
Relax	
Wash and brush teeth	Bathroom
Take a bath	
Take food	Refrigerator
Take tableware	Cupboard
Take food	Kitchen stove
Take tableware	
Cook	
Eat	Dining table-chair set
Put clothes in washing machine	Washing machine
Take clothes out of washing machine	
Go to toilet (short duration)	Toilet
Got to toilet (long duration)	
Watch TV	Sofa-TV set
Relax	
Relax	Writing desk-chair set
Read	
Get dressed	Wardrobe
Eat	Entrance
Go out	
Clean	Trash bin
Wander	None

Rule 2.3) Following the principle that MV_i should be generally unchanged after one period in an ideal case, ω_i can be determined by **D**, **T**, and *f*.

Note: e.g., for the 8th AS, watching TV, assuming that the resident watches TV for 4 h (D_8), and sleeps 8 h ($D_1 + D_2$) per day ($T_8 = 24$ h), ω_8 is determined by Eq. (2),

$$\omega_8 = \frac{\text{Norm\_MV}}{[T_8 - (D_1 + D_2) - D_8]}. \tag{2}$$

which means ω_8 should increase by Norm_MV in the remaining 12 h, while it decreases by Norm_MV during the 4 h (D_8).

Rule 2.4) MV_i increases step by step if $i = 7$ or 11. For the 7th AS, "going to toilet (long duration)", MV_7 increases by Norm_MV/($3 \times T_7$) 2.5 h after the resident starts eating. For the 11th AS, "taking clothes out of the washing machine", MV_{11} increases by Norm_MV 1 h after the resident puts their clothe into the washing machine.

Rule 3.1) MV_i will decrease if the *i*th AS has been performed except if $i = 13$.

Rule 3.2) The decrease of MV_i depends on the T_i and actual duration, AT. It is defined by Eq. (3) except if the AS is eating breakfast, the decrease is $(2AT/3T_i) \times$ Norm_MV.

$$MV_i(t + AT) = MV_i(t) - \frac{AT}{T_i} \text{Norm\_MV}. \tag{3}$$

Rule 3.3) AT is related to T_i, AT is sampled from $[0.97T_i, 1.03T_i]$ for $i = 1$, from $[0.4T_i, 0.9T_i]$ for $i = 5$, from $[0.3T_i, 0.7T_i]$ for $i = 8$ or 9, and from $[0.95T_i, 1.05T_i]$ for other cases.

Rule 3.4) The resident may perform the activities "eat" and "go to toilet" outside. When he/she is going out, if MV_3, MV_6 or MV_7 reach Norm_MV, and there is sufficient time to perform the corresponding AS, this MV decreases as the AS is performed.

Initialization of MVs. MVs should be initialized before evolution, which can be achieved by determining when each AS will be performed for first time. The time when the ith AS is first performed is approximately equal to the time when MV_i first reaches Norm_MV. We sample the initial time from 9:30 PM of one day to 1:00 AM of the next day, and the resident is going to sleep. MV_0 thus is Norm_MV, as D_i and ω_i is known, other initial MVs can be calculated with Eq. (1), e.g., assuming that $D_1 = 8$ h, and the resident will eat breakfast 1 h after waking up, initial MV_3 is calculated by Eq. (4).

$$MV_3 = \text{Norm\_MV} - 0.1\omega_3 \times 8\,\text{h} - \omega_3 \times 1\,\text{h}. \tag{4}$$

To keep the generated schedule stable in the long term, we need to avoid two MVs whose ASs require long durations to reach Norm_MV at the same time.

Relationship Between MV and P. The possibility of performing the ith AS depends on the motivation value, MV_i, as shown in Eq. (5)

$$P_i = \frac{\exp[\max(0, MV_i - 0.98\text{Norm\_MV})]}{\sum_{j=1}^{13} \exp[\max(0, MV_j - 0.98\text{Norm\_MV})]}. \tag{5}$$

3.3   Implementation

We wrote a Python3 program to achieve activity schedule generation. A sample of the indoor spatial attribute data (***Spatial_data***) and total generation duration (Total_Dur) were input into the program, and it returns a resident's daily activity schedule during the Total_Dur. The pseudocode of the program is shown below, where constants, variables, and variable vectors are in regular, italic, and bold italic styles, respectively.

```
program Schedule_Generation(Spatial_data, Total_Dur):
1 AS_canbe_perform := Process_Input(Spatial_data)
2 T, D, f := Generate_Resident_Profile()
3 ω := Calculate_Increse_rate(T, D, f)
4 MV, Init_time := Initialize_MVs&time(T, D, f)
5 Current_ASnum, time := 1, Init_time
6 ASnum_list, time_list := [], []
7 while time < Init_time + Total_Dur do:
8   AT := Determine_actual_duration(Current_ASnum, T)
9   MV := Update_MV(Current_ASnum, time, MV, ω, T, AT)
10  time := time + AT
11  Next_ASnum = Sample_next_ActSeq(MV)
12  If Next_ASnum != Current_ASnum do:
13    ASnum_list.append(Next_ASnum)
14    time_list.append(time)
15    Current_ASnum := Next_ASnum
16 Activity_Schedule = Post_Process(ASnum_list, time_list, Spatial_
data)
17 return Activity_Schedule
```

The program first processes the input spatial attribute data, analyzes the layout, and determines what ASs can be performed in the house in Line 1. The resident's profile is determined by sampling D, T, and f in Line 2. ω is calculated in Line 3 in accordance with *Rule 2.3)*. The original *MV* and the start time of the schedule generation are determined in Line 4. In Line 5, we assume the resident performs AS_1 at the beginning of the generation, and the variable *Time* records the current time. Two lists are created in Line 6, *ASnum_list* and *time_list*, which will record the number of all performed ASs and their start times chronologically, respectively. From Lines 7 to 15, the program determines the *AT* of performing each AS with *Rule 3.3)*, updates *MV* using the other rules, samples the next performed AS with Eq. (5), and stores the number of performed ASs and their start times in *ASnum_list* and *time_list*, respectively. The program converts these two lists into an activity schedule in Line 17. The schedule indicates the start times of all activities performed.

4   Performance of the Generator

We input indoor spatial data generated by the spatial attribute generator into the activity schedule generator, which then produces diverse activity schedule data. For example, a sample of spatial data whose layout is shown in Fig. 2 is input into the generator. As the places "desk" and "washing machine" do not exist in the house, AS_9 (read) and AS_{11} (take clothes) can not be performed. The activity schedule generator then determines the resident's profiles and generates their corresponding schedules. Two example schedules are shown in Fig. 3. Figure 3a) shows a schedule for a resident who sleeps around noon, goes out, watches TV, and takes a bath every day, while Fig. 3b) shows a schedule for who does not sleep around noon, watches TV, and takes a bath every day, but only goes out every four days.

We also tested the performance of our generator on PC with an Intel[R] core[TM] i7-8550U @1.80-GHz CPU. The generator ran 100 times in 3.987 s.

Additional generated schedules are available via this website [17].

5 Using Generated Activity Schedules for Simulation

Smart house are often equipped with passive infrared (PIR) sensors. When residents are in the detection range of one, it turns on, otherwise, it remains off. Each PIR sensor has a unique ID number which can be recorded when the sensor turns on or off. By placing several PIR sensors in the house and analyzing their records, a resident's movement trajectories can be acquired, which can be used to determine whether they contain wandering travel patterns associated with dementia [18].

In the simulation, the PIR sensor records were generated from simulated real-time location data. We built a generator that could convert an activity schedule, a sample of indoor spatial data, and several samples of travel pattern data into a sample of real-time location data. We developed an interface to convert the real-time location data into virtual PIR sensor records, which can be used to optimize the placement of the PIR sensors in a smart house.

Examples of the performance of the real-time location data generator and the interface are shown in figures and tables. Figure 2 shows a sample of spatial data. Table 2 shows part of an activity schedule. The travel pattern data are shown in Fig. 4. The above data are input into the generator to produce the real-time location data. Figure 4 also shows the positions of the five PIR sensors located in the virtual house. Their coordinates are [100, 0], [300, −150], [500, −200], [550, 50] and [850, 0]. The interface converts the real-time location data into the records of PIR sensors, which is shown in Table 3.

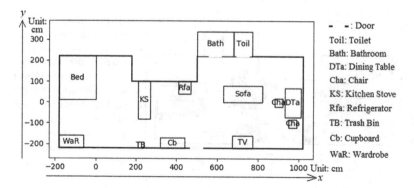

Fig. 2. Layout of input indoor spatial data.

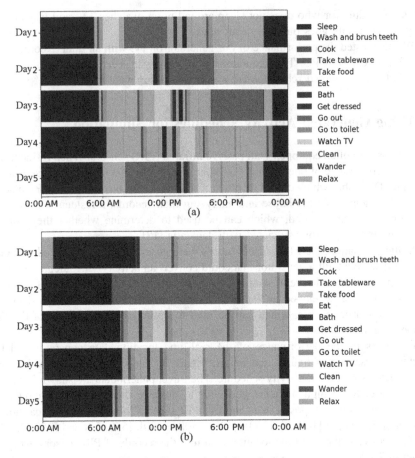

Fig. 3. Generated activity schedules.

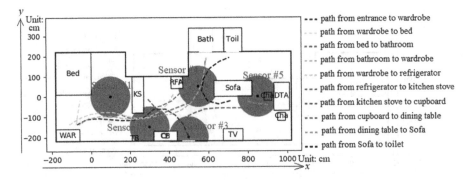

Fig. 4. Layout of input indoor spatial data with PIR sensors and travel pattern data.

Table 2. Part of the activity schedule shown in Fig. 3(a).

Activity	Start time	Activity	Start time
Go out	5d AM 8 h 17 m 7 s	Cook	5d PM 2 h 17 m 56 s
Get dressed	5d PM 1 h 13 m 59 s	Take tableware	5d PM 2 h 28 m 44 s
Sleep	5d PM 1 h 16 m 12 s	Eat	5d PM 2 h 29 m 46 s
Relax	5d PM 1 h 40 m 0 s	Relax	5d PM 2 h 49 m 20 s
Bath	5d PM 1 h 54 m 36 s	Watch TV	5d PM 3 h 15 m 1 s
Get dressed	5d PM 2 h 15 m 10 s	Go to toilet	5d PM 4 h 30 m 33 s
Take food	5d PM 2 h 17 m 18 s		

Table 3. Simulated records of virtual PIR sensors.

Time		Time	
5d PM 1 h 13 m 45 s 9	#3 ON	5d PM 2 h 17 m 7 s 5	#1 ON
5d PM 1 h 13 m 47 s 8	#3 OFF	5d PM 2 h 17 m 9 s 7	#1 OFF
5d PM 1 h 13 m 50 s 2	#2 ON	5d PM 2 h 17 m 10 s 9	#2 ON
5d PM 1 h 13 m 53 s 4	#2 OFF	5d PM 2 h 17 m 14 s 0	#2 OFF
5d PM 1 h 54 m 19 s 5	#1 ON	5d PM 2 h 17 m 50 s 5	#4 ON
5d PM 1 h 54 m 22 s 9	#1 OFF	5d PM 2 h 17 m 50 s 6	#4 OFF
5d PM 1 h 54 m 24 s 2	#2 ON	5d PM 2 h 17 m 53 s 6	#2 ON
5d PM 1 h 54 m 27 s 5	#2 OFF	5d PM 2 h 28 m 38 s 5	#2 OFF
5d PM 1 h 54 m 30 s 2	#4 ON	5d PM 2 h 28 m 39 s 7	#2 ON
5d PM 1 h 54 m 34 s 4	#4 OFF	5d PM 2 h 29 m 34 s 5	#2 OFF
5d PM 2 h 14 m 52 s 3	#4 ON	5d PM 2 h 29 m 34 s 5	#3 ON
5d PM 2 h 14 m 56 s 4	#4 OFF	5d PM 2 h 29 m 36 s 1	#3 OFF
5d PM 2 h 14 m 59 s 1	#2 ON	5d PM 2 h 29 m 41 s 9	#5 ON
5d PM 2 h 15 m 2 s 5	#2 OFF	5d PM 3 h 30 m 21 s 7	#5 OFF
5d PM 2 h 15 m 4 s 4	#1 ON	5d PM 3 h 30 m 23 s 8	#4 ON
5d PM 2 h 15 m 5 s 1	#1 OFF	5d PM 3 h 30 m 27 s 7	#4 OFF

6   Conclusion

Smart houses with a sensor network and domestic robots were built to take care elderly people living alone. Many simulation tools have been proposed to help smart house developers test and verify their designs, but it takes time and effort to build a simulation scenario, and developers need to repeat scenario-generation procedures if they want to use multiple simulators. To address these issues, we proposed a simulation tool that provides diverse simulation scenarios and enables developers to build scenarios automatically in multiple simulation platforms [11].

In this paper, we proposed an activity schedule generator that is an essential part of our simulator. With an improved motivation-driven method, the generator produces diverse daily activity schedules to mimic the daily lives of residents living alone. It outperforms existing generators in three aspects: 1) it is adaptive to the layout of a simulated smart house; 2) there is no unspecified time in the timeline of generated schedules; and 3) it generates stable, but not tedious schedules for a number of days.

A generated schedule includes a list of activities and their start time. The list of activities determines all starts and ends of indoor walking paths with spatial attributes of a virtual house, the travel pattern generator then generates all paths. The generated paths determine simulated real-time locations of a resident with the list of start time.

The real-time locations can be converted to records of virtual sensors with interfaces, and these records can be used to optimize designs of smart house. For example, we convert the real-time locations to records of virtual PIR sensors, and the records are useful for optimizing placement of these sensors.

Acknowledgments. This research was partially supported by a grant from the Japan Society for the Promotion of Science (JSPS KAKENHI 18H00968) and a scholarship of Mizuho International Foundation.

References

1. He, W., Goodkind, D., Smith, P.K.: An Aging World: 2015: International Population Reports, U.S. Census Bureau (2016)
2. Reher, D., Requena, M.: Living alone in later life: a global perspective. Popul. Dev. Rev. **44**(3), 427–454 (2018)
3. Pimouguet, C., et al.: Impact of living alone on institutionalization and mortality: a population-based longitudinal study. Eur. J. Public Health **26**(1), 182–187 (2016)
4. Simoens, S., Villeneuve, M., Hurst, J.: Tackling nurse shortages in OECD countries: Technology Report, Organisation for Economic Co-operation and Development (2005)
5. Vuong, N.K., Chan, S., Lau, C.T., Chan, S.Y., Yap, P.L., Chen, A.S.: Preliminary results of using inertial sensors to detect dementia-related wandering patterns. In: Proceedings of 37th International Conference on Engineering in Medicine and Biology Society (EMBC2015), Milan, pp. 3703–3706 (2015)
6. Das, B., Cook, D.J., Krishnan, N.C., Schmitter-Edgecombe, M.: One-class classification-based real-time activity error detection in smart homes. IEEE. JSTSP **10**(5), 914–923 (2016)
7. Do, H.M., Pham, M., Sheng, W., Yang, D., Liu, M.: RiSH: a robot-integrated smart home for elderly care. Rob. Auton. Syst. **101**, 74–92 (2018)
8. Fischinger, D., et al.: Hobbit, a care robot supporting independent living at home: first prototype and lessons learned. Rob. Auton. Syst. **75**(A), 60–78 (2016)
9. Alshammari, N., Alshammari, T., Sedky, M., Champion, J., Bauer, C.: OpenSHS: open smart home simulator. Sensors **17**, 1003 (2017)
10. Vaughan, R.: Massively multi-robot simulation in stage. Swarm Intell. **2**, 189–208 (2008)
11. Jiang, C., Mita, A.: Automatic spatial attribute and travel pattern generation for simulating living spaces for elderly individuals living alone. Build. Environ. **176**, 106776 (2020). https://doi.org/10.1016/j.buildenv.2020.106776
12. Jiang, C., Mita, A.: Automatic floorplan generation of living space for simulating a life of an elderly resident supported by a mobile robot. In: Proceedings of 36th International Symposium on Automation and Robotics in Construction (ISARC 2019), Banff, pp. 688–695 (2019)

13. Renoux, J., Klügl, F.: Simulating daily activities in a smart home for data generation. In: Proceedings of Conference on Winter Simulation (WSC2018), Gothenburg, pp. 798–809 (2018)
14. Bouchard, B., Gaboury, S., Bouchard, K., Francillette, Y.: Modeling human activities using behaviour trees in smart homes. In: Proceedings of 11th Conference on PErvasive Technologies Related to Assistive Environments (PETRA), Corfu, pp. 67–74 (2018)
15. Mshali, H., Lemlouma, T., Magoni, D.: Context-aware adaptive framework for e-health monitoring. In: IEEE International Conference on Data Science and Data Intensive Systems, Sydney (2015)
16. Lee, W., et al.: Automatic agent generation for IoT-based smart house simulator. Neurocomputing **209**, 14–24 (2016)
17. https://github.com/Idontwan/Activity-Schedule-Generator/tree/master/Schedules
18. Gochoo, M., Tan, T., Velusamy, V., Liu, S., Bayanduuren, D., Huang, S.: Device-free non-privacy invasive classification of elderly travel patterns in a smart house using PIR sensors and DCNN. IEEE Sens. J. **18**(1), 390–400 (2018). https://doi.org/10.1109/JSEN.2017. 2771287

A Novel On-Wrist Fall Detection System Using Supervised Dictionary Learning Technique

Farah Othmen[1,2,3(✉)], Mouna Baklouti[2,3(✉)], André Eugenio Lazzaretti[4(✉)], Marwa Jmal[3(✉)], and Mohamed Abid[2(✉)]

[1] Ecole Polytechnique de Tunisie, Universite de Carthage, La Marsa, Tunisia
farah.othmen@ept.rnu.tn
[2] Telnet Innovation Labs, Telnet Holding, Ariana, Tunisia
mouna.baklouti@enis.tn, med.abid@enis.tn
[3] CES Lab, National School of Engineers of Sfax, University of Sfax, Sfax, Tunisia
Marwa.Jmal@groupe-telnet.net
[4] Federal University of Technology, Paraná (UTFPR), Curitiba, Brazil
lazzaretti@utfpr.edu.br

Abstract. Wrist-based fall detection system provides a very comfortable and multi-modal healthcare solution, especially for elderly risking falls. However, the wrist location presents a very challenging and unstable spot to distinguish falls among other daily activities. In this paper, we propose a Supervised Dictionary Learning approach for wrist-based fall detection. Three Dictionary learning algorithms for classification are invoked in this study, namely SRC, FDDL, and LRSDL. To extract the best descriptive representation of the signal data we followed different preprocessing scenarios based on accelerometer, gyroscope, and magnetometer. A considerable overall performance was obtained by the SRC algorithms reaching respectively 99.8%, 100%, and 96.6% of accuracy, sensitivity, and specificity using raw data provided by a triaxial accelerometer, accordingly overthrowing previously proposed methods for wrist placement.

Keywords: Fall detection · Supervised Dictionary Learning · Machine learning · Wrist-based wearable · Signal processing

1 Introduction

The elderly population rate has witnessed dramatic growth over the last decades and is projected to be still increasing throughout the upcoming years to reach 35% by the year 2050, and thus, jointly increasing the population dependency

This research and innovation work is supported by MOBIDOC grants from the EU and National Agency for the Promotion of Scientific Research under the AMORI project and in collaboration with Telnet Innovation Labs.

rate [17]. Falling is one of the most crucial health risks faced by this fragile population, classified as a disease in the International Classification of Diseases [27]. According to [16], the risk of falling varies from 30% for elderly over 65 to 50% for those over 85 each year.

Wearable fall detection systems have captivated much interest in later years literature as they can fit easily into smart wearable accessories like wristbands assuring anywhere-anytime accessibility and comfortable use compared to other existing solutions, i.e the vision and ambient-based [22]. Commonly, state-of-the-art methods for wearable fall detectors are either threshold-based or machine learning-based, for which the latter received superior interest recently [29]. Abstracting an optimal combination between extracted features and classifiers, while enhancing system reliability, has been extensively researched in most related works [19,23]. However, classification performance can degrade substantially, as hand-crafted features may be very specific to the sensor, device placement, or dataset [2,8].

Dictionary learning approaches (DLA) have gained a lot of enthusiasm in image processing including sparse representation based classification algorithm for face recognition [30], as it has shown robustness especially for a limited number of channels and samples, thus reducing the need to select the best feature combination and classifier for the application. Therefore, DLA has been recently emerged into the biomedical signal processing field, of which some associated works have been proposed mainly for Electroencephalography (EEG) and electrocardiogram (ECG) signal classification [3,13].

In the same direction, we propose in this paper a novel on-wrist fall detection system based on Supervised Dictionary Learning (SDL), to autonomously generate optimal features selection that best represents acquired data. Indeed, the work presented here extends previous study [19] that implemented a movement decomposition method to extract features (direction components and body orientation) and machine learning algorithms for fall detection based on wrist wearable device. For evaluation purposes, three SDL and sparse representations algorithms with different experimental situations will be assessed throughout this paper, besides comparing it with previous related works. In this context, multiple sensors and features combinations in different experimental arrangements will be used. To the extent of our knowledge, such a dictionary-based approach is still underexplored in the related literature, so it is the main contribution of this work.

The remainder of this paper is organized as follows. Section 2 presents the main theoretical background behind our study. A detailed description of our proposed method is provided in Sect. 3. Section 4 illustrates the obtained results and compares them with prior works. Conclusion and future related work are provided in Sect. 5.

2   Theoretical Background and Related Work

2.1   Wearable Fall Detection System

Wearable-based fall detection systems illustrate all on-body attached garment devices that usually embed inertial measurement units (IMU) to inspect the body's motions, positions, and rotation movements in the space [22]. Commonly, inertial sensors such as accelerometers, gyroscopes, and magnetometers are the most used for fall detection to discriminate and notify the occurrence of a fall event as soon as possible [15]. It mostly presents an ideal solution for indoor and outdoor monitoring, especially with the emergence of nowadays advances in wearable technologies like a pendant, band, and glasses to make it more comfortable and tolerable to be wear.

Most of the analysis methods being employed in wearable fall detection are grounded on threshold and machine learning algorithms [10]. Threshold-based approaches usually compare the sensor's acquired data (or extracted features) with a predefined threshold(s) and a fall is detected when the predefined value is exceeded [26]. However, these algorithms are practically unreliable as fall is often confused with other activities like jumping. Additionally, a huge amount of soft falls are likely to be unidentified, due to their low threshold [6]. To enhance the accuracy limitation of the threshold algorithms, the literature proposed various machine learning-based solutions through classification algorithms like SVM, ANN, KNN, etc [1,23]. These algorithms are more efficient as they can globe a greater number of fall types, yet very dependent of the on-body placement. Thus, machine-learning algorithms have shown impressive practical results when placed in steady body location (near gravity point of the body) such as waist and chest-worn. Otherwise, they are less efficient especially when placed in extremities such as wrist, requiring further investigations to improve the performance in those cases, mainly because wrist-based solutions are the most comfortable from a user point of view and less associated to the stigma of using a medical device [12,18,19].

2.2   Dictionary Learning for Classification

Sparse Representation and Supervised Dictionary Learning Characteristics. DLA has received a lot of interest as a representation learning paradigm by achieving state-of-the-art performance in many practical fields in computer vision such as information retrieval, image restoration, and classification [5].

It has been observed that DLA intends to learn a dictionary directly from the training samples by generating the space where the given signal could be represented properly to provide improved processing and better results in fitted to the problem domain. In DLA models, given a set $\mathbf{X} = [\mathbf{x}_1,\dots,\mathbf{x}_m]$ of m samples, the objective is to generate a dictionary $\mathbf{D}$ which maps a high and sparse dimensional representation denoted $\mathbf{A}$ for each input sample. Generally, one can obtain this by solving an optimization problem defined by the following equation:

$$\min_{\mathbf{D},\mathbf{A}} \sum_{i=1}^{m} (\frac{1}{2}||\mathbf{x}_i - \mathbf{D}\mathbf{a}_i||_2^2 + \lambda_1||\mathbf{a}_i||_1), \tag{1}$$

where, λ_1 defines the regularization parameter that affects the number of nonzero coefficients.

To cover classification tasks, many techniques have been proposed in the literature [5]. The latter, exploit the label information in the learning of either the dictionary atoms, the coefficients of the sparse vector, or both. Based on [21], both extra restraint function $f_A(.)$ and $f_D(.)$ are added to Eq. (1) that satisfies:

$$\min_{\mathbf{D},\mathbf{A}} \{ \sum_{i=1}^{m} (\frac{1}{2}||\mathbf{x}_i - \mathbf{D}\mathbf{a}_i||_2^2 + \lambda_1||\mathbf{a}_i||_q) + \lambda_2 f_A(\mathbf{A}) + \lambda_3 f_D(\mathbf{D}) \}, \tag{2}$$

where, $f_A(.)$ could be a logistic function, a linear classifier, a label consistency term, a low-rank constraint, or the Fisher discrimination criterion. As for $f_D(.)$ is to force the incoherence of the dictionary for different classes. Hence, it is possible to jointly learn the dictionary and classification model, which attempt to optimize the learned dictionary for classification tasks [9]. λ_2 and λ_3 are two scalar parameter corresponding respectively to the associated function [5].

Assuming that SDL methods and sparse representation differ in the way they exploit class labels, we will detail three of the most popular SDL algorithms, namely, the SRC, FDDL, and LRSDL.

Sparse Representation-Based Classification (SRC). SRC was first proposed by Wright et al. in their work [28] with robust face recognition approach, and have accordingly proved its effectiveness for low to moderate amount of data based problems [5]. This approach aims to concatenate the training data from different classes into a single dictionary and uses class-specific residue for the recognition. Thus, the test samples are represented as a linear combination of just the training samples corresponding to the same class. Literally, no actual training is performed in his method, since the integrity of the training samples are used in the dictionary and the sparse representation is extracted and classified over the testing phase following two main stage process:

1. The SRC algorithm computes the sparse coefficient $\mathbf{a}$ of the test sample $\mathbf{x}_{test}$ via the *Lasso* equation as:

$$\min_{\mathbf{a}} \{ \frac{1}{2}||\mathbf{x}_{test} - \mathbf{D}\mathbf{a}||_2^2 + \lambda_1||\mathbf{a}||_1 \}, \tag{3}$$

Assuming that $\mathbf{D} = \mathbf{X}_{train}$.

2. Class label of each test sample is assigned while maintaining a minimum residual error of the classes according to:

$$Label(\mathbf{x}_{test}) = \min_i r_i(\mathbf{x}_{test}), \tag{4}$$

where, $r_i = ||\mathbf{x}_{test} - \mathbf{D}\sigma_i(\mathbf{a})||_2^2$, σ_i is the selective function of the coefficient vector associated to the class i.

Fisher Discrimination Dictionary Learning (FDDL). In [31], Yang et al. proposed an SDL method that learns class-specific structured dictionary while managing its discriminability through adding a Fisher criterion. Thus, the learned dictionary $\mathbf{D} = [\mathbf{D}_1, \mathbf{D}_2, .., \mathbf{D}_m]$, where $\mathbf{D}_i$ is a sub-dictionary corresponding to the class i, powerfully represents the inter-class similarity and the intra-class variance. To describe FDDL more formally, suppose $\mathbf{X} = [\mathbf{X}_1, \mathbf{X}_2, .., \mathbf{X}_c]$, such as the training samples are grouped according to the classes they belong and c is the total number of classes. The overall objective function of FDDL is written as shown by Eq. (5):

$$\min_{\mathbf{D},\mathbf{A}}\{r(\mathbf{X}, \mathbf{D}, \mathbf{A}) + \lambda_1 ||\mathbf{A}||_1 + \lambda_2 f(\mathbf{A})\}, \tag{5}$$

where, $\mathbf{A} = [\mathbf{A}_1, \mathbf{A}_2, .., \mathbf{A}_c]$ regroups the sparse representation of each training sample over $\mathbf{D}$; $r(\mathbf{X}, \mathbf{D}, \mathbf{A})$ is the Fisher fidelity term; $f(\mathbf{A})$ defines the discrimination constraint.

2.3   Low-Rank Shared Dictionary (LRSDL)

Vu et al. proposed an SDL framework in their works [24, 25], that aims to enhance the capability of capturing shared features of the FDDL approach. The LRSDL approach intent to simultaneously learn sub-dictionaries with discriminative and shared features of each class, as different classes often share common patterns. Accordingly, the main focus of the LRSDL is the shared part in which two intuitive constraints are added to the corresponding objective function. The first one is the low-rank structure constraint, that allows the shared dictionary to contain some discriminative features. As for the second, the sparse coefficients corresponding to the shared dictionary should be very similar.

3   Proposed Dictionary Learning Method

Considering that the wrist-worn devices are the most comfortable body location for the patient [18], they are yet very unstable for the IMU [32]. Since arms are usually very moving parts of the body, many hand movements, i.e clapping, rising, and releasing hands, may present similar motion patterns compared with fall movements. Thus, these movement similarities may present a bottleneck for the feature extraction task as it may become very specific to the collected data and the selected sensors.

To overcome this issue while bearing in mind the system reliability, we propose a fall detection approach based on the dictionary learning algorithms for classification. Therefore, different SDL classification algorithms will be evaluated and compared through their prediction performances with previous on-wrist solutions presented in the literature. The pipeline of the designed architecture is illustrated by Fig. 1. In this section, we will describe the main phases presented in the illustration, namely the preprocessing, the training, and the test phases.

3.1 Dataset

The data set has been collected throughout de Quadros et al. study [19]. In fact, the signal acquisition was done by the use of three main triaxial IMU sensors, i.e, accelerometer, gyroscope, and magnetometer which are embedded in the GY-80 IMU model device. To acquire and register data signals from the latter sensors, an Arduino Uno was integrated with the IMU device into a wrist-worn band at the non-dominant hand. The raw sensors data were obtained in a 100 Hz sampling rate and 4 g, 500 degrees/sec, and 0.88 Gs for the accelerometer, gyroscope, and magnetometer respectively.

In order to make the data set more generalized and accurate, twenty-two volunteers with different ages, heights, and weights were engaged in this experimental protocol. Each one performs two main event categories, namely, fall incidents and Activities of Daily Living (ADL). The recorded fall incident covers forward to fall, backward fall, right-side fall, left-side fall, fall after rotating the waist clockwise, and fall after rotating the waist counterclockwise. The ADL's performed activities enclose walking, clapping hands, moving an object, tying shoes and sitting on a chair. The average duration of the recorded activities is 9.2 s, assuming that each one starts with a resting arm (resting state) followed by a few steps before the activity's performance.

For the sake of removing any external influence that affects the accelerometer [6], the accelerometer data was preprocessed with a low pass filter with a window size of 40 and a subtraction of a fixed value equal to 1 g to eliminate the gravity-related information.

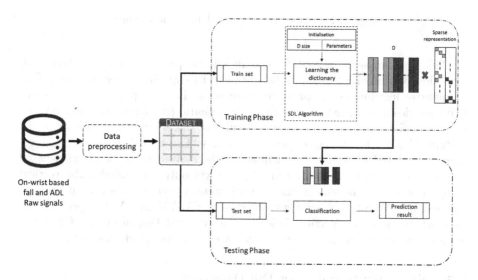

Fig. 1. Pipeline overview of the proposed SDL-based fall detection system.

3.2   Data Preprocessing

Most of the proposed wearable fall detection relies, mainly, on the data preprocessing phase, including feature extraction and feature selection, as it plays a
critical role in defining an accurate fall detector [14]. In this sense, one of the
faced challenges for this placement is extracting relevant features that better
describe raw data and discriminate ADL events from a fall event, especially for
overlapped and similar data. Finding significant attributes that better illustrate
the raw data has always been a challenge depending on the device's on-body
position. For instance, most on-wrist solution presented in the literature depends
mainly on accelerometer [4,11,20,34], while some others fuses it with other sensors like gyroscope [7,32,33], gyroscope and magnetometer [19], or heart rate
sensor [14].

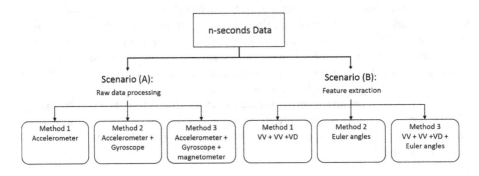

Fig. 2. Proposed scenarios for data preprocessing.

This work implements SDL for classification approaches in a wrist-based fall
detection system with the aim of benefiting of its capacity to generate more discriminative features using sparse representation. For this purpose, we consider
two scenarios as demonstrated in Fig. 2. In scenario (A), the system will process
a time window of raw data, where we will test the effect of each sensor in the
system efficiency by adding one sensor at a time. The second scenario (B) experiments extracted features, as we will adopt the movement decomposition-based
feature extraction method used in [19]. We will only acknowledge the vertical
component of the movement and the orientation decomposition as it reached
the best results in the latter work. We denote VA, VV, and VD respectively as
Vertical Acceleration, Vertical Velocity, and Vertical Displacement. The Euler
angles present the spacial orientation features, i.e. yaw, pitch, and roll.

3.3   Dictionary Learning for Fall Detection

As being a branch of Machine Learning, the classification based on SDL involves
two main phases, namely the training and the testing phases. In the training
phase, the goal of the SDL algorithm is to map the low dimensional training

data to a high and sparse dimensional representation using a learned dictionary $\mathbf{D}$, to make a more discriminated pattern and easier to be distinguished. In this paper, we consider three SDL algorithms, SRC, FDDL, and LRSDL, that we previously detailed in Sect. 2.2.

Considering the test phase, the testing sample can be classified by directly coding it over the obtained $\mathbf{D}$. Generally, the sparse code is then used as a feature descriptor of the data in order to calculate the reconstruction error associated to each class. The prediction is accorded to the class with the least error following the formula expressed by Eq. (4). However, the SDL performance is directly affected by the dictionary size. To abstract each SDL's higher performance we will inspect the impact of the Dictionary size into the system's accuracy.

4   Experimental Validation

4.1   Performance Metrics

This study is evaluated in terms of three common metrics, namely, Accuracy (AC), Sensitivity (SE), and Specificity (SP). AC represents the overall true detection, SE represents the ability to detect authentic falls among all detected falls, and SP represents the capacity to detect real ADL in all the detected ADL.

4.2   Experimental Configuration

In our experimental analysis, we assume that a 4-s time window is sufficient to extract a fall or an ADL event. We consider that the collected data set is subdivided such as 75% of the data (nearly 300 samples for each class) is for the training phase and 25% for the test phase. From our experiments, the SDL algorithms' hyper-parameters are set based on the best-achieved performances for our dataset using random training features. Thus, we initiate them as follows: SRC: $\lambda = 0.01$; FDDL: $\lambda_1 = \lambda_2 = 0.001$; LRSDL: $\lambda_1 = 0.001$, $\lambda_2 = 0.01$, $\eta = 0.02$. Throughout this study, the size of the dictionary $\mathbf{D}$ for the FDDL and the LRSDL algorithm will vary between 50 and 300 atoms per class depending on the experiment.

4.3   Experimental Result

In this study, we followed two main experimentation scheme to validate the high sensitivity and efficiency of our proposed method. Firstly, we fix the Dictionary size in order to assess the SDL classification performance behavior compared with each outline of both scenarios showcased in Fig. 2. Secondly, we evaluate the best performance of the previous experiment with multiple $\mathbf{D}$ sizes for the FDDL and LRSDL algorithms to exhibit for each the best-fitted size to our proposed system.

Table 1. Performance comparison for different methods of raw data scenario.

Algorithm	SRC			FDDL			LRSDL		
	AC	SE	SP	AC	SE	SP	AC	SE	SP
Acc	**99.8**	100	99.6	98.0	98.0	98.0	97.4	97.9	96.9
Acc, Gyr	**90.6**	90.6	90.6	**90.6**	93.8	87.5	90.1	93.8	86.5
Acc, Gyr, Mag	**97.4**	96.9	97.9	96.4	96.9	95.8	**97.4**	96.9	97.9

Table 2. Performance comparison for different methods of feature extraction scenario.

Algorithm	SRC			FDDL			LRSDL		
	AC	SE	SP	AC	SE	SP	AC	SE	SP
VA, VV, VD	**96.4**	97.9	94.8	95.9	99.0	92.7	95.8	99.0	92.7
Euler	**99.5**	99.0	100	98.4	100	96.9	98.4	100	96.88
(+Euler)	**96.9**	96.9	96.9	95.8	96.9	94.8	96.4	95.8	96.9

1st Experiment. The SRC algorithm generates a dictionary **D** with the size of the training samples, we set a **D** size of 300 atoms per class.

Table 1 and Table 2 exhibit respectively the performance of the tested SDL algorithms under Scenario (A) and Scenario (B). In Table 1, an impressive performance is achieved by the SRC algorithm using a single triaxial accelerometer raw data. Even though joining the gyroscope has significantly decreased efficiency, it has proved its convenience when fused with the magnetometer. Table 2 shows that the extracted spacial orientation angles present a better accuracy compared with it when fused with a vertical movement component. Overall, the SRC has reached the best accuracy of 99.8% compared to FDDL and LRSDL when processed with a raw data accelerometer.

2nd Experiment. In order to inspect the best performance of both SDL algorithms, i.e FDDL and LRSDL, we vary the **D** size in the range of $[50, \ldots, 300]$ atoms per class. As illustrated in Fig. 3, the change in SDL performance depends roughly on the patterns of the input set. Consequently, the LRSDL has reached the best accuracy of 99.5%, when processed with Euler angles an input data and **D** presents a total of 400 atoms.

Table 3. Comparison of performance for related on-wrist fall detectors.

	[34], 2014	[7], 2014	[14], 2016	[19], 2018	[11], 2018	[20], 2019	[32], 2019	[33], 2019	Our work
Accuracy	93.75	NA	92.9	99.0	95.47	98.1	98.36	99.86	**99.8**
Sensitivity	83.33	95.0	80.95	100	83.33	98.1	95.1	99.93	**100**
Specificity	95.4	96.7	98.35	97.9	95.96	98.1	100	99.8	**99.6**

We listed in Table 3 a full synthesis of performances, in terms of sensitivity, specificity, and accuracy of prior works related to the on-wrist fall detection system. Zheng et al. [33] achieved the best accuracy performance of 99.86% with the use of an accelerometer and gyroscope using the Convolution Neural Network (CNN) architecture, yet very close with the one accomplished with our proposed study using a single sensor adopting a simpler algorithm SRC. Moreover, our work reached the maximum sensitivity of 100% likewise the one obtained by de Quadros et al. [19] resulting in a maximum ability to distinguish real falls, thereafter a more reliable system.

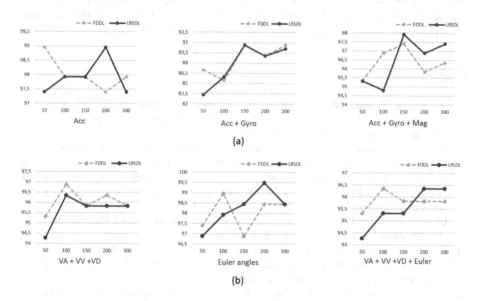

Fig. 3. Performance of the FDDL and LRSDL for different D size, (a) Scenario A, (b) Scenario B.

5   Conclusion

In this work, we introduced a new classification method, Dictionary Learning, for a wrist-based fall detection system. Thus, our contribution mainly lies in applying the Supervised Dictionary Learning approach into an on-wrist fall detection system as it has not been explored yet in literature. We explored three main SDL algorithms, namely SRC, FDDL, and LRSDL with different experiments in order to abstract the best performer and compares it to those reported in previous related work. The SRC has proved its efficiency reaching respectively 99.8%, 100%, and 96.6% of accuracy, sensitivity, and specificity. Indeed, our proposed method has proven the best capacity to classify real falls correctly and the higher accuracy with just one accelerometer mounted. This solution is energy efficient compared with the one presenting similar accuracy thanks to its simpler algorithm complexity compared with the CNN architecture.

Thorough experimentation will be conducted in future work, we expect an additional improvement of results even further. As being a popular representation based paradigm, we plan next to test the performance of the SDL on jointly learn a frame-like representation of further complex patterns like cepstral representations and classification parameters in order to enhance the system's reliability.

In our future related work, we will study a further advantage of the DLA benefits by testing its robustness in regards to noisy signals. For this proposal, we will be combining a Signal-to-Noise Ratio (SNR) to the raw signal and compare its performance behavior with traditional machine learning models.

References

1. Ansari, M., Mahmood, N., Nadeem, A., Mehmood, A., Rizwan, K.: Fall detection system for the elderly based on the classification of shimmer sensor prototype data. Healthc. Inform. Res. **23**, 147–158 (2017)
2. Aziz, O., Musngi, M., Park, E.J., Mori, G., Robinovitch, S.N.: A comparison of accuracy of fall detection algorithms (threshold-based vs. machine learning) using waist-mounted tri-axial accelerometer signals from a comprehensive set of falls and non-fall trials. Med. Biol. Eng. Comput. **55**(1), 45–55 (2016). https://doi.org/10. 1007/s11517-016-1504-y
3. Ceylan, R.: The effect of feature extraction based on dictionary learning on ECG signal classification. Int. J. Intell. Syst. Appl. Eng. **1**, 40–46 (2018)
4. Degen, T., Jaeckel, H., Rufer, M., Wyss, S.: SPEEDY: a fall detector in a wrist watch. In: Seventh IEEE International Symposium on Wearable Computers 2003, Proceedings, pp. 184–187, October 2003
5. Gangeh, M., Farahat, A., Ghodsi, A., Kamel, M.S.: Supervised dictionary learning and sparse representation-a review, February 2015
6. Genoud, D., Cuendet, V., Torrent, J.: Soft fall detection using machine learning in wearable devices. In: 2016 IEEE 30th International Conference on Advanced Information Networking and Applications (AINA), pp. 501–505 (2016)
7. Hsieh, S., Chen, C., Wu, S., Yue, T.: A wrist-worn fall detection system using accelerometers and gyroscopes. In: Proceedings of the 11th IEEE International Conference on Networking, Sensing and Control, pp. 518–523, April 2014
8. Igual, R., Medrano, C., Plaza, I.: A comparison of public datasets for acceleration-based fall detection. Med. Eng. Phys. **37**, 870–878 (2015)
9. Jiang, Z., Lin, Z., Davis, L.S.: Learning a discriminative dictionary for sparse coding via label consistent K-SVD, pp. 1697–1704, June 2011
10. Khel, M.A.B., Ali, M.: Technical analysis of fall detection techniques. In: 2019 2nd International Conference on Advancements in Computational Sciences (ICACS), pp. 1–8 (2019)
11. Khojasteh, S.B., Villar, J.R., Chira, C., González, V.M., De la Cal, E.: Improving fall detection using an on-wrist wearable accelerometer. Sensors **18**(5), 1350 (2018)
12. Krupitzer, C., Sztyler, T., Edinger, J., Breitbach, M., Stuckenschmidt, H., Becker, C.: Beyond position-awareness-extending a self-adaptive fall detection system. Pervasive Mob. Comput. **58**, 101026 (2019)

13. Mo, H., Luo, C., Jan, G.E.: EEG classification based on sparse representation. In: 2017 International Joint Conference on Neural Networks (IJCNN), pp. 59–62, May 2017

14. Nho, Y., Lim, J.G., Kim, D., Kwon, D.: User-adaptive fall detection for patients using wristband. In: 2016 IEEE/RSJ International Conference on Intelligent Robots and Systems (IROS), pp. 480–486, October 2016

15. Noury, N., et al.: Fall detection - principles and methods. In: 2007 29th Annual International Conference of the IEEE Engineering in Medicine and Biology Society, pp. 1663–1666, August 2007

16. World Health Organization: WHO Global Report on Falls Prevention in Older Age. NIH Publication, Bethesda (2008)

17. World Health Organization of Aging, U.N.I.: Global Health and Ageing. NIH Publication, Bethesda (2011)

18. Ozdemir, A.: An analysis on sensor locations of the human body for wearable fall detection devices: principles and practice. Sensors **16**, 1161 (2016)

19. de Quadros, T., Lazzaretti, A.E., Schneider, F.K.: A movement decomposition and machine learning-based fall detection system using wrist wearable device. IEEE Sens. J. **18**, 5082–5089 (2018)

20. Urresty Sanchez, J.A., Muñoz, D.M.: Fall detection using accelerometer on the user's wrist and artificial neural networks. In: Costa-Felix, R., Machado, J.C., Alvarenga, A.V. (eds.) XXVI Brazilian Congress on Biomedical Engineering. IP, vol. 70/1, pp. 641–647. Springer, Singapore (2019). https://doi.org/10.1007/978-981-13-2119-1_98

21. Suo, Y., Dao, M., Srinivas, U., Monga, V., Tran, T.D.: Structured dictionary learning for classification (2014)

22. Vallabh, P., Malekian, R.: Fall detection monitoring systems: a comprehensive review. J. Ambient Intell. Humaniz. Comput. **9**(6), 1809–1833 (2017). https://doi.org/10.1007/s12652-017-0592-3

23. Vallabh, P., Malekian, R., Ye, N., Capeska Bogatinoska, D.: Fall detection using machine learning algorithms, September 2016. https://doi.org/10.1109/SOFTCOM.2016.7772142

24. Vu, T.H., Monga, V.: Learning a low-rank shared dictionary for object classification, pp. 4428–4432, September 2016

25. Vu, T., Monga, V.: Fast low-rank shared dictionary learning for image classification. IEEE Trans. Image Process. **26**, 5160–5175 (2016)

26. Wang, F.T., Chan, H.L., Hsu, M.H., Lin, C.K., Chao, P.K., Chang, Y.J.: Threshold-based fall detection using a hybrid of tri-axial accelerometer and gyroscope. Physiol. Meas. **39**, 105002 (2018)

27. World Health Organization: ICD-11 for mortality and morbidity statistics (version 04/2019). http://icd.who.int/browse11/l-m/en#/id.who.int/icd/entity/134290789. Accessed 09 Nov 2019

28. Wright, J., Yang, A.Y., Ganesh, A., Sastry, S.S., Ma, Y.: Robust face recognition via sparse representation. IEEE Trans. Pattern Anal. Mach. Intell. **31**(2), 210–227 (2009)

29. Xu, T., Zhou, Y., Zhu, J.: New advances and challenges of fall detection systems: a survey. Appl. Sci. **8**, 418 (2018)

30. Xu, Y., Li, Z., Yang, J., Zhang, D.: A survey of dictionary learning algorithms for face recognition. IEEE Access **5**, 8502–8514 (2017)

31. Yang, M., Zhang, L., Feng, X., Zhang, D.: Fisher discrimination dictionary learning for sparse representation, pp. 543–550, November 2011

32. Zhang, H., Alrifaai, M., Zhou, K., Hu, H.: A novel fuzzy logic algorithm for accurate fall detection of smart wristband. Trans. Inst. Meas. Control **42**, 786–794 (2019). https://doi.org/10.1177/0142331219881578

33. Zheng, G., Zhang, H., Zhou, K., Hu, H.: Using machine learning techniques to optimize fall detection algorithms in smart wristband. In: 2019 25th International Conference on Automation and Computing (ICAC), pp. 1–6, September 2019

34. Zhou, C., et al.: A low-power, wireless, wrist-worn device for long time heart rate monitoring and fall detection. In: 2014 International Conference on Orange Technologies, pp. 33–36, September 2014

Combined Machine Learning and Semantic Modelling for Situation Awareness and Healthcare Decision Support

Amira Henaien[1](✉)(iD), Hadda Ben Elhadj[2](✉), and Lamia Chaari Fourati[2]

[1] King Khalid University, Abha, Kingdom of Saudi Arabia
aheniaen@kku.edu.sa
[2] Laboratory of Technology and Smart Systems (LT2S), LR16CRNS01, Digital Research Center of Sfax, Sfax, Tunisia
Hadda.Ibnelhadj@ESTI.rnu.tn, lamia.chaari@enis.rnu.tn

Abstract. The average of global life expectancy at birth was 72 years in 2016 [1], however, the global *healthy* life expectancy at birth was only 63.3 years in the same year, 2016 [2]. Living a long life is not any more as challenging as assuring active and associated life [25]. We propose in this paper an IoT based holistic remote health monitoring system for chronically ill and elderly patients. It supports smart clinical decision help and prediction. The patient heterogeneous vital signs and contexts gathered from wore and surrounding sensors are semantically simplified and modeled via a validated ontology composed by FOAF (Friend of a Friend), SSN (Semantic Sensors Network)/SOSA (Sensor, Observation, Sample and Actuator) and ICNP (International Classification Nursing Practices) ontologies. The reasoner engine is based on a scalable set of inference rules cohesively integrated with a ML (Machine Learning) algorithm to ensure predictive analytic and preventive personalized health services. Experimental results prove the efficiency of the proposed system.

Keywords: Active and assisted living · Ontologies · ML · Health monitoring · Preventive personalized health services

1 Introduction

Information revolution and wireless mobile technology growth have made a considerable contribution to the expansion and empowering of E-health services. In fact, smart remote and mobile healthcare applications are making an enormous shift in the health and social care workforce efficiency as well as patients' well-being. The main target of such applications is leveraging IoT, ML and Semantic Web technologies to ensure opportunities that enable people to be and do what they value throughout their lives despite illness. The headline goal of E-health is promoting elderly independence and sustaining cognitive and physical capability via multidisciplinary and user-friendly technology. [6] is one of the earliest

M. Jmaiel et al. (Eds.): ICOST 2020, LNCS 12157, pp. 197–209, 2020.
https://doi.org/10.1007/978-3-030-51517-1_16

studies that has highlighted the importance of the development of a powerful healthcare system. The study conclude that an integrated multidisciplinary infrastructure allowing interoperability and scalability is crucial. From that stage to nowadays, innovations in Information and Communication Technologies have radically changed healthcare services, created several manners for collecting and managing data effectively and provided several solutions to e-healthcare challenges [11]. The health sector is nowadays in its knowledge age: data, information, and knowledge are used in real time to support effective integration of prevention, treatment, and recovery services across healthcare services. Computers are not only used to provide health services but also to improve health itself through the management of the knowledge base and the automatic support of decisions. Therefore, healthcare applications are now exchanging and performing not only an enormous volume of data but also an important quantity of information and a large knowledge base Fig. 2. Thus, the semantic interoperability is becoming a crucial feature that is hard to imagine a healthcare or clinical system architecture without it [15]. The IoT ontologies appear as a suitable alternative to exchange knowledge per providing the required semantics to augment the data contained in the information model, and that to support service management operations [32]. Ontological models are becoming commonly used models in healthcare systems providing a flexible approach to integrate data and share meaning and able to assist inferring meaning [24,33]. Often ontology-based systems are using rule-based decision support system in order to assure an active and assisted monitors of patients [33]. However, a majority of those systems are not performing an automatic updates of the knowledge base. Hence, we propose in this paper a semantic-based healthcare monitoring system with seamless integration of many intricate existing knowledge, ontologies and ML technologies. It is a dynamic rule-based system, which infers information and medical recommendations based on the interaction of IoT input captured data, subjective and objective knowledge and a dynamic rule base updates by a ML algorithm based rules generator. The main contribution of this work is a combinations of semantic rules reasoning and ML reasoning to provide a new ubiquitous context awareness situation framework for healthcare monitoring systems. Those two highly modern and very powerful tools: semantic rules based reasoning and ML based reasoning, should provide complementary and supportive roles in the collection and processing of data, identification of clinical situations and automated decision making for supporting medical activities.

Paper Organization: The structure of this paper is as follows: Sect. 2 briefly introduces the related works and background. Section 3 outlines our methodology. Section 4 describes in details our proposed system. Section 5 presents context and situation awareness ontological modelling. Section 6 focuses on the knowledge and reasoning component engine. Section 7 evaluates the proposed system. Concluding remarks and perspectives are presented in Sect. 8.

2   Background and Related Works

Adoption of EHR[1] has increased almost 9 times since 2008 [12]. This huge amount of data circling in clinical information systems has formed new challenges as: semantic interoperability, standardization, automatic medical discovery, knowledge reuse, preventive personalized health services, etc. Aligned with this list of challenges, our work is based on three key concepts: Ontologies, Semantic Rules and ML; presented in the sequel:

Ontologies Based Semantic Healthcare Modelling: The conceptual model ontology is encouraging knowledge reuse and simplify problem solving in various fields. Healthcare applications are one of the systems that benefit from using ontologies: drug recommendations discovery [8], clinical support decisions [31], home personalized care to chronic patients [20], healthcare monitoring [33], etc. In Ontologies engineering, integration of ontologies is a useful process that consists on the combination of two or more standard validate ontologies from different disciplines in the aim to create a new multi-disciplinary ontology [23].

Semantic Rules Healthcare Reasoning: Semantic web and its technologies are providing efficient solutions in the information and system integration in any distributed information system environments including eHealth systems for which information integration and knowledge discovery are highly recommended [7]. The combination of Semantic Web Rules with Ontology are becoming a mature technology [14]. It use widespread in healthcare and clinical systems. A semantic rules are used in reasoning based approach for dieting and exercising management for diabetics [9]. OWL ontologies and SWRL are combined to integrate reasoning for decision support in alerting system [21].

ML Techniques for Healthcare: The high dimensional features and the availability of high quality software made the ML techniques widely used in all fields [4]. It refers to a set of algorithms used to extract useful knowledge or to learn by searching for interesting patterns in a large volumes of previously collected data. The use of ML algorithms in medicine is a hot research topic: disease progression [36,37], diagnosis prediction [5,19,35], and so on. However, those technologies are not mature enough and researchers are still working in the different possibilities and manners to integrate ML algorithms in healthcare systems [29]. One of the combination that appears successful and promising is the combination of ML techniques and ontologies [18,26,28].

3   Proposed Methodology

Our main goal is the integration of the ML Techniques in a combined ontology semantic modelling and semantic rules based reasoning healthcare framework for

---

[1] Electronic Health Records.

chronically ill and elderly patients. Our framework is build up in three keys stage: ontology for semantic modelling and representation, semantic rules for reasoning and machine learning techniques for learning; detailed in the following:

Semantic Representation and Ontological Modelling: The aim of this step is to find the best practices in semantic representation for holistic remote health monitoring system that is characterized by a large set of terminologies. Ontology modelling is one of the best choices, and as discussed before, the combination of different standard and valid ontologies is one of the recommended practice to build up an integrated multidisciplinary ontology.

Semantic Rules Reasoning Based Prediction: This step consists in the definition of primary knowledge base: a prediction based set of semantic rules. It exists two categories of rules: objectives and subjective. Objective knowledge contains medical rules defined in general medicine textbooks. Subjective knowledge is defined about the patient profile and context such as prior medical history, genetic diseases, personal lifestyle, etc.

Machine Learning Based Healthcare Reasoning: The outcome of this step is the best ML algorithm able to give the efficient support to the risk assessment system by providing the best and accurate new medical rules, detailed later in the Algorithm 1.

3.1 Information Life Cycle

In this subsection, we explain the information life cycle in our system: from a data, to an information, then finally a knowledge. The schema of Fig. 1 represents the different steps starting from the collection of data, passing by the different information uses in real-time ubiquitous healthcare monitoring, finally generating of knowledge. We have two main types of data sources: received data from smart devices and entered data by users (medical staff basically). All the data is collected and prepared to be analysed. The first step of the data preparation consists on highlighting the outliers and missing values: any abnormal value could be an alert. Then, in data selection, only contextual and health attributes are selected that are related to the environment or the health situation of a patient. un-selected data will be temporary removed from the data. Different transformations are required, viz, String to Nominal, Unify Date Format. The data mining step is our main contribution because it is not only processed using data mining techniques but also it is based on inferring meaning applied using a set of rules which consists on the subjective knowledge. In a first step, the inferring meaning is used in real-time by the system to determinate the current health situation of the patient, instantaneous alert, healthcare risk assessment and anomalous detection. Each applied rule is registered in the subjective knowledge. This knowledge base is able to grow in terms of number of rules. This

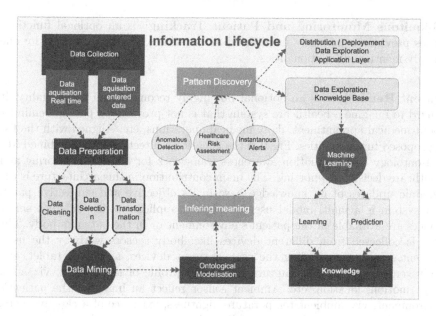

Fig. 1. The life cycle of information: data, information, knowledge

growth is assisted by a ML engine. The new learned rules will be dynamically and automatically provided to the objective knowledge. The system should allow the updates of the ML algorithm manually and the updates of the subjective knowledge automatically.

4 Detailed System Description

The main functionalities of the system are summarized in the following:

Electronic Health Record: is the basic functionality in our system since its the main way of the data collection. It is a systematic recording of contextual and environmental signs adequate to a multimodal, continuous and real-time user interactions.

Alerts for Instantaneous Rescue: is the main functionality of our system which consists in providing a help support system for elderly persons with chronic diseases. It awareness users about risks and emergency situations for an early and preventive health care.

Reasoning for Clinical Decision Support: is the major contribution of our system providing all necessary techniques that ensure predictive analytic and preventive personalized health services for a better clinical support system.

Ubiquitous Monitoring and Patient Tracking: is an optional function-alities provide an instantly monitoring and tracking that may be used for the already mentioned functionalities.

Patient Reminder: is an optional but highly recommended functionality. It is hard to imagine a healthcare system that is not providing a patient reminder about medical appointment, daily medical operations, etc. Aligned with the list of proposed functionalities, Fig. 2 is the generic architecture for a combined ML and ontology based situation awareness framework for clinical monitoring and healthcare decision supporting. The main contribution in this architecture is the dynamic updates of its knowledge base in its objective and subjective parts. Our system is a multi modal user interaction application, i.e. different smart devices are available in the patient's environment or in the patient's body. The data is collected from different devices like: body sensors worn by the user, ambient sensors surrounding the user or smart devices, as phone, tablet, etc. Body sensors are used to capture the health profile of the patient, viz, vital signs, motion, location, etc. Ambient sensor reflect an image of the patient's environment, viz, ambient temperature, lightness, existence of a caregiver, etc. Smart devices are basically used to allow the communication between the user and the system and between users, viz sending an alert to user about a patient's situation, monitoring a patient, etc. The architecture of the proposed system is layered and detailed in the following:

Active and Assisted Living Sensors Layer: contains all smart devices including the set of wearable and nearable sensors related directly to the user, his body and his environment. Its role is collecting data for a complete holis-tic health profile for each patient: health data, ambient data, location, motion, personal information, etc.

Networking and Communication Layer: a set of networking device allowing the communication between the different physical elements and the connection of those elements to the internet. **Ontological model based Data Layer:** it contains the set of the collected (current and previous) data and the ontology used in this system.

Multi-modal Interactions Application Layer: is the implementation of all the functionalities of the system providing all the services for ubiquitous and continuous medical monitoring and supporting the multi-modal interaction.

Semantic Rules Based Knowledge Layer: it is composed by the objective and the subjective knowledge. It is playing a fundamental role in our system since it contains the prediction component, i.e. prevention and detection of emergency cases and alert management.

ML Based Reasoning Layer: it is the layer performing the main contribution of our system which is the learning of new predictive and preventive medical or technical rules.

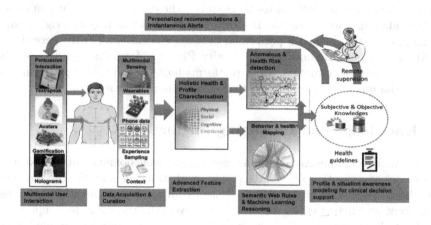

Fig. 2. Proposed architecture.

5   Context and Situation Awareness Modelling

Our ontology, Fig. 3, is composed from different valid and standard ontologies: ICNP, SSN/SOAS and FOAF. ICNP includes terminologies from the nurses' statements. And no doubt, nursing science has a significant contribution in healthcare services since nurses' statements are the early and important step in systematizing and prioritizing healthcare services [10]. In the following, we differentiate predefined classes and properties from ours by prefixing each one of them by the name of its original ontology. As One of the main classes in our application, we consider $icnp : Patient$ representing the patient, $icnp : VitalSign$ representing its vital signs and $icnp : Result$ representing all results of any diagnosis (measurement of vital sign, measurement from blood test, etc). The W3C, SSN is one of the popular ontologies in describing sensors. It describes the sensors capabilities, actuators observation and all the related concepts [3,27]. SOSA is the lightweight core of SSN that provide general purpose specification model for interaction between sensors. SOSA is an extension of the SSN ontology in semantic web community by providing a flexible framework and easy to use vocabulary [16]. The class $sosa : Observation$ represents any estimation or calculation of a value of a property of a feature of interest. FOAF declares the person profile in different fields such as health, finance, law, etc. [17]. It has four main categories of information: basic, personal, online accounts and personal documents and images. Those standard and valid ontologies are integrated together: merged, mapped and extended in order to provide the final ontology. In the following, some example of the mentioned operations: **Merging:** in our case this operation has poorly affect our ontology since, it is only linking class with the same name which are not many in the three ontologies. The outcome of this operation a set of equivalent axioms defining equivalence between components having the same name as the entity Person. **Mapping:** we are using FOAF to present the personal profile of users. However, the ontology ICNP has an entity called Individual presenting the health profile of a user as height, weight. So, a merging operation has been performed between the entities FOAF: person and ICNP: individual. **Extending:** The entity Platform from SSN gathers all the entities as sensors, actuators, other platforms hosted in the same platform. We created the property has Platform to link each user to his sensors.

6   Knowledge and Reasoning Engine

The knowledge component is defining: general medicine domain and context data using a set of semantic rules SWRL [14] in an abstract manner. So, the semantic rules based knowledge engine will be basically applying such medical knowledge to prevent and detect emergency cases. However, the reasoning techniques will be able to learn dynamically from the previous facts, i.e. previous applied rules, and provide new SWRL rules. The proposed system will allow a self-learning about new relations instances of cause & effect relations between data. Causes are the health situation represented by a set of signs and symptoms. Effects are the medical situation of a patient, viz, emergency case, disease, diagnosis, etc.

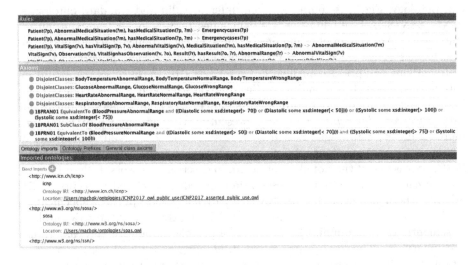

Fig. 3. Ontology overview

6.1   Semantic Rules Knowledge

Reasoner Engine (RE) applies the knowledge into the collected data in the order to determinate new facts about the current patient's situation in real-time way. RE will be in continuous search of causes which are any changes in the medical situation (signs and symptoms of each patient). Our preliminary set of SWRL is only containing a basic set of medical rules allowing to detect few emergency cases as: less blood pressure, height temperature, etc. To resume any abnormal value for a vital sign, we define the following SWRL[2] rule (GM): $icnp$: $VitalSign(?v) \land sosa$: $Observation(?o) \land VitalSignhasObservation(?v, ?o) \land icnp$: $Result(?r) \land sosa$: $hasResult(?o, ?r) \land AbnormalRange(?r) \rightarrow AbnormalVitalSign(?v)$. The rule is defining abnormal vital signs as the following: for a vital sign $?v$ and its observation $?o$, if the result $?r$ of the observation $?o$ is a value in an abnormal range, then $?v$ is an abnormal vital sign. $VitalSignhasObservation(?v, ?o)$ and $sosa$: $hasResult(?o, ?r)$ are expressing the relation between a vital sign and its observation and between an observation and its result. The class $AbnormalRange(?r)$ is representing abnormal ranges.

6.2   Learning and Prediction Reasoning

ML Engine (MLE) learns from previous patient's detected alarms to produce new reasoning rules in different steps from the Algorithm 1. The MLE is based on the Fast Decision Tree (FDT) Learning Algorithm [34]. Decision Tree (DT) Learning Algorithms are known because of their simplicity, comprehensibility, absence of parameters, and ability to handle mixed-type data. In addition, FDT is a well-known adapted version of DT that scales up well to large data sets with large number of attributes as a healthcare data set.

Algorithm 1. Compose Fast Decision Tree Learning Algorithm and Semantic rules reasoning based Healthcare System

---

Data: Medical Data set
Result: Medical Inference Rules
forall *patients* **do**
> Load data
> Apply preprocessing techniques
> Apply transformation techniques
> Classify per types of alarms using Fast Decision Tree Learner
> Learn new rules from generated tree

---

[2] We recommend [14] for further information about SWRL notation. The symbol ? is proceeding names of variables and $\land$ is the logical And.

7   Performance Evaluation and Results

In order to prove the feasibility of the proposed approach and to evaluate its performance, we have tested the general process previously proposed in Algorithm 1 to an electronic health recorded data set from [22,30]. This data is considered as preliminary data set. The different proposed steps have been realised with WEKA [13]. An example of new rule is the detection of a low level of SpO2-Oxygen Saturation- that is used to continuously monitor the oxygenation status of critically ill patients. Actually the SpO2 measurement provides: Pleth waveform (visual indication of patient's pulse), Oxygen saturation of arterial blood (SpO2) in percent, Pulse rate (derived from Pleth wave), Perfusion indicator (Perf)- numerical value for the pulsatile portion of the measured signal caused by arterial pulsation. Only a medical staff is able to read and to interpret such result, then to detect an emergency case. The result of Algorithm 1 applied to data from one patient allow the definition of the following new rule: Perf < 0.5 and AWV $<$ 3749.05 and AWF < 10.4 and NBP (Sys) < 105 is an emergency case with alarm labelled SpO2 LOW PERF, Fig. 4. Then, the different instances of non normal range of the following signs: Perf, AWV, AWF et NBP will be updated. For example, the following axioms will be defined (or update if it exists previously): **Axiom 1** $Perf AN$ $SubClassOf$ $Perf AbnoramlRange$ and **Axiom 2** $Perf AN$ $EquivalentTo$ $Perf AbnoramlRange$ and $somexsd : real[< 0.5]$. Then, the rule GM will be applicable to determinate a new alert.

Fig. 4. Example of Weka result

8   Conclusions

This paper presents a combined semantic rules reasoning and Fast Decision Tree Learner algorithm for a predictive, preventive and personalized medical framework. The main idea consists in a knowledge and reasoning engine able to apply SWRL medical rules on collected data to generate alerts and able to create new general medicine rules based in previous detected alerts. As a continuation of this work, we are aiming to develop a prototype of the proposed system and test it on a larger samples of data collected from an elderly population with chronic diseases.

References

1. World Health Organization. https://www.who.int/gho/mortality_burden_disease/life_tables/situation_trends/en/
2. World Health Organization. https://www.who.int/gho/mortality_burden_disease/life_tables/hale/en/
3. Alamri, A.: Ontology middleware for integration of IoT healthcare information systems in EHR systems. Computers **7**(4), 51 (2018). https://doi.org/10.3390/computers7040051
4. Baltrušaitis, T., Ahuja, C., Morency, L.P.: Multimodal machine learning: a survey and taxonomy. arXiv preprint arXiv:1705.09406 (2017)
5. Choi, E., et al.: Multi-layer representation learning for medical concepts. In: Proceedings of the 22nd ACM SIGKDD International Conference on Knowledge Discovery and Data Mining, pp. 1495–1504 (2016)
6. Detmer, D.E.: Building the national health information infrastructure for personal health, health care services, public health, and research. BMC Med. Inform. Decis. Mak. **3**(1), 1 (2003)
7. Dogdu, E.: Semantic web in ehealth, January 2009. https://doi.org/10.1145/1566445.1566542
8. Doulaverakis, C., Nikolaidis, G., Kleontas, A., Kompatsiaris, I.: GalenOWL: ontology-based drug recommendations discovery. Biomed. Semant. **3**, 1–9 (2012)
9. Faiz, I., Mukhtar, H., Qamar, A., Khan, S.: A semantic rules & reasoning based approach for diet and exercise management for diabetics, pp. 94–99, January 2015. https://doi.org/10.1109/ICET.2014.7021023
10. Félix, N.D.d.C., Ramos, N.d.M., Nascimento, M.N.R., Moreira, T.M.M., de Oliveira, C.J.: Nursing diagnoses from ICNP® for people with metabolic syndrome. Rev. Bras. Enferm. **71**(suppl 1), 467–474 (2018). https://doi.org/10.1590/0034-7167-2017-0125
11. Haluza, D., Jungwirth, D.: ICT and the future of healthcare: aspects of pervasive health monitoring. Inform. Health Soc. Care **43**(1), 1–11 (2018)
12. Henry, J., Pylypchuk, Y., Searcy, T., Patel, V.: Adoption of electronic health record systems among us non-federal acute care hospitals: 2008–2015. ONC Data Brief **35**, 1–9 (2016)
13. Holmes, G., Donkin, A., Witten, I.H.: WEKA: a machine learning workbench. In: Proceedings of ANZIIS 1994-Australian New Zealand Intelligent Information Systems Conference, pp. 357–361. IEEE (1994)
14. Horrocks, I., Patel-Schneider, P.F., Boley, H., Tabet, S., Grosof, B., Dean, M.: SWRL. https://www.w3.org/Submission/SWRL/
15. Iroju, O., Soriyan, A., Gambo, I., Olaleke, J.: Interoperability in healthcare: benefits, challenges and resolutions. Int. J. Innov. Appl. Stud. **3**(1), 262–270 (2013)
16. Janowicz, K., Haller, A., Cox, S.J.D., Le, D.: Web semantics : science, services and agents on the world wide web SOSA: a lightweight ontology for sensors, observations, samples, and actuators. Web Semant. Sci. Serv. Agents World Wide Web **56**, 1–10 (2019). https://doi.org/10.1016/j.websem.2018.06.003

17. Kalemi, E., Martiri, E.: FOAF-academic ontology. In: 2011 Third International Conference on Intelligent Networking and Collaborative Systems, pp. 440–445 (2011). https://doi.org/10.1109/INCoS.2011.94

18. Kassahun, Y., et al.: Automatic classification of epilepsy types using ontology-based and genetics-based machine learning. Artif. Intell. Med. **61**(2), 79–88 (2014). https://doi.org/10.1016/j.artmed.2014.03.001. http://www.sciencedirect.com/science/article/pii/S0933365714000207

19. Kourou, K., Exarchos, T.P., Exarchos, K.P., Karamouzis, M.V., Fotiadis, D.I.: Machine learning applications in cancer prognosis and prediction. Comput. Struct. Biotech. J. **13**, 8–17 (2015)

20. Lasierra, N., Alesanco, A., Guillén, S., García, J.: A three stage ontology-driven solution to provide personalized care to chronic patients at home. J. Biomed. Inform. **46**(3), 516–529 (2013). https://doi.org/10.1016/j.jbi.2013.03.006

21. Lezcano, L., Sicilia, M.A., Rodríguez-Solano, C.: Integrating reasoning and clinical archetypes using OWL ontologies and SWRL rules. J. Biomed. Inform. **44**(2), 343–353 (2011)

22. Liu, D., Görges, M., Jenkins, S.A.: University of Queensland vital signs dataset: development of an accessible repository of anesthesia patient monitoring data for research. Anesth. Analg. **114**, 584–589 (2012)

23. Liu, J., Li, Y., Tian, X., Sangaiah, A.K., Wang, J.: Towards semantic sensor data: an ontology approach. Sensors (Switzerland) **19**(5), 1–21 (2019). https://doi.org/10.3390/s19051193

24. Liyanage, H., Krause, P., de Lusignan, S.: Using ontologies to improve semantic interoperability in health data. BMJ Health Care Inform. **22**(2), 309–315 (2015). https://doi.org/10.14236/jhi.v22i2.159. https://informatics.bmj.com/content/22/2/309

25. Marcelino, I., Laza, R., Domingues, P., Gómez-Meire, S., Fdez-Riverola, F., Pereira, A.: Active and assisted living ecosystem for the elderly. Sensors **18**(4), 1246 (2018)

26. Martin, H., Tsymbal, A., Zillner, S.: Medical ontologies for machine learning and decision support. US Patent 7,899,764, 1 March 2011

27. Nachabe, L., Girod-genet, M., Hassan, B.E.: Unified data model for wireless sensor network. IEEE Sens. J. **15**(7), 3657–3667 (2015). https://doi.org/10.1109/JSEN.2015.2393951

28. Ongenae, F., et al.: A probabilistic ontology-based platform for self-learning context-aware healthcare applications. Expert Syst. Appl. **40**(18), 7629–7646 (2013). https://doi.org/10.1016/j.eswa.2013.07.038. http://www.sciencedirect.com/science/article/pii/S0957417413005174

29. Puri, C.A., Gomadam, K., Jain, P., Yeh, P.Z., Verma, K.: Multiple ontologies in healthcare information technology: motivations and recommendation for ontology mapping and alignment. In: ICBO (2011)

30. The University of Queensland: The University of Queensland vital signs dataset. http://dx.doi.org/102.100.100/6914/

31. Riaño, D., et al.: An ontology-based personalization of health-care knowledge to support clinical decisions for chronically ill patients. J. Biomed. Inform. **45**(3), 429–446 (2012). https://doi.org/10.1016/j.jbi.2011.12.008

32. Serrano, M., Barnaghi, P., Carrez, F., Cousin, P., Vermesan, O., Friess, P.: Internet of Things IoT semantic interoperability: research challenges, best practices, recommendations and next steps. European Research Cluster on the Internet of Things, Technical report, IERC (2015)

33. Sondes, T., Ben Elhadj, H., Chaari, L.: An ontology-based healthcare monitoring system in the internet of things. In: 2019 15th International Wireless Communications & Mobile Computing Conference (IWCMC), pp. 319–324. IEEE (2019)
34. Su, J., Zhang, H.: A fast decision tree learning algorithm. In: AAAI, vol. 6, pp. 500–505 (2006)
35. Suo, Q., et al.: A multi-task framework for monitoring health conditions via attention-based recurrent neural networks. In: AMIA Annual Symposium Proceedings, vol. 2017, p. 1665. American Medical Informatics Association (2017)
36. Wang, X., Sontag, D., Wang, F.: Unsupervised learning of disease progression models. In: Proceedings of the 20th ACM SIGKDD International Conference on Knowledge Discovery and Data Mining, KDD 2014, pp. 85–94. Association for Computing Machinery, New York (2014). https://doi.org/10.1145/2623330.2623754
37. Xiao, H., Gao, J., Vu, L., Turaga, D.S.: Learning temporal state of diabetes patients via combining behavioral and demographic data. In: Proceedings of the 23rd ACM SIGKDD International Conference on Knowledge Discovery and Data Mining, KDD 2017, pp. 2081–2089. Association for Computing Machinery, New York (2017). https://doi.org/10.1145/3097983.3098100

Improving Access and Mental Health for Youth Through Virtual Models of Care

Cheryl Forchuk[1,2(✉)], Sandra Fisman[3], Jeffrey P. Reiss[1,2],
Kerry Collins[4], Julie Eichstedt[4], Abraham Rudnick[5,6],
Wanrudee Isaranuwatchai[7], Jeffrey S. Hoch[8], Xianbin Wang[2],
Daniel Lizotte[2], Shona Macpherson[4], and Richard Booth[1,2]

[1] Lawson Health Research Institute, London, ON, Canada
cforchuk@uwo.ca
[2] Western University, London, ON, Canada
[3] St. Joseph's Health Care, London, ON, Canada
[4] London Health Sciences Centre, London, ON, Canada
[5] Department of Psychiatry and School of Occupational Therapy,
Dalhousie University Halifax, Halifax, NS, Canada
[6] Nova Scotia Operational Stress Injury Clinic, Nova Scotia Health Authority,
Halifax, NS, Canada
[7] St. Michael's Hospital, Toronto, ON, Canada
[8] Division of Health Policy and Management, Department of Public Health
Sciences, University of California Davis, Davis, CA, USA

Abstract. The overall objective of this research is to evaluate the use of a mobile health smartphone application (app) to improve the mental health of youth between the ages of 14–25 years, with symptoms of anxiety/depression. This project includes 115 youth who are accessing outpatient mental health services at one of three hospitals and two community agencies. The youth and care providers are using eHealth technology to enhance care. The technology uses mobile questionnaires to help promote self-assessment and track changes to support the plan of care. The technology also allows secure virtual treatment visits that youth can participate in through mobile devices. This longitudinal study uses participatory action research with mixed methods. The majority of participants identified themselves as Caucasian (66.9%). Expectedly, the demographics revealed that Anxiety Disorders and Mood Disorders were highly prevalent within the sample (71.9% and 67.5% respectively). Findings from the qualitative summary established that both staff and youth found the software and platform beneficial.

Keywords: Smart technology · Youth · Mental health · eHealth

1 Introduction

In Canada, the total cost of treatment, care and support services for mental health problems exceeds 42.3 billion Canadian dollars per year [1], with mental health services for young people being the second highest youth healthcare expenditure after injuries [2]. Although 70% of mental health problems develop during childhood and adolescence [3], only a quarter of the 10–20% of Canadian youth affected by mental

M. Jmaiel et al. (Eds.): ICOST 2020, LNCS 12157, pp. 210–220, 2020.
https://doi.org/10.1007/978-3-030-51517-1_17

illness will receive mental health services [4]. Suicide is the second leading cause of death among Canadian youth, accounting for 24% of the deaths among individuals aged 15–24 [4]. Research on the integrated use of information technologies has shown strong improvements in the accessibility, quality, and efficiency of health and mental healthcare services [5]. Mobile technologies, in particular, appear to be a promising avenue due to the ubiquitous and portable nature of mobile devices. Smart phones have been successfully used to complement the treatment of a wide range of illnesses such as schizophrenia [6], bipolar disorder [7], and social phobia [8].

This ongoing study is integrating a mobile technology solution into routine care for youth who have symptoms of anxiety and depression. This technology is expected to: 1) promote healthcare outcomes, community inclusion and quality of life; and 2) reduce healthcare system costs by preventing hospitalization and reducing the need for out-patient visits. This report focuses on baseline data and the initial set of focus group data with youth and their care providers.

2 Materials and Methods

Study Design
This participatory action research project utilized a pre-post, mixed methods design. This paper reports on the baseline data from interviews and the initial focus groups after the youth had been using the application for less than 3 months.

Semi-structured interviews are being conducted at baseline, 6, and 12 months respectively. Focus groups will be held with youth and separate groups with care providers. A standardized evaluation framework will be instituted to facilitate systematic effectiveness, economic, ethical, and policy analyses [9]. The primary outcome measure for effectiveness is the Community Integration Questionnaire – Revised.

Participants
This two-year project will recruit 125 youth participants and have recruited 115 youth (ages 14–25) from the caseloads of 46 mental healthcare providers in London and Woodstock, Ontario, Canada who are receiving hospital-based or community agency-based outpatient care.

Additional inclusion criteria for participants to participate in the study include:

1. Must be on a caseload of a participating staff or care provider.
2. Able to understand English to the degree necessary to participate.
3. Have symptoms of anxiety or depression.
4. Youth must be 14–25 years old.

Intervention
The study, called Youth Telemedicine and Patient-Reported Outcome Measurement (TELEPROM-Y), allows participants synchronous and asynchronous communication with their staff/care provider team through the Collaborative Health Record (CHR). The CHR integrates the workflow of the full spectrum of healthcare providers, while also having embedded patient engagement functionality. These functionalities include the ability to: book appointments online; track quality of health and health outcome scores using mobile devices; access tailored educational content pertaining to their mental health;

and engage in both synchronous (e.g. video-conferencing) and asynchronous (e.g. secure messaging) virtual visits with their healthcare providers. Youth participants used a smartphone application (app) to connect to the CHR. The intervention is designed to facilitate better care and engagement between the patient and their care team.

Collaborative Health Record (CHR)

TELEPROM-Y app

Measures

Measures included a demographic questionnaire, the Community Integration Questionnaire [10], Lehman's Quality of Life [11], EQ-5D, health and social services utilization, and Likert scales assessing perception of technology, a researcher-developed questionnaire that inquires about participants' attitudes and opinions of the smartphone provided, provided data plan, and the CHR. Common qualitative items included feedback from participants on what they do and do not like about the technology, as well as suggestions for improvement on ethical principles such as autonomy, privacy and beneficence. A thematic analysis [12] using an ethnographic [13] method of analysis will be used to observe the broader social and cultural contexts surrounding individual experiences as well as the impact on staff/care providers and how the intervention influenced their practice.

3   Results

Data Analysis

At present, a total of 115 participants have been recruited into the study (see Table 1). There was a wide range of ages among the participants on enrollment from 14 to 25. The majority of participants identified themselves as Caucasian (66.9%) as shown in Table 1. Expectedly, the demographics revealed that Anxiety Disorders and Mood Disorders were highly prevalent within the sample (71.9% and 67.5% respectively). Of this sub-population of the sample who reported prior psychiatric admissions, the mean number of days since their most recent hospitalization was 68. The Perception of Smart Technology found that a lot of the youth participants were not using the CHR, nor had they even downloaded it. The individuals who had used it found that it improved their healthcare. See Figs. 1 and 2 (Table 2).

Table 1. Demographics (N = 115)

Age (mean)	19.57 yrs
Sex	
Female	63 (55.3%)
Male	51 (44.7%)
Other	1 (0.9%)
Ethnicity	
Caucasian	77 (66.9%)
Indigenous	12 (10.4%)
Black	6 (5.2%)
Asian	2 (1.7%)
Latin American	2 (1.7%)
Arab	1 (0.8%)
Other	5 (4.3%)
Missing	6 (5.2%)
Psychiatric diagnosis	
Anxiety disorder	82 (71.9%)
Mood disorder	77 (67.5%)
Disorder of childhood/adolescence	42 (36.8%)
Personality disorder	17 (14.9%)
Psychotic disorder	14 (12.3%)
Substance-related disorder	13 (11.4%)
Developmental handicap	7 (6.1%)
Other	24 (21.0%)
Previous psychiatric hospitalization?	
Yes	71 (62.3%)
No	43 (37.7%)
Missing	1 (0.9%)
Age at first psychiatric hospitalization (mean) (n = 71)	15
Estimated total number of psychiatric hospitalizations (mean) (n = 70)	5.9

Table 2. Community Integration (N = 115)

Approximately how many times a month do you usually visit friends or relatives?	
Never	14 (12.3%)
1–4 times	50 (43.9%)
5 or more	50 (43.9%)
Missing	1 (0.9%)
When you participate in leisure activities do you usually do this alone or with others?	
Mostly alone	25 (21.9%)
Mostly with friends who have mental health challenges	22 (19.3%)
Mostly with family members	11 (9.6%)
Mostly with friends who do not have mental health challenges	18 (15.8%)
With a combination of family and friends	38 (33.3%)
Missing	1 (0.9%)
How often do you travel outside the home?	
Almost every day	85 (74.6%)
Almost every week	25 (21.9%)
Seldom/never (less than once per week)	4 (3.5%)
Missing	1 (0.9%)
How often do you write to people for social contact using the Internet (e.g., Facebook)?	
Every day/most days	83 (72.2%)
Almost every week	21 (18.3%)
Seldom/never	11 (9.6%)
How often do you make social contact with people by talking or text messaging using your phone?	
Every day/most days	80 (70.2%)
Almost every week	14 (12.3%)
Seldom/never	20 (17.5%)
Missing	1 (0.9%)

Initial Focus Groups

A staff focus group and 2 youth focus groups have been completed prior to 3 months of implementation.

Youth described the advantages of both the app as well as having a phone. For the application itself, youth identified increased communication with their care provider, primarily through the messaging function. They also appreciated having the availability of information on phone including safety plan, the ability to set up appointments and, reminders related to wellness plan, as well as medication prompts. They enjoyed using

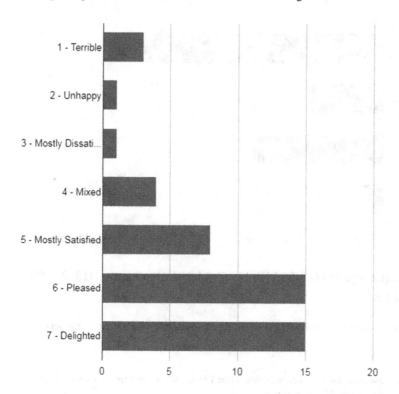

Counts/frequency: 1 - Terrible (3, 6.4%), 2 - Unhappy (1, 2.1%), 3 - Mostly Dissatisfied (1, 2.1%), 4 - Mixed (4, 8.5%), 5 - Mostly Satisfied (8, 17.0%), 6 - Pleased (15, 31.9%), 7 - Delighted (15, 31.9%)

Fig. 1. How do you feel about connecting with your care provider using your smartphone?

a paperless format for things such as completing forms on-line that were sent by the care provider. Examples of comments include:

I liked doing the little survey thing. Cause like when I'm bored and or like on a bus or something and I think, need to stop focusing on people, like, probably not staring at me but staring at me. I'll go on it. It gives me something to do so, and like it's helpful to so. I'll do like the surveys and questionnaires that pop-up ...

Well I mean just yesterday, I was able talk to Dr.(Name), who scheduled an a, an appointment for Friday, which I found really helpful because I wouldn't know how to contact her otherwise

The youth also described areas for improvement. They described that they initially had to take time to figure out the functions. There were several complaints about the cumbersome log-in process. Although they identified that they understood the log-in privacy concerns they thought it could still be streamlined. Some examples of quotes include:

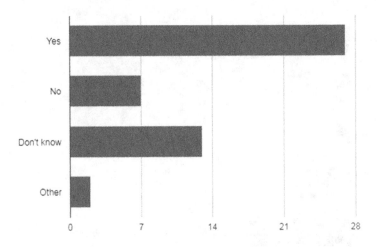

Counts/frequency: Yes (27, 55.1%), No (7, 14.3%), Don't know (13, 26.5%),
Other (2, 4.1%)

Fig. 2. Has the use of the Smartphone and CHR for personal health information improved your healthcare?

> *At first it was confusing, but then figured it out. I don't know, like I don't know exactly how it's confusing but like, it was like, it, it was new, ...*
> *Yeah randomly it signed me out the other day like it was signed in for like a good few weeks now and I was like thank you. And then it just randomly signed out and I was like damn. I remember my stuff but it's just annoying how you would put it in every single time but like I know that's for like confidentiality and like some people can't go on it. But, kinda sucks sometimes.*

The other major theme related to the importance of having a phone. Many of the youth in the study were experiencing poverty and twenty (17.5%) reported being homeless. The phones themselves helped youth feel comfortable and connected to other people. They reported the advantage of having a phone at all. Some examples of quotes include:

> *When I didn't have a phone like I just hate going places and not knowing where I'm going, or like I don't know, my anxiety's really bad.*
> *Then, the phones helped me to not only help myself, but to help others in like emergent situations... which I had to do a couple weeks ago and had I not gone to the study, like I wouldn't have been able to help them so it's helped in a lot of ways.*

Staff identified similar issues using the app in particular the ability to securely message their clients frequently. Specifically, staff identified the advantages were the ability to send questionnaires and to set appointments using the app. They discussed that sometimes youth felt more comfortable to first raise uncomfortable topics by phone/messaging and this resulted in strengthening the relationship between the youth and care provider and empowering the youth. Staff supporters also identified the importance of their clients having a phone at all.

Some examples of quotes include:

Yeah I use messaging, especially one time um one of my youth didn't have any minutes on their phone so we actually were a couple times messaging through the site

I think a good one for me is the mood Qnaire and the medication one. Um, because a lot of my youth, their mood fluctuates either in a single day – when I see them in the morning they could be doing amazing and then by the afternoon they're just doing horrible. So, I can send them one of those and then kind of see like maybe what a trend is and figure out the trend and then that way I can better support them as well

So that they do make it to their appointments on time, and at their like right day. I'm able to text them ahead of time to remind them

So, they don't want to like give away things in person like if its ... going to cause them to cry. It ... allows them to be more vulnerable

If anything it's increased the relationships and made them like stronger and better

For improvements they noted the app had a medical look to it that was not inviting to youth:

It does, like I feel like if I'm a 23-year-old and I'm just looking and it's this nice bright blue and white, but...it's just reminds me of a doctor's office and a lot of our youth may be triggered by doctor's offices, or have had really bad experiences...

They also noted that they do not spend much time on their computer so they really need a phone app themselves for the provider version.

4   Discussion

The demographic findings from the baseline interviews were characterized by a wide age range (14–25 years) with a comorbidity of psychiatric illnesses. There were 62.3% of participants who stated that they had been admitted to a hospital for psychiatric reason. When asked the estimate total number of psychiatric admissions, the average number of hospitalizations among youth who did report a hospitalization was 5.9 times.

With regards to community integration the sample appeared to be socially isolated as only 43.9% visiting friends or relatives at least weekly. The majority of the sample used social media on most days.

Based on the preliminary findings, we report that the use of smart technology was successfully deployed to a range of youth with symptoms of depression or anxiety. Both staff and youth identified strengths of both having the application as well as having a phone. The ability to communicate more easily was noted as a particular strength that has the potential to improve access to care and support the therapeutic relationship. As previously noted in the literature, smartphones have been found to be successful in assisting individuals with bipolar disorder [6], and social phobia [7]. It is anticipated that the TELEPROM-Y project will be able to provide greater assistance to individuals with mental illness through enhanced access to resources and supports, as well as further opportunities for communication with care providers. Moreover, the use of smartphones may represent a more convenient approach to mental healthcare as opposed to in-person appointments or printed resources (i.e. brochures, information sheets) that are easily lost or damaged. As described in the preliminary focus groups of this study, some individuals may not wish to visit a healthcare provider's office due to previous negative experiences. Some participants voiced that they like receiving care from the comfort of their own environment using the CHR app. This can also negate any potential missed appointments or concerns going unchecked, therefore providing early intervention and prevention.

From the perspective of care providers, the CHR also allows for greater monitoring of clients for early intervention and prevention. By using the app to complete the questionnaires in real time the care providers can be alerted to any potential mental healthcare crises that may have otherwise been unreported or unacknowledged. This approach could allow mental healthcare providers to see and communicate with more individuals in one day. By improving this connectivity with care providers, participants in this study can overcome barriers to care such as lack of money or transportation to attend appointments, and difficulty accessing much-needed services. In Canada alone, 64% of street-involved youth have reported difficulty accessing services [14].

A challenge for this project was encouraging hospital health care providers to adopt this technological approach. Although a number of hospital care providers embraced the technology and efficiency of the software available, others were skeptical. Due to the personal nature of the data being collected, some were concerned about the participants' privacy. Through the CHR is fully compliant with jurisdictional standards of practice, professional standards and guidelines, some care providers still did not want to participate in the study, so our team recruited from community agencies.

Another unanticipated expense was the amount of smartphones and data plans needed. In our proposal we anticipated purchasing 40 smartphones and 40 data plans but since a lot of the youth participants are living in poverty and/or homeless, an additional 55 had to be provided with a smartphone and 73 with a data plan to participate.

This study was limited by not being controlled other than by the pre/post-intervention design; future research could benefit from a comparison with a similar cohort of participants who do not receive the intervention during the study period, perhaps as part of a waiting list that could later receive the intervention.

5   Conclusion

The implications of this study could be far-reaching. This intervention may provide a more efficient approach that enhances connectivity with care services. Further, this intervention could represent a more efficient approach to mental healthcare by providing participants with greater opportunities to seek additional support and resources. We further anticipate that these extra supports will result in greater community integration among participants, which in turn could improve quality of life.

Acknowledgments. We would like to acknowledge St. Joseph's Health Care, the London Health Sciences, Woodstock General Hospital, Youth Opportunities Unlimited, WAYS Mental Health Support for facilitating the research environment. We would like to thank the participants and staff/care providers for their voluntary participation. In addition, we appreciate the commitment of the research assistants for data collection and auditing to make sure the quality of research is assured. Finally, we would also like to acknowledge the granting agency Ontario Centre for Excellence for making the funding available.

Conflicts of Interest. The authors declare no conflict of interest.

Reference

1. Mental Health Commission of Canada: Making the Case for Investing in Mental Health in Canada (2013). http://www.mentalhealthcommission.ca/English/node/5020
2. Mental Health Commission of Canada: Strengthening the Case for Investing in Canada's Mental Health System: Economic Considerations. Mental Health Commission of Canad (2017)
3. Gill, P.J., Saunders, N., Gandhi, S., et al.: Emergency department as a first contact for mental health problems in children and youth. J. Am. Acad. Child Adolesc. Psychiatry. **56**(6), 475–482 (2017). e4pmid:28545752
4. Canadian Mental Health Association: Fast Facts about Mental Illness (2016). http://www.cmha.ca/media/fast-facts-aboutmental-illness/#.VsosVjbSl3g
5. E-Mental Health in Canada: Transforming the Mental Health, January 2014. https://www.researchgate.net/publication/275210722_E-Mental_Health_in_Canada_Transforming_the_Mental_Health_System_Using_Technology
6. Ben-Zeev, D., Kaiser, S.M., Brenner, C.J., Begale, M., Duffecy, J., Mohr, D.C.: Development and usability testing of FOCUS: a smartphone system for self-management of schizophrenia. Psychiatric Rehabil. J. **36**(4), 289–296 (2013). https://doi.org/10.1037/prj0000019
7. Nicholas, J., Larsen, M.E., Proudfoot, J., Christensen, H.: Mobile apps for bipolar disorder: a systematic review of features and content quality. J. Med. Internet Res. **17**(8), e198 (2015). https://doi.org/10.2196/jmir.4581
8. Dagöö, J., et al.: Cognitive behavior therapy versus interpersonal psychotherapy for social anxiety disorder delivered via smartphone and computer: a randomized controlled trial. J. Anxiety Disord. **28**, 410–417 (2014). https://doi.org/10.1016/j.janxdis.02.003
9. Forchuk, C., Reiss, J.P., O'Regan, T., Ethridge, P., Donelle, L., Rudnick, A.: Client perceptions of the mental health engagement network: a qualitative analysis of an electronic personal health record. BMC Psychiatry **15**, 250 (2015). https://doi.org/10.1186/s12888-015-0614-7
10. Wilier, B., Ottenbacher, K.J., Coad, M.L.: The community integration questionnaire a comparative examination. Am. J. Phys. Med. Rehabil. **73**(2), 103–111 (1994). https://doi.org/10.1097/00002060-199404000-00006
11. Lehman, A.: A quality of life interview for the chronically mentally ill. Eval. Program Plann. **111**, 51–62 (1988). https://doi.org/10.1016/0149-7189(88)90033-X
12. Alhojailan, M.I.: Thematic analysis: a critical review of its process and evaluation. In: WEI International European Academic Conference, pp. 8–21 (2012). https://www.westeastinstitute.com/wp-content/uploads/2012/10/ZG12-191-Mohammed-Ibrahim-Alhojailan-Full-Paper.pdf

13. Leininger, M.M.: Ethnography and ethnonursing: models and modes of qualitative data analysis. In: Leininger, M.M. (ed.) Qualitative Research Methods in Nursing, pp. 33–71. Grune and Stratton, Orlando (1987). https://doi.org/10.1177/160940691201100306. https://www.researchgate.net/publication/277198481_Ethnonursing_A_Qualitative_Research_Method_for_Studying_Culturally_Competent_Care_Across_Disciplines
14. Barker, B., Kerr, T., Nguyen, P., Wood, E., DeBeck, K.: Barriers to Health & Social Services for Street-Involved Youth in a Canadian Setting. J. Public Health Policy **36**(3), 350–363 (2015). https://doi.org/10.1057/jphp.2015.8. https://www.ncbi.nlm.nih.gov/pmc/articles/PMC4515178/

Short Contributions: IoT and AI Solutions for E-Health

Study of Middleware for Internet of Healthcare Things and Their Applications

Ghofrane Fersi[1,2(✉)] iD

[1] Laboratory of Development and Control of Distributed Applications (ReDCAD),
University of Sfax, Sfax, Tunisia
ghofrane.fersi@redcad.org
[2] Higher Institute of Applied Sciences and Technology of Sousse (ISSAT),
University of Sousse, Sousse, Tunisia

Abstract. The rapid proliferation and miniaturization of the wireless and embedded devices has led to the invasion of the Internet of Things in many domains and has reached the healthcare sector to form what is called the Internet of Healthcare Things (IoHT). The growing number of the applications in the Internet of Healthcare Things as well as the overwhelming number of heterogeneous medical devices that should interact in this network has put the researchers and developers in front of lot of challenges: How to facilitate the implementation of the various healthcare applications? And how to ease the integration of new devices and make their interoperation a transparent task for the developers? To fulfill these requirements, lot of middleware have been proposed. In this paper we provide a complete study on the existing middleware for IoHT and specify their applications, we propose a taxonomy for them and we present their main advantages and drawbacks.

Keywords: Middleware · Healthcare · Internet of Healthcare Things

1 Introduction

The interest to the healthcare digitalization is growing during these last years due to its multiple benefits [1]. Effectively, there is a growing need to monitor the patients behavior and/or status and notify the doctors and the relatives of any danger according the patient's health. Such tight monitoring cannot be ensured by nurses or caregivers. Internet of Things (IoT) represents here a suitable and efficient solution for this [2]. Effectively, IoT is made up of tiny devices that can easily communicate and cooperate together to achieve a common task. This is exactly what is needed in healthcare: tiny devices that might be portable (off the body), wearable (on the body) or implantable (in the body), track the patient's status. The application of IoT in the healthcare is called Internet of Healthcare Things. This new concept has certainly improved the healthcare services and increased its efficiency. However, it is facing lot of challenges. Effectively,

© The Author(s) 2020
M. Jmaiel et al. (Eds.): ICOST 2020, LNCS 12157, pp. 223–231, 2020.
https://doi.org/10.1007/978-3-030-51517-1_18

healthcare applications are compelled to deal with medical devices having different protocols, various capabilities and working with different standards. These devices are also mobile and prone to failure. So it is important to conceive a layer between the physical devices and the application layer that hides all these diversities and deals with these challenges transparently to the end devices. This layer is called middleware [15]. We study in this paper the various middleware that have been proposed for IoHT and discuss them.

Our paper is organized as follows: We present in the second section a study of the existing middleware for IoHT. In the third section, we discuss the proposed solutions. And finally, section four concludes the paper.

2   Existing Middleware for IoHT and Their Corresponding Applications

We present in this section the most important middleware that have been proposed during these last years for the IoHT. We propose to classify them according to their main technical directives.

2.1   Fog-Based Middleware

Fog computing is considered by many researches as a middleware between the IoT and the cloud computing. This intermediate layer [3] reduces drastically the latency and affords the required processing and storage needs to the healthcare IoT devices. Effectively, many healthcare situations require a timely reaction. A IoT security middleware for use between IoT, fog and cloud computing, has been proposed in [4]. The main aim of this middleware is to ensure security and better network performance during churns. 'Session resumption' algorithm has been used by the authors to help a recently disconnected node to regain its encrypted session. This middleware can be applied in rural healthcare and public safety applications. In [5], fog nodes that are placed near to the patient's location will host a privacy middleware that ensures the user's privacy. In these nodes, data are stocked in clear and are accessed rapidly. Authors in [6] argue that using fog-based middleware in healthcare ensures the agregation of data that are generated from the patients with ensuring their privacy and confidentiality. Hence, this will lighten the burden of security processing in IoT healthcare devices.

2.2   Publish/Subscribe-Based Middleware

The multiplicity of events in the healthcare domain favors the use of Publish/Subscribe middleware due to their ability to deliver asynchronously multiple events from their sources to their subscribers. In [7], an IoT middleware has been proposed to help people with special needs. In this middleware, there is only one powerful component (NCeH) that will be deployed to every node that belongs to the network, in order to have a uniform configuration. This component is made up of various modules that ensure the communication between it and the other nodes and also to enable it to self-configure itself based on remote commands, and to analyze the received data so that the appropriate decision can be taken.

The proposed middleware [8] is used to classify the patients movements and count their steps number. The required materials are 2 sensors with triaxial accelerometer that should be placed on the knee and on belt, and a PDA or a smart phone to acquire the collected data by the sensors and process the classification. VIRTUS uses XMPP to know if the message is delivered to the destination or not. Also, the use of XMPP allows to verify if the destination is not connected when the message is received or not. This middleware is adaptable to modules composition changes without the need to restart the system.

2.3 Web of Things-Based Middleware

Authors in [20] and [10] argue that Web of Thing-based middleware are suitable to ensure interoperability since all the devices can be abstracted as a web resource.The ECOHelath middleware proposed in [10], connects doctors and patients to ease the health monitoring system and offers more accurate patients diagnosis. This middleware is based on the Web of Things (WoT) paradigm in which the physical devices are digitalized to ensure the efficient use of their data in different applications. In this middleware, there are body sensors that send their related data through a web interface that is provided by a Visualization and Management module. This interface helps doctors to track their patients' status. All the medical data are stored by the storage module in a relational database with the possible support of cloud computing. The proposed middleware has been applied to monitor the patients' heartbeats and blood pressure. ECG sensors are used to measure the heartbeats and discover heart pathologies. Blood pressure oscillometer sensor measures the arterial pressure. μWoTOP (micro Web of Things Open Platform) [11] has the ability to integrate heterogeneous biometric sensors. The data collection and notifications transmission are ensured by gateways. This middleware relies on Web technologies such as Html, REST. Its web of things strategy offered it the ability to be suitable at the same time for many healthcare applications like: Fall detection for elderlies, faint detection, abnormal behavior detection and freezing detector for Parkinson patients.

The main aim of the Sphere [12] middleware is to offer a flexible platform to integrate different sensors types and ensure their cooperation to achieve a given objective such as fall detection, Activity of Daily Living (ADL) recognition, and behavior anomaly detection.

2.4 SOA Based Middleware

SOA-based middleware rely mainly on services that offer a public functionnality through an interface while hiding their internal details. The main advantage of these middleware is their ability to reuse multiple devices with ensuring their communication as providers and requestors independently from any underlying architecture. Linksmart [14] is a SOA-based middleware that has proved its ability to interoperate with various devices. This middleware is widely used in healthcare to monitor patients. The Smart Homes for All (SM4All) middleware framework [13] has been proposed to help people with special needs in their homes. This middleware integrates multiple protocols such as UPnP into the OSGi framework and is able to interoperate with devices employing Zigbee, Bluetooth. This allows heterogeneous devices to connect dynamically and interact with each other in person-centric surrounding.

The main objective of Uranus middleware [16] is to afford Ambient Assisted Living (AAL) for users with vital signs monitoring. This ensures a rapid prototyping for multiple applications working on healthcare and users wellness. Authors presented two case studies that have been tested using Uranus middleware. In the first, the oxygen level in the blood of a chronically ill patient is monitored at his home. To fulfill the requirements of this case study, an oximeter should be attached to the patient to measure the oxygen level and send it to a smart phone which transmits it to the doctor. The second case study aims to monitor patients that should be injected with radioactive substance. This monitoring alerts nurses in the case of patient's complications after injection and also supervise the radiation level in order to specify the convenient examination time (Each examination type requires a specific radiation level to deliver the accurate results). To achieve this, each patient is equipped with an RFID tag, a PDA and an ECG sensor. These equipments in addition to the service discovery ensured by the middleware enable to monitor the patient's heart beats. The patient location is updated when he moves from a room to another in order to track his status (still waiting, in the examination state, injected and awaiting that the radiation level reduces). These events are traduced using semantic information.

The contribution [9] is mainly used in sleep monitoring and bedsore prevention. The patient's positions in the bed are specified and classified according to the collected RSSI of the sensors using SVM classification method. These positions give an idea about the patient's sleep and can prevent from bedsore risks. This middleware helps the caregivers and eases their job by keeping track of the patient's position in the bed and decides when and how the patient should change his position to avoid bedsores. It is made up of two layers. The middleware [17], is able to monitor and offer assistance to disabled people. The system functionalities are dispatched and divided into independent services. An ECG sensor monitors the heart activity.

2.5 Event-Driven Middleware

In the event-driven middleware, all the middleware functionnalities are based on events going from events production to the reaction to events. Authors in [18] consider that event driven middleware is suitable to the context of healthcare, since the sensors reading according to the patient's status and/or activity change over the time. Also, the majority of medical devices work according to the event driven process. For example, when the heartbeats rate exceeds a predefined value, a notification is triggered. Furthermore, the event driven process reinforces the data abstraction that is needed to ensure applications interoperability. The proposed middleware is dedicated for smartphone like devices that are compelled to interact with a changing set of wireless nodes in a medical environment. The proposed middleware has the ability to multiplex the received data from the various sensors in order to fit multiple applications simultaneously.

The contribution has been applied in three applications. The first is the fitness support in which the user's physical activity is tracked by dedicated sensors: a wearable accelerometer to track the user's status (walking, sitting, standing etc.) and a chest strap and two embedded sensors in the weightlifting gloves to figure out the user's body exercise. This application motivates the user and helps him to track his sports activities. The second application is the telemonitoring. The main objective of this application is to monitor remotely the patient's status. To this end, the middleware collects information about the patient's weight, pressure, heart rate, ECG, etc. When the heart rate of the patient is not suitable (abnormal) to his activities, an alarm is sent. The third application is elderly care that monitors the elderly daily activities and reminds him whenever he forgets an important task.

2.6 Message Oriented Middleware (MoM)

Message oriented middleware have the ability to exchange important number of messages between distributed applications. A MoM in [21] is proposed to unify the access to all the medical devices in order to ease the data collection from the patients to the doctors. To this end, "Advanced Message Queuing Protocol (AMQP)" is employed to ensure data transfer according predefined standards with the required interoperability. To increase the security of the middleware, a RESTful application has been added to verify which manager is allowed to access which data.

2.7 Real Time Publish Subscribe Based Middleware

The Real-Time Publish Subscribe (RTPS) middleware is well suited for the real-time distributed applications. That's why authors in [19] decided to port this middleware to healthcare. In this middleware, each medical device such as temperature probe, Capnometer, ElectroCardiogram, has the function of a publisher. It collects and publishes the patient's measurements via fast Ethernet LAN. The published information is sent to the corresponding subscribers.

3   Discussion

As we have stated in the previous sections, the middleware for healthcare of things have covered lot of healthcare domains. Table 1 gives an overview of these middleware, their applications and their required medical devices (NM means not mentioned in the related paper). We notice that a same application can be ensured in many cases by different middleware belonging to different classes. For example, patients monitoring applications are implemented using SOA-based or Event-driven or Web of things or Publish/subscribe middleware. There are also some middleware solutions like [11] and [9] that offered a very flexible architecture that allowed them to be applied in a wide applications range. So, we should now answer at this crucial question: What is the most suitable middleware for Internet of healthcare things?

The answer at this question is not trivial. Effectively, we see that there is no 'perfect' solution since there are miscillaneous applications in the healthcare that have different uses cases with different constraints. For example, in some healthcare applications, there are lot of events that occur and require a quick

Table 1. Taxonomy of middleware for IoHT

Healthcare domain	Contribution	Required devices	Middleware class
Patients privacy preservation	[3–6]	NM	Fog-based
Fall/Faint detection	[12]	Wearable sensors with accelerometers	
	[11]	Accelerometer, blood pressure wristband	Web of Things
	[17]	Air pressure sensor, triaxial accelerometer	SOA
Freezing detection	[11]	Accelerometer	Web of Things
Patients monitoring	[13, 14]	NM	SOA
	[18]	Wearable accelerometer, chest strap	Event-driven
	[10]	ECG sensors, blood Pressure oscillometer, Cooking health sensor, biometric chest belt	Web of Things
	[11]	Blood pressure, accelerometer, Mood ring	Web of Things
	[8]	Sensors, accelerometer	Publish/Subscribe
AAL+ADL	[16]	ECG sensor, Oximeter, Zigbee, THL Sensor	SOA
	[9]	NM	
	[12]	Environmental sensors, video sensors, RGB-D sensors	Web of Things
Bedsore prevention	[9]	Bed pressure pad, wireless PIR detectors, luminance sensors	SOA
Radio activity injection monitoring	[16]	RFID tag, ECG sensor	SOA

reaction, such the case of an application that monitors the vital signs of a patient in a reanimation unit. Any modification in these signs (heart beats rate decrease, respiration problem, etc.) should trigger an event that must be handled rapidly. In these situations, an event-based middleware is a suitable candidate.

In SOA, there are service providers, service consumers and service registry. The service consumers search their required service from a service registry. They inform the corresponding service provider if the service is found. This architecture is well-suited for heterogeneous devices. And it ensures efficient service composition. However it does not fit real time applications. Many health scenario rely on one to many communication like the dissemination of a relevant healthcare information to a group of patients. In these situations, Publish/Subscribe is more suitable than the request/response strategy because it offers lower delays. But, if many situations are present simultaneously, how to choose the best middleware?

The answer is: Why to choose if we can combine? Effectively, most of these middleware classes are not mutually exclusive! We can conceive a middleware that is at the same time an event-based and a Web of Things-based for example. A middleware can even contain multiple components and each component can be based on different middleware class.

Based on the studied middleware, we can confirm that there are up to now lot of challenges that are not overcame. Indeed, the majority of the proposed middleware are conceived to a specific application and are not able to be adaptable to other applications without applying core modifications. Also, interoperability is still a crucial issue due to the continuous emergence of new medical devices with new technologies and new standards. Furthermore, the progress of the security middleware is countered by the progress of the security attacks, which lets security one of the most leading open issues that need more investigation.

4   Conclusion

We studied in this paper existing middleware for the Internet of Healthcare Things and specified their various applications. This study conducted us to conclude that in spite of the diversity of the proposed middleware, none of them has the ability to fulfill all the healthcare requirements. This urges to the openess and the collaboration between these middleware to have a more robust middleware verifying the trade off between the IoHT needs and devices technical limits.

References

1. Menvielle, L., Audrain-Pontevia, A.F., Menvielle, W.: The Digitization of Healthcare: New Challenges and Opportunities. Palgrave Macmillan, London (2017)
2. Wilk, S., et al.: An ontology-driven framework to support the dynamic formation of an interdisciplinary healthcare team. Int. J. Med. Inf. **136**, 1–12 (2020)
3. Shukla, S., Hassan, M.F., Khan, M.K., Jung, L.T., Awang, A.: Ananalytical model to minimize the latency in healthcare internet-of-things in fog computing environment. PLoS One **14**(11), 1–31 (2019)

4. Mukherjee, B., et al.: Flexible IoT security middleware for end-to-end cloud-fog communication. Future Gener. Comput. Syst. **87**, 688–703 (2018)

5. Elmisery, A.M., Rho, S., Botvich, D.: A fog based middleware for automated compliance with OECD privacy principlesin internet of healthcare things. IEEE Access **4**, 8418–8441 (2016)

6. Elmisery, A.M., Rho, S., Aborizka, M.: A new computing environment for collective privacy protection from constrained healthcare devices to IoT cloud services. Clust. Comput. **22**(1), 1611–1638 (2017). https://doi.org/10.1007/s10586-017-1298-1

7. Cecílio, J., Furtado, P.: Middleware solution for healthcare IoT applications. In: Mumtaz, S., Rodriguez, J., Katz, M., Wang, C., Nascimento, A. (eds.) WICON 2014. LNCS, vol. 146, pp. 53–59. Springer, Cham (2015). https://doi.org/10.1007/978-3-319-18802-7_8

8. Bazzani, M., Conzon, D., Scalera, A., Spirito, M.A., Trainito, C.I.: Enabling the IoT paradigm in e-health solutions through the VIRTUS middleware. In: Proceedings IEEE 11th International Conference on Trust, Security Privacy Computing Communication (TrustCom), pp. 1954–1959, June 2012

9. Palumbo, F., Barsocchi, P., Furfari, F., Ferro, E.: AAL middleware infrastructure for green bed activity monitoring. J. Sens. **2013**, 1–15 (2013)

10. Maia, P., et al.: A web platform for interconnecting body sensors and improving health care. Procedia Comput. Sci. **40**, 135–142 (2014)

11. Corredor, I., Metola, E., Bernardos, A.M., Tarrıo, P., Casar, J.R.: A lightweight web of things open platform to facilitate context data management and personalized healthcare services creation. Int. J. Environ. Res. Public Health **11**, 4676–4713 (2014)

12. Zhu, N., et al.: Bridging e-health and the internet of things: the sphere project. IEEE Intell. Syst. **30**(4), 39–46 (2015)

13. Warriach, E.U., Kaldeli, E., Lazovik, A., Aiello, M.: An interplatform service-oriented middleware for the smart home. Int. J. Smart Home **7**, 115–142 (2013)

14. Souza, A.M.C., Amazonas, J.R.A.: A novel smart home application using an internet of things middleware. In: Proceedings of 2013 European Conference on Smart Objects, Systems and Technologies (SmartSysTech), pp. 1–7 (2013)

15. Fersi, G.: Middleware for internet of things: a study. In: Proceedings of IEEE International Conference on Distributed Computing in Sensor Systems (DCOSS), Fortaleza, Brazil, pp. 230–235 (2015)

16. Coronato, A.: Uranus: A middleware architecture for dependable aal and vital signs monitoring applications. Sensors **12**(3), 3145–3161 (2012)

17. Corchado, J.M., Bajo, J., Tapia, D.I., Abraham, A.: Using heterogeneous wireless sensor networks in a telemonitoring system for healthcare. IEEE Trans. Inf. Technol. Biomed. **14**(2), 234–240 (2010)

18. Seeger, C., Van Laerhoven, K., Buchmann, A.: MyHealthAssistant: an event-driven middleware for multiple medical applications on a smartphone-mediated body sensor network. IEEE J. Biomed. Health Inform. **19**(2), 752–760 (2015)

19. Almadani, B., Saeed, B., Alroubaiy, A.: Healthcare systems integration using real time publish subscribe (RTPS) middleware. Comput. Electr. Eng. **50**, 67–78 (2016)

20. Bhawiyuga, A., Pramukantoro, E.S., Kirana, A.P.: A web of thing middleware for enabling standard web access over BLE based healthcare wearable device. In: IEEE LifeTech (2019)

21. Bellagente, P., Depari, A., Ferrari, P., Flammini, A., Sisinni, E., Rinaldi, S.: M^3 IoT - message-oriented middleware for M-health internet of things: design and validation. In: IEEE International Instrumentation and Measurement Technology Conference (I2MTC) (2018)

Uncertainty in IoT for Smart Healthcare: Challenges, and Opportunities

Anis Tissaoui[(⊠)] and Malak Saidi

VPNC Lab, FSJEG, University of Jendouba, Jendouba, Tunisia
anis.tissaoui@fsjegj.rnu.tn, malaksaidi16@gmail.com

Abstract. According to Knight, uncertainty signifies deviations from the expected states, which prevent us from the use of any probability for the determination of a result for a given action or decision [1]. This paper describes the phenomenon of uncertainty in the face of technological mega-trends and challenges associated with them. The article focuses on the analysis of the uncertainty in one of the most important technology trends – the Internet of Things (IoT) – on the example of Healthcare. The right decisions are not always equivalent to good results. Sometimes, the decision taken in accordance with general rules brings worse results than the one who breaks them. Such a situation is possible as a result of the uncertainty accompanying the predictions of the future. In this article the concept of the IoT is treated as a big, complex, dynamic system with specific characteristics, dimensions. structures and behaviors. The aim of the article is to analyze the factors that may determine the uncertainty and ambiguity of such systems in the context of the development of Healthcare, and recommendations are made for future research directions.

Keywords: Uncertainty · Internet of Things · Smart Healthcare

1 Introduction

The basic idea of the Internet of Things is the pervasive presence around us of a variety of things or objects – such as Radio-Frequency IDentification (RFID) tags, sensors, actuators, mobile phones, etc. – which, through unique addressing schemes, are able to interact with each other and cooperate with their neighbors to reach common goals [7].

This The advent of the Internet of Things is changing people's lives and their integration with the surrounding environment. It is estimated that the number of connected IoT devices will outgrow the world population and increase to 50 billion by end 2020 [2]. The technical evolution of IoT also stimulates the development of smart homes. It not only makes people's daily living more convenient, but also can contribute solutions for challenges in healthcare system [3, 4].

Key fields and applications (This can be portrayed in Fig. 1) for applying IoT solutions encompass [5]: smart cities, smart power networks, smart transport

M. Jmaiel et al. (Eds.): ICOST 2020, LNCS 12157, pp. 232–239, 2020.
https://doi.org/10.1007/978-3-030-51517-1_19

and smart buildings (intelligent solutions for living). This list also includes smart health care, one of the main subjects of this article.

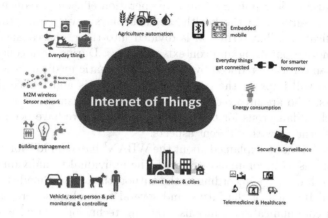

Fig. 1. Figure showing the Internet of Things application areas

The IoT field is a long-range technological area which presents great opportunities for development. Since the Internet of Things is a relatively new domain it carries a high level of uncertainty, both in relation to IoT technologies as well as to the aspects which are (or will be) correlated to this field, such as social, economic, technological, legal, etc. aspects [6]. Various characteristics, structures and behaviors of the IoT system are beyond areas which, so far, have been observed and are within verified knowledge, which creates significant uncertainty regarding future situations.

Healthcare is undergoing a rapid transformation from traditional hospital and specialist focused approach to a distributed patient-centric approach. The IoT applications are obscurity essential in remodeling lives of individuals than in health care. Internet of Things indicates to physical devices, like a measuring system, weight scale and patients very important watching devices (glucose, force per unit area, vital sign, and activity watching, etc.) connect with the web and transforms data from the physical to the digital world.

At present, healthcare widely uses IoT are continually evolving to accommodate the needs of future intelligent healthcare applications. This will place complex demands in terms of heterogeneity of devices, scalability, wide scale use of wireless data transfer technology, optimum energy use, data management, privacy protection bandwidth, data rate and latency, among other factors.

In the field of healthcare, various types of uncertainty are distinguished in the assessment of innovative programmes: parameter uncertainty, structural uncertainty, methodological uncertainty, variability, heterogeneity and decision uncertainty [12]. The article addresses the phenomenon of uncertainty occurring in large, developing systems namely the Internet of Things through the use of the example of the smart Health care.

2   The IoT in Health Care

There is a great potential for applying IoT technology across all sectors including both industrial and public to improve operation efficiency, reduce cost, and provide better service. In the healthcare, IoT plays a very important role in various applications. This criterion is divided into three phases, such as clinical care, remote monitoring and context awareness. During data collection, the risks of human error are reduced by means of automatic medical data collection method. This will improve the quality of the diagnosis and reduce the risk of human errors, who are involved in the collection or transmission of false information which is dangerous for the patients' health. There have been efforts for reviewing healthcare with different aspects.

This Arcadius et al. explained about the WBAN[1] based on IoT for the healthcare applications as it communicated with the individual to individual and the individual to things [13]. According to the author, the IoT was made to be a part of the overall Internet of the future and several technologies were used in the IoT such as communication solutions, tracking technology, wired and wireless sensor identification etc.

Jara et al. described the interconnection framework for m- healthcare application based on IoT [14]. The process of communication and the information access process had a personalized health end to end framework. The personalized data was complex and was found to be in an incomplete manner. So, the authors introduced interconnection framework for m-healthcare applications based on IoT. It made continuous and real-time vital sign monitoring system which introduced technological innovations for the health monitoring of patient's devices by means of Internet system.

Qi et al. [7] explored various applications of IoT in smart healthcare from different perspectives (i.e., Blood pressure monitoring, monitoring of oxygen saturation, heartbeat monitoring etc.). Islam et al. focused on IoT-based healthcare technologies and present architecture for healthcare network and platforms which support access to the IoT backbone and enable medical data reception and data transmission. Secondly, the paper delivers detailed research events and how the IoT can address chronic disease supervision, pediatric, care of elderly and fitness management [8].

Catarinucci et al. modeled a smart healthcare system based on IoT aware architecture [15]. The authors introduced the IoT aware architecture for automatic monitoring and tracking of patient's biomedical information. They also proposed smart hospital system, with enabling technologies, especially for wireless networks and smart mobile to enable network infrastructure. Thus, it provided highly efficient real-time monitoring of patient's biomedical information. Furthermore, privacy was an open issue in this system; Baker et al. [9] presented a new model for future smart healthcare systems, which can be used for both special (i.e., special condition monitoring) and general systems. Nowadays, all over the world, there are many people whose health might suffer due to lack of

---

[1] Wireless Body Area Network.

effective healthcare monitoring. Elderly, children or chronically ill people needed to be examined almost daily. Remote monitoring is an important paradigm for many real- world applications.

Context-awareness is a major criterion in the healthcare IoT applications. As it has the ability to find the patient's condition and the environment where the patient was located it will greatly assist the healthcare professionals to understand the variations that can influence the health status of these patients. In addition to, the change of physical state of the patient may increase the percentage of its vulnerabilities to diseases and be a cause for his/her health deterioration [10].

Mahmoud et al. [11] focused on different IoT-based healthcare systems for Wireless Body Area Network (WBAN) that can enable smart healthcare data reception and data transmission. the author presented a detailed of resource management, power, energy, security and privacy related to IoT-based smart healthcare.

3   Characteristics of the Phenomenon of Uncertainty

3.1   Defining Uncertainty

The concept of uncertainty encompasses multiple aspects and meanings. The widely spread use of the concept of uncertainty throughout various scientific disciplines, as well as in everyday language, has caused it to acquire many definitions.

According to F.H. Knight, uncertainty signifies deviations from the expected states, which prevent us from the use of any probability for the determination of a result for a given action or decision [1]. E. Ostrowska follows F. Knight with the measurable and immeasurable uncertainty theory which defines the former as risk and the latter as immeasurable uncertainty in its strict sense.

According to A.H. Willet uncertainty concerns changes which are difficult to estimate, or events whose probability cannot be predicted because the amount of available information is too limited [16]. A. Jøsang [17] proves that uncertainty in its strict sense can be measured using subjective logic. Subjective logic is a type of probabilistic logic that allows probability values to be expressed with degrees of uncertainty. The idea of subjective logic is to extend probabilistic logic by also expressing uncertainty about the probability values themselves, meaning that it is possible to reason with argument models in the presence of uncertain or incomplete evidence.

3.2   Types of Uncertainty in the Field of Healthcare

Depending on the contexts being studied in the field of healthcare, various types of uncertainty are distinguished in the assessment of innovative programmes: parameter uncertainty, structural uncertainty, methodological uncertainty, variability, heterogeneity and decision uncertainty [12].

Structural uncertainty refers to uncertainty surrounding the structure of a decision model. Variability relates to the fact that individuals are unique and therefore vary in their outcomes, which may partly be explained by individual characteristics [19]. Parameter uncertainty relates to the fact that the true value of a parameter is not known [18]. In practice, it mostly refers to imprecise estimates and standard errors surrounding a mean value, which corresponds to measurement error. Decision uncertainty is the umbrella term for all uncertainty surrounding a decision, and can be caused by any other type of uncertainty [12]. Methodological uncertainty can be defined as disparities in the choice of analytic methods that underpin an assessment [18].

3.3 Sources of Uncertainty in IoT Systems

Several of other factors could influence the occurrence of uncertainty in IoT. Key characteristics of IoT which influence uncertainty include:

- *heterogeneity of devices or Interoperability*: Interoperability plays an important role in smart healthcare, providing connectivity between different devices using different communication technologies. Interoperability between different devices in different domains is a key limitation for IoT success due to lack of universal standards. the large number of devices used means high diversity in their calculation and communication capabilities.
- *Resources constraints (energy and computational and storage capabilities)*: the issue of power use is crucial. IoT devices used for healthcare are connected with a collection of sensors. A continuous source of energy is required to drive these devices, which presents a severe challenge in term of cost and battery life. Their computational and storage capabilities do not allow complex operations support (e.g. cryptographic operations, etc.).
- *privacy protection*: The security protection is not about encrypting/decrypting user data, but about how a user in a heath community can use trust information to filter out untrustworthy input when gathering health information to enhance IoT health security. Due to constrained nature of IoT device (limited processing and battery life) it is difficult to implement complex security protocols and algorithms. This leads to numerous attacks and threats in term of security and privacy.
- *scalability (connectivity in IoT)*: connectivity of a growing number of devices being used every day. A smart healthcare network consists of billions of devices. can succeed only if it can provide capabilities of sensing to produce important information.
- *data management*: In smart healthcare, billions of devices are connected, which can produce a huge amount of data and information for analysis. in IoT it will be crucial to utilize appropriate data models and semantic descriptions of their content, appropriate language and format.
- *Network*: Intermittent loss of connection in the IoT is fairly frequent. In fact, IoT is seen as an IP network with more constraints and a higher ratio of packet loss problems connected with overcoming this issue are related to transfer speeds and delays in delivery of data;

- *Quality of Services (QoS)*: the quality of services is an important parameter used in the healthcare services which is a highly time-sensitive system. Numerous challenges exist to meet the quality requirements of IoT-based applications in terms of energy efficiency, sensing data quality, network resource consumption, and latency. The quality of body sensors determines the accuracy and sensitivity measurements provided by a sensor.

3.4 Causes of Uncertainty in IoT Systems

Uncertainty is one of the key problems for most IoT systems based on RFID (Radio Frequency IDentification) technology. Listed below are causes of uncertainty relating to the following fields [20]:

- *Inconsistent data (unbounded data, data conflict)*: RFID tags can be read using various readers at the same time therefore it is possible to get inconsistent data about the exact location of tags;
- *Incomplete data (Noisy data, data loss)*: tagged objects might be stolen or forged and generate fake data.
- *Ambiguity Data (plausibility, imprecision)*: sometimes radio frequencies might cause data to be reflected in reading areas, so RFID readers might read those reflections;
- *Missing readings*: tag collisions, tag detuning, metal/liquid effect, tag misalignment;
- *Redundant data*: captured data may contain significant amounts of additional information;

4   Findings and Recommendations

4.1   Research Challenges

a) How to guarantee connectivity of massive IoT devices in a wide range during high mobility?
b) How to guarantee resource management in highly dense network?
c) How to utilize power/energy of IoT devices?
d) How to extend IoT devices battery life?
e) Incorporating devices for retailer locked-in services.
f) Secure integration and deployment of services (cloud-based) at both device and network levels.
g) Early detection of both outsider and insider threats.
h) Standardized security solutions without delaying data integrity.

4.2   Major Requirements

- adaptation of trust management mechanisms, similarly to what was already adopted for P2P and grid systems and technical security policies;

– Identification of vulnerabilities at a various level in the network. which work as entry points for numerous attacks.
– adaptation of trust relationships on the following levels:
  • IoT entities;
  • data perception (sensor sensibility, preciseness, security, reliability, persistence, data collection efficiency);
  • privacy preservation (user data and personal information);
  • data fusion and mining;
  • data transmission and communication;
  • quality of IoT services;
  • acceptance of shared standards to cope with the diversity of devices and applications;
– creation of simulations and models of uncertainty phenomena;

References

1. Knight, F.H.: Risk: Uncertainty and Profit, pp. 224–225. Beard Books, Washington (2002)
2. Evans, D.: The internet of things: how the next evolution of the internet is changing everything, vol. 1, pp. 1–11. Cisco Internet Business Solutions Group (IBSG), San Jose (2011)
3. Gietzelt, M., et al.: Home-centered health-enabling technologies and regional health information systems an integration approach based on international standards. Methods Inf. Med. 53, 160–166 (2014)
4. Wu, W., Pirbhulal, S., Sangaiah, A.K., Mukhopadhyay, S.C., Li, G.: Optimization of signal quality over comfortability of textile electrodes for ECG monitoring in fog computing based medical applications. Future Gener. Comput. Syst. 86, 515–526 (2018)
5. Schatten, M.: Smart residential buildings as learning agent organizations in the internet of things. Bus. Syst. Res. 5(1), 34–46 (2014)
6. Brad, B.S., Murar, M.M.: Smart buildings using IoT technologies. Constr. Unique Build. Struct. 5(20), 15–27 (2014)
7. Qi, J., Yang, P., Min, G., Amft, O., Dong, F., Xu, L.: Advanced internet of things for personalised healthcare systems: a survey. Pervasive Mob. Comput. 41, 132–149 (2017)
8. Islam, S.R., Kwak, D., Kabir, M.H., Hossain, M., Kwak, K.S.: The internet of things for health care: a comprehensive survey. IEEE Access 3, 678–708 (2015)
9. Baker, S.B., Xiang, W., Atkinson, I.: Internet of things for smart healthcare: technologies, challenges, and opportunities. IEEE Access 5(C), 26521–26544 (2017)
10. Perera, C., Zaslavsky, A., Christen, P., Georgakopoulos, D.: Context aware computing for the Internet of things: a survey. IEEE Commun. Surv. Tutor. 16(1), 414–454 (2014)
11. Dhanvijay, M.M., Patil, S.C.: Internet of things: a survey of enabling technologies in healthcare and its applications. Comput. Netw. 153, 113–131 (2019)
12. Bilcke, J., Beutels, P., Brisson, M., Jit, M.: Accounting for methodological, structural, and parameter uncertainty in decision-analytic models: a practical guide. Med. Decis. Making 31(4), 675–692 (2011)

13. Arcadius, T.C., Gao, B., Tian, G., Yan, Y.: Structural health monitoring framework based on internet of things: a survey. IEEE Internet Things J. **4**(3), 619–635 (2017)
14. Jara, A.J., Zamora-Izquierdo, M.A., Skarmeta, A.F.: Interconnection framework for mHealth and remote monitoring based on the internet of things. IEEE J. Sel. Areas Commun. **31**(9), 47–65 (2013)
15. Catarinucci, L., et al.: An IoT-aware architecture for smart healthcare systems. IEEE Internet Things J. **2**(6), 515–526 (2015)
16. Janasz, K.: Ryzyko i niepewność w gospodarce - wybrane aspekty teoretyczne. Studia I Prace Wydziału Nauk Ekonomicznych iZarzadzania **14**, 87–98 (2009)
17. Jøsang, A.: Subjective logic. University of Oslo (2013)
18. Briggs, A.H., et al.: Model parameter estimation and uncertainty analysis: a report of the ISPOR-SMDM modeling good research practices task force working group-6. Med. Decis. Making **32**(5), 722–732 (2012)
19. Grutters, J.P., et al.: Acknowledging patient heterogeneity in economic evaluation: a systematic literature review. Pharmaco Econ. **31**(2), 111–23 (2013)
20. Dong, X., Yongrui, Q., Quan, Z.S., Yong, X.: Managing uncertainties in RFID applications: a survey. In: IEEE 11th International Conference on e-Business Engineering (2014)

Secure E-Health Platform

Karima Djouadi$^{(\boxtimes)}$ and Abdelkader Belkhir$^{(\boxtimes)}$

Department of Computer Science, Computer Systems Laboratory,
USTHB BO 32, Bab Ezzouar 16111, Algiers, Algeria
kdjouadi1@usthb.dz, kaderbelkhir@hotmail.com

Abstract. Currently, the Internet has become a service hosting infrastructure through its interconnection of a very large number of heterogeneous objects, thus offering users several types of services implemented by different sectors. Although these services make people's lives easier and provide them with a means of communication between their real and virtual worlds, they risk being a path of intrusion into their private lives, or in some cases an easy target for malicious individuals aiming to endanger human life. To avoid this, we have designed a secure e-health platform based on IoT that serves to monitor patients' medical profiles remotely by collecting their medical records while ensuring their confidentiality and integrity.

Keywords: Internet of things (IoT) · E-health · Security · Confidentiality

1 Introduction

With the interconnection of billions of objects around the world, IoT offers several services to individuals through many types of applications deployed in several domains, including smart grid [1], smart home, smart city, smart healthcare and applications dedicated to vehicle monitoring [2,3].

Healthcare Systems have emerged to address some of the problems facing the health sector, mainly the lack of medical staff caused by the ever-increasing population and the lack of timely diagnosis of diseases [4] by allowing constant medical monitoring of chronic patients or residents of isolated or underserved locations. In this development and deployment of e-health systems, information management by mobile devices require very short response times and latency, it introduces also several challenges including data storage and management, security and confidentiality (e.g. authorization control and anonymity) [8]. The integration of fairly strong security mechanisms is necessary for this systems where a successful security attack results in several human lives being subjected to false diagnosis or delayed surgical procedures.

We are interested to problems of storage, confidentiality and data integrity by ensuring minimal response time and low latency. Several authors have conducted works aimed at setting up remote patient monitoring platforms such as [13–16]. Nevertheless, this works present some limitations such as neglecting the security

M. Jmaiel et al. (Eds.): ICOST 2020, LNCS 12157, pp. 240–248, 2020.
https://doi.org/10.1007/978-3-030-51517-1_20

of the monitoring systems, the privacy of its users, the availability and the storage of data.

To address the aforementioned issues, we propose a solution to provide the healthcare community and patients with a secure medical service. Our platform offers continuous medical monitoring with the integration of medical data backup mechanisms at the Cloud level, thus ensuring the notion of fault tolerance through data replication and thus the availability of information while guaranteeing the integrity and confidentiality of the data exchanged (using sh1 and MD5 protocols for hashage and DES ,RSA for encryption), a minimal response time and low latency due to the implementation of fog computing. The remainder of this paper is organized as follows. Section 2 reviews related works on healthcare systems. Section 3 describes the proposed solution. Section 4 presents the experiments. Finally, Sect. 5 concludes the paper.

2 Related Works

In this section, we discuss the related work of healthcare systems. In [5], The authors present a cloud computing solution for patient's data collection in healthcare institutions. The system uses sensors attached to medical equipment to collect patient data and sends it to cloud for providing ubiquitous access. In [6], the proposed architecture is dedicated to data acquisition via several personal health devices via USB, ZigBee or Bluetooth. But the disadvantage of the above-mentioned work is that the response time and latency increases due to the long path to the cloud, which influences the user's access time to the data. In [7] who have implemented an IoT- healthcare system architecture which benefits from the concept of fog computing, thus ensuring low latency data processing and low bandwidth usage. The main disadvantage of the above works is the neglect of the notion of security. In [15] authors have proposed a robust solution in terms of response time by ensuring the confidentiality of data via an authentication protocol except that it only authenticate LPU (Local Process Unit) and not identify the users and neglects the property of data availability by centralizing storage at the level of a single server, in the event of failure of the latter, access to medical records will be suspended, which could endanger human life. While the authors of [16] Propose a secure healthcare system with the same drawback as the previous one with neglect of the quality of service criteria (response time and latency). On the other hand, our approach maintains a backup procedure to ensure continuity of service while guaranteeing the unique identity rule via the NIN [12]. According to [17] that uses Blockchain as a security method offers several advantages by allowing an agreement without the use of a trusted third party and thus avoiding the bottleneck, the antecedent medical data are also complete and coherent thanks to the chaining. However, this technology requires a significant investment which is very costly. It should also be noted that the blockchain consumes a lot of computing time, which is not ideal for e-health platforms.

3   E-Health Platform

In this section we present the architecture of our IoT system which is based on fog-enabled cloud computing as described in [10]. Then we will present the two main processes of our system and we finish by presenting the different security aspects available on our platform.

3.1   System Architecture

As illustrated in Fig. 1, the architecture of our system is mainly based on (N) local servers distributed geographically over (N) zones, in which patients and medical institutions can be located, medical sensors used for the collection of patients data and IoT equipment (smartphones); as well as a central server (cloud) dealing with global data storage.

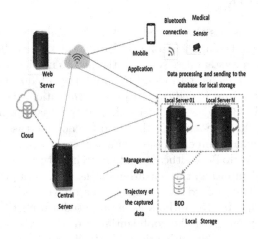

Fig. 1. E-health platform

The different actors and components of our architecture are explained as follows:

- **Medical sensors:** it is planted in, on or around a human body to capture the patient's health data and send it to the system periodically.
- **User:** consists of two categories of users, each of them has a unique identifier (NIN) [12]:

  1. *The Patient*: person with whom one or more sensors are associated to monitor its health status.
  2. *The practitioner*: person who is in charge of setting up the association between the patient and his sensor.

- **Mobile application:** a User Interface (UI); it authenticates users by submitting their identifiers (NIN) [12] with their relative passwords. It also allow the Patient/sensor association procedure, which only the practitioner is authorized to do, it allows him to consult the medical records of his patients and make diagnoses.
- **Local servers:** a distributed computing paradigm that acts as an intermediate between Cloud datacenters and IoT sensors. Its role is to lightly process the medical data collected by the sensors associated with the different patients geographically distributed over the (N) zones, followed by the backup of this data on local databases.
- **Web server:** administrates and maintains the system, including the management of the accounts of the administrator of the (N) area. All this is done by the super administrator, while each administrator is responsible for creating and managing the accounts of the users in his or her zone.
- **Cloud:** a central server, which is responsible for the global storage of medical and personal data of users in all areas, with the possibility of transferring this data to an area X to which the patient has moved, if the attending physician wants to consult the file of his new patient, who has just arrived in his new area.

3.2 The Main Operating Processes

Among the most important processes for the realization of our IoT service platform, the following two processes driving the operating principle of the mobile application, the association of sensors to patients and sends it as well as data storage.

- **Process of association's creation**
  The practitioner first searches the patient's profile at the local level by introducing his identifier, otherwise, the local server sends a request to the central server of the Cloud to retrieve and save it at its level.
  After retrieving the patient's profile, practitioner checks the availability of the sensor to associate it with the right patient; This procedure can be summarized by the following steps:

  1. Initiation of the association process by the practitioner.
  2. Sensor search procedure and availability test.
  3. Beginning of capture of the patient's medical constants.

  In the case of healing of the patient or the end of his or her followup by his practitioner, the latter ends this association by disassociating the patient's sensor.
- **Process of detection and data transmission by sensors**
  After the patient sensor association is established, the sensor begins to capture the patient's data and sends it through the mobile application to the local server for storage.

3.3   Security of the E-Health Platform

We introduced security mechanisms to protect the captured user data as it will be sent to processing equipment and then to storage spaces, which will make them subject to theft or alteration attempts [3]which represent very high risks for the functioning of IoT applications.

- **Data integrity:** Data integrity refers to the state of data that, at the time of processing, storage or transmission is not intentionally or accidentally altered or destroyed and maintains a format that allows its use. For this purpose, the programmed SQL queries will be used, and data will be encrypted using the RSA asymmetric encryption algorithm, to ensure such data integrity.
- **Backup and logging of the cloud database:** To preserve the data within our database, we have opted for the backup strategy which consists of making copies of existing data in order to improve reliability, fault tolerance, or availability. Every day, our database will be automatically replicated to the cloud to ensure continuity of service in the event of a local server failure.
- **Authentication:** The authentication process will allow us to prevent privacy breaches, unauthorized access to data, identity theft, and password attacks by limiting authentication and login attempts to the private areas of practitioner and patient users. This is done by using small gadgets called "smart cards", which each user has. These cards have the above-mentioned user ID (NIN) and a corresponding password [12].
- **Data encryption:** To prevent human attacks from the middle, the following encryption mechanisms are applied to the exchanged data in our system.

    - Encryption of data within the database, using md5 and DES encryption protocols.
    - Encryption of data circulating in the network, using SSL Sockets with certificates and Data hash by applying the SH1 protocol [9].

4   Implementation and Results

In this section we present the basic implementation setup, then we introduce the mobile prototype to validate our solution as well as some simulations and discussion of results.

The experiments were conducted on an IoT sensor Xiaomi Mi Band3 [11] is an intelligent IoT-based electronic bracelet that incorporates an HR (Heart Rate) heart rate sensor. The user interface (UI) was built using an Android Studio V4.4+. We have used the Google Cloud Platform for the creation of our local servers and the global server for the data storage.

4.1   Mobile Application Prototype

The mobile application is used to communicate with the IoT device in order to collect the data. It will be installed at the practitioner and the patient having a profile for each one of them (see Fig. 2). Both types of users will be entitled to the following functionalities:

- **For the practitioner:** Patient/Sensor Association, Monitoring,Transfer, and patients update.
- **For the patient:** consultation of his various medical information.

As can be seen in Fig. 2, each time the sensor registers a new value; it sends it to the mobile application to which it is connected. In the case of a heart defect as shown in the following figure, notifications and alerts are sent to the practitioners treating the patient, and a telephone call is made from the patient's home to the toll-free civil protection number.

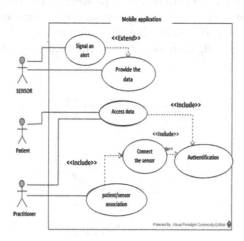

Fig. 2. Use case of the mobile application

4.2 Simulation and Discussion of Results

In order to test the performance of our system, and see how it will react to changes in the number of users, simultaneous access to the server through the use of "Threads" and the data encryption operation; we launched a simulation with a series of tests based on the response time of the local server for requests issued by the users, whether patients or practitioners, as this time may be a factor in the favorable to saving a human life.

Test 1: Incrementing the number of users with the use of Threads and encryption: First, we start by testing the incrementation of the number of users with the activation of simultaneous access to the server using "Threads", and the encryption and data encryption operation.

Test 2: Incrementing the number of users with the use of Threads without encryption: Secondly, we test the incrementation of the number of users with the activation of simultaneous access to the server using "Threads", and by disabling the encryption and data encryption operation.

Test 3: Incrementing the number of users without Threads and encryption: Finally, we tested the incrementation of the number of users without the activation of simultaneous access by using "Threads", and without encryption.

After completing the series of tests, and as illustrated in Fig. 3 We noticed that the encryption operation will not have much influence on the system's response time. Whilst, the use of Threads will have an impact on the load on the communication network. After analyzing the simulation results, we conclude that as the number of users increases, the number of requests to be processed by the server increases too, which will lead to congestion at the server level and additional traffic on the network, thus prolonging the response time, which is not tolerable in our system in the event of an extreme emergency. Whilst with the use of Threads, We notice that the different requests will be processed simultaneously, which will, therefore, reduce the response time, as well as the load on the network.

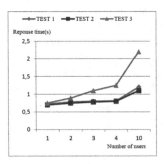

Fig. 3. Simulation's tests

5   Conclusion and Perspectives

We have developed a service platform based on IoT, with a secure online health application to establish the medical profiles of patients from distributed information, allowing their continuous monitoring in order to improve and modernize health services by ensuring the security of the data exchanged on our platform, thus guaranteeing the preservation of patients' privacy.As a future work, We plan to expand the real deployment of integrated sensors to better evaluate our system.

References

1. Lu, R.: Privacy-Enhancing Aggregation Techniques for smart Grid Communications. Wireless Networks. Springer, Heidelberg (2016). https://doi.org/10.1007/978-3-319-32899-7

2. Gubbi, J., Buyya, R., Marusic, S., Palaniswami, M.: Internet of Things (IoT): a vision, architectural elements and future directions. Future Gener. Comput. Syst. **29**(7), 1645–1660 (2013)
3. Atamli, A.W., Martin, A.: Threat based security analysis for the internet of things. In: International Workshop on Secure Internet of Things, pp. 35–43 (2014)
4. Zhao, W., Wang, C., Nakahira, Y.: Medical application on internet of things, pp. 660–665 (2011)
5. Rolim, C.O., Koch, F.L., Westphall, C.B., Werner, J., Fracalossi, A., Salvador, G.S.: A cloud computing solution for patient's data collection in health care institutions. In: Second International Conference eHealth, Telemedicine, and Social Medicine, ETELEMED 2010, pp. 95–99. IEEE (2010)
6. Park, K., Pak, J.: An integrated gateway for various phds in healthcare environments. BioMed. Res. Int. **2012** (2012)
7. Gia, T.N., Jiang, M., Rahmani, A.-M., et al.: Fog computing in healthcare internet of things: a case study on ECG feature extraction. In: 2015 IEEE International Conference on Computer and Information Technology; Ubiquitous Computing and Communications; Dependable, Autonomous and Secure Computing; Pervasive Intelligence and Computing, pp. 356–363. IEEE (2015)
8. Doukas, C., Maglogiannis, I.: Bringing IoT and cloud computing towards pervasive healthcare. In: 2012 Sixth International Conference on Innovative Mobile and Internet Services in Ubiquitous Computing, pp. 922–926. IEEE (2012)
9. Mukherjee, M., Matam, R., Shu, L., et al.: Security and privacy in fog computing: challenges. IEEE Acces **5**, 19293–19304 (2017)
10. Gill, S.S., Arya, R.C., Wander, G.S., et al.: Fog-based smart healthcare as a big data and cloud service for heart patients using IoT. In: Hemanth, J., Fernando, X., Lafata, P., Baig, Z. (eds.) ICICI 2018. LNDECT, vol. 26. Springer, Cham (2018). https://doi.org/10.1007/978-3-030-03146-6_161
11. https://www.mi.com/fr/mi-band-3/. Accessed 20 Jan 2020
12. Berbar, A., Belkhir, A.: A universal identification code for e-health services. In: 2019 Third World Conference on smart Trends in Systems Security and Sustainablity (WorldS4), pp. 327–332. IEEE(2019)
13. Ng, J.W.P., Lo, B.P.L., Wells, O., et al. Ubiquitous monitoring environment for wearable and implantable sensors (UbiMon). In: International Conference on Ubiquitous Computing (Ubicomp) (2004)
14. Chakravorty, R.: A programmable service architecture for mobile medical care. In: Fourth Annual IEEE International Conference on Pervasive Computing and Communications Workshops (PERCOMW 2006), p. 5pp.-536. IEEE (2006)
15. Gope, P., Hwang, T.: BSN-care: a secure IoT-based modern healthcare system using body sensor network. IEEE Sens. J. **16**(5), 1368–1376 (2015)
16. Ren, Y., Werner, R., Pazzi, N., et al.: Monitoring patients via a secure and mobile healthcare system. IEEE Wirel. Commun. **17**(1), 59–65 (2010)
17. Esposito, C., de Santis, A., Tortora, G., et al.: Blockchain: a panacea for healthcare cloud-based data security and privacy? IEEE Cloud Comput. **5**(1), 31–37 (2018)

Hybrid and Secure E-Health Data Sharing Architecture in Multi-Clouds Environment

Tayssir Ismail[1,2(✉)], Haifa Touati[1,2], Nasreddine Hajlaoui[1,2], and Hassen Hamdi[3]

[1] Hatem Bettahar Research Unit IResCoMath, Gabes, Tunisia
taissirism88@gmail.com, haifa.touai@cristal.rnu.tn,
hajlaoui.ing@gmail.com
[2] Faculty of Science of Gabes, Gabes, Tunisia
[3] MIRACL Laboratory, FSEG-Sfax, Sfax, Tunisia
hhassen2006@yahoo.fr

Abstract. Healthcare is among the sectors showing efforts in adopting cloud computing to its services considering the provided cost reduction and healthcare process efficiency. However, outsourcing patient's sensitive data increases the concerns regarding security, privacy, and integrity of healthcare data. Therefore, there is a need for building a trust relationship between patients and e-health systems. In this paper, we propose a privacy-preserving framework, called Hybrid and Secure Data Sharing Architecture (HSDSA), to secure data storage in e-health systems. Our approach improves security in healthcare by maintaining the privacy and confidentiality of sensitive data and preventing threats. In fact, in the upload phase, Multi-cloud environment is used to store Rivest–Shamir–Adleman (RSA) encrypted medical records. We adopt a Shamir's secret sharing approach for the distribution of shares to different independent cloud providers. In the retrieval phase, the reconstruction operation is based on the (t, n) strategy. To check the requester identity and to prove the hash possession, we used a zero-knowledge cryptography algorithm, namely the Schnorr algorithm. The patient has a total control over the generation and management of the decryption keys using Diffie-Hellman algorithm without relying on a trusted authority.

Keywords: E-health system security · Privacy preservation · Multi-cloud · Data storage · Data share · Data encryption

1 Introduction

Cloud computing is a new promising technology that leverages the user from the burden of hardware maintenance and offers dynamically flexible and scalable computational resources accessible from any place where a network is available. The emergence of this paradigm has deeply influenced many domains and especially the healthcare sector. However, the usage of this model in the healthcare

M. Jmaiel et al. (Eds.): ICOST 2020, LNCS 12157, pp. 249–258, 2020.
https://doi.org/10.1007/978-3-030-51517-1_21

domain needs the reinforcement of security measures because data are susceptible to lose, leakage or theft. Therefore, confidentiality and integrity of the stored
Electronic Health Records (EHR) are deemed as one of the major challenges
elevated by the external storage. Besides, the privacy of sensitive data must be
guaranteed. To overcome the above cited challenges, cryptographic techniques
for securing e-health systems are widely adopted. But the reliance on a single
cloud storage provider has shown many drawbacks like a single point of failure,
vendor lock-in and malicious insiders. To narrow down the listed disadvantages,
it is advisable to use multi-cloud architecture. One of the key concepts of this
model is to store data on different cloud server providers where an insider is not
able to reconstruct the original data from a single share [1].

In this context, several solutions have been proposed in the literature to
ensure secure multi-cloud storage in e-health systems [2–5]. They mainly have
two phases: *storage* and *retrieval.* They also all use cryptographic primitives to
ensure EHRs security. Authors of [2] use an Attribute Based-Encryption (ABE)
for selective access authorisation and cryptographic secret sharing. The EHRs
split and reconstruction is done through a proxy. In [3], ABE is used for selective data sharing with physicians without allowing them to know the precise
description of the patient's illnesses. Biometrics based authentication and Ker-
beros tickets session are used in [4] to guarantee secure interaction with the
EHR system. In addition, a steganographic technique is used to store EHR. In
[5], authors propose the use of Shamir's Secret Sharing not only to distribute
EHR shares among cloud servers but to retrieve the requested EHR from partial cloud servers. In summary, the main drawback of [2–5] is the reliance on a
trusted third party which may not be adequate for practical use as they show
security risks. Hence, a secure privacy-preserving data storage solution is still
needed to improve the patient role to monitor his data on the cloud.

In this paper, we present a Hybrid and Secure Data Sharing Architecture
(HSDSA), for secure and privacy-preserving storing and sharing of patient's
sensitive data in a Multi-cloud environment without relying on a trusted third
party. In HSDSA, cloud providers are assumed to be semi-trusted: honest but
curious. HSDSA gives the patient total control over the generation and management of the decryption keys without relying on a trusted authority and thus
it is more applicable for public cloud environments. To protect the data from
external attackers, Rivest–Shamir–Adleman (RSA) encryption is applied before
outsourcing EHR. To secure data against cloud providers curiosity, Shamir's
secret sharing is adopted. The resulted shares are distributed to multiple clouds.
To download an EHR, HSDSA recovers its shares using an outsourcing reconstruction operation based on the (t, n) strategy. To complete the file decryption,
a Schnorr-based technique is used to prove data possession and to verify the
requester identity. Then a session, using the Diffie Hellman (DH) algorithm, is
created to securely exchange the decryption key. Finally, the key is extracted
and the original EHR could be recovered. Outsourcing reconstruction operation
based on the (t, n) strategy is used.

The remainder of the paper is organised as follows. Section 2 gives an overview of the overall architecture of the proposed framework and its components. Sections 3 and 4 detail the different techniques used in the storage and retrieval processes. Finally, Sect. 5 concludes the paper and highlights some open issues.

2 Architecture Overview of the Proposed Scheme

We recall that our goal is to securely store EHRs in multi-cloud environment and to securely share them among healthcare organisations staff. In the following, we will give an overview of the HSDSA framework in which we focus on the context of medical data storage, share and retrieval. The basics of HSDSA are shown in Fig. 1. Our system compromises three different entities: Data Owner (DO), Data Requester (DR) and n CSP ($CSP_1,...,CSP_n$). The key components of the HSDSA framework include:

- **The storage process** which is composed of two phases, namely the **registration** phase and the **storage** phase.
- **The retrieval process** which is composed of two phases, namely the EHR **reconstruction** and the EHR **recovery** phases.

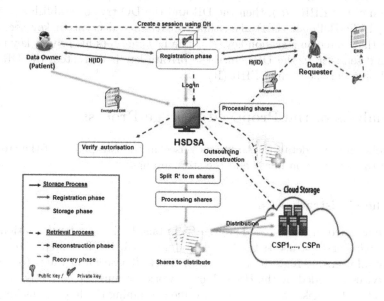

Fig. 1. Architecture overview

As shown in Fig. 1, the workflow of HSDSA is as follows:

- **The registration phase** starts when a DO or a DR signs in to the Framework Interface. After being signed to HSDSA, a DO or a DR receives in response the hash of his identity H($ID_{DO,DR}$).

- **The storage phase** starts when a DO wants to store his EHRs, he calculates the digital signature of his EHR (R), encrypts R using Rivest–Shamir–Adleman (RSA) algorithm for both and logs in to the HSDSA. Then, the DO uploads his encrypted record (R') and the hash value of the original record H(R). HSDSA generates a unique identifier (ID_R) of the EHR to guarantee the anonymity of stored data in Cloud servers and stores H(ID_{DO}), H(R) and ID_R. The framework calculates the hash of the uploaded EHR (R') and splits it into m shares. Then, it performs an exclusive OR operation between each share (S_i') and the hash value of R'. The distribution is done using Shamir's secret sharing algorithm and the resulted shares are sent to n different Cloud Server Providers $CSP_1, ... CSP_n$.
- **The reconstruction phase** starts when a DO or an authorised user DR wants to get the EHR, he sends a request to the framework. After confirming the request, HSDSA assigns a CSP (CSP_R) to perform the reconstruction step. The CSP_R gets t shares or more from $CSP_1, ... CSP_n$. Once the reconstruction is done, the CSP_R returns the resulted shares to the framework.
- Finally, **the recovery phase**, when the DR wants to get the DO's private key, he has to prove that he is the right DR and he has the correct hash value of R. To this end, the Schnorr algorithm is used. Once, the DO makes sure that the DR is an authorised requester and that he possesses the encrypted version of the EHR (R'), then the DR and the DO try to establish a session using Diffie-Hellman (DH) algorithm to exchange decryption key securely. Once they agree on a session key, K_s. The DO encrypts his private key using K_s and sends it to the DR. Once the private key is extracted, the DR can finally recover the desired EHR (R).

3   Analysis of the Proposed Storage Process

In the following, we detail the techniques used in the two phases of the storage process: the registration phase and the storage phase.

3.1   The Registration Phase

As recommended in cloud-based storage solutions, building a trust relationship between partners is a necessity. To achieve this goal, the first step is to make sure that all users are registered to the framework. If a new user wants to benefit from services provided by the HSDSA framework, he must be correctly authenticated. Once he registers, he receives a value containing the hash of his identity H($ID_{DO,DR}$) in order to maintain the anonymity of user identities.

3.2   The Storage Phase

HSDSA acts as an intermediary between DO and CSPs. Our goal is to provide a secure storage facility to authorised users. This phase involves Shamir's secret sharing technique to make sure that the multi-cloud environment, used to store shares, is a collusion-safe. By collusion-safe we mean that if two or more CSPs combine their keys, they cannot decrypt the data. Ten steps, illustrated in Table 1, describe the storage phase.

When a DO wants to store an EHR, he calculates the digital signature of the original EHR (R). Then the RSA is used to split the selected EHR into blocks and encrypt them. Sequential execution of RSA needs a lot of calculation. Therefore, we use the enhancement proposed in [6] where authors have parallelized the process of encryption and decryption of a large number of data blocks. The resulted file R' and H(R) are sent to HSDSA.

$$R' = E_{PK_R}(R) \tag{1}$$

When the framework receives R' and H(R), it generates a unique identifier ID_R corresponding to the file R'. This is used to guarantee the unlinkability between DO and EHR. After that, HSDSA computes the hash of R' (H(R')) and stores ID_R, H(R) and H(R'). Next the framework splits R' into m shares $[S_1, ... , S_m]$, performs the exclusive OR operation of each split of R' with H(R').

$$
\begin{aligned}
[S'_1, ..., S'_m] &= R' \oplus H(R') \\
&= [S_1, ..., S_m] \oplus H(R') \\
&= [S_1] \oplus H(R'), .., [S_m] \oplus H(R')
\end{aligned}
\tag{2}
$$

$[S'_1, ... , S'_m]$ are the shares to be stored in independent CSPs. To securely distribute the shares, we adopted Shamir's secret sharing protocol. It represents a so-called (t,n) threshold scheme with $1 \leq t \leq n$. This mechanism permits the distribution of a document among n parts in a way that reconstruction is possible if at least t shares are present. Suppose a share S'_i (for i i $= 1 ... m$), Shamir's secret sharing algorithm sets $a_{i0} = S'_i$, chooses $a_{i1}, ..., a_{it-1}$ at random, takes distinct values $x_1, x_2,..., x_m$ with $m \geq t$-1 and computes the shares to distribute, as follows:

$$
\begin{cases}
S_{1i} = (x_i, f_1(x_i)) \\
\quad .... \\
S_{mi} = (x_i, f_m(x_i))
\end{cases}
, \ for \ i = 1..n
$$

In the proposed architecture, HSDSA selects m polynomials.

$$
\begin{cases}
f_1(x) = a_{10} + a_{11}x + a_{12}x^2 + ... + a_{1t-1}x^{t-1} \ mod \ p \\
\qquad\qquad ... \\
f_m(x) = a_{m0} + a_{m1}x + a_{m2}x^2 + ... + a_{mt-1}x^{t-1} \ mod \ p
\end{cases}
$$

Where

$$
\begin{bmatrix}
a_{11}, ..., a_{1t-1} \\
... \\
a_{m1}, ..., a_{mt-1}
\end{bmatrix}
\in \ \mathbb{Z}_1
$$

The HSDSA computes n shares $S_{1i}, ..., S_{mi}$ ($i = 1, ..., n$) and distributes them to $CSP_1, ..., CSP_n$.

Table 1. Scenario of the storage phase

User	HSDSA	$CSP_1, \dots CSP_n$
1. Calculate H(R) = $E_{PU_R}(R)$ 2. Encrypt R: $R' = E_{PK_R}(R)$ 3. Log in $\xrightarrow{\text{upload } R'}$ $H(R)$	4. Generate an identifier of R' : ID_R 5. Calculate H(R') 6. Split R' to m shares: $R' = S_1, \dots, S_m$ 7. Calculate S'_i for $i=(1\dots m)$ $S'_i = S_i \bigoplus$ H(R') 8. Select polynomials: $f_i(x)$ $i=(1\dots m)$ 9. Compute shares: $S_{1i}, \dots, S_{mi}$ $\xrightarrow{\text{Send shares}}$ ID_R	10. Store shares and ID_R

4   Analysis of the Proposed Retrieval Process

File retrieval, also known as file reconstruction, is the reversal process of file distribution and file slicing. In this framework the retrieval process starts when a data requester DR needs to get an EHR. He must log in and submit the EHR identifier (ID_R). HSDSA checks if the DR has the right to get the requested EHR. If the authorisation succeeded, then the reconstruction phase starts.

4.1   The Reconstruction Phase

Since the reconstruction of R' requires a massive amount of computation and that client resources are limited, we will use the reconstruction outsourcing scheme proposed in [5]. The framework assigns a CSP (CSP_R) to reconstruct shares S'_j. The reconstruction is considered successfull only if CSP_R gets at least t shares from $CSP_1, ..., CSP_n$. We assume that CSP_R gets k shares.

$$\begin{bmatrix} S_{11}, ... S_{m1} \\ ... \\ S_{1k}, ..., S_{mk} \end{bmatrix}, (k \geq t)$$

CSP_R computes S'_j for $j = (1, ..., m)$ using Lagrange interpolation polynomial and sends them to HSDSA:

$$S'_j = \sum_{i=1}^{k} S_{ji} \prod_{l=1, l\neq i}^{k} \frac{x_i}{x_i - x_l} \ mod \ p \ (j = 1, ..., m) \tag{3}$$

To make sure that CSP_R could not reveal any useful information, knowing that he is a curious and dishonest party, doing an exclusive OR operation helps to blind the content. Upon receipt of the shares, the HSDSA framework performs the exclusive OR operation between S'_j and H(R') to get S_j.

4.2   The Recovery Phase

This phase aims to securely transfer the Data Owner's private key to the right Data Requester. Table 2 illustrates the main steps related to this phase.

Once the reconstruction phase is done, HSDSA sends ID_{DO}/ID_{DR} to the Data Owner and to the Data Receiver. First the DR has to prove to the DO that he holds the right hash value of the original file $(H(R))'$ and that he is the correct DR. For this purpose, a Schnorr's identification protocol [7] is used not only to prove the hash possession but also to verify the DR identity. In the process of the latter algorithm the DO checks if H(R) $\overset{?}{=} (H(R))'$), and verifies if the n first bits of the DR identity match the ID_{DR} previously sent by FI. Then the DO and the DR must establish a secure connection for key exchange, based on Diffie-Hellman (DH) scheme Ephemeral version [8], reinforced with the hash value of the original file (H(R)). Establishing a session means that the two partners have agreed on session key (K_s) that will be used to crypt partners

Table 2. Scenario of the recovery phase

Data Requester	Data Owner
Schnorr algorithm	
$\alpha = (H(R))'$, s: secret key	
$v = \alpha^{-s}$	
1. Choose r and calculate	
$x = \alpha^r \bmod p$	
$\xrightarrow{x}$	
	2.Choose e, n $(3 \le n \le 20)$
$\xleftarrow{e,\ n}$	
3.Calculate $y = r + es \bmod p$	
Calculate $F = n$ first bits of ID_{DR}	
Calculate $Y = y \oplus F$	
$\xrightarrow{Y}$	
	4.Calculate $y = Y \oplus F$
	5.Verify $x \overset{?}{=} H(R)^y.v^e \bmod p$
Diffie Hellman algorithm	
s, p, g	b
6.Calculate $A = g^s \bmod p$	
$F_1 = $ premier n bits de $H(R)$	
$A_1 = A \oplus F_1$	
$\xrightarrow{A_1,p,g}$	
	7.Calculate $B = g^b \bmod p$
	$B_1 = B \oplus F_1$
$\xleftarrow{B_1}$	
$\xrightarrow{\text{Calculate } K_s}$	
$B = B_1 \oplus F_1$	8. Calculate $\qquad A = A_1 \oplus F_1$
$K_s = B^s \bmod p$	$K_s = A^s \bmod p$
	9.Encryt private key PU
	$PU' = E_{K_s}(PU)$
$\xleftarrow{PU'}$	
10.Extract PU	
$PU = D_{K_s}(PU')$	
11. Recover R $= D_{PU_R}(R')$	

metadata. Next, the DO encrypts his private key (PU) using K_s and sends the resulted value PU' to the DR.

$$PU' = E_{K_s}(PU) \tag{4}$$

The DR decrypts PU' using K_s to extract the DO private key. Possessing PU, the DR decrypts R' to finally recover the original EHR (R).

$$PU = D_{K_s}(PU') \tag{5}$$

$$R = D_{PU}(R') \tag{6}$$

5   Conclusion

In this paper, we presented HSDSA, a novel architecture for secure EHR. HSDSA includes several techniques, namely (i) RSA algorithm to guarantee the security of outsourced data, (ii) Shamir's secret sharing to securely distribute data across multiple clouds, (iii) a secure outsourcing reconstruction based on the (t, n) strategy, (iv) a Schnorr-based technique to prove data possession and to verify the requester identity and (v) a Diffie-Hellman algorithm to securely exchange decryption key. The proposed scheme allows the patient to get total control over the generation and management of the decryption keys without relying on a trusted authority. In a future work, we plan to add governmental organisation as Data Requester. These latter need to access data without the Data Owner authorisation. Hence, we aim to protect privacy while giving them access to EHR.

References

1. AlZain, M.A., et al.: Cloud computing security: from single to multi-clouds. In: 45th International Conference on System Sciences (2012)
2. Fabian, B., Ermakova, T., Junghanns, P.: Collaborative and secure sharing of health-care data in multi-clouds. Inform. Syst. **48**, 132–150 (2015)
3. Xhafa, F., Li, J., Zhao, G., Li, J., Chen, X., Wong, D.S.: Designing cloud-based electronic health record system with attribute-based encryption. Multimed. Tools Appl. **74**(10), 3441–3458 (2015)
4. Premarathne, U.S.: Hybrid cryptographic access control for cloud based electronic health records systems. IEEE Cloud Comput. **2**, 1–7 (2017)
5. Zhang, H., Yu, J., Tian, C., Zhao, P., Xu, G., Lin, J.: Cloud storage for electronic health records based on secret sharing with verifiable reconstruction outsourcing. IEEE Access **6**, 40713–40722 (2018)
6. Gupta, P., Verma, D.K., Singh, A. K.: Improving RSA algorithm using multi-threading model for outsourced data security in cloud storage. In: 8th International Conference on Cloud Computing, Data Science & Engineering, pp. 14–15 (2018)
7. Smart, N.P.: Zero-knowledge proofs. In: Smart, N.P. (ed.) Cryptography Made Simple. Information Security and Cryptography, pp. 425–438. Springer, Cham (2016). https://doi.org/10.1007/978-3-319-21936-3_21
8. Blake-Wilson, S., Menezes, A.: Authenticated Diffie-Hellman key agreement protocols. In: Tavares, S., Meijer, H. (eds.) SAC 1998. LNCS, vol. 1556, pp. 339–361. Springer, Berlin (1998). https://doi.org/10.1007/3-540-48892-8_26

Blockchain for Internet of Medical Things: A Technical Review

Fatma Ellouze[1]([✉]), Ghofrane Fersi[1,2], and Mohamed Jmaiel[1,3]

[1] ReDCAD laboratory, National School of Engineers of Sfax, University of Sfax,
B.P. 1173, 3038 Sfax, Tunisia
`fatma.ellouze@redcad.org`
[2] Higher Institute of Applied Sciences and Technology (ISSAT), University of Sousse,
Sousse, Tunisia
[3] Digital Research Center of Sfax, B.P. 275, Sakiet Ezzit, 3021 Sfax, Tunisia

Abstract. The Internet of Medical Things (IoMT) represents a network of implantable or wearable medical devices that continuously collect medical data about the patient's health status. These data are heavy, sensitive and require high level of security. With the emergence of blockchain technology, researchers are focusing on using blockchain strategies to bring security to healthcare applications. However, such integration is very difficult and challenging due to the different requirements in these two technologies. We present in this paper a technical review of existing solutions applying blockchain technology on IoMT. We analyze these studies, discuss the proposed architectures and how they managed the integration challenges. The open issues regarding the application of blockchain over IoMT are also specified.

Keywords: Healthcare · Internet of Medical Things · Security ·
Blockchain

1 Introduction

Recently, with the rapid development of wearable/implantable sensors and wireless communication, researchers are increasingly interested in improving the health sector in response to human needs by digitizing and decentralizing healthcare institutions and providing continuous and remote medical monitoring. Generated medical data are very critical and must be dealt with care to prevent any kind of data tampering. In this context, blockchain has emerged as the most secured, decentralized platform. It provides many powerful features without third party dealing including tamper-proof, immutability, traceability, data integrity, confidentiality and privacy.

Several research studies have identified blockchain effectiveness for the healthcare ecosystem. The papers [1, 8, 10, 11, 16] reviewed existing works related to using blockchain technology in healthcare to bring security. However, none of these works has focused on the integration of blockchain technology to the Internet of Medical Things. In this context, we propose our paper that reviews existing

© The Author(s) 2020
M. Jmaiel et al. (Eds.): ICOST 2020, LNCS 12157, pp. 259–267, 2020.
https://doi.org/10.1007/978-3-030-51517-1_22

works related to the integration of blockchain with the IoMT and discuss the technical details of each work.

The remainder of this paper is structured as follows. Section 2 presents a detailed technical analysis of existing articles dealing with the integration of blockchain with IoMT. Section 3 provides an in-depth discussion based on our study and presents research gaps, while Sect. 4 concludes the paper.

2   Internet of Medical Things (IoMT)-Blockchain Challenges

Certainly, blockchain technology is beneficial to the internet of medical things in terms of security. However, integrating both technologies is not trivial at all and is facing several challenges due to the conflicting requirements in these two technologies:

- **Processing:** Mining process and complex cryptography in blockchain are resource-hungry, demanding intensive computation and high energy consumption which cannot be afforded by resource-constrained IoMT devices that already suffer from resource shortage and energy limitations.
- **Storage:** IoMT devices generate huge amount of data with large flow. These data must be treated and stored in the blockchain to ensure their integrity which poses a significant challenge. In fact, blockchain technology relies on its nodes to provide a distributed storage which is not affordable by IoMT devices that have limited storage capabilities.
- **Mobility:** Blockchain was designed for a fixed network topology. However, implantable/wearable medical devices are in movement all the time which continuously change the topology.
- **Real Time:** IoMT applications are generally critical and require a real time and immediate response. Whereas, blocks creation is time consuming. In Bitcoin [15], 1MB per block is created every 10 min. Grouping these streams of data on blocks while respecting real time requirement is challenging.
- **Traffic Overhead:** Blockchain nodes communicate continuously to synchronize which creates significant overhead traffic. This is not affordable by bandwidth-limited IoT devices.

3   Blockchain-Based Approaches in IoMT

We present in this section, the most recent researches that have applied blockchain on IoMT. We classify these researches according to the most leading technique used to integrate blockchain into IoMT.

3.1   Ethereum-Based Contributions

In [12], a private Ethereum-based architecture is proposed to implement smart contracts in order to manage the users/devices requests and control access based on a set of attributes including the credentials, role and the domain. It uses IPFS for data storage. An interPlanetary File (IPFS) is used to store patient health records and devices technical information. The consensus mechanism is performed by a smart contract. The authors proposed a proof of medical stack (PoMS) as an alternative to PoS consensus model to protect smart contracts from malicious actions. PoMS allows stakeholders with huge amount of medical data presented as tokens to validate and create blocks.

A private blockchain-based system for medical data management has been proposed in [9]. It works on Ethereum smart contracts to manage data access permission between entities including patients, hospitals, doctors, research organizations and other stakeholders. The smart contract contains smart representations of medical records including permissions, record ownership metadata and data integrity. The medical record data are stored in external server (off-chain) and a cryptographic hash of the record is kept on the blockchain ensuring data integrity. The proposed system eliminates mining for simplification.

In [3], authors developed a cloud-based framework to monitor the progression of a neurological disorder disease using IoMT devices. They used cloud computing to store and process IoMT data and deploy Ethereum-based Blockchain network to securely exchange and share data between healthcare users. Smart contracts are employed to control users access to data in the cloud. No technical details about integrating blockchain in the system are presented.

In [6], authors proposed a permissioned blockchain-based architecture for secure remote patient monitoring. They used Ethereum to implement smart contracts in order to analyze data and send alerts to patient and healthcare providers. They proposed the use of Practical Byzantine Fault Tolerance (PBFT) as an alternative to PoW consensus model. The proposed architecture lacks techniques to meet challenges related to IoMT-Blockchain integration. And in SMEAD [13], an Ethereum-based architecture for remotely monitoring diabetes patients, smart contracts are used to manage access to data.

3.2   Modified Consensus Protocol

In order to fit the IoMT specificities, some works like [12] have proposed to modify the consensus protocol. In [20], authors proposed a consortium blockchain-based architecture in order to record data generated from IoMT in a secure way while ensuring the patient's privacy. The proposed architecture implements a patient agent software (PA) that defines the Blockchain functionalities. It is deployed on the Edge computing network to perform lightweight tasks and on a cloud server to provide tamper proof storage of the large volume of health data. The authors also proposed a modified PoS consensus which consists in choosing a leader for a group of nodes to validate and create the blocks. Smart contracts are used to manage health data including filtering clinically useless health data, generating alarm for some events, migrate data to the cloud if necessary, classify data and others. Compared to PoS, authors affirm that the modified PoS is more efficient in term of energy consumption and block generation time.

3.3   Modified Cryptographic Technique

The authors in [14] use some features of the standard version of blockchain to provide privacy and data integrity when sharing IoMT data. They use the hashing technique and propose a newly encryption algorithm to encrypt the transactions containing personal and sensitive data about patients. The main advantage of this algorithm is its ability to cover large number of uniquely identified medical objects and its very low time complexity which fits the real time requirement of IoMT. All transactions are stored in a blockchain maintained by the healthcare providers.

In [5], Authors proposed a customized blockchain-based framework suitable for IoMT devices. First, the proposed blockchain is private: nodes must be certificated to be able to join the network and send transactions. Second, authors eliminate the POW consensus protocol. To deal with the high volume generated by IoMT devices, they group encrypted data in blocks and store the interconnected blocks in the cloud. The hashes of blocks are kept on the blockchain to ensure tamper proof storage. For anonymity and the authenticity of the user, they use a 'A lightweight privacy-preserving ring signature scheme' which allows a group of nodes to participate in the data signature. To secure data and ensure its integrity during the transmission and storage, the authors used double encryption scheme besides the digital signature. The data are encrypted using lightweight ARX algorithms and the key is encrypted using the receiver's public key. To secure the transfer of public keys, authors proposed the Diffie-Hellmman key exchange technique. To meet scalability and network delay challenges, nodes are grouped in clusters. A cluster head is chosen to verify and store hash blocks, verify digital signatures and manage interactions between nodes in the cluster. The proposed work is not implemented and not evaluated.

In addition to their modified consensus protocol, authors in [20] proposed the ring signature as an alternative to the standard public key based digital signature to ensure patient privacy.

3.4   Hyperledger-Based Contributions

In [2], the authors proposed an IoT-blockchain based architecture to allow healthcare remote monitoring. The architecture contains two types of blockchain: (1) Medical Devices Blockchain to store medical data generated by medical devices during treatment period, (2) Consultation Blockchain maintained by hospitals to permanently store patients records. The transactions are verified and validated using smart contracts (Chaincodes in Fabric) executed by endorsing peers following Practical Byzantine Fault Tolerance algorithm. The authors developed a user interface to visualize the patient health data.

3.5   General Blockchain Concept Without Technical Specifications

In [7], the authors took benefit of tamper proof feature of blockchain to securely store and share IoMT data through patients and healthcare providers.

The patient data are stored as strings in blocks in the blockchain and the IoMT data are stored in blocks in off-chain database like IPFS. Smart contracts are used to ensure the privacy and security of blockchain.

MedChain [18] is a consortium blockchain-based framework proposed to meet challenges related to efficiently sharing data streams continuously generated from medical sensors. This includes handling time-series data streams, managing mutable and immutable medical data, and allowing an efficient storage and sharing of big and sensitive data. The MedChain network includes two separate decentralized sub-networks: (1) Blockchain network to store immutable data including users identity, data digest, session and operation, and (2) P2P network to store mutable data that facilitates data query including the description of data and session. MedChain uses the BFT-SMaRt as a consensus protocol

BIoMT [17] is an optimized, lightweight blockchain-based framework proposed to meet security and privacy challenges in developing solutions for IoMT systems. The proposed architecture is made up of four stratum: (1) Device layer consists of IoMT devices and implements the Elliptic Curve Cryptography (ECC) [9] key establishment protocol and the identity-based credential (IBC) mechanism to provide decentralized privacy, (2) Facility layer for managing IoMT devices and providing unique identity based on their attributes, (3) Cloud layer that runs anonymization algorithms to allow an identity-free data analysis and storage, and (4) Cluster layer groups several entities including medical facilities, service providers, and cloud servers into clusters. Each cluster has a cluster head that manages communication with other cluster heads to decrease the network overhead and delay. This work does not provide any technical details. It is not implemented and not evaluated. In [4] and [19], a blockchain-based architecture is proposed to allow secure transmission and storage of large amount of sensitive data generated by IoMT.

4   Discussion and Open Issues

Table 1 presents a classification of the existing contributions having integrated blockchain to IoMT (NM means Not Mentioned). Most of the proposed solutions are private blockchain-based and used Ethereum infrastructure thanks to its flexibility that is offered by the implementation of smart contracts for management purposes. Many issues have been treated when integrating blockchain with IoMT. For storing the big IoMT data, most of works [3] proposed an off-chain storage: Some researches [7,12] proposed to use IPFS because of its distributed data structure. Other works [3,5,9,17,20] used the cloud computing to store encrypted data while keeping hash references of that data in the blockchain. Such solutions do not guarantee immutability which is the essential feature of blockchain. In fact, if data have been modified/altered, this will be detected thanks to their hash stored in the blockchain but not recovered as it is only stored in the cloud (centralized storage). Other studies proposed an on-chain storage without precising technical details about dealing with the huge amount of data streams generated by IoMT devices. In the other hand, healthcare applications require real time responses which require a fast consensus protocol. However, IoMT are constrained devices and produce huge amount of data. The majority of studied works [9] have eliminated the consensus protocol to meet IoMT requirements. Some authors [12] use smart contract to self-verify and self-execute transactions. These smart contracts are protected using a lightweight consensus mechanism. Some others [6] proposed a lightweight consensus protocol: Researchers in [12,20] modified the PoS protocol to adapt it to the IoMT requirements, other works [5,20] grouped the nodes in clusters and chose a header for each cluster to manage transactions between nodes, validate and create the blocks. For security requirements in healthcare domain, some existing works proposed solutions to manage and control access rights. The majority [3,9,12,13] implement smart contracts to allow access to only authorized users based on some attributes of the IoMT ecosystem and their interaction with the users/stakeholders. Some other works [5,14,20] focused on maintaining patient privacy by proposing a lightweight privacy-preserving algorithms like ring signature scheme.

The literature review shows that there are some significant research gaps. There are several challenges that must be addressed to reach maturity and be efficient. These challenges include:

- **Lack of standards:** The proposed solutions are proprietary. They do not define standard protocols to adapt heterogeneous technologies and promote interoperability which prevent the adoption of such solutions. It is crucial to provide universal and platform-agnostic solutions that govern the interaction between IoMT devices, blockchain, cloud computing and end-users.
- **Programming Abstractions:** The integration of blockchain technology into the IoMT opens the way to many relevant applications in the health field. However, the adoption of such technology (Blockchain-IoMT) is complex and requires in-depth interdisciplinary knowledge from low-level including the management of IoMT devices and configuring blockchain to meet IoMT requirements, to high-level knowledge including sharing, storing and treating IoMT data. In this context, it is crucial to conceive an abstraction layer hiding all these complexities and to provide developers with new application programming interfaces (APIs) and middleware allowing them to easily implement decentralized and secure applications for healthcare using IoMT.
- **Limited Application Scope:** The majority of existing works are only focusing on healthcare applications related to remote patient monitoring and IoMT data management including data sharing and storage. It is crucial to conceive tracking applications that prevent counterfeit drugs and medical errors. In this context, the use of blockchain technology accompanied by the IoMT can be an effective solution to control the activity of doctors as well as for the management of the drug supply chain.
- **Lack of Technical Details:** The integration of blockchain with the IoMT is challenging. Most of existing solutions did not reveal any technical details. There is a need that researchers demystify all the technical details of the blockchain integration into IoMT.

Table 1. Classification of researches applying blockchain in IoMT

Contribution	Framework	Type	Consensus	Storage	Digital signature	Smart contract	Use case
[20]	NM	Consortium	Cluster head verifies and adds blocks	Off-chain (cloud)	Ring signature	Analyze and manage data	Manage IoMT data
[14]	NM	Private	NM	On-chain (hospitals)	NM	NM	Privacy and data integrity preservation
[9]	Ethereum	Private	NM	Off-chain (external server)	NM	Smart representations of medical records	Manage IoMT data
[7]	Ethereum	Public	NM	Off-chain (IPFS)	NM	Manage interactions between patients and their data and doctors	Manage IoMT data
[12]	Ethereum	Private	Proof of medical stake	Off-chain (IPFS)	NM	Manage access control	Manage access control to IoMT data and devices
[2]	Hyperledger Fabric	Private	NM	On-chain (hospitals and medical devices)	NM	Verifying and validating transactions	Healthcare remote monitoring
[18]	NM	Consortium	BFT-SMaRt	On-chain	NM	NM	Manage IoMT data
[5]	NM	Private	Cluster head verifies and adds blocks	Off-chain (cloud)	Lightweight ring signature	Analyze IoMt data and control patient health	Remote patient monitoring
[17]	NM	Private	NM	Off-chain(cloud)	NM	NM	Manage IoMT data and devices
[3]	Ethereum	Private	NM	Off-chain(cloud)	NM	Manage access control	Monitor the progression of a neurological disorder
[4]	NM	Private	PoW	NM	NM	NM	Manage IoMT data
[6]	Ethereum	Private	PBFT	On-chain	NM	Analyze data and send alerts to patients and healthcare providers	Remote patient monitoring
[19]	NM	NM	NM	Hybrid	NM	NM	Manage IoMT data
[13]	Ethereum	NM	NM	NM	NM	Manage access control	Remote monitoring of diabetes patients

5   Conclusion

With the strict and severe requirements of security in the healthcare domain, several researches focused on adopting Blockchain in the Internet of Medical Things (IoMT). Majority of them were focusing on providing privacy, data integrity, confidentiality and authentication. They proposed different use cases including remote monitoring of patients (RMP) and medical data management. Our research review shows that the proposed solutions lack many technical details when integrating Blockchain in the IoMT. Majority of them did not deal with high volume of data streams generated by resource-constrained IoMT devices and did not propose technical modifications on the Blockchain architecture in order to feet these challenges.

References

1. Agbo, C.C., Mahmoud, Q.H., Eklund, J.M.: Blockchain technology in healthcare: a systematic review, in healthcare. Multidisc. Digit. Publ. Inst. **7**, 56 (2019)
2. Attia, O., Khoufi, I., Laouiti, A., Adjih, C.: An IoT-blockchain architecture based on hyperledger framework for healthcare monitoring application. In: 2019 10th IFIP International Conference on New Technologies, Mobility and Security (NTMS), pp. 1–5, June 2019
3. Nguyen, D.C., Pathirana, P., Nguyen, K.: A mobile cloud based iomt framework for automated health assessment and management, vol. 2019, August 2019
4. Dilawar, N., Rizwan, M., Ahmad, F., Akram, S.: Blockchain: securing internet of medical things (IoMT). Int. J. Adv. Comput. Sci. Appl. **10** (2019)
5. Dwivedi, A., Srivastava, G., Dhar, S., Singh, R.: A decentralized privacy-preserving healthcare blockchain for IoT. Sensors **19**, 326 (2019)
6. Griggs, K.N., Ossipova, O., Kohlios, C.P., Baccarini, A.N., Howson, E.A., Hayajneh, T.: Healthcare blockchain system using smart contracts for secure automated remote patient monitoring. J. Med. Syst. **42**, 1–7 (2018)
7. Gupta, S., Malhotra, V., Singh, S.N.: Securing IoT-driven remote healthcare data through blockchain. In: Kolhe, M., Tiwari, S., Trivedi, M., Mishra, K. (eds.) Advances in Data and Information Sciences. LNNS, vol. 94, pp. 47–56. Springer, Singapore (2020). https://doi.org/10.1007/978-981-15-0694-9_6
8. Hussien, H.M., Yasin, S., Udzir, N., Zaidan, A., Bahaa, B.: A systematic review for enabling of develop a blockchain technology in healthcare application: taxonomy, substantially analysis, motivations, challenges, recommendations and future direction. J. Med. Syst. **43**, 320 (2019)
9. Khatoon, A.: A blockchain-based smart contract system for healthcare management. Electronics **9**, 94 (2020)
10. Kassab, M.H., DeFranco, J., Malas, T., Laplante, P., destefanis, G., Graciano Neto, V.V.: Exploring research in blockchain for healthcare and a roadmap for the future. IEEE Trans. Emerg. Top. Comput. 1 (2019)
11. Khezr, S., Moniruzzaman, M., Yassine, A., Benlamri, R.: Blockchain technology in healthcare: a comprehensive review and directions for future research. Appl. Sci. **9**, 1736 (2019)

12. Malamas, V., Dasaklis, T., Kotzanikolaou, P., Burmester, M., Katsikas, S.: A forensics-by-design management framework for medical devices based on blockchain. In: 2019 IEEE World Congress on Services (SERVICES), vol. 2642–939X, pp. 35–40, July 2019
13. Mohan, S., Shubha, R., Marks, A., Iyer, V.: SMEAD: a secured mobile enabled assisting device for diabetics monitoring, pp. 1–6, December 2017
14. Natarajan, B., Abilashkumar, P., Aboorva, S.: A Blockchain Based Approach for Privacy Preservation in Healthcare IoT. In: Gunjan, V., Garcia, Diaz V., Cardona, M., Solanki, V., Sunitha, K. (eds.) ICICCT 2019, pp. 465–473. Springer, Singapore (2020). https://doi.org/10.1007/978-981-13-8461-5_52
15. Reyna, A., Martín, C., Chen, J., Soler, E., Díaz, M.: On blockchain and its integration with IoT. Challenges and opportunities. Future Gener. Comput. Syst. **88**, 173–190 (2018)
16. Saha, A., Amin, R., Kunal, S., Vollala, S., Dwivedi, S.K.: Review on "blockchain technology based medical healthcare system with privacy issues". Secur. Priv. **2**, e83 (2019)
17. Seliem, M., Elgazzar, K.: BIoMT: blockchain for the internet of medical things. In: 2019 IEEE International Black Sea Conference on Communications and Networking (BlackSeaCom), pp. 1–4, June 2019
18. Shen, B., Guo, J., Yang, Y.: MedChain: efficient healthcare data sharing via blockchain. Appl. Sci. **9**, 1207 (2019)
19. Uddin, M.A., Stranieri, A., Gondal, I., Balasubramanian, V.: A patient agent to manage blockchains for remote patient monitoring, April 2018
20. Uddin, M.A., Stranieri, A., Gondal, I., Balasubramanian, V.: Blockchain leveraged decentralized iot ehealth framework. Internet Things **9**, 100159 (2020)

Application of Blockchain Technology in Healthcare: A Comprehensive Study

Rim Ben Fekih[1,2(✉)] and Mariam Lahami[1,2(✉)]

[1] ReDCAD Laboratory, National School of Engineers of Sfax, University of Sfax,
BP 1173, 3038 Sfax, Tunisia
{rim.benfekih,mariam.lahami}@redcad.org
[2] Digital Research Center of Sfax, B.P. 275, Sakiet Ezzit, 3021 Sfax, Tunisia

Abstract. Blockchain technology has been emerged in the last decade and has gained a lot of interests from several sectors such as finance, government, energy, health, etc. This paper gives a broad ranging survey of the application of blockchain in healthcare domain. In fact, the ongoing research in this area is evolving rapidly. Therefore, we have identified several use cases in the state of art applying the blockchain technology, for instance for sharing electronic medical records, for remote patient monitoring, for drug supply chain, etc. We have focused also on identifying limitations of studied approaches and finally we have discussed some open research issues and the areas of future research.

Keywords: Blockchain · Healthcare · Review

1 Introduction

In the last decade, blockchain is emerging as one of the most promising technology that captures attentions of several academic researches and industry. This concept was originally introduced by Satoshi Nakamoto in a white paper in 2008 [19]. It is defined as a decentralized, distributed, immutable ledger which is used to securely record transactions across many computers in a peer-to-peer network, without the need of third party.

The first generation of blockchain, Blockchain 1.0, is underlying on Bitcoin [19] which is the first implementation of blockchain based on cryptocurrency applications[1]. The next generation, called Block chain 2.0, is emerged with the concept of smart contract that it is considered as a piece of code defined, executed and recorded in the distributed ledger. The third generation of blockchain technology, Blockchain 3.0, deals essentially with non financial applications such as government, energy, health, etc. In fact, several organisations have adopted this technology and applied it for several use cases in the healthcare domain. The most interesting features in blockchain that are beneficial to healthcare

---

[1] Other blockchain 1.0 technologies have been appeared such as Dash, Litecoin, etc.

M. Jmaiel et al. (Eds.): ICOST 2020, LNCS 12157, pp. 268–276, 2020.
https://doi.org/10.1007/978-3-030-51517-1_23

applications is decentralization, privacy and security since blockchain technology may ensure for example a secure access to medical data for patients and various stakeholders (insurance companies, hospitals, doctors, etc.).

In this survey, we present the most relevant researches applying blockchain in healthcare sector. The studied approaches are classified according to a wide range of use cases such as electronic medical records [2, 6–8, 16, 22, 25], remote patient monitoring [11, 14, 21], pharmaceutical supply chain [4, 5, 12, 15, 20] and health insurance claims [10, 26]. Additionally, this study discusses the applicability of these solutions and their technical limitations. Moreover, lessons learnt and some research directions are identified.

The remainder of this paper is organized as follows. Section 2 introduces the key concepts to understand blockchain technology. In Sect. 3, we provide some medical uses cases in healthcare that use this promising technology. At the end of this section, we will sum up the main results. In Sect. 4, research challenges and opportunities are highlighted. Finally, Sect. 5 concludes the paper and gives suggestions for future work.

2 Key Concepts on Blockchain

In this section, we discuss the core features of blockchain technology to help understanding the rest of this paper.

2.1 Overview and Architecture of Blockchain

Essentially, blockchain is a peer-to-peer network that sits on top of the internet [13], which was introduced in 2008 as part of a proposal for Bitcoin [19]. The blockchain is a public ledger made up of a sequence of blocks, which holds a full history of transaction records that occurred within the network. A block is consisted essentially by a header and a body. The header of each block contains the hash of the previous block. Therefore, the blocks form a chain or a linked list where each block structure is based on the previous one.

Block headers also contain a *timestamp* indicating the time of when the block was published, *a nonce*, which is an arbitrary number that miners would change frequently to get a certain hash value to solve a mathematical puzzle and a *Merkle tree* that fundamentally decreases the exertion required to check transactions inside a block.

A Blockchain transaction can be defined as a small unit of task that is stored in public blocks. Each transaction is verified by consensus of a majority of the system participants. This way, tamperproof is ensured once transactions are packed into the blockchain. In regards to blockchain immutability, a same copy of the ledger is replicated, hosted and maintained by all participants [13].

Regardless of the type of blockchain, the business logic is encoded using smart contracts, a self-executing code on the blockchain framework that allow for straight-through processing. When embedded in the blockchain, smart contracts becomes permanently *tamper-proof*, as no one can change what's been programmed, *self-verifying* due to automated possibilities and *self-enforcing* when the rules are met at all stages.

Among the important features of Blockchain, decentralization by making the ledger accessible by all participants, immutability, so blockchain is nearly impossible to tamper and is censorship-resistant, availability by providing all peers a copy of the blockchain to get access all timestamped transaction records, and anonymity, where each user can interact with the blockchain with a generated address, that does not reveal the real identity of the user.

2.2 Taxonomy of Blockchain Systems

Current blockchain systems are categorized into four types: public, private, consortium and hybrid blockchains [21].

- **Public Blockchains**: Public blockchains provide a fully decentralized network, where every member can access the blockchain content and could take part in the consensus process (e.g. Bitcoin and Ethereum [23]).
- **Private Blockchains**: Private blockchains are dedicated for single enterprise solutions and utilized to keep track of data exchanges occurring between different departments or individuals. Every participant need consent to join the network and considered as a known member once it has been adhered.
- **Consortium Blockchains**: A consortium blockchain is a permissioned network and public only to a privileged group. It is used as an auditable and reliably synchronized distributed database that keeps track of participant's data exchanges.
- **Hybrid Blockchains**: Hybrid blockchains combine the benefits of private and public blockchains. Therefore, a public blockchain is employed to make the ledger fully accessible, with a private blockchain running in the background that can control access to the modifications in the ledger.

3 Blockchain Use Cases in Healthcare

One of the fields where blockchain is considered to have great potential is healthcare. Understanding the pertinence and importance of blockchain in healthcare, in 2016, the Office of the National Coordinator for Health Information Technology (ONC), composed an ideation challenge for requesting white papers on the potential utilization of blockchain in healthcare. This challenge brought about a few proposed healthcare applications for blockchain.

In this section, we focus on the most important studies classified by several use cases such as electronic medical records, remote patient monitoring, pharmaceutical supply chain and health insurance claims.

3.1   Electronic Medical Records

To transform healthcare, the focus should be attributed to the management of health data that could be improved from the potential to connect heterogeneous systems and increase Electronic Health Records (EHRs) accuracy. While Electronic medical records (EMRs) and EHRs are used interchangeably, there is a difference between the two terms. EMRs term came along first, which is a digital version of the paper charts in the clinician's office. An EMR contains the medical and treatment history of the patients in one practice. However, EHRs focus on the total health of the patient-going beyond standard clinical data collected in the provider's office and inclusive of a broader view on a patient's care [1].

From the mapping study, blockchain technology supports the management of EHRs. In this context, Ekblaw et al. present [7] MedRec, an EHR-related implementation that proposes a decentralized approach to manage authorization, permissions, and data sharing between healthcare stakeholders. MedRec uses ethereum platform to enable patients to have knowledge and information on who can get to their healthcare information.

A second application that integrates EHR, is FHIRChain (Fast Health Interoperability Records + Blockchain) [25]. It's a blockchain-based application implemented using ethereum for sharing clinical data that focuses on healthcare record management. FHIRChain provides solutions for patients that meet the requirements from the ONC.

Similarly, Xia et al. present Medshare [24] an ethereum application for systems that struggle with a lack of collaboration for sharing data between cloud services due to the adverse risks towards displaying the contents of private data. Medshare provides data provenance, auditing, and control between big data entities for sharing medical data in cloud repositories.

Other blockchain-based EMR applications include MedBlock [8] and BlocHIE [16]. MedBlock [8] provides a mechanism for a record search. The proposed system maintains the address of blocks containing the records of a patient, grouped by a healthcare provider or department. Each patient inventory contains a reference to the corresponding record on the blockchain. BlocHIE [16] proposed by Jiang et al. where they present a healthcare platform based on blockchain technology.

To keep exploiting existing databases, BlocHIE combines both off-chain storage, where data is stored in external hospitals' databases, and on-chain verification. The blockchain system stores a hashed value of external records. Authors improve fairness and throughput by proposing FAIR-FIRST and TP&FAIR, two fairness-based transaction packing algorithms. There is also another healthcare blockchain-based framework, Ancile [6] which uses ethereum smart contracts to achieve data privacy, security, access control and interoperability of EMRs.

Roehrs et al. [22] present omniPHR, a distributed model that maintain an interoperable single-view of Personal Health Records (PHR). The proposed solution is based on an elastic, interoperable and scalable architecture of PHR data. Furthermore, omniPHR evaluation could ensure the division of PHR into data blocks and its distribution in a routing overlay network.

3.2   Remote Patient Monitoring

To be able to remotely monitor the status of the patient, remote patient monitoring covers the collection of medical data through mobile devices, body area sensors and IoT (Internet of Things) devices. Blockchain play an important role in storing, sharing and retrieving the remotely collected biomedical data.

In this context, Ichikawa et al. [14] present an application where mobile devices are used to transmit data to a blockchain-based application on Hyperledger Fabric.

Griggs et al. [11] demonstrate how Ethereum smart contracts provides automated interventions in a secure environment by supporting real-time patient monitoring application. Other proposed approaches present the great potentials of Internet of Things (IoT) in many domains, especially it's being heavily exploited and used in e-health. In this direction, Ray et al. propose IoBHealth [21], a data-flow architecture that combines the IoT with blockchain and can be used for accessing, storing and managing of e-health data.

3.3   Pharmaceutical Supply Chain

One other identified use case of blockchain is in the pharmaceutical industry. The delivery of counterfeit or inadequate medications can have critical consequences for the patients. Blockchain technology has been identified as having the capability to address this problem.

Bocek et al. [4] present Modum.io AG, a startup that uses blockchain to achieve data immutability. To verify the compliance to quality control temperature requirements, this startup creates public accessibility of the temperature records of pharmaceutical products during their transportation.

Counterfeit drugs also have been addressed by [5,12,20] where authors prevent counterfeiting by proposing a secure, immutable and traceable pharmaceutical supply chain based on blockchain technology.

With regards to drug regulations issues, Jamil et al. [15] addressed drugs standardization problems. Authors have highlighted the difficulties to detect falsified drugs and proposed a blockchain-based solution to detect counterfeits.

While there is a minority of papers that present an implementation of the proposed system, some interesting reviews discuss pharmaceutical supply chain issues [9,17].

3.4   Health Insurance Claims

Health Insurance claims are one of healthcare fields that can benefit from blockchain's immutability, transparency and auditability of data stored on it.

While Healthcare insurance claim processing is an important area where blockchain has potentials [10]. However, prototypes implementations of such systems are very limited. We can find MIStore [26], a blockchain-based medical insurance system that provides medical insurance industry with encrypted and immutably stored medical insurance data.

Table 1. Major contributions classified by use cases

Use cases	Paper	Framework	Data Storage	Contribution	Year
Electronic medical records	[7]	Ethereum	Off-chain	Provides a patient-centric system for a transparent and accessible view of medical history	2016
	[24]	Ethereum	Off-chain	Propose a platform for shared medical data in cloud repositories	2017
	[22]	Specific	Off-chain	A PHR distributed model that propose solutions for latency issues	2017
	[25]	Ethereum	Hybrid	Proposes a blockchain-based EMR application that meets ONC requirements	2018
	[8]	Proprietary	Off-chain	Provides a blockchain-based EMR management system	2018
	[16]	Proprietary	Off-chain	A healthcare system that Combines both off-chain storage and on-chain verification	2018
	[6]	Ethereum	Hybrid	Proposes an electronic health records system that protects personal health information	2018
Remote patient monitoring	[14]	Hyperledger Fabric	Off-chain	A mobile Health blockchain-based system for cognitive behavioral therapy for insomnia	2017
	[11]	Ethereum	Hybrid	Proposes to use blockchain-based smart contracts to perform real-time data analysis	2018
	[21]	–	–	Propose an architecture that integrates blockchain and IoT sensory data collected from patients	2020
Pharmaceutical supply chain	[4]	Ethereum	Off-chain	Maintains public temperature records' accessibility of drugs during their transportation	2017
	[12]	–	–	Explains blockchain usability to add traceability and visibility to drugs supply	2018
	[5]	Hyperledger Fabric	On-chain	Design a blockchain-based control system for the control of drugs turnover	2019
	[20]	Hyperledger Fabric	On-chain	Design a secure, immutable and traceable pharma supply chain	2019
Health insurance claims	[26]	Ethereum	On-chain	Proposes a blockchain-based medical insurance storage system	2018

We present a summary of the studied papers in Table 1. We have noticed that the majority of these applications are developed on popular blockchain frameworks, such as Ethereum and Hyperledger Fabric.

4   Research Challenges and Opportunities

Based on the proposed prototypes and developed applications, we can identify different limitations of the healthcare Blockchain-Based applications.

First, EMR systems do not address semantic interoperability [3]. Consequently, manual inspection and mapping of predefined ontologies from medical and health data experts are required. Second, clinical malpractice cannot be controlled at this level. Moreover, scalability and interoperability issues represent the main focus of current and future studies in this field. Interoperability challenge reveals the fact of missing standards for developing healthcare applications based on blockchain technology. Thus, the different developed applications may not be able to interoperate. In addition, scalability is a major issue in blockchain-based healthcare systems [18] especially towards the volume of medical data involved. Due to high-volume healthcare data, it is not practicable to store it on-chain i.e. on blockchain, as this is may lead to serious performance degradation. Furthermore, there is a problem of latency caused by the speed of transactions' processing and off-chain data load in a blockchain-based system. Finally, another weakness is related to blockchain immutability and self-execution of code, since smart contracts could become vulnerable to hackers. Just between 2016 and 2018, attacks such as the decentralized autonomous organization (DAO) attack cause a loss of millions of dollars as part of the assets held by the smart contracts.

5 Conclusion

The present study gave an overview about the application of Blockchain in Healthcare. In fact, due to the exponential growth of this technology, blockchain has been applied in several use cases with the aim of enhancing the automation of medical services.

Our study shows that the majority of researches applying blockchain in healthcare are concentrated towards sharing Electronic Health Records. Other investigations should be considered by blockchain researchers in domains such as biomedical research, pharmaceutical supply chain, insurance. Furthermore, we noticed that rarely are papers dealing with implementation details.

Even though, blockchain technology offers promising features, there is still a need for more research to better understand, efficiently and securely develop and evaluate this technology. Ongoing efforts have been conducted to overcome limitations in scalability, security and privacy in order to improve stakeholders' confidence in using this technology and to increase its adoption in healthcare.

References

1. Electronic health and medical records. https://www.healthit.gov/buzz-blog/electronic-health-and-medical-records/emr-vs-ehr-difference
2. Ahram, T., Sargolzaei, A., Sargolzaei, S., Daniels, J., Amaba, B.: Blockchain technology innovations. In: IEEE Technology & Engineering Management Conference (TEMSCON), pp. 137–141. IEEE (2017)
3. Bender, D., Sartipi, K.: HL7 FHIR: an agile and restful approach to healthcare information exchange. In: Proceedings of the 26th IEEE International Symposium on Computer-based Medical Systems, pp. 326–331. IEEE (2013)
4. Bocek, T., Rodrigues, B.B., Strasser, T., Stiller, B.: Blockchains everywhere - a use-case of blockchains in the pharma supply-chain. In: IFIP/IEEE Symposium on Integrated Network and Service Management (IM), pp. 772–777, May 2017

5. Bryatov, S., Borodinov, A.: Blockchain technology in the pharmaceutical supply chain: researching a business model based on hyperledger fabric. In: International Conference on Information Technology and Nanotechnology (ITNT), Samara, Russia (2019)

6. Dagher, G.G., Mohler, J., Milojkovic, M., Marella, P.B.: Ancile: privacy-preserving framework for access control and interoperability of electronic health records using blockchain technology. Sustain. Cities Soc. **39**, 283–297 (2018)

7. Ekblaw, A., Azaria, A., Halamka, J.D., Lippman, A.: A case study for blockchain in healthcare: "MedRec" prototype for electronic health records and medical research data. In: Proceedings of IEEE Open & Big Data Conference, vol. 13, p. 13 (2016)

8. Fan, K., Wang, S., Ren, Y., Li, H., Yang, Y.: Medblock: efficient and secure medical data sharing via blockchain. J. Med. Syst. **42**(8), 136 (2018)

9. Fernando, E., et al.: Success factor of implementation blockchain technology in pharmaceutical industry: a literature review. In: 6th International Conference on Information Technology, Computer and Electrical Engineering (ICITACEE), pp. 1–5. IEEE (2019)

10. Gatteschi, V., Lamberti, F., Claudio, D., Víctor, S.: Blockchain and smart contracts for insurance: Is the technology mature enough?, February 2018

11. Griggs, K.N., Ossipova, O., Kohlios, C.P., Baccarini, A.N., Howson, E.A., Hayajneh, T.: Healthcare blockchain system using smart contracts for secure automated remote patient monitoring. J. Med. Syst. **42**(7), 130 (2018)

12. Haq, I., Esuka, O.M.: Blockchain technology in pharmaceutical industry to prevent counterfeit drugs. Int. J. Comput. Appl. **975**, 8887 (2018)

13. Iansiti, M., Lakhani, K.R.: The truth about blockchain. Harv. Bus. Rev. **95**(1), 118–127 (2017)

14. Ichikawa, D., Kashiyama, M., Ueno, T.: Tamper-resistant mobile health using blockchain technology. JMIR mHealth uHealth **5**(7), e111 (2017)

15. Jamil, F., Hang, L., Kim, K., Kim, D.: A novel medical blockchain model for drug supply chain integrity management in a smart hospital. Electronics **8**(5), 505 (2019)

16. Jiang, S., Cao, J., Wu, H., Yang, Y., Ma, M., He, J.: BlocHIE: a blockchain-based platform for healthcare information exchange. In: IEEE International Conference on Smart Computing (SMARTCOMP), pp. 49–56. IEEE (2018)

17. Mackey, T.K., Nayyar, G.: A review of existing and emerging digital technologies to combat the global trade in fake medicines. Expert Opin. Drug Saf. **16**(5), 587–602 (2017)

18. Mazlan, A.A., Daud, S.M., Sam, S.M., Abas, H., Rasid, S.Z.A., Yusof, M.F.: Scalability challenges in healthcare blockchain system-a systematic review. IEEE Access **8**, 23663–23673 (2020)

19. Nakamoto, S., et al.: Bitcoin: A Peer-to-peer Electronic Cash System (2008)

20. Raj, R., Rai, N., Agarwal, S.: Anticounterfeiting in pharmaceutical supply chain by establishing proof of ownership. In: TENCON 2019–2019 IEEE Region 10 Conference (TENCON), pp. 1572–1577. IEEE (2019)

21. Ray, P.P., Dash, D., Salah, K., Kumar, N.: Blockchain for IoT-based healthcare: background, consensus, platforms, and use cases. IEEE Syst. J. (2020)

22. Roehrs, A., da Costa, C.A., da Rosa Righi, R.: OmniPHR: a distributed architecture model to integrate personal health records. J. Biomed. Inform. **71**, 70–81 (2017)

23. Wood, G., et al.: Ethereum: a secure decentralised generalised transaction ledger. Ethereum Project Yellow Paper **151**(2014), 1–32 (2014)

24. Xia, Q., Sifah, E.B., Asamoah, K.O., Gao, J., Du, X., Guizani, M.: MeDShare: trust-less medical data sharing among cloud service providers via blockchain. IEEE Access **5**, 14757–14767 (2017)
25. Zhang, P., White, J., Schmidt, D.C., Lenz, G., Rosenbloom, S.T.: FHIRChain: applying blockchain to securely and scalably share clinical data. Comput. Struct. Biotech. J. **16**, 267–278 (2018)
26. Zhou, L., Wang, L., Sun, Y.: MIStore: a blockchain-based medical insurance storage system. J. Med. Syst. **42**(8), 149 (2018)

Trust Execution Environment and Multi-party Computation for Blockchain e-Health Systems

Feriel Yahmed$^{(\boxtimes)}$ and Mohamed Abid

Unit Hatem Bettaher IRESCOMATH, University of Gabes, Gabes, Tunisia
yahmedferiel@gmail.com, mohamed.abid@enig.rnu.tn

Abstract. Blockchain is a rich and attractive domain for researchers since it is independent of "third party" such as Bank or government. This "open" phenomenon does not respect all the security criteria such as private data protection and confidentiality; hence, we cannot trust this approach despite its contributions. Blockchain technology has gained considerable progress in recent years in fields such as e-health. The medical data contains personal and sensitive information that must be preserved. The current Blockchain systems suffer from serious practical limitations, e.g. poor performance, high-energy consumption and lack of confidentiality. On the other hand, *Trust Execution Environment* TEE is imperfect; it is based on the centralization of data. To avoid data centralization and its limitations, an approach based on collecting the necessary data from distributed database is presented in this paper. Our goals are to protect the user's privacy and to execute it in TEE combined with *Multi-party computation* MPC. We proof by security analysis that our new solution meets the fundamental criteria of security such as confidentiality and privacy.

Keywords: E-health · MPC (Multi-party computation) · BC (Blockchain) · TEE (Trust Execution Environment) and Smart Contract (SC) · IPFS (Interplanetary File System)

1 Introduction

Technological evolution is bringing a profound change to the core of business. Nowadays IT(Information Technology) is not only a productivity tool but also a means of administration and management. It is becoming a strategic and a necessary mean to manage the evolutionary processes of the company's business lines. Therefore, the field of information and communication technologies has become one of the pillars of business.

The information system is an essential element for the company; hence, its innovation must be almost permanent and exploits to the best the new technologies. New network technologies open up new potential for communication and data exchange in different geographical areas. This context has motivated the IT community to take an interest in distributed architectures such as the Blockchain.

Modern systems like Blockchain have become increasingly complex, open, connected and are leading to new challenges. User requirements for security are increasingly demanding. The Blockchain has affected several sectors such as finance, health care, public services, electronic voting, music and the government sector. The reason

© The Author(s) 2020
M. Jmaiel et al. (Eds.): ICOST 2020, LNCS 12157, pp. 277–286, 2020.
https://doi.org/10.1007/978-3-030-51517-1_24

for this enhanced interest is the disappearance of the trusted medium, to operate in a decentralized manner with an acceptable degree of confidence.

The IT community hails the Blockchain as the next great technological innovation. According to Marc Andreessen, co-founder of Netscape and co-writer of Mosaic the Blockchain: "When we sit here in 20 years, we will talk about [Bitcoin and Blockchain technology] the way we talk about the internet today" [1].

1.1 Blockchain

The Blockchain is a new technology for storing and transmitting data in a secure and transparent way, it works without a central control body. This technology takes the form of a transaction log in a peer-to-peer P2P network. These transactions grouped together in the form of blocks, which are linked together. Each block contains data, the hash of the previous block, and a time stamp. Figure 1 represents an example of Blockchain structure.

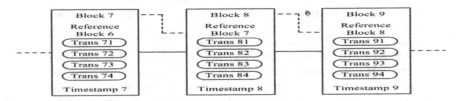

Fig. 1. Blockchain structure [17]

All network nodes back up and verify the data stored in the Blockchain, and consequently provides a strong resilience against attacks that can tamper the integrity of the data.

As this great feature leads to a Blockchain-based implementation of smart contract platforms such as Ethereum [2], several developers have been attracted to build decentralized applications using smart contracts that avoid the need for a central server to manage and maintain the data [3].

The first cryptocurrency based on a Blockchain was Bitcoin in 2008 [7], however the Blockchain has evolved to meet and serve a variety of purposes. The difference between a traditional database and the Blockchain is essentially the storage policy. The Blockchain resides on computer networks However, databases are stored on centralized servers (see Fig. 2). Each one of them has its own advantages and limitations.

Fig. 2. Traditional DATABASE VS Blockchain

1.2   Smart Contract

Szabo first introduced the term *smart contract* in 1994, where the smart contract is defined as "a computerized transaction protocol that executes the terms of a contract" [4].

Smart contracts are compiled as byte codes and executed in EVM (Ethereum Virtual Machine) located in miners' computers, which is very similar to Java executed in JVM. When the smart contract operates, it must be packaged by the miner and written into the Blockchain. Each Blockchain in Ethereum has various functions and purposes [5]. Compared with traditional contract, a smart contract is an executable code stored and running in Blockchain. The smart contract may execute independently and automatically without third parties, and these running results are irreversible on Blockchain and are traceable by each participant. The main features of smart contract are given as follows [6]: stability and deterministic features, the same input always produces the same output. Because smart contracts are executable codes stored in Blockchain, every network participant can inspect them. Meanwhile, all the interactions with a smart contract occur via signed messages on the Blockchain and thus every participant can verify and trace the contract's operations.

The structure of this paper is as follows. Section 2 presents a state of the art by analyzing the current situation and motivation. Section 3 describes the steps of the new solution and an e-health use-case. We present the security analysis of the proposed solution in Sect. 4. Conclusion is drawn in Sect. 5.

2   State of the Art

We have conducted an intensive research to get the state of the art of Blockchain and smart contracts applications. In the following, we present the existing solutions based on the technologies chosen by researchers.

2.1   Centralized Database

The researchers in [8] propose a solution for digitizing certificates, in university use case, in order to improve the conditions and make life much easier using the Blockchain and intelligent contracts. Therefore, it will be possible to have a certificate, wherever the student is and whatever the time, with full security since the access to the data will be done only when people are authorized.

It is true that this solution has contributions in terms of time and speed. However, in our opinion, it does not ensure total security since it puts in danger the private data when they are published in the Blockchain. In addition, the weak point of the solution is the centralization since the data are recorded in the database of the university and if it is broken down, nothing can be done.

2.2   PKI Public Key Infrastructure

Existing certificate mechanisms do not dynamically ensure the trustworthiness of a certificate, to solve this weakness Ahmed et al. [9] offer the "smart contract assisted

PKI". This solution manages trust dynamically in a distributed way and provides better trust experience for users. Despite its contribution, this solution neglects the protection of private data.

2.3 TEE Trust Execution Environment

TEE (Trust Execution Environment) [16] is a tamper-proof trusted execution processing environment. It runs on a separate kernel and it can be safely updated.

TEE resists all software and physical attacks. It represents a space for storage execution and secure execution.

In this context, Hawk [10], which is the first TEE, is a smart contract system that provides confidentiality by executing contracts off-chain and posting only zero-knowledge proofs on-chain. The zero-knowledge proofs in Hawk incurs very high computational overhead. Additionally, it was designed for a single compute node called the "manager" which must be trusted for privacy.

There are also some technical inefficiencies such as limited block size and transfer cost. In addition, once the data is stored in the Blockchain, it cannot be modified. This poses certain problems such as falsification during the execution of the contract. In some cases, the contract needs data in real time. The most relevant solution is to store the data off-chain and choose another execution platform more secure and more relevant.

To ensure confidentiality and private data protection, Rifi et al. [11] offer a solution that combines two technologies: *Trust Execution Environment* TEE and Blockchain, from where data is stored and executed in TEE. It is a platform that ensures data integrity; confidentiality and protection, but it is based on the centralization of data storage. In [11], authors concluded that in order to apply Blockchain technology to E-Health, it should be public, and has three main keys: scalability, secure access to medical data, and data privacy. In this article, the researchers prove that the Blockchain does not have good performances in terms of storage. Therefore, they proposed to store the data off-chain using the IPFS (*Interplanetary File System*). The new Blockchain technology [15] applied in e-Health identifies new ways to share the distributed view of health data and promotes the advancement of precision medicine, improving health and preventing diseases.

2.4 IPFS

IPFS [12] (*Interplanetary File system*) is a decentralized file sharing platform. It identifies files by their contents. To retrieve file locations and connectivity information from the nodes, this system uses Distributed Hash Table (DHT).

As described in [13], the DHT is primarily a distributed key value store. It uses node identifiers and keys. They must have the same length and a distance metric to easily store and retrieve the information. A node tries to find the nodes in its vicinity, when searching a value and a key. To do this; it uses buckets to keep track of the nodes in the network. The spaces are organized so that each node in the network has precise information about its immediate environment.

Blockchain and IPFS [14] are based on similar concepts of decentralized networks. However, each one of them has its own characteristics. IPFS is a file-sharing system that chops its files. The search for files within IPFS is based on these hashes. Blockchain and IPFS perform very different tasks for their users. It is possible to store files in IPFS while the hashes are stored in Blockchain.

As discussed before, the TTE has many advantages but it is not based on multi-party computation. Therefore, to eliminate the centralization of data, we try to link between IPFS, TEE and the Blockchain to have efficient results that respect the security rules.

The use of TEE allows the user to store his/her data in TEE and to execute his/her smart contract. To access to the latter, the user must enter his/her public hash key; TEE compares it with the list of public hash keys; if it is compatible with a public hash key, he/she can access to it. The Blockchain is used to transfer smart contract from user to TEE (see Fig. 3 Smart contract with TEE). To import data from IPFS, the user should put the IPFS Hashes and a time stamp in the smart contract (see Fig. 3 Smart contract with IPFS). As a conclusion, executing smart contract in Blockchain suffers from many problems such as poor performance, high-energy consumption.

Fig. 3. Smart contract with TEE VS Smart contract with IPFS

3 The Proposed Solution

With the technical progress, many technologies are developing, a huge amount of exchanged data will appear, and the exchange of data is carried out from different locations and different sources. In order to ensure all these criteria, we must have a solution that provides: Confidentiality, Authenticity, Integrity, Decentralization and privacy in two phases: Data Storage and Smart contract' execution.

3.1 Architecture and Security Parameters

Figure 4 presents the architecture of the new solution which is composed by two phases:

a) Data Storage

In this phase, the user stores his\her encrypted data in different places. To access to it, we need to process some cryptographic steps.

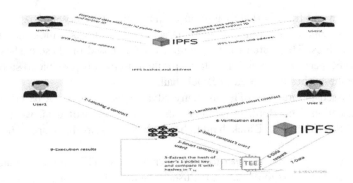

Fig. 4. Proposed architecture

b) Smart contract's execution

Before this operation, we need to transfer the smart contract using Blockchain. After that, the TEE "imposes" some protocols to access to it. Also, TEE controls missing data and imports them from DDB (Distributed Data Base) The approach proposed in Article [18] can be used to collect data either from IPFS or from users. After that, it executes the smart contract and returns the result to the Blockchain.

Table 1 contains all the security parameters of the communicating parties in e-health scenario.

Table 1. Security parameters

Parameters	Description
H_{IPFS}	Hashes IPFS
H_{Kpub}	Hashes public key
K_{pub}	Public key
K_{priv}	Private key
$@_{IPFS}$	IPFS address
T_{ht}	Hashes table in TEE
L_{DD}	List of demanded data
EN_{Kpub}	Encrypt with public key

3.2 Steps of the New Solution

Next, we describe, step by step, the exchanges in the new solution:

a) *User's subscription (Data Storage)*

A user accesses an IPFS and stores his/her encrypted message with homomorphic cryptography. The encryption ensures data security since only authorized persons have the right to access encrypted data. IPFS sends to the user its $@_{IPFS}$ and H_{IPFS}.

1 - User 1 sends his\her Id and $EN_{Kpubuser2}$(Data) to the IPFS.
2 - IPFS sends $@_{IPFS}$ and H_{IPFS} to User2
3 - User 2 sends his\her Id and $EN_{Kpubuser1}$(Data) to the IPFS.
4 - IPFS sends $@_{IPFS}$ and H_{IPFS} to User1

b) *Smart contract execution*
   1 - User 1 signs his\her smart contract with his/her private key K_{priv} (this smart contract demands $@_{IPFS}$ and H_{IPFS} from the acceptation smart contract) and sends it to the Blockchain.
   2 - The Blockchain sends the signed Smart Contract to the TEE
   3 - TEE extracts the hash H_{kpub} and compares it with the hashes in T_{ht}
   4 - User 2 signs his\her contract that contains his\her $@_{IPFS}$ and H_{IPFS} with his \her K_{priv} and sends it to the Blockchain.
   5 - The Blockchain sends the signed Smart contract to the TEE. The latter extracts the H_{Kpub} of User 2 and compares it with the hashes in T_h. After that, it builds a file that contain missing data.
   6 - TEE sends the file that contains the L_{DD} (List of demanded data), $@_{IPFS}$, H_{IPFS} and timestamp (from acceptation smart contract) to IPFS
   7 - IPFS verifies the TEE request that contains $@_{IPFS}$, H_{IPFS}, L_{DD} and timestamp after that it sends missing data to the TEE.
   8 - TEE executes the smart contract
   9 - TEE sends the executed results to the Blockchain.

3.3 E-Health Use Case

We present in the following the steps of our solution when applied to e-health scenario. In this use case, we have two actors, the doctor and the patient. Figure 5 shows the steps of this use case.

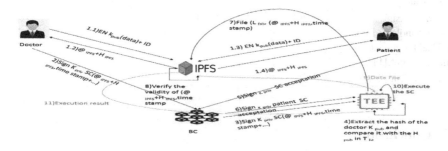

Fig. 5. All the exchanges in e-health scenario

1.1, 1.2, 1.3 and 1.4: Both doctor and patient send EN_{Kpub} (data) + ID and receive $@_{IPFS}$ + H_{IPFS}

2 - The doctor sends his/her ID and signed smart contract to the Blockchain.
3 - The Blockchain sends this smart contract to TEE

4 - The TEE receives the smart contract, after it verifies the state of the doctor. Then, it extracts the public key of the doctor and calculates its hash and compares it with the hashes in T_{ht}

5 - The patient signs smart contract acceptance with his\her private key and sends it to the TEE using Blockchain.

6 - The Blockchain sends the signed SC patient with K_{priv} to the TEE.

7 - TEE creates a file that contains a list of demanded data with IPFS hashes, $@_{IPFS}$ and the time stamp and send it to the IPFS.

8 - IPFS verifies the validity of ($@_{IPFS} + H_{IPFS}$, time stamp).

9 and 10 - TEE executes the SC and returns the execution result to the Blockchain.

4 Security Analysis

Table 2 presents a comparison between three previous solutions and our proposed solution. We observe that the others solution does not respect all the criteria of security.

When using this approach, the 5 key criteria of security are guaranteed or maintained. in short, user data can only be modified, accessed or deleted by authorized persons (integrity; privacy and integrity).

The IPFS contains the data in a homomorphic way (decentralization) and the execution in TEE will be based on the encrypted data, without forgetting that the TEE and IPFS platforms only allow access to authorized persons.

Table 2. Comparison approaches

Articles	Confidentiality	Privacy	Authenticity	Integrity	Decentralization
Hawk [10]	+	+	+	+	−
BC and SC for digital certificate [8]	+	−	+	+	+
Towards using BC technology for e-Health data access management [11]	+	−	+	+	+
Our solution	+	+	+	+	+

5 Conclusion

The Blockchain technology has reached a great boom in many sectors such as e-health, e-commerce; e-vote… The main important Blockchain [11] characteristics are: Transparency, no need for third parties and instant access to data since it is replicated on all nodes. To create a secure smart contract based on Blockchain, a new solution is presented which combines three technologies: Blockchain, TEE, and IPFS in order to take advantage of their benefits. This approach is based on collecting the necessary data from distributed database while protecting the user's privacy and executing it in TEE.

This approach meets the various security criteria such as confidentiality, authentication, integrity, decentralization and protection of private data. this approach can be applied in different domains such as e-health to show the strong points of this one in the e-health domain it is necessary to link it with the Internet of Things domain [19].

As future work, we need to implement the new solution in order to study its feasibility and measure its performance.

References

1. Kim, H., Laskowski, M.: A perspective on blockchain smart contracts: reducing uncertainty and complexity in value exchange. In: 2017 26th International Conference on Computer Communication and Networks (ICCCN) (2017). https://doi.org/10.1109/icccn.2017. 8038512
2. Wood, G.: Ethereum: a secure decentralized generalized transaction ledger. Ethereum Proj. Yellow Paper **151**, 1–32 (2014)
3. McCorry, P., Shahandashti, S.F., Hao, F.: A smart contract for boardroom voting with maximum voter privacy. In: Kiayias, A. (ed.) FC 2017. LNCS, vol. 10322, pp. 357–375. Springer, Cham (2017). https://doi.org/10.1007/978-3-319-70972-7_20
4. Szabo, N.: Smart contracts (1994). http://www.fon.hum.uva.nl/rob/Courses/ InformationInSpeech/CDROM/Literature/LOTwinterschol2006/szabo.best.vwh.net/smart. contracts.html
5. Magazzeni, D., McBurney, P.: Validation and verification of smart contracts: a research agenda. Computer **50**, 50–57 (2017)
6. Braghin, C., Cimato, S., Damiani, E., Baronchelli, M.: Designing smart-contract based auctions. In: Yang, C.-N., Peng, S.-L., Jain, L.C. (eds.) SICBS 2018. AISC, vol. 895, pp. 54–64. Springer, Cham (2020). https://doi.org/10.1007/978-3-030-16946-6_5
7. Nakamoto, S.: Bitcoin: a peer-to-peer electronic cash system (2008). https://bitcoin.org/ bitcoin.pdf
8. Cheng, J.-C., Lee, N.-Y., Chi, C., Chen, Y.-H.: Blockchain and smart contract for digital certificate. In: 2018 IEEE International Conference on Applied System Invention (ICASI) (2018)
9. Ahmed, A.S., Aura, T.: Turning trust around: smart contract-assisted public key infrastructure. In: 2018 17th IEEE International Conference on Trust, Security and Privacy in Computing and Communications/12th IEEE International Conference on Big Data Science and Engineering (TrustCom/BigDataSE) (2018)
10. Kosba, A., Miller, A., Shi, E., Wen, Z., Papamanthou, C.: Hawk: the blockchain model of cryptography and privacy-preserving smart contracts. In: IEEE Security and Privacy (S&P) (2016)
11. Rifi, N., Rachkidi, E., Agoulmine, N., Taher, N.C.: Towards using blockchain technology for eHealth data access management. In: 2017 Fourth International Conference on Advances in Biomedical Engineering (ICABME) (2017)
12. Benet, J.: IPFS - Content addressed, versioned, p2p file system (draft 3) (2014). https://ipfs. io/ipfs/QmR7GSQM93Cx5eAg6a6yRzNde1FQv7uL6X1o4k7zrJa3LX/ipfs.draft3.pdf
13. Maymounkov, P., Mazières, D.: Kademlia: a peer-to-peer information system based on the XOR metric. In: Druschel, P., Kaashoek, F., Rowstron, A. (eds.) IPTPS 2002. LNCS, vol. 2429, pp. 53–65. Springer, Heidelberg (2002). https://doi.org/10.1007/3-540-45748-8_5. http://dl.acm.org/citation.cfm?id=646334.687801

14. https://www.edureka.co/community/30534/what-is-the-difference-between-ipfs-and-ethereum

15. Alonso, S.G., Arambarri, J., López-Coronado, M., de la Torre Díez, I.: Proposing new blockchain challenges in eHealth. J. Med. Syst. **43**, 64 (2019)

16. https://www.trustonic.com/news/technology/what-is-a-trusted-execution-environment-tee/

17. https://www.researchgate.net/figure/The-composition-ofblockchain_fig2_327277530

18. El Houda, Z.A., Hafid, A.S., Khoukhi, L.: Cochain-SC: an intra- and inter-domain DDoS mitigation scheme based on blockchain using SDN and smart contract. IEEE Access **7**, 98893–98907 (2019)

19. Moudoud, H., Cherkaoui, S., Khoukhi, L.: An IoT blockchain architecture using oracles and smart contracts: the use-case of a food supply Chain. In: 2019 IEEE 30th Annual International Symposium on Personal, Indoor and Mobile Radio Communications (PIMRC) (2019)

A Fuzzy-Ontology Based Diabetes Monitoring System Using Internet of Things

Sondes Titi[1,2]([⊠]) (ID), Hadda Ben Elhadj[1,2], and Lamia Chaari Fourati[1,2]

[1] Laboratory of Technology and Smart Systems (LT2S), LR16CRNS01, Sfax, Tunisia
contact@crns.rnrt.tn
[2] Digital Research Center of Sfax, Sfax, Tunisia

Abstract. The majority of the Internet-of-things (IoT)-based health monitoring systems adopt ontologies to represent and interoperate the huge quantity of data collected. Classical ontologies cannot appropriately treat imprecise and ambiguous knowledge. The integration of Fuzzy logic theory with ontology can effectively resolve knowledge problems with uncertainty. It considerably raises the accuracy and the precision of healthcare decisions. This paper presents a fuzzy-ontology based system using the internet of things and aims to ensure continues monitoring of diabetic patients. It mainly describes the ontology-based model and the semantic fuzzy decision-making mechanism. The system is evaluated using semantic querying. The results indicate its feasibility for effective remote continuous monitoring for diabetes.

Keywords: Fuzzy · Ontology · Internet of thing · Healthcare · Diabetes

1 Introduction

The increasing number of diabetic patients place a severe burden on healthcare systems and makes their monitoring a very difficult task. According to [17], the total number of diabetic patients is expected to rise from 171 million in 2000 to 366 million in 2030. Diabetes is a group of metabolic disorders of carbohydrate metabolism characterized by the variation of blood glucose level that results from insufficient production of the hormone insulin (type 1 diabetes) or an ineffective response of cells to insulin (type 2 diabetes). It requires remote continuous monitoring to prevent emergencies and long-term complications such as cardiovascular diseases. Therefore, its treatment should focus mainly on controlling and managing blood glucose levels constantly with diet, physical exercises, and medications. New healthcare systems based on IoT offer a new effective perspective in diabetes management based on the IoT data collected. They are enable to sufficiently handle imprecise and vague information related to patient and therefore fail in describing his health condition and to recommend the appropriate drug

M. Jmaiel et al. (Eds.): ICOST 2020, LNCS 12157, pp. 287–295, 2020.
https://doi.org/10.1007/978-3-030-51517-1_25

and food, because they adopt conventional approaches such as classical ontology and fuzzy logic. The combination of ontologies and fuzzy-logic approaches can effectively resolve the problem of uncertainty of data related to diabetic patients and thus ameliorate the accuracy of system when performing decisions related to the current health condition and recommendations. This paper introduces a fuzzy-ontology-based healthcare system integrating IoT technologies. The system provides certain and precise diabetes-related decisions that allow patients to maintain a lifestyle in which the diet is coordinated with exercise and activities. The remainder of this paper is organized as follows. Section 2 presents related works. Section 3 then describes the architecture of the proposed system and the knowledge construction mechanism. Next, Sect. 4 introduces the fuzzy-ontology generating model. Section 5 describes the semantic fuzzy decision-making process for diabetes system and summarizes the evaluation results. Conclusions and perspectives are finally drawn in Sect. 6.

2   Related Works

The increasing number of chronically ill aged people worldwide has drawn the attention of a diverse array of fields including Internet of Things (IoT) and Artificial Intelligence (IA), explaining why IoT based healthcare systems using ontology and fuzzy-logic have been adopted for continues real-time monitoring. For instance, Mumtaj et al. [10] proposed an IoT-based system combining ANN and fuzzy logic and aims to ensure the monitoring of elderly and supports caregivers to diagnose diseases by sending alerts in case of any abnormalities. Huang et al. [6] introduced predictive symptom checker system based fuzzy logic that helps the elderly to decisively determine the most appropriate illness and any health-related threats. Another system presented in [11] aims to evaluate the likelihood of developing heart diseases in patients. Another work presented in [3] introduced an expert fuzzy system for heart disease diagnosis. IoT allows users to share information everywhere and every time. However, the huge exploitation of the connected objects becomes a source of a mass of heterogeneous data. Ontologies play an important role to deal with the huge quantity of data by offering a semantic representation of the domain knowledge. Recently, different ontologies related to IoT based healthcare are proposed. For instance, [12] describes an ontology-based framework using the semantic IoT that provides continuous monitoring of patient status. Another work in [14] presents an IoT based system where an ontology is introduced to provide semantic interoperability among heterogeneous devices and users to ensure remote control of patient affected by chronic diseases. In [2], the authors proposed a context management system for smart environments that uses an ontology to model the uncertainty and vagueness of the contextual information collected to reach a richer inference process. Authors in [9], propose an ontology-based context management system that allows the monitoring of the elderly citizens' behavior and the detection of risks related to mild cognitive impairments and frailty. The work proposed in [8] describes a decision support system aiming to ensure the treatment and care delivery pathways for patients with Head and Neck Cancer. In [15] a personalized ontology-based food recommendation system is proposed for supporting travelers with long-term diseases and follow a strict diet. Although classical ontologies provide a formalized and accumulated knowledge base for users to investigate and share, they cannot appropriately treat imprecise and vague knowledge for healthcare applications [18]. Thus, the combination of fuzzy logic theory with ontology is considered the solution for uncertainty. For example, the system presented in [5] enables elderly citizens suffering from chronic diseases to live safely and independently by generating more effective and accurate recommendations. [7] proposed a fuzzy expert decision system for diabetic patients. The system aims to model diabetes knowledge with uncertainty. [1,13] propose recommender fuzzy-ontology based systems that efficiently monitor the diabetic patient and recommend appropriate foods and drugs.

3 Architecture of Fuzzy Ontology-Based Healthcare System

This section describes the overall architecture of the proposed system (Fig. 1). Different medical and ambient sensors and devices are used to monitor the patient's vital signs and his home surroundings. These measurements data combined with patient profile data, lifestyle data including diet, physical exercises and medication intake constitute the sensing layer. The data collected is transferred to the server using the interconnected IoT technologies that constitute the network layer. On the server-side, the middleware management layer, which acts as the central part of the system, is deployed. It is responsible for data collection and management, sensors and devices control and services generation. Its main Components are:

- Collection and fusion engine: receives data from medical and ambient IoT devices and other data related to patient's profile and lifestyle (foods, medication, and exercise) and extracts features/inputs to send them to the fuzzification component and to the knowledge base.
- Database: stores patients' profile data, symptoms, medical history, medication intake, exercises, meals and foods, examination results, etc.
- The knowledge base: comprises the fuzzy-ontology that formulates data representing the patient, his environment, his lifestyle, his examinations and rule-based reasoning model fusing SWRL and fuzzy-logic theory to deal with vagueness and uncertainty and thus ameliorates the efficiency of decisions making results.
- Fuzzification: transforms raw feature/input values to fuzzy variables. This is to determine the membership function of each variable in the set.
- Fuzzy inference: maps input variables to output variable through a number of fuzzy if-then rules.
- Defuzzification: transforms fuzzy variables to output values. These crisp values are necessary for the generation of healthcare services.

– Query engine: handles queries received from the application layer.
– Reasoning Engine: checks the consistency of raw data and deduces the high-level data from low-level data.

The results of diagnosis representing healthcare services are delivered to the end users (doctors, patient, nurses, and family members). Multiple programming interfaces are developped to display the results that answer users' queries.

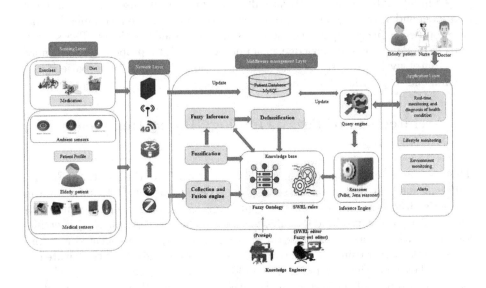

Fig. 1. The architecture of fuzzy ontology-based healthcare system

4   Proposed Fuzzy-Ontology

Ontologies have been adopted in IoT-based healthcare applications, as they are capable of modeling and representing the whole concepts related to the health domain and describing the relationships among them. However, classical ontologies are unable to handle imprecise and vague knowledge and thus fail to provide accurate and efficient diagnoses. This limitation has leading us to develop a fuzzy-ontology capable of managing health-related knowledge. The ontology proposed uses fuzzy members and gives a semantic description related to diabetes disease. It supports the patient in monitoring their health condition and their lifestyle and generating efficient recommendations. It is an extension of our classic ontology proposed in [14]. Protege tool is used to develop and maintain our proposed fuzzy-ontology. It allows reasoning through different plugins: Fuzzy owl is used to add fuzzy sets to fuzzy variables. SWRL is adopted to manage fuzzy rules. DL and SPARQL queries are employed to retrieve the results and answers. The ontology includes multiple classes representing the concepts, data and object properties and fuzzy data types representing the intervals of the membership fuzzy variables. The fuzzy concepts define concepts and relations to describe uncertain and vague knowledge. The main difference between fuzzy and classic concepts is that in classic concepts the membership degree of each property is equal to 1 or 0 while in fuzzy concepts it is equal to a certain degree belongs the interval [0, 1]. The classes extended are the following:

- Fuzzy patient class: represents all the information required to supervise the condition of the diabetic elderly. It describes 5 fuzzy variables which are height, weight, gender, disease history and age. The fuzzy variable weight has the fuzzy sets "Light", "Normal", and "Heavy" and "Obese". The fuzzy variable gender has the fuzzy set "Male" and "Female". The fuzzy variable age has these sets, "Young", "Adult" and "Old".
- Fuzzy MedicalProperty class: describes and manages the medical observations. It has the following Fuzzy sub-classes: blood pressure, blood glucose, BMI, heart rate, temperature. These measurements are used as the input variables to identify the health condition of the patient which is the output variable. Each fuzzy variable has several fuzzy terms. For example, the blood sugar glucose variable has the fuzzy sets: (very-low 0–90, low 71–130, medium 125–154, high 142–180, very-high 165–250).
- Fuzzy Health condition class defines the patient's health condition calculated based on medical data collected. The health condition is the output variable determined based on fuzzy input variables defining the medical measurements and the fuzzy rules. This variable has fuzzy sets "Healthy", "Moderate" and "Serious". The system acts automatically based on the patient's health condition: If it is healthy, the system indicates to the patient to maintain his lifestyle. If it is moderate, the system recommends the appropriate drugs, foods and physical exercises required for the patient to establish his normal health condition and notify the corresponding caregiver to do the regular health services. If it is serious, the system generates alarms to call the medical staff and recommends different foods and drugs.
- Fuzzy Food class: defines the food eaten by a diabetic patient. Foods are distributed in meals. According to the nutritionists, a diabetic patient should maintain a healthy diet that allows him to maintain a normal blood glucose level. The meal eaten is considered healthy or UnHealthy based on the percentage of carbohydrate PC, protein PP, and fat consumed PF, BMI, the difference between the calories consumed by the patient and the planned total calories required for patient's body defined by nutritionists DCP. The total calories needed to maintain or lose weight is calculated based on the basal metabolic rate BMR and the activity level. The BMR is calculated based on patient' age, gender, weight and height using Mifflin St Jeor formula [4]. The nutritionists recommend that the planned total calories should be divided into the five meals: Breakfast, breakfast, snack 1, lunch, snack 2, and dinner with the respective percentage: 25%, 12.5%, 25%, 12.5%, and 25%. For each meal, the number of calories should be distributed in three nutrients, which are carbohydrates, fat, and protein with the respective percentage 50%, 30%, and 20%. Therefore, four fuzzy variables are described by this class which are

PC, PP, PF, DPC. These variables are considered as inputs variables combined with the fuzzy variables Age, BMI and physical activity to deduce if the diet is healthy or not which is expressed by the fuzzy variable Diet status.
- Fuzzy physical activity: expresses the level of physical activity practiced by the diabetic patient. The level of physical activity is used to calculate the total calories needed by the diabetic patient to maintain or lose weight. In fact, according to the level of activity, a factor is multiplied by the BMR as following: little = BMR * 1.2, light = BMR * 1.375, moderate = BMR * 1.55, strenuous = BMR * 1.725, extra strenuous = BMR * 1.9.

5   Health Condition and Diet Status Calculation Process

This section details the process calculation of health condition and diet status values for the diabetic patient using the following components: fuzzy-ontology, fuzzification, fuzzy rule-base, fuzzy inference, and defuzzification. The crisp inputs related to patient's profile and sensors data are collected and then fuzzified using the fuzzy sets of each variable. Health condition is calculated using blood glucose, blood pressure, BMI, heart rate, body temperature fuzzy inputs. Diet Status is calculated based on PC, PP, PF, DCP, activity, Age, BMI. The fuzzification step is proceeded by the fuzzy inference step. This later uses the fuzzy-ontology and a fuzzy-rule base that includes a set of fuzzy-rules. The proposed fuzzy rules are categorized in: (1) Rules to determine the health condition of the patient (2) Fuzzy rules to determine the status of diet consumed by the patient. (3) Rules to determine the BMR and planned calories needed by the patient according to his physical activity level, height, weight, and age. (4) Rules to recommend drugs, foods and physical activity according to health and diet conditions calculated. Following, are example of two SWRL rules. Rule 1 deduces the health status of the patient based on his physiological signs and generates Health services. Rule 2 deduces the diet status based on the composition of meals eaten by the patient, his activity and the difference between the planned and consumed calories, and generates appropriate recommendations. The rules determining the status of diet are implemented according to these two conditions: (1) the diet is more healthy if PC, PF, PP, activity are more balanced and (2) the planned caloric intake is closer to the one consumed. The Fuzzy inference is based on Mamdani's method to determine the fuzzy output variable and send it to the defuzzyfier. The defuzzyfier adopts 'Center of gravity' [16] method to deduce the crip value of the output variable.

Rule 1: Patient(?p), HasBloodGlucose(?p, HighBG), HasBloodPressure(?p, HighBP), HasHeartBeat(?p, HighHB), HasBMI(?p, OverweightBMI), HasBody Temperature(?p, NormalBT), greaterThan(?HighBG, 180), SystolicBPValue (?HighBP, ?s), DiastolicBPValue(?HighBP,?d), greaterThan(?d, 86), lessThan (?d, 90), greaterThan(?s, 131), lessThan(?s, 139), greaterThan(?NormalBT, 37), lessThan(?NormalBT, 38), greaterThan(?HighHB, 100), greaterThan(?Over weightBMI, 38), lessThan(?OverweightBMI, 40), Alarm(?a), EmergencyButton(?e), UseActuatingDevice(?p, ?e) -> HasHealthCondition(?p, Serious),

HasAlarm(?p, ?a), HasServiceMessage(?a, "You are in danger, Call a doctor"), HasActuatorState(?e, "Device is swiched On")

Rule 2: Patient(?p), HasAge(?p, Old), HasBMI(?p, OverWeight), HasPC(?p, HighPC), HasPP(?p, HighPP), HasPF(?p, LowPF), HasDCP(?p, MLUnAcceptableCDP), greaterThan(?Old, 65), HasActivity(?P, LightAC), Recommandation (?R), greaterThan(?OverWeight, 38), lessThan(?OverWeight, 40), greaterThan (?HighPC, 65), lessThan(?HighPC, 100), greaterThan(?HighPP, 20), lessThan (?HighPP, 100), lessThan(?LowPF, 25), greaterThan(?LightAC, 8), lessThan (?LightAC, 30), greaterThan(?MLUnAcceptableCDP, 50), lessThan(?MLUn AcceptableCDP, 200)-> HasDietStatus(?p, UnHealthy), HasRecommandation (?p, ?R), HasServiceMessage(?R, "Do more exercises, Eat More Fat, Less Carbohydrate, Less Protein"), NeedFood(?p, LowCalorie).

The proposed system is implemented on java. Fuzzy components are implemented using jfuzzylogic plugin to calculate the output variables, which are health condition and diet status. The ontology is evaluated based on the querying-answering approach using DL and SPARQL queries and is then integrated into the java application using Jena API. The evaluation includes: (1) Technical evaluation to check the consistency and the coherence of the ontology using Jena reasoner as well as the response time that the system takes to execute user queries and display the result. Results show that the time consumed depends on the number of inputs that the query needs to calculate the output. The more the inputs are, the more the response time is. (2) Functional evaluation, which evaluates the efficiency of the system and the accuracy level of the decisions for which the system was queried. Results demonstrate that the accuracy of our system can reach 100% for diet status related queries, 96% for health condition related queries and on average 94% for queries related recommandations. Therefore our system is capable of acting more similar to human expertise.

6   Conclusion

This paper proposes a fuzzy-ontology based diabetic monitoring system using IoT technology. The fuzzy-logic is adopted to infer the health condition and the diet status for the patient and then presents the result to the ontology to generate convenient recommendations. Evaluation indicates that the performance of the system is increased considerably and the system gives results with more accuracy compared to the system using classic ontology.

References

1. Ali, F., et al.: Type-2 fuzzy ontology-aided recommendation systems for IoT-based healthcare. Comput. Commun. **119**, 138–155 (2018)
2. Almeida, A., López-de Ipiña, D.: Assessing ambiguity of context data in intelligent environments: towards a more reliable context managing system. Sensors **12**(4), 4934–4951 (2012)
3. Alqudah, A.M.: Fuzzy expert system for coronary heart disease diagnosis in Jordan. Health Technol. **7**(2–3), 215–222 (2017)
4. Amirkalali, B., Hosseini, S., Heshmat, R., Larijani, B., et al.: Comparison of harris benedict and mifflin-st jeor equations with indirect calorimetry in evaluating resting energy expenditure. Indian J. Med. Sci. **62**(7), 283–290 (2008)
5. Chiang, T.C., Liang, W.H.: A context-aware interactive health care system based on ontology and fuzzy inference. J. Med. Syst. **39**(9), 105 (2015)
6. Huang, Y.P., Basanta, H., Kuo, H.C., Huang, A.: Health symptom checking system for elderly people using fuzzy analytic hierarchy process. Appl. Syst. Innov. **1**(2), 10 (2018)
7. Lee, C.S., Wang, L., Wang, M.-H.: A fuzzy expert system for diabetes decision support application. IEEE Trans. Syst. Man Cybern.—Part B: Cybern. **41**(1), 139–153 (2011)
8. Lopez-Perez, L., et al.: BD2Decide: big data and models for personalized head and neck cancer decision support. In: 2019 IEEE 32nd International Symposium on Computer-Based Medical Systems (CBMS), pp. 67–68. IEEE (2019)
9. Mulero, R., Urosevic, V., Almeida, A., Tatsiopoulos, C.: Towards ambient assisted cities using linked data and data analysis. J. Ambient Intell. Humaniz. Comput. **9**(5), 1573–1591 (2018). https://doi.org/10.1007/s12652-018-0916-y
10. Mumtaj, S., Umamakeswari, A.: Neuro fuzzy based healthcare system using IoT. In: 2017 International Conference on Energy, Communication, Data Analytics and Soft Computing (ICECDS), pp. 2299–2303. IEEE (2017)
11. Nazari, S., Fallah, M., Kazemipoor, H., Salehipour, A.: A fuzzy inference-fuzzy analytic hierarchy process-based clinical decision support system for diagnosis of heart diseases. Expert Syst. Appl. **95**, 261–271 (2018)
12. Saad, S., Zafar, B.A., Mueen, A.: Developing a framework for e-healthcare applications using the semantic internet of things. Int. J. Comput. Appl. **975**, 8887 (2018)
13. Selvan, N.S., Vairavasundaram, S., Ravi, L.: Fuzzy ontology-based personalized recommendation for internet of medical things with linked open data. J. Intell. Fuzzy Syst. **36**(5), 4065–4075 (2019)
14. Sondes, T., Elhadj, H.B., Chaari, L.: An ontology-based healthcare monitoring system in the internet of things. In: 2019 15th International Wireless Communications and Mobile Computing Conference (IWCMC), pp. 319–324. IEEE (2019)
15. Subramaniyaswamy, V., et al.: An ontology-driven personalized food recommendation in iot-based healthcare system. J. Supercomput. **75**(6), 3184–3216 (2019)
16. Van Broekhoven, E., De Baets, B.: A comparison of three methods for computing the center of gravity defuzzification. In: 2004 IEEE International Conference on Fuzzy Systems (IEEE Cat. No. 04CH37542), vol. 3, pp. 1537–1542. IEEE (2004)
17. Wild, S., Roglic, G., Green, A., Sicree, R., King, H.: Global prevalence of diabetes: estimates for the year 2000 and projections for 2030. Diabetes Care **27**(5), 1047–1053 (2004)
18. Zhang, F., Cheng, J., Ma, Z.: A survey on fuzzy ontologies for the semantic web. Knowl. Eng. Rev. **31**(3), 278–321 (2016)

Short Contributions: Biomedical and Health Informatics

A Hybrid Approach for Heart Disease Diagnosis and Prediction Using Machine Learning Techniques

Fatma Zahra Abdeldjouad[1(✉)], Menaouer Brahami[1(✉)],
and Nada Matta[2(✉)]

[1] National Polytechnic School of Oran - Maurice Audin, Oran, Algeria
fatma.abdeldjouad@gmail.com, mbrahami@gmail.com
[2] University of Technology of Troyes, Troyes, France
nada.matta@utt.fr

Abstract. Heart disease is considered as one of the major causes of death throughout the world. It cannot be easily predicted by the medical practitioners as it is a difficult task which demands expertise and higher knowledge for prediction. Currently, the recent development in medical supportive technologies based on data mining, machine learning plays an important role in predicting cardiovascular diseases. In this paper, we propose a new hybrid approach to predict cardiovascular disease using different machine learning techniques such as Logistic Regression (LR), Adaptive Boosting (AdaBoostM1), Multi-Objective Evolutionary Fuzzy Classifier (MOEFC), Fuzzy Unordered Rule Induction (FURIA), Genetic Fuzzy System-LogitBoost (GFS-LB) and Fuzzy Hybrid Genetic Based Machine Learning (FH-GBML). For this purpose, the accuracy and results of each classifier have been compared, with the best classifier chosen for a more accurate cardiovascular prediction. With this objective, we use two free software (Weka and Keel).

Keywords: Machine learning · Data mining · Healthcare informatics · Heart disease · Classification · Prediction models · Medical decision support system

1 Introduction

One of the most common reasons of death in Algeria or other Maghreb countries is chronic disease. Nevertheless, chronic disease is a vital issue to be fixed for a healthy human life. More recently, Cardiovascular Disease (CVD) is the leading cause of death for both men and women globally. Though real-life consultants can be able to predict the disease with an enormous number of tests and requiring a huge processing time, sometimes, their prediction may be incorrect because of lack of skilled knowledge [1]. Meanwhile, the introduction of artificial intelligence and machine learning has helped to extract relevant data from large databases which are available in hospitals to make a good decision. It involves data mining techniques to analyze medical data [2]. For this reason, data mining has gained popularity due to its tools with the potential to identify trends within data and turn them into knowledge that could serve as the strong basis for the analysis [3]. To that end, the key issue in the field of CVD prevention is to give an accurate

© The Author(s) 2020
M. Jmaiel et al. (Eds.): ICOST 2020, LNCS 12157, pp. 299–306, 2020.
https://doi.org/10.1007/978-3-030-51517-1_26

prediction of whether a person is probable to have this disease. Motivated by the growing mortality of CVD patients every year and the accessibility to a huge amount of patient data from which to obtain valuable knowledge, we found it useful to use data mining methods for assisting healthcare professionals in the diagnosis of CVD. The objective of this research work is not to replace the specialist physician, but to assist the doctor in obtaining an alternative opinion and its various feasibility in critical situations.

The rest of this paper is organized as follows. Section 2 describes the literature review. Section 3 presents the proposed approach used for predicting heart disease. Experimental results are analyzed in Sect. 4 and Conclusion and References are given in Sect. 5 and 6.

2   Literature Review

In previous studies, researchers expressed their efforts in finding the best model for predicting cardiovascular disease. In the meantime, various studies give only a glimpse into predicting heart disease using machine learning techniques and fuzzy logic systems. This section explores the research works that are related to the proposed approach. A machine learning model has been proposed in [2] by combining five different algorithms. In fact, the integration of the machine learning model with medical information systems would be useful to predict the Heart Failure (HF) or any other disease using the live data collected from patients. A new hybrid approach for heart disease prediction that combines all techniques into one single algorithm has been proposed in [4]. The result confirms that accurate diagnosis can be made using a combined model from all techniques. An "Optimal Multi-Nominal Logistic Regression (OMLR) algorithm has been proposed in [5] and is used to train the data set for heart disease. Experiments are conducted on the dataset of UCI heart disease and the results show 92% accuracy in the detection of heart severity. The Fast Correlation-Based Feature Selection (FCBF) method has been exploited in [6], to filter redundant features in order to improve the quality of heart disease classification. Then, the authors performed a classification based on different algorithms such as K-Nearest Neighbour, Support Vector Machine, Random Forest and a Multilayer Perception optimized by Particle Swarm Optimization (PSO) combined with Ant Colony Optimization (ACO) approaches. A predictive model for heart disease diagnosis using a fuzzy rule-based approach with decision tree has been proposed in [7]. In this study, the authors have obtained the accuracy of 88% which is statistically significant for diagnosing the heart disease patient and also outperforms some of the existing methods. A new method namely Hybrid Differential Evolution based Fuzzy Neural Network (HDEFNN) which can predict the heart disease occurrence fastly and accurately has been proposed in [8]. The performance of this method in terms of accurate diagnosis of heart disease is attained by improving the initial weight updating of a neural network which is done by introducing the genetic algorithm. The genetic algorithm can select the most optimal weight values for the hidden layers of the neural network. A neuro-fuzzy genetic approach has been proposed in [9], to predict chances of cardiovascular disease. The proposed approach also helps to make the system more accurate and efficient with the help of a genetic algorithm.

3 Proposed Approach

(See Fig. 1).

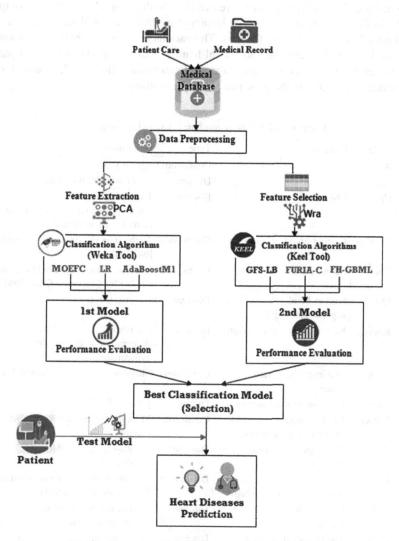

Fig. 1. General architecture of the proposed approach

3.1 Description of the Dataset and Attributes

The dataset used in this article is taken from the UCI Repository Of Machine Learning Databases[1]. Formally, it is named Heart Disease Dataset. The Cleveland (Cleveland Clinic Foundation) database was selected for this research because it is a commonly used database for machine learning researchers with comprehensive and complete records. In this field, the dataset is a collection of medical analytical reports with a total of 303 records with 14 medical features. The various features and their description are shown in Table 1. Besides, the categorical feature "Class" contains whether a patient has a presence or absence of heart disease. Its original values 1, 2, 3 and 4 were transformed in one that is the presence (1) of heart disease.

Table 1. UCI dataset attributes detailed information

Num.	Code	Feature	Type	Description
1	Age	Age	Continuous	Age in years
2	Sex	Sex	Discrete	sex (1 = male; 0 = female)
3	Cp	Chest pain type	Discrete	1 = typical angina; 2 = atypical angina; 3 = non-angina pain; 4 = asymptomatic
4	Trestbps	Resting boold pressure (mg)	Continuous	At the time of admission in hospital [94, 200]
5	Chol	Serum cholesterol (mg/dl)	Continuous	Multiple values between [Minimum Chol: 126, Maximum Chol: 564]
6	Fbs	Fasting bood sugar > 120 mg/dl	Discrete	1 = yes; 0 = no
7	Restecg	Resting electrocardiographic results	Discrete	0 = normal; 1 = ST-T wave abnormal; 2 = left ventricular hypertrophy
8	Thalach	Maximum heart rate achieved	Continuous	Maximum heart rate achieved [71, 202]
9	Exang	Exercise induced angina	Discrete	1 = yes; 0 = no
10	Oldpeak	ST depression induced by exercise relative to rest	Continuous	Multiple real number values between 0 and 6.2.
11	Slope	The slope of the peak exercise ST segment	Discrete	1 = upsloping; 2 = flat; 3 = downsloping
12	Ca	Number of major vessels (0–3) colored by fluoroscopy	Discrete	Number of major vessels coloured by fluoroscopy (values 0–3)
13	Thal	Exercise thallium scintigraphy	Discrete	3 = normal; 6 = fixed defect; 7 = reversible defect
14	Class (Target)	The predicted attribute	Discrete	0 = no presence; 1 = presence

[1] Repository Of Machine Learning (UCI Databases). Heart Disease Data Set. [Online]. Available: https://archive.ics.uci.edu/ml/machine-learning-databases/heart-disease/heart-disease.names [Accessed: June 20, 2019].

3.2   Data Pre-processing

In medical informatics, the diagnosis of diseases becomes quicker and easier if data is free from missing, redundant and irrelevant data. In this study and after collection of various records, we begin the preprocessing process. The dataset contains a total of 303 patients records, where 7 records are with some missing values. Those 7 records have been removed from the dataset and the remaining 296 records are used in the process.

3.3   Feature Selection

Feature selection is a process of selecting a relevant feature of original features according to definite condition. Further, feature collection algorithms intended with different evaluation criteria mostly fall into three categories: the filter, wrapper, and hybrid models [10]. In our work, we used only the wrapper method under Keel tool. As per our objective, from among the 14 attributes of the dataset, two attributes pertaining to age and sex are used to identify the personal information of the patient. The remaining 12 attributes are considered important as they contain vital clinical records.

3.4   Feature Extraction

Feature extraction is a process that extracts a subset of new features from the original set by means of some functional mapping. In order to meet the goal of the work, we used PCA as one of the most widely used dimensionality reduction technique for the medical applications under Weka tool, where the extracted information is represented by a set of new variables, termed components or features. With PCA, we reduced the attributes number to 6 which contributes more towards the diagnosis of the CVD.

3.5   Classification Algorithms

Under Weka tool, different predictive algorithms were chosen to build the first model, namely: Multi-Objective Evolutionary Fuzzy Classifier (MOEFC), Logistic Regression (LR), Adaptive Boosting (AdaBoostM1), while Genetic Fuzzy System-LogitBoost (GFS-LB), Fuzzy Unordered Rule Induction Algorithm (FURIA) and Fuzzy Hybrid Genetic Based Machine Learning (FH-GBML) were used under Keel tool to build the second model. Therefore, we selected the best model in order to achieve the highest possible performance on medical datasets and allow effective data classification.

3.6   Test Model

In the second stage, we tested our selected model only when the model is completely trained. Its accuracy on the test data gives a realistic estimate of the model performance on completely unseen patient data and confirms the actual predictive power of the model.

4   Experimental Results

In this paper, the experimental effects of the cardiovascular diseases' diagnosis and the following algorithms LR, AdaBoostM1, MOEFC, FURIA, GFS-LB and FH-GBML are examined in this phase with the use of Keel and Weka tools. Meanwhile, machine learning algorithm efficiency is derived using values like True Positive (TP), True Negative (TN), False Positive (FP) and False Negative (FN). These measures are used for the calculation of the sensitivity, specificity, accuracy and error rate.

$$\text{Sensitivity (Recall) or True positive rate (TPR)} = TP/(TP + FN). \qquad (1)$$

$$\text{Specificity} = TN/(TN + FP) \qquad (2)$$

$$\text{Accuracy (ACC)} = (TP + TN)/(TP + TN + FP + FN). \qquad (3)$$

$$\text{Error rate} = (FP + FN)/(P + N). \qquad (4)$$

4.1   Evaluation of Results

Setting up the Experiment under WEKA Software. In our experiment, the problem has been transformed into binary classification with 0 presents absence and 1 presence of heart disease. For this, Table 2 shows the results obtained by binary classification and 10-fold cross-validation. The highest accuracy 80.20 is gained by majority voting, while LR obtained lowest accuracy and AdaBoostM1 has the highest accuracy when applied without ensemble.

Table 2. Multi-class classification results by 10-fold cross-validation

Algorithm	Sensitivity	Specificity	Accuracy
MOEFC	79.96	75.44	79.42
LR	78.22	71.34	78.77
AdaBoostM1	80.11	75.40	80.01
Vote	84.76	74.82	80.20

Setting Up the Experiment under KEEL Software. Our purpose is to make a comparison of three methods that belong to different ML techniques. In this step, we have used a GFS-LogitBoost-C classifier with a previous pre-processing stage of prototype selection guided by a Generational Genetic Algorithm for Feature Selection (GGA-FS) model. We have also used a FURIA classifier with a previous preprocessing stage of replacing missing values guided by a KNN-MV (K-Nearest Neighbor Imputation) algorithm as well as prototype feature selection guided by SSGA-Integer-knn-FS (Steady-state GA with integer coding scheme for wrapper feature selection with K-NN) and an FH-GBML that uses a Generational Genetic Algorithm for Feature

Selection (GGA-FS). After the models are trained, the instances of the dataset are classified according to the training and test files. These results are the inputs for the visualization and test modules. The module Vis-Clas-Tabular receives these results as inputs and generates output files with several performance metrics computed from them, such as confusion matrices for each method. There is also another type of results flow which interconnects each possible pair of methods with a test module. In this case, the test module used is the signed-rank Wilcoxon non-parametrical procedure Clas-Wilcoxon-ST which compares two samples of results. The experiment establishes a pair-wise statistical comparison of the three methods. Once the experiment has been run we can reach results shown in Table 3 and Table 4.

Table 3. Performance of the KEEL model - training datasets

Evaluation criteria	FURIA-C	GFS-LogitBoost-C	FH-GBML-C
Sensitivity	88.62	94.99	87.47
Specificity	76.26	93.20	78.66
Error rate	0.17	0.06	0.17
Accuracy	82.95	94.17	83.44

Table 4. Performance of the KEEL model - testing datasets

Evaluation criteria	FURIA-C	GFS-LogitBoost-C	FH-GBML-C
Sensitivity	84.76	80.49	82.82
Specificity	74.82	80.58	74.26
Error rate	0.20	0.19	0.21
Accuracy	80.20	80.53	78.93

5   Conclusion

Efficient classification of healthcare dataset is a major machine learning problem then and now. Diagnosis, Prediction of cardiovascular diseases and the precision of results can be improved if relationships and patterns from these complex healthcare datasets are extracted efficiently. This paper analyses some of the different classification algorithms like Logistic Regression (LR), Adaptive Boosting (AdaBoostM1), Multi-Objective Evolutionary Fuzzy Classifier (MOEFC), Fuzzy Unordered Rule Induction (FURIA), Genetic Fuzzy System-LogitBoost (GFS-LB) and Fuzzy Hybrid Genetic Based Machine Learning (FH-GBML). The performance evaluation of these algorithms is done based on Accuracy, Sensitivity, Specificity and Error rate using WEKA and KEEL tools.

References

1. Pouriyeh, S., Vahid, S., Sannino, G., Pietro, G. D., Arabnia, H., Gutierrez, J.: A comprehensive investigation and comparison of machine learning techniques in the domain of heart disease. In: IEEE Symposium on Computers and Communication, Heraklion, Greece, pp. 1–4 (2017)
2. Alotaibi, F.S.: Implementation of machine learning model to predict heart failure disease. Int. J. Adv. Comput. Sci. Appl. **10**(6), 261–268 (2019)
3. Safdari, R., Samad-Soltani, T., GhaziSaeedi, M., Zolnoori, M.: Evaluation of classification algorithms vs knowledge-based methods for differential diagnosis of asthma in iranian patients. Int. J. Inform. Syst. Serv. Sect. **10**(2), 22–26 (2018)
4. Tarawneh, M., Embarak, O.: Hybrid approach for heart disease prediction using data mining techniques. ACTA Sci. Nutrit. Health **3**(7), 147–151 (2019)
5. Satyanandam, N., Satyanarayana, C.: Heart disease detection using predictive optimization techniques. Int. J. Image Graph. Signal Process. **11**(9), 18–24 (2019)
6. Khourdifi, Y., Bahaj, M.: Heart disease prediction and classification using machine learning algorithms optimized by particle swarm optimization and ant colony optimization. Int. J. Intell. Eng. Syst. **12**(1), 242–253 (2018)
7. Pathak, A.K., Arul Valan, J.: A predictive model for heart disease diagnosis using fuzzy logic and decision tree. In: Elçi, A., Sa, P.K., Modi, Chirag N., Olague, G., Sahoo, Manmath N., Bakshi, S. (eds.) Smart Computing Paradigms: New Progresses and Challenges. AISC, vol. 767, pp. 131–140. Springer, Singapore (2020). https://doi.org/10.1007/978-981-13-9680-9_10
8. Bhaskaru, O., Sree, M.: Accurate and fast diagnosis of heart disease using hybrid differential neural network algorithm. Int. J. Eng. Adv. Technol. **8**(3S), 452–457 (2019)
9. Nikam, S., Shukla, P., Shah, M.: Cardiovascular disease prediction using genetic algorithm and neurofuzzy system. Int. J. Latest Trends Eng. Technol. **8**(2), 104–110 (2017)
10. Khare, P., Burse, K.: Feature selection using genetic algorithm and classification using weka for ovarian cancer. Int. J. Comput. Sci. Inform.Technol. **7**(1), 194–196 (2016)

Context-Aware Healthcare Adaptation Model for COPD Diseases

Hamid Mcheick[1(✉)], John Sayegh[2], and Hicham Ajami[1]

[1] Department of Computer Sciences and Mathematics,
University of Québec at Chicoutimi, Chicoutimi, QC G7H 2B1, Canada
{Hamid_mcheick,Hicham.ajami1}@uqac.ca
[2] Lebanese University, Hadath-I, Beirut, Lebanon
johnsayegh1994@gmail.com

Abstract. Nowadays, ubiquitous computing and mobile applications are controlling all our life's aspects, from social media and entertainment to the very basic needs like commerce, learning, government, and health. These systems have the ability to self-adapt to meet changes in their execution environment and the user's context. In the healthcare domain, information systems have proven their efficiency, not only by organizing and managing patients' data and information but also by helping doctors and medical experts in diagnosing disease and taking precluding procedure to avoid serious conditions. In chronic diseases, telemonitoring systems provide a way to monitor the patient's state and biomarkers within their usual life's routine. In this article, we are combining the healthcare telemonitoring systems with the context awareness and self-adaptation paradigm to provide a self-adaptive framework architecture for COPD patients.

Keywords: Software architecture · Self-adaptation · Context-aware system · COPD · Healthcare systems

1 Introduction

Chronic obstructive pulmonary diseases (COPD) have attracted research interest as a major public health problem, because according to the World Health Organization (WHO) [1], COPD is currently considered the fourth, and will soon become the third, most frequent cause of death worldwide. It is also a disabling disease and therefore associated with high costs for treating and managing patients. As the disease progresses, patients become more susceptible to respiratory exacerbations which cause frequent hospital admissions and, thus, have a huge impact on patients' quality of life and healthcare costs [2, 3]. Monitoring patient's health conditions from home and transmitting these data to a healthcare center could be a great solution that facilitates the management of the growing number of patients with COPD and reduce the burden on health services. This approach is called Home Tele-monitoring, which can be used for a timely assessment of acute exacerbation or as a mechanism to generate alarms to the patients and/or healthcare professionals when clinical changes that may constitute a risk to the patient occur [4]. There are many systematic reviews and studies on the topic of telemonitoring in respiratory patients, specifically in patients with COPD [5–8]. All these

M. Jmaiel et al. (Eds.): ICOST 2020, LNCS 12157, pp. 307–315, 2020.
https://doi.org/10.1007/978-3-030-51517-1_27

studies are focusing on proving the effectiveness of applying home telemonitoring on COPD patients, by studying the services that could be provided and their impacts on the patient's quality-of-life. However, none of these studies has provided a comprehensive proposal for a telemonitoring system that helps to control the burden of COPD.

We aim to design a telemonitoring healthcare application that helps COPD patients with self-management and improve their quality of life, therefore reducing pressures on healthcare resources. We must develop a system that uses this data to provide an effective intervention that prevents exacerbation through the early recognition of symptoms and prompt treatment which may reduce the risk of hospitalization and control the burden of COPD. Based on this healthcare requirement, we realized the need of combining context awareness and self-adaptation with health telemonitoring, which will give our system the ability to be aware of the patient's data and context, then to adapt the required changes and act accordingly.

The remainder of this paper is structured as follows. Section 2 introduces the concept of context-awareness and reviews the most common forms of self-adaptation frameworks. Section 3 highlights the characteristics of self-adaptive systems. Section 4 presents our self-adaptation healthcare system for COPD. Section 5 then validates the proposed approach. Finally, Sect. 6 presents our conclusions.

2 Context Awareness and Self-adaptation Systems

2.1 Background

The notion of context has appeared implicitly for the first time in the ubiquitous computing area in 1993 by Weiser "all the information that should be taken into consideration for an adjustment" [9]. Lieberman et al. [10] proposed another interpretation of the context that exists within the field of computing: "context can be considered to be everything that affects the computation". This definition focuses on the application instead of the user, but nowadays with the widespread of mobile applications that focus on the user's lifestyle, health, and activities the factors that affect the user and these that affect the computation process become almost the same.

In software systems, context awareness notion is mostly coupled with self-adaptation capability otherwise, there is no point in collecting contextual data. Self-adaptation is a set of simultaneous and successive processes as an organized reaction to changes in the resources or environment of the system [11]. Self-adaptive systems dynamically modify their behaviors to respond effectively to changes in their operational environment [12]. In the next section, an overview of many self-adaptation frameworks is provided.

2.2 Self-adaptations Frameworks

Rainbow framework provides general mechanisms for developing reusable self-adaptive systems at a variety of different levels [13]. Model-Driven Approach is an automated self-adaptive model that supports adding and removing technical resources at run-time [14]. Meta-Self is a service-oriented framework that provides a solid platform for the development of SAS [15]. This framework allows designers to identify system properties, architectural patterns, and different adaptation mechanisms. FUSION is a reusable feature architecture that incorporates a learning-based adaptive cycle. The adaptation cycle consists of three main steps—detect, plan, and effect [14]. MOSES is a service-oriented framework that focuses on quality of service (QoS) requirements at runtime. MOSES provides a reusable implementation strategy of the adaptation logic following the MAPE cycle (Monitoring, Analysis, Planning, and Execution) [14]. The Contract-Based Adaptive Software Application framework (CASA) [16] is specialized in handling resources instability. The framework assumes that a system should not make any assumptions about the resources that will be available and should be prepared for any resource availability scenario cases. Service-Oriented Architectures (SSOA) is a software framework that specifies any kind of adaptation by decomposing of functionalities [17]. Each of these functionalities shall be specialized to fit a particular purpose. CareDroid is an adaptation framework for android context-aware applications [18]. This framework CareDroid monitors the contexts at run-time, and active methods only when it intercepts calls to sensitive methods.

3 System Requirements and Self-adaptation Characteristics and Taxonomy

3.1 Requirements Extraction and Gathering

The first step to designing a self-adaptive system is to well identify the system requirements; we will depend on W5H-Pattern [19], which presents six questions that would help us in eliciting adaptation requirements (Table 1).

Table 1. Requirements extraction

Where	Where do we need to make a change inside our system when a context's change does happen? Depending on the model presented by Ajami and Mcheick [20], the change needs to be done in the Application layer on both sides: user interface and physician interface
When	When do we need to make these changes? Whenever an urgent update happens in the user contextual data like vital signs, environmental risk factors, and planned activities or periodical changes like the evaluation of treatment and decision support suggestions
What	What do we need to change? We need to update some system attributes that present the system state and these attributes in its turn could trigger new functions or activate new components
Why	Why these changes are required? In healthcare monitoring applications especially these related to chronic diseases, taking precluding actions is crucial in treatment plans. Also being able to notify the patient and the medical experts about any threatening situation or abnormal signs make these kinds of applications more efficient
Who	Is any human intervention is required in the adaptation process? From the patient side, all his biomedical data and surrounding environments data will be collected from sensors. However, because physical activities do affect the COPD patient's state, he needs to detect his planned physical activity (running, swimming)
How	How to determine what changes and actions are needed to be done in the adaptation process? Ajami and Mcheick [20] provided a rule-based reasoning engine, depending on these generated rules all the required actions and changes can be deduced

3.2   Adaptation Characteristics and Taxonomy

Christian et al. [21] presented a taxonomy of the different properties of self-adaptive software. We will analyze this work and do a projection on our system requirements and use the results to build our system.

Time: Handte et al. [22] provided two perspectives of temporal aspects: (i) Reactive is when we have to adapt whenever a change in the context does happen. (ii) Proactive is when the monitored data is used to forecast system behavior or environmental state [21]. In our case, the adaptation will be reactive depending on the changes that happen in the user contextual data.

Reason: The adaptation could be triggered for three reasons: (i) change of the context, (ii) change in the technical resources, and (iii) change in the users. In our case, the adaptation is triggered due to contextual changes, which provide a potential solution for the multiscale nature of COPD.

Level: In our system, the change needs to be done on the application layer, where we need to update the acceptable range for the different datasets or we need to activate new components or call new functions.

Technique: McKinley [23] provided two techniques for adaptive software: parameter adaptation and compositional adaptation. Parameter adaptation achieves a modified system behavior by adjusting system parameters. Whereas compositional adaptation enables the exchange of algorithms or system components dynamically at runtime. We will use the first approach because it is suitable for a rule-based system.

Adaptation Control: Two approaches for implementing the adaptation logic can be found in the literature. The internal approach, which twists the adaptation logic with the system resources. The external approach splits the system into adaptation logic and managed resources, The IBM Autonomic Computing Initiative provided MAPE Model [24], which is an external, feedback control approach. Another aspect of the adaptation logic is the degree of decentralization. We will follow a decentralized approach by implementing independent units that control different aspects of adaptation.

4   Self-adaptation Healthcare System for COPD

4.1   Proposed System

Ajami and Mcheick [20] have proposed an ontology-based approach to keep track of the physical status of patients, suggest recommendations and deliver interventions promptly, by developing a decision support system based on an ontological formal description that uses SWRL rules. The main goal of this paper is to provide an adaptation architecture design for the application layer, which will address the connection between three different entities:

1 - The end-user application: which is supposed to provide a certain service for both patient and physician.

2 - The data sources (sensors and patient's records): that provides a continuous stream of contextual data and historical data about the patient.

3 - The rules base: which presents the knowledge base in our system (Fig. 1)

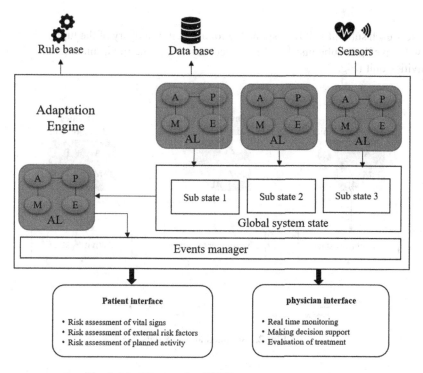

Fig. 1. Architecture for COPD context-aware system

4.2   The Adaptation Engine and Monitoring Units

The adaptation engine consists of a central adaptation unit and multiple sub adaptation units. Each subunit is responsible for monitoring and managing changes for a specific category tuple (data, rules, services).

The system variables will be saved in a shared memory called the global state, which is a composition of sub-states. Each sub-state is considered as a container for saving category-specific data and it will be updated and managed by the adaptation subunit that is responsible for monitoring the same category. We will divide all our sets of data, rules, and services into three categories (Table 2):

Table 2. Categorization of data

	Biometrics	Environmental	Activities
Data	Biometrics data	Environmental data	Activities data
Rules	Biometrics rules	Environmental rules	Activities rules
Services	Biometrics services	Environmental services	Activities services

Now each subunit will be responsible for a specific category of the tuple. Therefore, we will have three subunits: 1 - The biometrics unit 2 - The Environmental unit 3 - The Activities unit (Fig. 2).

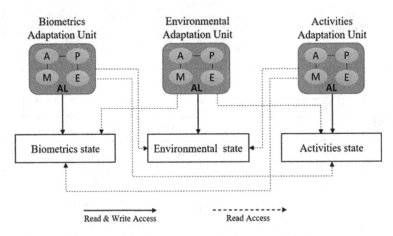

Fig. 2. Subunits and sub stats

- The Biometrics Unit will be responsible for monitoring all the patient's biomarkers upcoming from the biometrics sensors, and it will read all the stored data in the other two sub-states (the environmental state & the activities state), then depending on the vital related rules in the rules engine, it will update The Biometrics State with the safe ranges for all the vital biomarkers and the current measurements for them. The same workflow will be applied in both the Environmental Unit and the Activities Unit.
- The Central Adaptation Unit: it is considered the main core of our system; it will be responsible for monitoring the global state, which will get rid of the burden of dealing with the continuous streaming of the patient's biometrics and the environmental data. By collecting all the contextual data in the global state, each category in its sub-state, we will have access to all the current biometrics and external factors value with the safe range for each one of them as well the current physical activity and the planned list of activities.

Depending on the previous data, the central unit will be able to detect any potential risk or abnormal situations by comparing the current value of each factor in the sub-states with its normal range, which had been adapted by every sub adaptation unit.

When an abnormal situation is detected, the central unit will detect what action should be taken to prevent an exacerbation in the patient's health state.

5 Validation

In order to test and validate our proposed system, we implemented a simulation app using some data obtained from medical records to simulate the streamed data and a set of COPD rules extracted in [25] to create some testing scenarios. The main focus of the validation process was on the efficiency of the system to provide continuous monitoring of the patient status, and the ability to apply and adapt the required changes to prevent any dangerous exacerbation. The testing scenarios we had performed, proofed the ability of our system to handle the complexity of monitoring the enormous amount of contextual data, and keep track of the latest updates in the global state. Also, following an aspect-oriented approach facilitates the implementation of the adaptation logic, by separating the categories of data that each Adaptation Unit needs to be responsible for observing. After testing some rules that lead to call a sequential set of actions and multiple updates in the state units, the system was able to adapt the safe ranges for the different environmental and biometrical factors and detect suitable action in an abnormal situation. Nevertheless, our system still needs to be tested when it is connected to the whole rules engine when all COPD rules are inserted into the engine, which will be done in future work.

6 Conclusion

In this paper, we have presented an architecture for a context-aware self-adaptive system that is used to develop a COPD healthcare telemonitoring system. The system is backed out by a medical rules engine in the COPD domain that is used as the knowledge base to determine the safe ranges for patient's biomarkers and external factors, then detect the precluding actions needed to be taken to prevent severe exacerbations in patient's health state.

Our main contribution in this work is providing a context-aware self-adaptive system architecture that is dealing with the huge variety and complexity of contextual data and different sets of services by implementing a decentralized adaptation unit, which makes the monitoring and adaptation task easier and less complex by applying the separation of concerns principle.

References

1. The top 10 causes of death. In: World Heal. Organ. http://www.who.int/mediacentre/factsheets/fs310/en/. Accessed 3 Jun 2017
2. Casas, A., et al.: Integrated care prevents hospitalisations for exacerbations in COPD patients. Eur. Respir. J. **28**(1), 123–130 (2006)
3. Global Strategy for the Diagnosis Management and Prevention of COPD, Global Initiative for Chronic Obstructive Lung Disease (GOLD) (2011)
4. McKinstry, B.: The use of remote monitoring technologies in managing chronic obstructive pulmonary disease (2013)
5. Bolton, C.E., Waters, C.S., Peirce, S., Elwyn, G.: Insufficient evidence of benefit: a systematic review of home telemonitoring for COPD. J. Eval. Clin. Pract. **17**(6), 1216–1222 (2010)
6. Polisena, J., et al.: Home telehealth for chronic obstructive pulmonary disease: a systematic review and meta-analysis. J. Telemed. Telec. **16**, 120–127 (2010)
7. Jaana, M., Pare, G., Sicotte, C.: Home telemonitoring forrespiratory conditions: a systematic review. Am. J. Manage. Care **15**(5), 313–320 (2009)
8. Bartoli, L., Zanaboni, P., Masella, C., Ursini, N.: Systematicreview of telemedicine services for patients affected by Chronic Obstructive Pulmonary Disease (COPD). Telemed. J. E Health **15**(9), 877–883 (2009)
9. McLean, S., Nurmatov, U., Liu, J.L., Pagliari, C., Car, J., Sheikh, A.: Telehealthcare for chronic obstructive pulmonary disease: Cochrane Review and meta-analysis. Br. J. Gen. Pract. **62**(604), e739–e749 (2012). https://doi.org/10.3399/bjgp12X658269
10. Lieberman, H., Selker, T.: Out of context: computer systems that adapt to, and learn from, context. IBM Syst. J. **39**, 617–632 (2000)
11. Krupitzer, C., Roth, F.M., VanSyckel, S., Schiele, G., Becker, C.: A survey on engineering approaches for self-adaptive systems. Pervasive Mob. Comput. J. **17**(Part B), 184–206 (2015)
12. Oreizy, P., et al.: An architecture-based approach to self-adaptive software. IEEE Intell. Syst. **14**(3), 54–62 (1999)
13. Cheng, S.-W.: Rainbow: cost-effective software architecture-based self-adaptation. Ph.D. Dissertation. Carnegie Mellon University (2008)
14. Becker: Comparison of approaches for developing self-adaptive systems. In: Proceedings of ACM, New York, NY, USA, 14 p. (2018)
15. Di Marzo Serugendo, G., Fitzgerald, J., Romanovsky, A.: MetaSelf - an architecture and a development method for dependable self-* systems. In: Proc SAC, pp. 457–461. ACM (2010)
16. Mukhija, A., Martin G.: CASA a contract-based adaptive software architecture framework. In: Proceedings of the 3rd IEEE Workshop on Applications and Services in Wireless Networks (ASWN 2003), Berne, Switzerland, pp. 275–286, July 2003
17. Andr, F., Daubert, E., Gauvrit, G.: Towards a generic context-aware framework for self-adaptation of service-oriented architectures (2010)
18. Elmalaki, S., Wanner, L., Srivastava, M.: CAreDroid: adaptation framework for android context-aware applications. In: Proceedings of Annual International Conference on Mobile Computind Network (2015)
19. Gaasbeek, J.R., Martin, J.N.: Getting to requirements: the W5H challenge. In: Proceedings of the 11th International Symposium of the International Council on Systems Engineering (2001)

20. Ajami, H., Mcheick, H.: Ontology-based model to support ubiquitous healthcare systems for COPD patients. Electronics **7**, 371 (2018). https://doi.org/10.3390/electronics7120371
21. Krupitzer, C., Roth, F.M., Van Syckel, S., Schiele, G., Becker, C.: A survey on engineering approaches for self-adaptive systems. Pervasive Mob. Comput. **17**(Part B), 184–206 (2015)
22. Handte, M., Schiele, G., Matjuntke, V., Becker, C., Marrón, P.J.: 3PC: System support for adaptive peer-to-peer pervasive computing. ACM Trans. Auton. Adapt. Syst. **7**(1) (2012). Art. 10
23. McKinley, P., Sadjadi, S., Kasten, E., Cheng, B.H.C.: Composing adaptive software. IEEE Comput. **37**(7), 56–64 (2004)
24. IBM: An architectural blueprint for autonomic computing (2004)
25. Ajami, H., Mcheick, H., Mustapha, K.: A pervasive healthcare system for COPD patients. Diagnostics **9**, 135 (2019)

Study of Healthcare Professionals' Interaction in the Patient Records Based on Annotations

Khalil Chehab[1(✉)], Anis Kalboussi[2,3], and Ahmed Hadj Kacem[1]

[1] ReDCAD Research Laboratory, Faculty of Economics and Management,
University of Sfax, Sfax, Tunisia
khalilisig@gmail.com, ahmed.hadjkacem@fsegs.rnu.tn
[2] Higher Institute of Computer Science and Management, University of
Kairouan, Kairouan, Tunisia
anis.kalboussi@isigk.rnu.tn
[3] ReDCAD Research Laboratory, University of Sfax, Sfax, Tunisia

Abstract. The annotation practice is an almost daily activity; it is used by healthcare professionals (PHC) to analyze, collaborate, share knowledge and communicate, between them, information present in the healthcare record of patients. These annotations are created in a healthcare cycle that consists of: diagnosis, treatment, advice, follow-up and observation.

Due to an exponential increase in the number of medical annotation systems that are used by different categories of health professionals, we are faced with a problem of lack of organization of medical annotation systems developed on the basis of formal criteria. As a result, we have a fragmented image of these annotations tools which make the mission of choice of an annotation system by a PHC, in a well-defined context (biology, radiology...) and according to their needs to the functionalities offered by these tools, are difficult.

In this article we present a classification of thirty annotation tools developed by industry and academia based on 5 generic criteria. We conclude this survey paper with model proposition.

Keywords: E-heath · Annotation · Classification · Health record · Annotation system · Healthcare professionals

1 Introduction

The paper annotation practice is very common. Indeed, during our reading we are all accustomed to scribble our comments in a margin of document, to highlight, to circle sections, to paste post-it..., which aims to enrich and add value to information [40, 43]. Annotation is a central practice in many professions: teachers annotate copies of students; professors exchange annotated documents during their work; Engineers co build engines by annotating sketches of plans to make them evolve, doctors comment on patient folder, etc. [39, 44].

Annotations thus, take various forms and are used for different functions [28]. Moreover, computerization of documents offers us new perspectives to use these annotations (indexation, creation, document, assistance, etc.) which do not exist on paper [41]. Assistance is a very important function that can be related to the annotation activity.

© The Author(s) 2020
M. Jmaiel et al. (Eds.): ICOST 2020, LNCS 12157, pp. 316–328, 2020.
https://doi.org/10.1007/978-3-030-51517-1_28

Annotative activity is different when dealing with the professional annotator case. These annotations are created in a specific context, will follow a path, developed for the purpose of determining a specific task etc.

The annotation is expanded in a document flow. The latter is a carrier of the ratings. These annotations processed in this context are complementary. They provide us with information scattered over different documents. In fact, if we try to understand each one separately, in other words; if we separate an annotation from its creative context, we find that it does not make sense. In short, the annotation can be understood only in its semantic field.

For this reason, the study of annotation in a professional context obliges us to implement an annotation model that describes what actually happens. This model must provide us with the necessary links either at the level of the annotated documents or at the level of the tasks made without forgetting to take into account the specificity of the annotation's production domain. The documents that usually belong to a folder that is made for the purpose of carrying out a task has a definite circuit that repeats itself each time one needs to do this task. The proper understanding of annotations can be done in its creative context.

Doctors in/after consultation [45] use internet to search information that can help him. Based on their annotations it's possible to assist doctors and to gives him automatically pertinent information, from the net, after studying and analyzing their annotations.

This paper is organized as follows: Sect. 2 gives a classification of these tools based on several criteria; Sect. 3 gives a model proposition. Finally, Sect. 4 concludes this article.

2 Health Record Annotations and Medical Annotation Systems

In this work, we started with an exhaustive reading for the available papers on medical annotation systems (academic annotation system) and viewing the existing industrial annotation systems in the e-health domain. Although the medical annotation systems have already been studied in a variety of contexts, yet when it comes to the PHC to choose which system to use it is not a trivial task neither for a researcher to identify future research areas. This is because the annotation systems are so common and many of them share similar objectives. Moreover, there are no formal criteria to facilitate the comparison between those systems and to guide PHC choice or a researcher. As a result, there is a fragmented picture of these annotation tools. As far as we know, this is the first work to consider the classification of medical annotation system. When we determined the study of these systems we deduced that there are several common criteria which can classify these later. Several studies have proposed classifications of annotation systems in several fields [34, 35, 37] or in the field of e-health [42, 43]. We propose a classification based on 5 criteria which are: type of medical annotation object, the medical annotation activity, healthcare professional (Practitioner), type of annotation system, type of annotated resource.

2.1   Type of Medical Annotation Object (Cognitive/Computational)

- **Cognitive:** this annotation is created to be used by a human agent. In this case, the annotation requires a cognitive and intellectual effort to be interpreted. This annotation has a visible visual form on the document [34].
- **Computational:** this annotation is intended to be processed and manipulated by software agents. These annotations are also called meta-data. They allow us to annotate computer resources to facilitate their exploitation by machines.

2.2   The Medical Annotation Activity (Manual, Automatic, Semi-automatic)

Annotation activity begins with the choice of anchor and annotation form in the annotation toolbar related to the annotation software. Then, the annotation must complete the properties of the annotation; this process ends with the attachment of the annotation to a well-defined target. Based on this process we can classify the annotative activity as: manual, semi-automatic or automatic [38].

- **Manual:** the process already mentioned will be carried out totally by the user himself, who selects the form of the annotation, selects the anchor and creates the annotation. This process is similar to the process of annotation when a paper support is available.
- **Automatic:** the annotation process already mentioned is carried out totally by the machine. These annotations are based on either context sensors or pattern recognition techniques, etc.
- **Semi-automatic:** in this case, the process will be done from the start by the user. After a while, the system acquires and understands the way the user annotates. It moves to a suggestion of annotations that are automated, based on an annotation model built with rules under development. At this stage, human intervention remains just to validate or not validate and to refine the annotation rules created at a certain level, where there are no corrections and there is complete acceptance of the suggested rules, human intervention is canceled and the process becomes totally automated.

2.3   Healthcare Professional (Practitioner)

It is the annotator that is equipped with an annotation system to use all the functionalities offered by the latter. In our case, the practitioners are healthcare professionals (doctor, nurse, biologist, and radiologist). The healthcare cycle is composed of four phases (diagnostic, treatment, advice, follow up and observation). Each practitioner, with a medical annotation system, intervenes in one or many phases, according to their role, to accomplish a specific task in which annotation is made.

2.4 Type of Annotation System

- **Application:** an application is created to annotate the resources already consulted. These applications offer several functionalities as the types below.
- **Plug-in:** these are the expansion modules, an external module that is added to a website or software and which will make it possible to provide annotation functionalities to the latter.
- **Website:** these are specialized websites to annotate consulted resources by registered users on the web.

Knowing the type of annotation system facilitates the development of a patient record model which will be proposed in future research. This model allows communicating with different types of medicals annotations systems.

2.5 Type of Annotated Resource

Annotated resources can be: word document, pdf, image, text, video, html, audio, etc.

Table 1 presents a comparative study of the medical annotation systems seen in the bibliographical study using the 5 criteria already explained.

Table 1 presents a comparative study of thirty medical annotation systems seen in the bibliographical study using the 5 criteria already explained. These annotation systems are ranged on the table according of the chronological order of their publication year.

3 Model Proposition

Several models are already seen in the literature [33, 35, 36] and [37], these models present many problems, like the inexistence of the modeling of the cycle of care, the consideration of the annotation as an objective, no invocation of the services linked to the annotation, that not allows to use it in the healthcare domain. For this reason and based on the classifications already seen (Sect. 2) we propose an annotation model that preserve the semantic of annotative activity in the health domain.

3.1 Concept of Model

Our model must reflect the annotation process actually done; it must contain the following concepts:

- Basic_Concept: This group contains the concepts that can exist in each domain.
    - Place: this is the physical place where the annotation is produced by the annotator.
    - Anchor: this is the position of the annotation on the document.
    - Shape: represents the visual aspect of the annotation.
    - Annotated_content: this is the annotated passage.
    - Annotating_content: this is the comment written by the annotator about the Annotated_content.

Table 1. Comparative study of the medical annotation systems using 5 criteria

Name of annotation system		Year	Healthcare professional (Practitioner)	Annotated resource type	Category of annotation system			Annotation type		Type of annotation activity		
					Application	Plug-in	Web	Cognitive	Computational	Manual	Automatic	Semi-automatic
Santo	[1]	2018	D	Text			×	×			×	
Clean tools	[2]	2018	D	Image 3D	×			×		×	×	
Epivizr	[3]	2018	B	Document	×			×		×	×	
ODMSummary	[4]	2017	D	HTML			×	×			×	
3dBionote	[5]	2017	B	Image			×		×	×		
Verdant	[6]	2017	B	Text			×		×		×	
Best slice	[7]	2017	R, D	Image	×		×	×		×		
MicroMD	[8]	2017	R, D	Image	×			×		×		
GIDAC	[9]	2016	R	Image	×			×		×		
Vcf-miner	[10]	2016	B	Text			×	×	×	×		
Plexo	[11]	2016	R	Image		×		×		×		
BioDigital human	[12]	2016	D	Image 3D	×			×		×		
Icare	[13]	2015	N	Document	×			×		×		
Heideltime	[14]	2015	A	Time	×			×		×		
Domeo Annotation	[15]	2014	B	HTML		×			×	×	×	×
BioR	[16]	2014	B	Text			×		×	×	×	
3dmarkup radiologist	[17]	2014	R	Image		×			×	×	×	
Vita	[18]	2014	R	Image, video	×			×		×		
Marky	[19]	2014	R	All type	×				×			×

(continued)

Table 1. (*continued*)

Name of annotation system	Year	Healthcare professional (Practitioner)	Annotated resource type	Category of annotation system			Annotation type		Type of annotation activity		
				Application	Plug-in	Web	Cognitive	Computational	Manual	Automatic	Semi-automatic
Cliosoft dental [20]	2014	D	Image	X		X	X		X		
Medetect [21]	2013	D	HTML					X			X
Flersa [22]	2012	R	Image	X			X	X	X		X
SMltag [23]	2012	R	Image			X		X	X		
Mammoapplet [24]	2012	R	Image			X	X		X		
Brat [25]	2012	A	Text	X			X		X		
Idash [26]	2012	D	Text	X			X		X		
MedAt [27]	2011	D	Document	X				X			X
@note [28]	2009	B	text	X				X		X	
Arthemis [29]	2007	R	Video	X			X		X		
DocAnnot [30]	2006	D, N	Document	X							X

B: Biologist, D: Doctor, N: Nurse, R: Radiologist, A: all healthcares professional

- Type: the annotated content can have a type that enhances its content and facilitates access, filtering, searching later.
- Device: it is the device used to read and annotate the document.
- Date: represents the creation date of the annotation.
- Name: the name of PHC.
- Department: it is a part of decomposing the tasks of an organization (Hospital) according to the functions or the nature of these activities. This appointment is used in the professional field.
  - Service: It is a part of decomposing the tasks of a department according to the functions or the type of these activities.
  - Professional (PHC): it is the person (professional healthcare) who reads a document and makes the annotations.
  - Role: it is the function occupied by a professional.
  - Authority: it's the set of tasks that can be done by a professional in his role.
  - Name: it's the name and surname of the annotator.
- Package_document: it's a grouped document set.
  - Document: it's the annotated document.
  - Part_document: professional documents are usually divided into parts.
  - Element: each Part_document consists of a set of elements.
  - Part_element: it is the smallest granularity of document; it is a word, letter etc. In short, it is the annotated passage.
- Specific_concept: in each domain where the annotators are professionals, there are specific concepts related to the latter.
  - Validity: annotation can be associated with date which contains: Start_date, Finish_date, and Cyclic_date. Example: control the vital parameters of the patient today from 8 h (Start_date) to 19 h (Finish_date) every 2 h (Cyclic_date).
  - Scope: specifies the professional that can view the annotation.
  - Importance: a value affected to the annotation which valorizes it.
- Medical_care: each healthcare cycle consists of a set of Healthcare_cycle. Each Healthcare_cycle consists of a:
  - Diagnostic: Contain a detailed anamnesis of:
    - Patient history
    - Family history
    - Socio-economic question
    - Symptom of illness
    - Date of illness
    - Treatment already followed
    - Physical examination of patient
    - Complementary examination: medical image, biological analysis....
- Treatment: it contains the treatment written by the doctor.

- Advice: patient education: how to live with this disease, how to act in case of emergency, how to take their drugs...
- Follow up and observation: this is the last step of the care cycle in which the doctor follows his patient until the stabilization of his condition. In this step, it can also make a strengthening of advice....
- Service aspect: this aspect allows us to clarify the semantic of the annotation. It is used to interpret the meaning of the annotation by the annotator himself or by the software agents.
  - Effect: the effect of annotation is the result of web service called from this annotation.

3.2 Relationships Between Concepts

The relationships between the concepts of ontology are described through the data model presented in Fig. 1 as follows. There are only three type of cardinalities used in this model 1..*, 1 and *. An annotation is created by the PHC with a device, at a date and in a place. This annotation is presented by a particular shape. It is pointed to an anchor and related to an annotated content that can be related to another annotated content. This annotated content is a part of the read document. The annotation contains an annotating content that can be related to others annotating contents. An annotating content can have a type. An annotation has an annotated content that is alone, and at the base of this content, annotating content can be created for one or more professionals since this content can be written differently for each destination. Each domain has some specific concept. An annotation is related to Specifics concept.

The annotator, which is a PHC, is identified by a name. The place is a location in a medical department especially in a specific service. Each service has its own PHCs that are classified into categories (medical, paramedic). In the category a PHC can have a role and each role is related to a specific authority. A document is an element of a document package. A document package consists of the already known set of documents grouped together to perform a specific task. A document decomposed to parts, each one of it contains a set of elements (text box, radio button...). The annotated content can be an element or a part of an element (word, sentence...). A professional can have a power to launch tasks (Medical_care). Each healthcare cycle is divided into healthcare phases (Diagnostic – Treatment – Advice - Follow up and observation); the latter are linked together so we can fuse them once again when they are completed and we can follow the annotations of a healthcare cycle at the level of its phase. Each healthcare phase can be divided itself. A healthcare cycle can also be linked to other healthcare cycle that has a relationship between them.

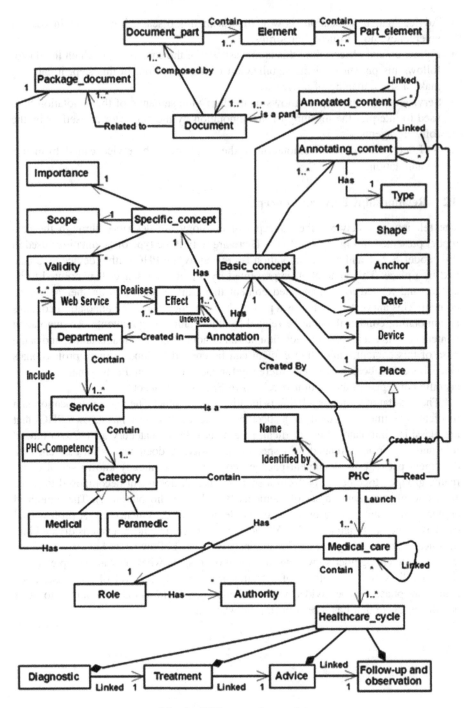

Fig. 1. PHC annotation model

4 Conclusion and Future Work

In this paper, we studied annotation systems of the digital health domain available in industrial and research areas in order to propose a unified classification of this kind of system that is omnipresent in hospital information systems. This panoramic view provided is based on the classification of thirty different annotation systems developed in the literature over the past two decades. This organization of annotation tools is built on the basis of five criteria: type of annotation (computational/cognitive); category of annotation system (application/plug-in/website); type of annotative activity (manual/ semi-automatic/automatic); type of annotated resource (text/Web page/video/image/ database) and practitioner (biologist/doctor/radiologist/nurse, etc.). This classification based on criteria, already explained in our study, which are transversal organizational criteria, facilitates the identification of limitations and possible challenges in the area of the medical annotation systems. Based on this, we proposed an ontology that covers the identified challenges and lead to a more intelligent annotation system. In future research, we try to use the results of this study to create an annotation template for PHCs and then try to generalize them to be functional for all professionals in different domains. We are also trying to create the computer services which allow the PHC to be assisted throughout the care cycle.

References

1. http://aclweb.org/anthology/P18-4012
2. Clean tools. https://arxiv.org/ftp/arxiv/papers/1808/1808.03806.pdf
3. Ma, J., Meng, J.: Interactive genomic visualization for R/bioconductor. In: International Conference on Biological Information and Biomedical Engineering, BIBE 2018, pp. 1–4. VDE, June 2018
4. Storck, M., Krumm, R., Dugas, M.: ODM summary: a tool for automatic structured comparison of multiple medical forms based on semantic annotation with the unified medical language system. PLoS ONE **11**(10), e0164569 (2017)
5. Segura, J., et al.: 3DBIONOTES v2. 0: a web server for the automatic annotation of macromolecular structures. Bioinformatics **33**(22), 3655–3657 (2017)
6. McKain, M.R., Hartsock, R.H., Wohl, M.M., Kellogg, E.A.: Verdant: automated annotation, alignment and phylogenetic analysis of whole chloroplast genomes. Bioinformatics **33**(1), 130–132 (2016)
7. https://www.best.edu.au/s/5njv62ar?data=8%400!9%4028320!10%40-27251.5&version=1
8. https://www.micromd.com/emr/
9. Vizza, P., Guzzi, P.H., Veltri, P., Cascini, G.L., Curia, R., Sisca, L.: GIDAC: a prototype for bioimages annotation and clinical data integration. In: 2016 IEEE International Conference on Bioinformatics and Biomedicine (BIBM), pp. 1028–1031. IEEE, December 2016
10. Hart, S.N., Duffy, P., Quest, D.J., Hossain, A., Meiners, M.A., Kocher, J.P.: VCF-Miner: GUI-based application for mining variants and annotations stored in VCF files. Brief. Bioinform. **17**(2), 346–351 (2016)
11. https://diegocantor.com/projects/
12. Qualter, J., et al.: The BioDigital human: a Web-based 3D platform for medical visualization and education. Stud. Health Technol. Inform. **173**, 359–361 (2016)

13. Marrast, P.: Equipement informatique des annotations et des pratiques d'écriture professionnelles: une étude ancrée pour l'organisation des soins en cancérologie (Doctoral dissertation, Université de Toulouse, Université Toulouse III-Paul Sabatier) (2015)

14. Zell, J., Strötgen, J.: HeidelTime Standalone Manual Version 2.1 (2015)

15. Clark, T., Ciccarese, P.N., Goble, C.A.: Micropublications: a semantic model for claims, evidence, arguments and annotations in biomedical communications. J. Biomed. Semant. **5**(1), 28 (2014)

16. Kocher, J.P.A., et al.: The Biological Reference Repository (BioR): a rapid and flexible system for genomics annotation. Bioinformatics **30**(13), 1920–1922 (2014)

17. Moreira, D.A., Hage, C., Luque, E.F., Willrett, D., Rubin, D.L.: 3D markup of radiological images in ePAD, a web-based image annotation tool. In: 2015 IEEE 28th International Symposium on Computer-Based Medical Systems (CBMS), pp. 97–102. IEEE, June 2015

18. Roy, S., Brown, M.S., Shih, G.L.: Visual interpretation with three-dimensional annotations (VITA): three-dimensional image interpretation tool for radiological reporting. J. Digit. Imaging **27**(1), 49–57 (2014)

19. Pérez-Pérez, M., Glez-Peña, D., Fdez-Riverola, F., Lourenço, A.: Marky: a lightweight web tracking tool for document annotation. In: Saez-Rodriguez, J., Rocha, M.P., Fdez-Riverola, F., De Paz Santana, J.F. (eds.) 8th International Conference on Practical Applications of Computational Biology & Bioinformatics (PACBB 2014). AISC, vol. 294, pp. 269–276. Springer, Cham (2014). https://doi.org/10.1007/978-3-319-07581-5_32

20. https://sotaimaging.com

21. Tian, L., et al.: Medetect: a lod-based system for collective entity annotation in biomedicine. In: 2013 IEEE/WIC/ACM International Joint Conferences on Web Intelligence (WI) and Intelligent Agent Technologies (IAT), vol. 1, pp. 233–240. IEEE, November 2013

22. Navarro-Galindo, J.L., Samos, J.: The FLERSA tool: adding semantics to a web content management system. Int. J. Web Inf. Syst. **8**(1), 73–126 (2012)

23. Federico, L., Néstor, D., Oscar, C.: SMITag: a social network for semantic annotation of medical images. In: 2012 XXXVIII Conferencia Latinoamericana En Informatica (CLEI), pp. 1–7. IEEE, October 2012

24. Mata, C., Oliver, A., Torrent, A., Marti, J.: MammoApplet: an interactive Java applet tool for manual annotation in medical imaging. In: 2012 IEEE 12th International Conference on Bioinformatics & Bioengineering (BIBE), pp. 34–39. IEEE, November, 2012

25. Stenetorp, P., Pyysalo, S., Topić, G., Ohta, T., Ananiadou, S., Tsujii, J.I.: BRAT: a web-based tool for NLP-assisted text annotation. In: Proceedings of the Demonstrations at the 13th Conference of the European Chapter of the Association for Computational Linguistics, pp. 102–107. Association for Computational Linguistics, April 2012

26. Ohno-Machado, L., et al.: iDASH: integrating data for analysis, anonymization, and sharing. J. Am. Med. Inform. Assoc. **19**(2), 196–201 (2011)

27. https://nit.felk.cvut.cz/drupal/projects/medical-annotation-tool-medat

28. http://anote-project.org

29. Liu, D., et al.: Arthemis: annotation software in an integrated capturing and analysis system for colonoscopy. Comput. Methods Programs Biomed. **88**(2), 152–163 (2007)

30. Tech-CICO UTT, LARIA U, Jury A: Les annotations pour supporter la collaboration dans le dossier patient électronique

31. Kalboussi, A., Omheni, N., Mazhoud, O., Kacem, A.H.: An interactive annotation system to support the learner with web services assistance. In: Proceedings of the 15th IEEE International Conference on Advanced Learning Technologies (ICALT 2015), pp. 409–410. IEEE (2015)

32. Kalboussi, A., Mazhoud, O., Hadj Kacem, A., Omheni, N.: A formal model of learner's annotations dedicated to web services invocation. In: Proceedings of the 21st International Conference on Computers in Education (ICCE 2013), pp. 166–169. APSCE (2013)
33. Charlet, J., Bachimont, B., Brunie, V., El Kassar, S., Zweigenbaum, P., Boisvieux, J.F.: Hospitexte: towards a document-based hypertextual electronic medical record. In: Proceedings of the AMIA Symposium, p. 713. American Medical Informatics Association (1998)
34. Kalboussi, A., Mazhoud, O., Kacem, A.H.: Annotative activity as a potential source of web service invocation. In: Proceedings of the 9th International Conference on Web Information Systems and Technologies (WEBIST 2013), pp. 288–292. SciTePress (2013)
35. Azouaou, F.: Modèles et outils d'annotations pour une mémoire personnelle de l'enseignant (Doctoral dissertation, Université Joseph-Fourier-Grenoble I) (2006)
36. Caussanel, J., Cahier, J. P., Zacklad, M., Charlet, J.: Les Topic Maps sont-ils un bon candidat pour l'ingénierie du Web Sémantique? In: Actes des 13e journées francophones d'ingénierie des connaissances (IC). Prix AFIA de la meilleure présentation (2002)
37. Kalboussi, A., Mazhoud, O., Kacem, A.H.: Comparative study of web annotation systems used by learners to enhance educational practices: features and services. Int. J. Technol. Enhanc. Learn. (IJTEL) 8(2), 129–150 (2016)
38. Sophie Clément, P.: Quels sites internet utilisent les médecins généralistes en consultation? Enquête de pratique auprès de 100 médecins généralistes. Thèse de doctorat en médecine (2016)
39. Iroju, O., Soriyan, A., Gambo, I., Olaleke, J.: Interoperability in healthcare: benefits, challenges and resolutions. Int. J. Innov. Appl. Stud. 3(1), 262–270 (2013)
40. Ryan, A.: Towards semantic interoperability in healthcare: ontology mapping from SNOMED-CT to HL7 version 3. In: Proceedings of the Second Australasian Workshop on Advances in ontologies, vol. 72, pp. 69–74. Australian Computer Society, Inc. (2006)
41. Lau, L.M., Shakib, S.: Towards data interoperability: practical issues in terminology implementation and mapping. In: HIC 2005 and HINZ 2005: Proceedings, vol. 208 (2005)
42. Chehab, K., Kalboussi, A., Kacem, A.H.: Study of annotations in e-health domain. In: Mokhtari, M., Abdulrazak, B., Aloulou, H. (eds.) ICOST 2018. LNCS, vol. 10898, pp. 189–199. Springer, Cham (2018). https://doi.org/10.1007/978-3-319-94523-1_17
43. Chehab, K., Kalboussi, A., Hadj Kacem, A.: An annotation model for patient record. Health Inf. 2019, 272–280 (2019)
44. Mille, D.: Modèles et outils logiciels pour l'annotation sémantiquede documentspéda-gogiques (Doctoral dissertation, Université Joseph-Fourier-Grenoble I) (2015)
45. Caussanel, J., Cahier, J.P., Zacklad, M., Charlet, J.: Les Topic Maps sont-ils un bon candidat pour l'ingénierie du Web Sémantique?. In: Actes des 13e journées francophones d'ingénierie des connaissances (IC). Prix AFIA de la meilleure présentation (2002)
46. Azouaou, F.: Modèles et outils d'annotations pour une mémoire personnelle de l'enseignant (Doctoral dissertation, Université Joseph-Fourier-Grenoble I) (2006)
47. Dublin Core Metadata Initiative. Dublin core metadata element set, version 1.1 (2012)
48. Kahan, J., Koivunen, M.R., Prud'Hommeaux, E., Swick, R.R.: Annotea: an open RDF infrastructure for shared Web annotations. Comput. Netw. 39(5), 589–608 (2002)

328 K. Chehab et al.

Multirate ECG Processing and k-Nearest Neighbor Classifier Based Efficient Arrhythmia Diagnosis

Saeed Mian Qaisar[1](✉), Moez Krichen[2,3], and Fatma Jallouli[4]

[1] College of Engineering, Effat University, Jeddah, Kingdom of Saudi Arabia
sqaisar@effatuniversity.edu.sa
[2] Faculty of CSIT, Al-Baha University, Al Bahah, Saudi Arabia
[3] ReDCAD Laboratory, University of Sfax, Sfax, Tunisia
moez.krichen@redcad.org
[4] Faculty of Medicine of Sfax, Sfax, Tunisia
fatma.jallouli@gmail.com

Abstract. The goal of this work is to make a contribution to the development of computationally efficient multirate Electrocardiogram (ECG) automated detectors of arrhythmia. It utilizes an intelligent combination of multirate denoising plus wavelet decomposition for an effective realization of the ECG wireless implants. The decomposed signal subband features are mined and in next step these are utilized by the mature k-Nearest Neighbor (KNN) classifier for arrhythmia diagnosis. The multirate nature substantially reduces the processing activity of the system and thus allows a dramatic decrease in energy consumption compared to traditional counterparts. The performance of the system is estimated also in terms of the classification performance. Obtained results reveal an overall 22.5-fold compression gain and 4-folds processing outperformance over the traditional equals while securing 93.2% highest classification accuracy and specificity of 0.956. Findings confirm that the proposed solution could potentially be embedded in contemporary automatic and mobile cardiac diseases diagnosis systems.

Keywords: Multirate processing · ECG · Arrhythmia · Wavelet · Features extraction · Classification

1 Introduction

Cardiovascular diseases have drawn global attention. This is due to its increasing prevalence and incidence [1, 14]. Electrocardiogram (ECG) measures electrical activities with respect to time. Manual examination of cardiac arrhythmias can be time consuming and complicated. This challenge may be solved using computer-aided automatic cardiac decision tools. The computer-aided or pattern-based recognition systems could increase the effectiveness of cardiac health analysis by detecting subtle differences in frequency and amplitude components of the heartbeat [2].

Many scientists have previously explored computer-assisted solutions for cardiac health monitoring as reviewed in [7]. Preprocessing is the first ECG processing stage. The popular ECG denoising methods are the finite impulse response (FIR) filtering,

© The Author(s) 2020
M. Jmaiel et al. (Eds.): ICOST 2020, LNCS 12157, pp. 329–337, 2020.
https://doi.org/10.1007/978-3-030-51517-1_29

principle component analysis (PCA) and Kalman filtering [2, 8]. The extraction of features is one of the essential steps of computer-aided ECG diagnostic solutions. Certain extensively used ECG signal feature extraction approaches are the "Wavelet Transform" (WT), "Discrete Cosine Transform" (DCT) and "Short Time Fourier Transform" (STFT). The pertinent signal features are afterward employed for the classification purpose. Techniques adopted for this purpose are the "Naïve Bias", the "K-Nearest Neighbor" (KNN), the "Artificial Neural Networks" (ANN) and the "Support Vector Machine" (SVM).

Classical ECG systems are by definition time-invariant [3, 4]. This can lead to inefficient use of system resources and energy consumption [2, 5]. For such signals, an effective solution can be achieved by diminishing the rates of data collection, processing and transmission [5]. In this framework, multirate signal processing tactics have been employed [6]. The subsampling is intelligently employed in the suggested framework. It allows overcoming the downsides of the counter fix rate ECG processing approaches [3, 4]. Therefore, it allows realizing a simplified and power efficient ECG wireless implant with a real-time compression of data.

2 Materials and Methods

Figure 1 illustrates the adopted system block level diagram. A description of the different modules of the system is given in the coming subsections.

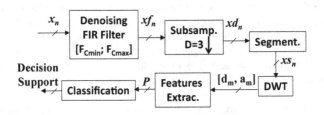

Fig. 1. Block diagram of the adopted system

2.1 Dataset

In this study, the ECG signals, obtained from a standard ECG dataset are used [1]. 3 different ECG classes the "Wolff-Parkinson-White" (WPW), "Right Bundle Branch Block" (RBBB) and the "Normal Sinus Rhythm" (N) are considered. ECG analog signals are band limited up to 60 Hz and each channel is recorded via an 11-Bit resolution analog to digital converter (ADC). The employed sampling frequency is of 360 Hz. The digitized versions of intended ECG signals are splitted into fixed length segments to split the continuous time signals into ECG impulses. Each impulse is considered as an instance. In order to avoid any biasing an equal representation is selected for each considered class. In this framework, 150 instances are considered for each class. It results in total 450 instances from 3 ECG classes.

2.2 Denoising

The digitized signal x_n is denoised by using an offline designed band-pass FIR filter. The denoising diminishes the noise like the "Power Line Interference" (PLI) and "Baseline Wander" (BW) from the ECG signal. It improves the efficiency of collection and classification of the features. The ECG signal's useful frequency range lies between [0.5; 50] Hz [9, 10]. Accordingly, a band-pass linear phase filter is configured offline for the cut-off frequencies of [$Fc_L = 0.5$; $Fc_H = 50$] Hz it resulted in a 122nd order filter designed for $F_S = 360$ Hz. For proper filtering, Fc_H is kept less than half of the signal sampling rate [5]. Therefore, $F_S = 360$ Hz fulfils this criterion.

2.3 Subsampling

The functioning of conventional ECG acquisition and analysis processes is of time-invariant nature [2–4]. Consequently, a worst-case parameterization is enforced [5]. It causes the processing ineffectiveness in the case of time-varying and sporadic ECG signals. These inadequacies can be diminished by using multirate processing approaches [2, 5, 6]. In this framework, the denoised signal xf_n is subsampled with a factor of $D = 4$ to obtain $xd_n = xf_{Dn}$. Subsampling without a prior digital antialiasing filtering can cause aliasing [6]. However, a proper choice of D allows to perform subsampling without prior filtering. In this case, the selected value of D should respect the condition: $D \leq \frac{F_S}{F_{Nyq}} = 3.6$. Here, $F_S = 360$ Hz, $F_{Nyq} = 2.f_{max}$ and f_{max} is the bandwidth of xf_n and is equal to $Fc_H = 50$ Hz. It shows that for the chosen $D = 3$ subsampling does not cause aliasing.

2.4 Segmentation

In order to split the continuous time ECG records into ECG pulses, xd_n is divided in 0.9-s length segments. Each segment, xs_n, contains one ECG pulse. The segmentation is realized by using fixed length rectangular windows [6]. The process can be mathematically depicted as:

$$ys_n = \sum\nolimits_{n=\tau-\frac{L_T}{2}}^{\tau+\frac{L_T}{2}} yd_n w_{n-\tau}.$$

Here, L_T and τ are respectively the length in seconds and the central time of an intended segment.

2.5 Discrete Wavelet Transform

The "Wavelet Transform" (WT) can be mathematically expressed by Eq. (1) where, s and u respectively represent the dilation and the translation parameters.

$$W_x^\psi(u, s) = \frac{1}{\sqrt{S}} \int_{-\infty}^{+\infty} x(t)\psi * \left(\frac{(t-u)}{s}\right) dt. \tag{1}$$

A discrete time wavelet transform (DWT) is used for decomposing the xs_n. A translation-dilation representation is attained by employing digital filters. In this case, each segment xs_n is decomposed through the "Daubechies Algorithm" based wavelet decomposition process. It consists of half-band low-pass filter and high-pass filter with subsampling with a factor of two. It allows the computation of approximation, a_m and detail, d_m, coefficients at each level of decomposition.

The mathematical processes of computing a_m and d_m are respectively depicted by Eq. (2) and Eq. (3). Where, m represents the level of decomposition. In this study a third level of decomposition is employed. Therefore, $m \in \{1, 2, 3\}$. g_{2n-k} and h_{2n-k} are respectively the half-band low-pass and high-pass filters using a subsampling factor of two.

$$a_m = \sum_{k=1}^{K_g} ys_n \cdot g_{2n-k}. \tag{2}$$

$$d_m = \sum_{k=1}^{K_g} ys_n \cdot h_{2n-k}. \tag{3}$$

2.6   Features Extraction

The wavelet coefficients, obtained for each intended subband, $d_1 = [60, 120]$ Hz, $d_2 = [30, 60]$ Hz, $d_3 = [15, 30]$ Hz and $a_3 = [0, 15]$ Hz are used for mining the discriminative and classifiable features. 4 statistical features are extracted from each subband. These are described in the following.

Energy (E) is calculated by adding all the absolute values of subband coefficients. *Kurtosis of the signal (K)* is a measure of the curvature of the considered subband coefficients. *Peak positive value (PV)* is the maximum positive value of the intended subband coefficients. *Peak negative value (NV)* is the maximum negative value of the intended subband coefficients.

2.7   Classification

After features extraction, each instance is presented in the form of a reduced data matrix, composed of 16 features. The intended dataset is composed of 3 ECG classes namely the "Normal Sinus Rhythm (N), the "Right Bundle Branch Block" (RBBB) and the "Wolff-Parkinson-White" (WPW). For equal representation, 150 instances are taken into consideration for every class. Thus, in total 450 ECG instances are considered. After features extraction, the resulting data matrix has a size of 450 × 16. To classify this data matrix, the "k-Nearest Neighbor" (KNN) classification algorithm is employed.

The KNN is well known for its ability of delivering high quality results even for applications wit high complexity [16]. In a data set, the features' distance is used by KNN to decide which data belongs to what class. When the distance in the data is near, a group is formed, and when the distance in the data is far, other groups are formed. A category membership might be the output of the KNN classifier. The categorization of an object is done through the majority vote by its neighbors. That is, the object is added to the class which is most common among its k closest neighbors (k could generally be a small positive whole number). The object is assigned solely to the nearest neighbor's single classification if the k equals one [11].

2.8   Evaluation Measures

Compression Ratio compares the designed system performance in terms of reduction in the amount of information to be classified compared to the conventional approach where acquired ECG data points are transmitted towards classifier without performing any features selection. If N_r and P are respectively the count of data points to be classified, for a given time length of L_T-Sec., in the conventional and the devised approach then the compression ration, R_{COMP}, can be calculated as:

$$R_{COMP} = \frac{N_r}{P}.$$

Computational Complexity compares the designed system performance with the fixed-rate counter equals in terms of the count of required standard operations like additions, multiplications and divisions [12]. In conventional case, the denoised signal is segmented by employing a rectangular window. It splits the incoming samples sequence in L_T-Sec. segments. Each segment is composed of N_r samples. The processing cost of this process is negligible compared to operations like additions and multiplications [12]. Each segment is further split into subbands by using the 3rd level Daubechies wavelet decomposition. It consists of half-band FIR high-pass and low-pass filters with a subsampling factor of two. Let Kg be the order of half-band filters and same filters are employed at all levels of decomposition. It is well known that a Kg order filter performs Kg additions and Kg multiplications [5]. Therefore, the computational complexity of this fixed rate wavelet decomposition process C_{FR-WD} can be mathematically expressed by Eq. (4). This mathematical derivation is also clear from Fig. 2.

$$C_{FR-WD} = \underbrace{3.5 \times Kg.N_r}_{Additions} + \underbrace{3.5 \times Kg.N_r}_{Multiplications}. \tag{4}$$

For the case of designed solution xf_n is firstly subsampled and then xd_n is segmented by employing a rectangular window. Each segment is composed of $N = 0.25 \times N_r$ samples. If Kg is the order of half-band filters and same filters are employed at all levels of decomposition then the computational complexity of this process C_{P-WD} can be mathematically expressed by Eq. (5). If $M = 0.5 \times M_r$ is the count of samples processed by the denoising module then the total computational complexity for the designed front-end processing chain can be expressed by using Eq. (10).

$$C_{P-WD} = \underbrace{0.875 \times Kg.N_r}_{Additions} + \underbrace{0.875 \times Kg.N_r}_{Multiplications} \tag{5}$$

Classification Accuracy and Specificity are used to evaluate the overall system precision. The processes may be formally described by means of Eq. (6) and Eq. (7). Where, "True Positives" (TP) and "True Negatives" (TN) are correct classifications. "False Negatives" and "False Positives" (FP) (FN) are wrong classification results [13].

$$Accuracy = \frac{T_P + T_N}{T_P + T_N + F_P + F_N} \times 100\%. \tag{6}$$

$$Specificity = \frac{T_N}{T_N + F_P}. \tag{7}$$

3   Results and Discussions

Examples of the considered ECG signal classes are shown in Fig. 2. These incoming signals x_n are denoised by employing the band-pass FIR filter. It improves the expected signal SNR ("Signal to Noise Ratio") and results in an increased classification precision. An example of the filtered version of signal for the (RBBB) class is shown in Fig. 3-a. The de-noised signal xf_n is down-sampled with a factor of $D = 3$. An example of the subsampled versions of signal for the RBBB class is shown in Fig. 3-b.

The decimated signal xd_n is splitted into fixed length segments of 0.9 s durations. Onward each segment is decomposed into subbands via the application of a 3 stages wavelet decomposer. Computational Gain of the designed front-end processing chain over the fixed-rate counterpart is calculated by using Eq. (4) and Eq. (5). It results in 4-fold reduction in terms of count of additions and multiplications of the designed solution compared to the fixed-rate counterpart.

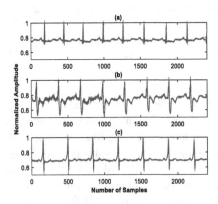

Fig. 2. Examples of the ECG signals. (a) (N), (b) (RBBB) and (c) (WPW).

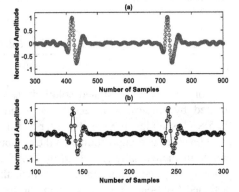

Fig. 3. Example of denoised RBBB signal (a) and example of decimated RBBB signal (b).

In next step, four statistical features are extracted from each subband. In this way each intended instance is presented by 16 parameters. The compression gain of the designed framework over the conventional equal is computed by using $R_{COMP} = \frac{N}{P}$. It results in 22.5-fold real-time compression gain of the proposed solution over the conventional equal.

Above results show that the devised solution outperforms the conventional equals in terms of processing efficiency and compression gain. However, due to the multirate processing feature it may lose its performance in terms of the precision. Therefore, the overall performance of the system is measured in terms of the accuracy of the classification process. The KNN classifier is employed with $k = 5$ configuration. Training and testing sets are made of 3 distinct classes. Total 450 instances are used. The 10-fold cross validation technique is used for all experiments. Classifier's performance is quantified in terms of the accuracy and the specificity by using Eq. (6) and Eq. (7). The obtained results are summarized in Table 1. It shows that for the studied case, the obtained classification accuracies are high. The highest classification accuracy is obtained for the (WPW) class, 93.2%. The average classification accuracy of the designed framework is 91.87% with an average specificity of 0.947. It concludes that the suggested approach not only attains the outperformance in terms of compression gain and processing efficiency but it also secures an appropriate ECG arrhythmia classification precision.

Table 1. Classification performance for 3 class ECG dataset

ECG class	Classification accuracy (% age)	Specificity	Average accuracy (% age)	Average specificity
Normal (N)	90.3	0.935	91.87	0.947
RBBB	92.1	0.951		
WPW	93.2	0.956		

4 Conclusion

In this paper a novel multirate ECG processing, subbands decomposition and classification framework is designed. The decomposed signal subband features are mined and in next step these are utilized by the mature k-Nearest Neighbor (KNN) based classifier for an effective arrhythmia diagnosis. The multirate feature diminishes the system processing load. It is shown that because of the multirate feature the system has attained the 4 folds diminishing in the count of processing load as compared to the conventional equals. Additionally, the features extraction process has induced 22.5 times compression gain in the system. It also assures a same factor of processing load diminishing at the post classification stage. The overall performance of the system is quantified in terms of the accuracy of the classification process. For the studied case the designed framework has attained the highest classification accuracy of 93.2% and specificity of 0.956. It assures that the devised solution is a potential candidate to be embedded in contemporary automatic and mobile cardiac diseases diagnosis systems.

A possible future direction of work is to adopt a model-based testing methodology for validating the proposed approach [15–18]. Integration and investigation of event-based processing modules [19–22] in this system is another prospect.

Acknowledgement and Ethical Approval. Authors are thankful to anonymous reviewers for their useful feedback. This article does not contain any studies with human participants or animals performed by any of the authors.

References

1. Pławiak, P.: Novel methodology of cardiac health recognition based on ECG signals and evolutionary-neural system. Expert Syst. Appl. **92**, 334–349 (2018)
2. Qaisar, S.M., Subasi, A.: An adaptive rate ECG acquisition and analysis for efficient diagnosis of the cardiovascular diseases. In: 2018 IEEE 3rd International Conference on Signal and Image Processing (ICSIP), pp. 177–181. IEEE, July 2018
3. You, I., Choo, K.K.R., Ho, C.L.: A smartphone-based wearable sensors for monitoring real-time physiological data. Comput. Electr. Eng. **65**, 376–392 (2018)
4. Lian, Y.: Energy efficient system architecture for wireless wearable biomedical sensors. In: 2017 IEEE Custom Integrated Circuits Conference (CICC), pp. 1–33. IEEE, April 2017
5. Qaisar, S.M.: Efficient mobile systems based on adaptive rate signal processing. Comput. Electr. Eng. **79**, 106462 (2019)
6. Gopi, E.S.: Multirate digital signal processing. In: Gopi, E.S. (ed.) Multi-Disciplinary Digital Signal Processing, pp. 121–146. Springer, Cham (2018). https://doi.org/10.1007/978-3-319-57430-1_4
7. Jahmunah, V., et al.: Computer-aided diagnosis of congestive heart failure using ECG signals–a review. PhysicaMedica **62**, 95–104 (2019)
8. Rakshit, M., Das, S.: An efficient ECG denoising methodology using empirical mode decomposition and adaptive switching mean filter. Biomed. Signal Process. Control **40**, 140–148 (2018)
9. Kærgaard, K., Jensen, S.H., Puthusserypady, S.: A comprehensive performance analysis of EEMD-BLMS and DWT-NN hybrid algorithms for ECG denoising. Biomed. Signal Process. Control **25**, 178–187 (2016)
10. Sharma, R.R., Pachori, R.B.: Baseline wander and power line interference removal from ECG signals using eigenvalue decomposition. Biomed. Signal Process. Control **45**, 33–49 (2018)
11. Serpen, G., Aghaei, E.: Host-based misuse intrusion detection using PCA feature extraction and kNN classification algorithms. Intell. Data Anal. **22**(5), 1101–1114 (2018)
12. Kulisch, U.W., Miranker, W.L.: Computer arithmetic in theory and practice. Academic Press, Cambridge (2014)
13. Paluszek, M., Thomas, S.: MATLAB Machine Learning. Apress, New Jersey (2016)
14. Nowbar, A., Gitto, M., Howard, J., Francis, D., Al-Lamee, R.: 112 global and temporal trends in mortality from ischaemic heart disease: statistics from the World Health Organisation. Heart **105**(Suppl 6), A93 (2019)
15. Krichen, M.: Model-based testing for real-time systems. Doctoral dissertation, Ph.D. thesis, Universit Joseph Fourier (2007)
16. Krichen, M., Maâlej, A.J., Lahami, M.: A model-based approach to combine conformance and load tests: an eHealth case study. IJCCBS **8**(3/4), 282–310 (2018)

17. Maâlej, A.J., Krichen, M., Jmaïel, M.: Conformance testing of WS-BPEL compositions under various load conditions. In: 2012 IEEE 36th Annual Computer Software and Applications Conference, p. 371. IEEE, July 2012
18. Krichen, M.: A formal framework for conformance testing of distributed real-time systems. In: Lu, C., Masuzawa, T., Mosbah, M. (eds.) OPODIS 2010. LNCS, vol. 6490, pp. 139–142. Springer, Heidelberg (2010). https://doi.org/10.1007/978-3-642-17653-1_12
19. Qaisar, S.M., Aljefri, R.: Time-domain identification of the power quality disturbances based on the event-driven processing. In: 2019 3rd International Conference on Energy Conservation and Efficiency (ICECE), pp. 1–5. IEEE, October 2019
20. Qaisar, S.M., Laskar, S., Lunglmayr, M., Moser, B.A., Abdulbaqi, R., Banafia, R.: An event-driven approach for time-domain recognition of spoken English letters. In: 2019 5th International Conference on Event-Based Control, Communication, and Signal Processing (EBCCSP), pp. 1–4. IEEE, May 2019
21. Qaisar, S.M., Subasi, A.: Efficient epileptic seizure detection based on the event driven processing. Procedia Comput. Sci. **163**, 30–34 (2019)
22. Qaisar, S.M., Niyazi, S., Subasi, A.: Efficient isolated speech to sign conversion based on the adaptive rate processing. Procedia Comput. Sci. **163**, 35–40 (2019)

Comparative Study of Relevant Methods for MRI/X Brain Image Registration

Marwa Abderrahim[1]([✉]), Abir Baâzaoui[1], and Walid Barhoumi[1,2]

[1] Institut Supérieur d'Informatique d'El Manar, LR16ES06 Laboratoire de recherche en Informatique, Modélisation et Traitement de l'Information et de la Connaissance (LIMTIC), Université de Tunis El Manar, 2080 Ariana, Tunisia
Abderrahimmarwa1@outlook.fr, a.baazaoui@hotmail.fr
[2] Ecole Nationale d'Ingénieurs de Carthage, Université de Carthage, Tunis-Carthage, Tunisia
walid.barhoumi@enicarthage.rnu.tn

Abstract. Several methods of brain image registration have been proposed in order to overcome the requirement of clinicians. In this paper, we assess the performance of a hybrid method for brain image registration against the most used standard registration tools. Most traditional registration tools use different methods for mono- and multi-modal registration, whereas the hybrid registration method is providing both mono and multi-modal brain registration of PET, MRI and CT images. To determine the appropriate registration method, we used two challenging brain image datasets as well as two evaluation metrics. Results show that the hybrid method outperforms all other standard registration tools and has achieved promising accuracy for MRI/X brain image registration.

Keywords: MRI/X brain image registration · Hybrid method · Standard registration tools · Brain diagnosis

1 Introduction

Hundreds of millions of people worldwide suffer from neurological disorders, and early detection coupled with appropriate treatment can generally cure these diseases. In this context, Computer Aided Diagnosis (CAD) explains the need to design automatic and semi-automatic tools to effectively process brain medical imaging. This could help clinicians to detect affected organs in order to specify appropriate treatments. However, there are still many challenges (*e.g.* noise, resolution, partial volume effect ...) that need to be investigated. There are several brain medical imaging modalities, and each of them has a different aspect of anatomy and/or functionality. Anatomical medical imaging (*e.g.* Magnetic Resonance Imaging (MRI), Computed Tomography (CT) ...) provides information on the structure, the shape, the edge, and the contents of organs. Functional medical imaging (*e.g.* Positron Emission Tomography (PET) ...) focuses on the function of organs, tissues or cells. In clinical routines, experts generally

M. Jmaiel et al. (Eds.): ICOST 2020, LNCS 12157, pp. 338–347, 2020.
https://doi.org/10.1007/978-3-030-51517-1_30

refer to both functional and structural aspects conjointly. In particular, MRI is frequently coupled with CT, MRI atlas and PET. However, a registration step is required in order to ensure effectively the complementarity of structural and functional images. Research on registration process is driven either by the type of attributes (geometric *vs.* iconic methods), the type of transformation (rigid *vs.* non-rigid) or the involved images (monomodal *vs.* multimodal) (Fig. 1). The principle of geometric registration methods consists in extracting geometric primitives from the two images to be registered (*e.g.* points, curves, surfaces ...), whereas iconic registration methods operate directly on the intensities. Furthermore, the rigid registration methods aim to correct the geometric transformations, including translation, rotation, shear, and scaling, whereas the non-rigid registration methods are carried out using localized stretch of the images. In this type of transformation, all kinds of deformation fields can be used (*e.g.* splines, B-spline, elastic model ...) [1]. For the monomodal registration methods, the two images are coming from the same modality (*e.g.* MRI scans, CT scans ...), whilst in the multimodal registration ones, the two images come from two different modalities (*e.g.* MRI and PET, MRI and CT ...) [2]. Generally, one of the key challenges in brain image registration is its veracity. This is because of the limitations in the registration methods, which are dependent on the quality of MRI/X parameters as well as the inaccuracy on the non-linear transformations. In addition to the registration errors, several registrations methods suffer from the extensive computational cost. To circumvent these limits, atlas-based registration coupled with standard softwares (such as SPM, ITK ...) are commonly used. Indeed, various studies are using this framework in order to investigate Parkinson disease [3], brain tumors using CT/MRI [4] or PET/MRI [5], and Alzheimer disease [6]. Additionally, challenges can arise where mono- and multimodal registration is required sequentially. To this end, we evaluate a hybrid method that may handle mono- and multi-modal registration according to the same technique. In fact, this paper is dedicated to determine the best tool for mono- and multi-modal registration for MRI/X brain images, such that X refers in our case to PET, CT and MRI atlas. We compare three widely brain image registration tools (SPM, ITK-Snap, 3D Slicer) against an accurate hybrid registration method from the state-of-the-art.

The rest of this paper is organized as follows. Section 2 shows the studied registration methods. Then, we present the clinical datasets and the evaluation protocol in Sect. 3. We detail experimental results in Sect. 4. Finally, a conclusion with some directions for future work are discussed in Sect. 5.

2   Registration Methods

ITK-Snap. Insight Segmentation and Registration Toolkit (ITK-Snap) is a popular tool for segmenting and registering medical images such as MRI, PET and CT [7]. It is an open source software widely used by clinicians and non-computer researchers. ITK-Snap allows manual and automatic medical image registration. This software groups several methods of registration based on the intensity. For

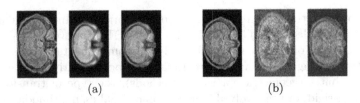

Fig. 1. MRI/X brain image registration: (a) mono-modal MRI/MRI atlas (from left to right: MRI image, MRI atlas and superposed images), (b) multi-modal MRI/PET (from left to right: MRI image, PET image and superposed images).

the automatic registration, the similarity measures included in ITK-Snap are mutual information, cross-correlation, and intensity difference. The transformation model included is affine and rigid transformation. This tool helps the users to locally find optimal rigid and affine transformations dynamically. For the manual registration, it is enough to determine the values of x, y, and z for the translation, rotation, and scaling. In our case, we used the same settings as [8].

SPM. Statistical Parametric Mapping (SPM) is an open source software for analysing functional brain imaging data (*e.g.* fMRI, PET, SPECT ...). It uses several setting options, which are referred to the Powell optimization algorithm. These options are: objective function, separation, tolerance and histogram smoothing. For the objective function, SPM uses either mutual information, normalized mutual information, or entropy correlation coefficient for multimodal registration, and normalised cross-correlation for monomodal registration. Separation, which is the average distance between sampled points, is of 8 mm for fMRI and 12 mm for PET [9]. SPM applies Gaussian smoothing to the 256×256 joint histogram. For similarity measurement, SPM includes the Nearest Neighbor, trilinear, and B-spline interpolation, and trilinear interpolation proved to be the most adequate for MRI and PET. For monomodal registration, SPM presents other parameters for estimating deformations (*e.g.* bias regularisation). Also, a mutual information-based affine registration with the tissue probability maps is used to obtain approximate alignment, with a smoothness value of 0 mm.

3D Slicer. 3D Slicer [10] supports rigid, affine and deformable registration. It includes point-surface and intensity-based registration. In fact, individual intensity-based registration modules depend on the used similarity metric (mutual information and cross-correlation) and flexibility of the transformation settings (rigid, affine, B-spline and dense deformation fields) [11]. The choice of algorithms depends on the organs' anatomy (*e.g.* brain, lungs ...), modality (multimodal *vs.* monomodal), performance (robustness *vs.* speed), and level of interaction. Besides, 3D Slicer uses parametric maps in order to align anatomical volumes. The registration process consists of three steps (Fig. 2). Firstly, it allows to align subject B: T2 according to the MRI mode T1 of the same subject. Secondly, it aligns subject A: T2 according to A: T1. Lastly, the registration is performed between the registered subject B: T1 and the fixed subject A: T1.

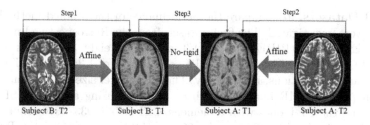

Fig. 2. Flowchart of 3D Slicer.

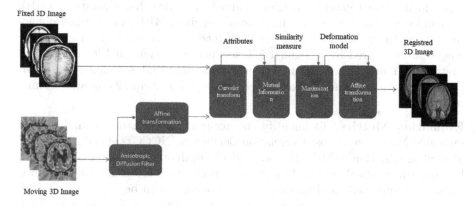

Fig. 3. Flowchart of the hybrid method.

Hybrid Method. The hybrid method is a unified tool for mono- and multi-modal 3D brain image registration. In fact, we extended the multi-modal 2D brain image registration work of [2]. The method is composed of five steps (Fig. 3) and its main contribution lies in adopting adaptive mutual information based on curvelet coefficients. Firstly, an anisotropic diffusion filter [12] denoises the moving image. Secondly, an affine transformation is applied on the moving image using transformation matrices (translation, rotation, scaling and shear). Thirdly, features from the two images are extracted using curvelet transform [13], and the Gaussian probability density function [14,15] is used to model the distribution of curvelet coefficients. Then, an adaptive mutual information, based on a conditional entropy between the coefficients of curvelet, aligns the images, and mutual information parameters are optimized using the maximum likelihood [16]. Finally, to align the moving image on the reference one, an affine transformation is adapted in order to deal with common distortions.

3   Materials

In this section, we present the used 3D medical image datasets and the evaluation protocol that we adopted in order to evaluate the compared registration methods.

Clinical Datasets. To compare the performance of the studied methods, two datasets were investigated. The first dataset, from the Retrospective Image Registration Evaluation (RIRE) project [17], consists of eight 3D triplets of PET, MRI and CT images of brain. The MRI voxel size is of 1.25, 1.28 and 4 mm in the x, y and z directions, respectively. The PET voxel size is (2.59 mm, 8 mm, 8 mm) in *(x, y, z)*. MR images have been obtained using a Siemens SP 1.5 T scanner, and the PET ones with a Siemens/CTI ECAT 933/0816 scanner. The CT voxel size is equal to (0.65 mm, 0.65 mm, 4.0 mm) in *(x, y, z)*. CT images have been acquired using a Siemens Somatom Plus scanner. The second dataset is provided by the Center for Addiction and Mental Health of Canada (CAMH). It includes a collection of nine 3D images. For fixed MRI images, voxel dimensions along the x, y, and z axes are 0.86, 0.86, and 3 mm, respectively. These images are captured by a Signa 1.5-T scanner from General Electric Medical System. PET images are captured by a Scanditronix PET scanning system, GE 2048-15B, with x, y and z voxel dimensions equal to 2 mm, 2 mm and 6.5 mm, respectively.

Evaluation Metrics. To quantify the accuracy of the studied methods, we measured Normalized Cross-Correlation Coefficient (NCCC) (1) and Normalized Mutual Information (NMI) (2) scores. NCCC evaluates the degree of similarity between two medical images. In fact, cross correlation is less sensitive to linear changes in amplitude and illumination in the images to be compared. A high value of NCCC shows the high accuracy of the registration. Furthermore, NMI, which is a measure of the quality of the registration, is defined in terms of the entropy H of the image. It measures the proximity between the fixed source image I_f and the moving one I_m. The more the value of normalized mutual information is, the more the accuracy of the registration process is.

$$NCCC = \frac{\sum_X^{x=1} \sum_Y^{y=1} \left(I_m(x,y)-\overline{I_m}\right)\left(I_f(x,y)-\overline{I_f}\right)}{\sqrt{\sum_X^{x=1} \sum_Y^{y=1} \left(I_m(x,y)-\overline{I_m}\right)^2 \left(I_f(x,y)-\overline{I_f}\right)^2}}, \tag{1}$$

$$NMI = \frac{2(H(I_f)+H(I_m))}{H(I_f)+H(I_m)+H(I_f|I_m)+H(I_m|I_f)}, \tag{2}$$

where, $H(\ )$ and $H(\ |\ )$ denote marginal and conditional entropies, respectively.

4   Results

We compare qualitatively and quantitatively the studied hybrid method against the other aforementioned softwares for MRI/MRI, MRI/CT, and MRI/PET images.

Qualitative Evaluation. Figures 4 and 5 show some samples of 3D slices before and after mono- and multi-modal registrations. For the multimodal case, PET and CT refer to the moving image and the MRI image is the fixed one. Obtained results prove the performance of the Hybrid Method (HM) comparatively to SPM, ITK-Snap and 3D Slicer (Fig. 4). Monomodal registration is similar to multimodal registration, in except for the modality of the moving image (Template MRI image), which is the same of the source image (Fig. 5). We conclude that the registered images by the hybrid method show a slight improvement in the accuracy of image registration and sharpness, since that contours in these images are better represented than those of registered images using SPM, ITK-Snap and 3D Slicer. Indeed, the representative cases of the superposition of the source image and the registered one based on the hybrid method allow good boundary estimation. The visual evaluations of the outputs show that the hybrid method allows a reliable registration of MRI/PET, MRI/CT or MRI/MRI scans. This can be explained by many reasons. In fact, the use of an anisotropic diffusion filtering ensures the maximization of PET image homogeneity and the minimization of the diffusion at the edges. Furthermore, the aim behind the use of a multi-scale and multidirectional geometric transform, which is the curvelet transform, is the optimal sparse representation of smooth objects with discontinuities along curves. Then, adaptive mutual information coupled with curvelet coefficients ensures the insensitivity to the permutations of intensity while handling simultaneously the positive and negative intensity correlations.

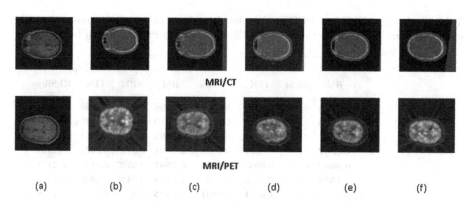

Fig. 4. Examples of MRI/X multimodal registration: (a) MRI image, (b) X image, superposed images using (c) HM, (d) SPM (e) ITK-Snap, and (f) 3D Slicer.

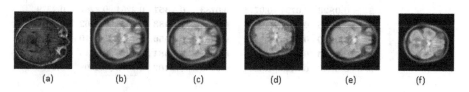

Fig. 5. Example of MRI/MRI monomodal registration: (a) MRI image, (b) MRI atlas image, registered images using (c) HM, (d) SPM, (e) ITK-Snap, and (f) 3D Slicer.

Quantitative Evaluation. The average NCCC and NMI values resulting from the analysis of different mono- and multi-modal registration methods of MRI brain images from the CAHM dataset are summarized in Table 1, whilst Table 2 illustrates MRI(T1)/PET registration results using the RIRE dataset. It is clear that both NMI and NCCC values given by the HM for the mono- and multi-modal registrations are better than those given by the other three widely used tools. The superiority of HM is confirmed by the boxplots of the four compared methods for registering MRI/CT and MRI(PD)/PET scans (Fig. 6). It should be pointed out that the nature of the images to be aligned can be very diverse and it affects considerably the choice of the registration method to be adopted. The hybrid method allows to align effectively images from the same modality as well as from different modalities. The nature of the modalities considered, as well as the type of the imaged organ, also influences the choice of the method. Likewise, the dimensionality of the input images could also be taken into consideration. Although no available registration method is perfect, research is being done to improve the results, while reducing the rate of registration error. This could increase the diagnosis confidence by improving the diagnosis accuracy.

Table 1. Average NMI and NCCC values resulting from the studied mono and multi-modal registration methods using the CAHM dataset (best values are in bold).

	Image pair	NMI				NCCC			
		HM	SPM	ITK	3D Slicer	HM	SPM	ITK	3D Slicer
Monomodal	1	**0.0344**	0.0087	0.0089	0.0630	**0.2666**	0.2226	0.0050	0.2623
	2	**0.0085**	0.0047	0.0032	0.0072	**0.2010**	0.1718	0.0215	0.1995
	3	**0.0561**	0.0075	0.0064	0.0495	**0.2609**	0.0259	0.0054	0.2520
	4	**0.0887**	0.0093	0.0081	0.0802	**0.2381**	0.0103	0.0078	0.2358
	5	**0.0930**	0.0075	0.0063	0.0912	**0.2567**	0.0505	0.0126	0.2468
	6	**0.1333**	0.0526	0.0526	0.1140	**0.2518**	0.0430	0.2318	0.2566
	7	**0.1102**	0.0351	0.0281	0.1021	**0.2135**	0.1270	0.0512	0.2048
	8	**0.1011**	0.0513	0.0426	0.0977	**0.2017**	0.0334	0.1882	0.1975
	9	**0.0284**	0.0476	0.0440	0.0469	**0.2543**	0.1345	0.1567	0.2491
Multimodal	1	**0.0766**	0.0578	0.0598	0.0690	**0.2408**	0.2329	0.2395	0.2343
	2	**0.0331**	0.0161	0.0165	0.0122	**0.2682**	0.1839	0.1858	0.1561
	3	**0.0972**	0.0728	0.0741	0.0641	**0.2486**	0.2373	0.2301	0.2362
	4	**0.0603**	0.0356	0.0344	0.0323	**0.2580**	0.2115	0.1884	0.1777
	5	**0.0823**	0.0794	0.0774	0.0783	**0.2351**	0.2264	0.2287	0.2279
	6	**0.0963**	0.0831	0.0813	0.0602	**0.2483**	0.2405	0.2462	0.2444
	7	**0.0719**	0.0623	0.0619	0.0457	**0.2556**	0.1627	0.2310	0.2131
	8	**0.0845**	0.0674	0.0678	0.0678	**0.2381**	0.1376	0.2115	0.2099
	9	**0.0643**	0.0439	0.0511	0.0589	**0.2467**	0.1873	0.2098	0.2125

Table 2. Average NMI and NCCC values resulting from the different multimodal registration methods using the RIRE dataset (best values are in bold).

Image pair	NMI				NCCC			
	HM	SPM	ITK	3D Slicer	HM	SPM	ITK	3D Slicer
1	**0.0830**	0.0798	0.0740	0.0790	**0.2473**	0.2255	0.2363	0.2457
2	**0.0780**	0.0723	0.0671	0.0723	**0.2651**	0.2451	0.2478	0.2537
3	**0.0498**	0.0387	0.0352	0.0405	**0.2726**	0.2343	0.2275	0.2336
4	**0.0391**	0.0288	0.0266	0.0340	**0.2139**	0.1799	0.1554	0.2066
5	**0.0643**	0.0459	0.0406	0.0591	**0.2401**	0.2246	0.1965	0.2251
6	**0.0765**	0.0576	0.0520	0.0657	**0.2542**	0.2394	0.2378	0.2474
7	**0.0605**	0.0553	0.0510	0.0515	**0.2726**	0.2419	0.2539	0.2522
8	**0.0763**	0.0698	0.0631	0.0607	**0.2642**	0.2446	0.2487	0.2542

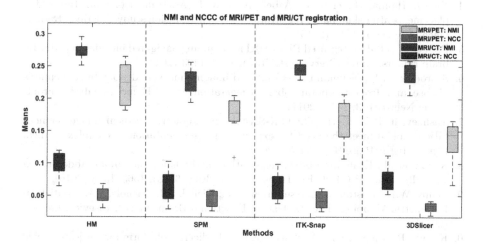

Fig. 6. Comparing boxplot distributions of the four studied methods for the registration of MRI(PD)/PET and MRI/CT brain images from the RIRE dataset.

5   Conclusion

In this work, a comparative study of a hybrid registration method with standard registration tools is investigated for 3D brain images. The hybrid method uses mutual information based on conditional entropy for the detection of the similarity criteria, while ensuring mono- as well as multi-modal registrations. However, the standard tools use different methods to align different brain image modalities. Qualitative and quantitative evaluations show the effectiveness of the hybrid method against all other studied methods. For the brain case, rigid registration is sufficient, but for other organs, non-rigid registration is required. For that, we plan to test the hybrid method on other organs using diverse medical imaging tools while comparing it with non-rigid registration tools.

References

1. Crum, W.R., Hartkens, T., Hill, D.L.G.: Non-rigid image registration: theory and practice. Br. J. Radiol. **77**(2), 140–153 (2004)
2. Baâzaoui, A., Berrabah, M., Barhoumi, W., Zagrouba, E.: Multimodal registration of PET/MR brain images based on adaptive mutual information. In: Blanc-Talon, J., Distante, C., Philips, W., Popescu, D., Scheunders, P. (eds.) ACIVS 2016. LNCS, vol. 10016, pp. 361–372. Springer, Cham (2016). https://doi.org/10.1007/978-3-319-48680-2_32
3. Barthel, H., Schroeter, M.L., Hoffmann, K.-T., Sabri, O.: PET/MR in dementia and other neurodegenerative diseases. Semin. Nucl. Med. **45**(3), 224–233 (2014)
4. Xu, Q., Hanna, G., Zhai, Y., Asbell, A., Fan, J.: Assessment of brain tumor displacements after skull based registration: a CT/MRI fusion study. Austin J. Radiat. Oncol. Cancer **1**, 1011 (2015)
5. Preuss, M., et al.: Integrated PET/MRI for planning navigated biopsies in pediatric brain tumors. Child's Nerv. Syst. **30**(8), 1399–1403 (2014)
6. Schroeter, M.L., Neumann, J.: Combined imaging markers dissociate Alzheimer's disease and frontotemporal lobar degeneration–an ALE meta-analysis. Front. Aging Neurosci. **3**, 1–10 (2011)
7. Yushkevich, P.A., Gerig, G.: ITK-SNAP: an interactive medical image segmentation tool to meet the need for expert-guided segmentation of complex medical images. IEEE Pulse **8**(4), 54–57 (2017)
8. Xu, Z., et al.: Evaluation of six registration methods for the human abdomen on clinically acquired CT. IEEE Trans. Biomed. Eng. **63**(8), 1563–1572 (2016)
9. Penny, W.D., Friston, K.J., Ashburner, J.T., Kiebel, S.J., Nichols, T.E.: Statistical Parametric Mapping: The Analysis of Functional Brain Images. Elsevier, London (2011)
10. Kikinis, R., Pieper, S.D., Vosburgh, K.G.: 3D slicer: a platform for subject-specific image analysis, visualization, and clinical support. In: Jolesz, F.A. (ed.) Intraoperative Imaging and Image-Guided Therapy, pp. 277–289. Springer, New York (2014). https://doi.org/10.1007/978-1-4614-7657-3_19
11. Pieper, S., Lorensen, B., Schroeder, W., Kikinis, R.: The NA-MIC Kit: ITK, VTK, pipelines, grids and 3D slicer as an open platform for the medical image computing community. In: International Symposium on Biomedical Imaging, pp. 698–701 (2006)
12. Xia, T., Qi, W., Niu, X., Asma, E., Winkler, M., Wang, W.: Quantitative comparison of anisotropic diffusion, non-local means and Gaussian post-filtering effects on FDG-PET lesions. J. Nucl. Med. **56**(3), 1797 (2015)
13. Dhahbi, S., Barhoumi, W., Zagrouba, E.: Breast cancer diagnosis in digitized mammograms using curvelet moments. Comput. Biol. Med. **64**, 79–90 (2015). https://doi.org/10.1016/j.compbiomed.2015.06.012
14. Rajwade, A., Banerjee, A., Rangarajan, A.: A new method of probability density estimation with application to mutual information based image registration. In: Conference on Computer Vision and Pattern Recognition, pp. 1769–1776 (2006)

15. Alam, M.M., Howlader, T., Rahman, S.M.M.: Entropy-based image registration method using the curvelet transform. Signal Image Video Process. **8**(3), 491–505 (2012). https://doi.org/10.1007/s11760-012-0394-1
16. Kline, R.B.: Principles and Practice of Structural Equation Modeling. The Guilford Press, New York (2016)
17. West, J., Fitzpatrick, J.M., Wang, M.Y., et al.: Comparison and evaluation of retrospective intermodality brain image registration techniques. J. Comput. Assist. Tomogr. **21**, 554–566 (1997)

Machine Learning Classification Models with SPD/ED Dataset: Comparative Study of Abstract Versus Full Article Approach

Mayara Khadhraoui[1,2(✉)], Hatem Bellaaj[2(✉)],
Mehdi Ben Ammar[3(✉)], Habib Hamam[4(✉)],
and Mohamed Jmaiel[1,2(✉)]

[1] ENIS, ReDCAD Laboratory, University of Sfax, B.P. 1173, Sfax, Tunisia
khadhraouimayara@gmail.com
[2] Digital Research Center of Sfax, 3021 Sfax, Tunisia
{hatem.bellaaj,mohamed.jmaiel}@redcad.org
[3] Solutions Galore Inc., Moncton, NB, Canada
mehdi.benammar@gmail.com
[4] Faculty of Engineering, Moncton University, Moncton, NB, Canada
habib.hamam@gmail.com

Abstract. In response to the researchers need in the bio-medical domain, we opted for automating the bibliographic research stage. In this context, several classification models of supervised machine learning are used. Namely the SVM, Random Forest, Decision Tree, KNN, and Gradient Boosting. In this paper, we conduct a comparative study between experimental results of full article classification and abstract classification approaches. Furthermore, we evaluate our results by using evaluation metrics such as accuracy, precision, recall and F1-score. We observe that the abstract approach outperforms the full article approach in terms of learning time and efficiency.

Keywords: Text classification · Data mining · Supervised machine learning · Medical informatics · Public health

1 Introduction

In the vast field of artificial intelligence, machine learning is called upon to play a central role allowing machines to learn automatically in the context of scientific research. In fact, the field of scientific research seems to be a challenging task and can generate difficulties for researchers. In this paper, we are interested in the epidemiological research domain. Here is a list of some of today's challenges; 1) Research in medicine requires an efficient working methodology to better attain pertinent results, confirm/affirm or complete a hypothesis or theory, evaluate a procedure or a program, minimize bias, etc., 2) Medical researchers face challenges in epidemiological research, such as the choice of population, sample size, time of study, and target knowledge base; the selection of reference subjects; the required budget, data collection, 3) Developing coherent epidemiological research requires the integration of knowledge and skill, 4) Based on the results of [2], one of the major challenges of this specified

© The Author(s) 2020
M. Jmaiel et al. (Eds.): ICOST 2020, LNCS 12157, pp. 348–356, 2020.
https://doi.org/10.1007/978-3-030-51517-1_31

domain is the literature review task which should be exhaustive. In this paper, we focus on the last aforementioned challenge. To overcome this problem, machine learning techniques and algorithms are recommended. In our work, we are concerned with several machine learning methods namely the Support Vector Machine (SVM), K Nearest Neighbor (KNN), Gradient Boosting (GB), Random Forest (RF), Decision Tree (DT), Multi-Nominal Naive Bayes (MNB) and Logistic Regression (LR).

The originality of our work lies in the creation of a new public database SPD/ED in the biomedical domain based on title, abstract, keywords and full scientific papers. Our database is a collection of several scientific papers classified into four different categories according to the taxonomy of the epidemiological studies (Analytic, descriptive, Meta-Analysis and Others) [5]. Based on the aforementioned machine learning methods, we will conduct a comparative study between the text classification task based on the abstract versus the full article.

The paper is organized as follows. Section 2 explains basic concepts of machine learning methods. Related work is discussed in Sect. 3. In Sect. 4, we present our method. Section 5 discusses the experimental results. Section 6 concludes the paper and outlines areas for future research.

2 Machine Learning

In our work, we are interested on text classification, defined as the process of associating a category (or class) with free text, based on the information it contains, is an important element of information retrieval systems. In our work, we deal with the text classification challenge and accuracy problem. In fact, the main challenge consists in, for each new entry, being able to determine to which category this entry belongs. Associating a class with free text is a costly and difficult task, therefore the automation of this task has become a challenge for the scientific community. To help the scientific community the task of Text classification is assisted by the machine learning.

2.1 Different Types of Approaches

There are several Machine learning methods: supervised, unsupervised, reinforcement and semi-supervised learning. In our work, we are interested on the supervised learning.

2.2 Machine Learning Algorithms

The objective of machine learning is to recognize among data structures that are difficult to detect manually. From these structures, we seek to classify new textual data. In our work, we focus on the classification of scientific papers in the epidemiological domain based on the taxonomy of the epidemiological studies.

2.2.1 Decision Tree (DT)

Decision trees are classification rules which base their decisions on a series of tests associated with a set of attributes. These tests are organized in a tree structure. The internal nodes are called decision nodes. Each decision node is labeled by a test which can be applied to any description of an individual in the population.

2.2.2 Support Vector Machine (SVM)

Support Vector Machines is a phenomenon f (possibly non-deterministic) which, from a certain set of inputs x, produces an output y = f (x). This approach, often translated by the name of Support Vector Machine (SVM), is a class of learning algorithms initially defined for discrimination and prediction of a binary qualitative variable. The main objective is to find f from the only observation of a certain number of input-output pairs $\{(xi, yi): i = 1, \ldots, n\}$. Among its advantages, SVM overcomes various common problems related to the recognition of shapes.

2.2.3 K-Nearest Neighbors (KNN)

The principle of this model consists in choosing the k data closest to the point studied in order to predict its value. The objective is to make a classification without making a hypothesis on the function $y = f (x1, x2, \ldots, xn)$ which links the dependent variable y to the independent variables $x1, x2, \ldots, xn$. Otherwise, the idea of the KNN algorithm is for a new observation $(u1, u2, \ldots, up)$ to predict the k observations that are most similar to it in the training data [1].

2.2.4 Multi-nominal Naïve Bayes (MNNB)

The Multi-Nominal Naïve Bayes classifier is derived from Bayesian decision theory. It is a fundamental statistical approach in pattern recognition. Bayesian decision theory chooses the best decision among the possible decisions based on these laws and the costs associated with each decision. The objective consists in finding a decision rule which minimizes an average cost and in defining which decision (action) to take according to the observed entity.

2.2.5 Random Forest (RF)

The algorithm of "random forests" was proposed by Leo Breiman and Adèle Cutler in 2001 [3]. It performs parallel learning on multiple decision trees randomly constructed and trained on subsets of data different. The ideal number of trees, which can go up to several hundred or more, is an important parameter: it is very variable and depends on the problem.

2.2.6 Gradient Boosting (GB)

This boosting technique is mainly used with decision trees (it is then called Gradient Tree Boosting). Again, the main idea is to aggregate several classifiers together but to create them iteratively. These "mini-classifiers" are generally simple and parameterized functions, most often decision trees, each parameter of which is the split criterion of the branches.

3 Related Work

In reference [5], the authors presented the various classic and new techniques for classifying texts: the preprocessing of documents such as tokenization, the removal of stop words, stemming; Lemmatizing, machine learning algorithms for document modeling; representation of document characteristics, optimal data representation; learning based on machine learning classifiers; measuring the performance of the classification model based on evaluation methods and performance metrics.

The authors of reference [5], presented five classifiers (SVM, NB, KNN, Decision Tree and Decision Table) with three different versions of the database. In addition, accuracy and scalability are calculated to evaluate and examine the advantages and disadvantages of them for Arabic TC based on the efficient tools of machine learning (Weka and RapidMiner).

In reference [4], the authors summarized the eminent multi-class classifiers, based on the literature, in order to apply them to evaluate on a new benchmark dataset of Vietnamese News (VNNews-01). In the data collect process, they are referred to more than thirty Vietnamese online newspaper websites and grouped into twenty-five categories. They added that their work might promote the text mining research in Vietnam.

Some authors present a comparative study of three machine learning algorithm to do the task of classifying human facial expression. Then, they analyzed the main performance. In the experimental study process, they introduced 23 variables calculated from the distance of facial features as the input in the classification phase. As output, they defined seven categories, such as: angry, disgust, fear, happy, neutral, sad, and surprise. As experimental results, they recorded 75.15% of K-Nearest Neighbor (KNN)'s accuracy, 80% for Support Vector Machine (SVM), and 76.97% for Random Forest algorithm. As for the result using the largest amount of data, the accuracy is 98.85% for KNN, 90% for SVM, and 98.85% for Random Forest algorithm [6].

4 Method

4.1 Data Collection

In our work, we focused on supervised learning. To do so, we collected a set of labeled scientific articles from different scientific journals including Science direct, PubMed, Google scholar, etc. In addition, scientific articles were classified in 4 different predefined classes related to the taxonomy of epidemiological study, including Descriptive, Analytic, Meta-Analysis and Experimental. The several categories' definitions are presented in Table 1.

Data collection was performed on the basis of two different approaches. The first approach is only interested in the Abstract part. We notice that, in the field of epidemiology, the Abstract part is composed of different parts in particular Aim/Introduction/ Purpose, Methods, Results and discussion and conclusion. The first approach reveals a first database made up of 300 abstracts per category. The second approach is to collect the full article without omitting any section from Abstract to the references. This exercise led us to the creation of a second extended database of 300 articles by category. Figures 1 and 2 exemplify the distribution of scientific papers according to their categories.

Table 1. Label encoding

Category code	Category name	Definition
0	Analytic study	Raise etiological hypotheses by comparing the prevalence of the event in exposed and unexposed subjects
1	Descriptive study	Describe phenomena and their geographic distribution and temporal
2	Meta-Analysis study	Assess the effect of a treatment used on comparable populations, by combining the results of multiple studies
3	Experimental study	Intervene on the exhibition status of subjects. It can affect the factor (s) of exposure, the time of exposure and the people exposed

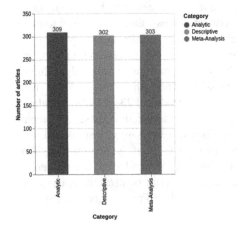

Fig. 1. The distribution of articles across the different values of labels/article.

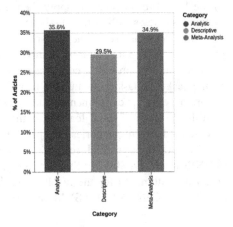

Fig. 2. Histogram representation of the articles/label Percentage

It is worth noting, that this is a critical step since this task is normally performed manually. The state of the art of existing databases shows that there is no standard corpus containing scientific articles classified according to the taxonomy of epidemiological studies. Scientific papers are labeled according to different predefined classes according to the taxonomy of the epidemiological study. For that reason, in the data collect process, we were aware that the quality of data plays a vital role in the training data process and the calculation of the accuracy score of any machine learning classification algorithm. Based on the carefully selected data, the machine learning algorithms can learn the patterns and correlations in the data.

4.2   Data Preprocessing

In order to transform raw data into an understandable format, we aim to apply data preprocessing techniques to build machine learning classifier. In fact, the data should be cleaned and preprocessed to eliminate characteristics of less important data and improve accuracy. For this purpose, we used machine learning techniques such as lowercasing which defines a common approach to reduce all the text to lower case for simplicity, Tokenization which assumes splitting text into tokens, Punctuation Removal which is a form of pre-processing to filter out useless data and Stop words Removal.

4.3   Data Representation

The TF * IDF (for Term Frequency * Inverse Document Frequency) is the result of a calculation, in the algorithm of search engines, allowing to obtain a weight, an evaluation of the relevance of a document compared to a term, taking into account two factors: the frequency of this word in the document (TF) and the number of documents containing this word (IDF) in the corpus studied. The TF * IDF is expressed as follows:

$$w_{i,j} = tf_{i,j} \times log\left(\frac{N}{df_i}\right)$$

Where $tf_{i,j}$ = number of occurrences of i in j, d_i = number of documents containing of i, N = total number of documents.

4.4   Method

In our work, we compared 6 classifiers of supervised learning that learn and predict a categorical response that includes 4 categories as mentioned before. We adopted performance measures to assess the performance of classifiers, in particular accuracy, precision, recall and f1-score. We studied the performance measures of each classifier compared to all scientific papers. The performance measurement values reflect the careful selection of data from our database from the various scientific journals. We compared classifiers based on their respective best performance.

4.5   Performance Metrics

In this subsection, we will focus on indicators that measure the quality of the model. To measure the performance of this classifier, we must distinguish 4 types of elements classified for the desired class namely: True Positive, False Positive, True Negative and False Negative. In the following, we present the performance metrics adopted to assess the performance of the different machine learning models used. Indeed, our assessment is based on 4 different measures including: Accuracy, Precision, Recall, F1-Score.

5 Results

This section summarizes the experimental results obtained using our Dataset SPD/ED in two version, the extended and the closed one. In fact, we used several machine learning classifiers, aforementioned detailed. In each approach, the dataset is divided into train and test dataset with the ratio of 25% of test data and 75% of training data. Both train and test data need to be preprocessed and converted into feature vectors.

As depicted in Table 2, we present a comparative table of two approaches proposed at the level of this paper.

Table 2. Comparative table of machine learning algorithms based on our database in the case of 300 Full papers and 300 abstracts.

Machine learning methods	300 full papers				300 abstracts			
	Accuracy	Precision	Recall	F1-score	Accuracy	Precision	Recall	F1-score
SVM	**80%**	75%	81%	78%	**81%**	74%	72%	73%
KNN	**62%**	53%	58%	55%	**65%**	49%	56%	52%
RF	**81%**	85%	72%	78%	**83%**	81%	70%	75%
MN_NB	**74%**	82%	58%	68%	**79%**	83%	58%	69%
DT	**86%**	79%	86%	82%	**75%**	65%	74%	69%
GB	**78%**	81%	78%	79%	**81%**	75%	69%	71%

From Table 2, we can see that each algorithm shows high performance. In another side, we can see, from Table 2, that using the abstract (Aims, Methods, Results and Conclusion) only from the whole paper, is more fruitful and efficient in terms of accuracy. Then, we conclude that SVM, RF and GB are more accurate than the others used algorithms.

Based on the experimental results, we first concluded that the best scores obtained are justified by the relevant choice of scientific papers in the learning phase. Second, we can see, according to Table 2, that the training data process with the Abstract approach is more efficient and fruitful in terms of accuracy than the Full paper approach. We recorded that SVM, KNN, RF and MN Naïve Bayes present motivating performances.

We explored both methods: Machine learning and Deep learning. In contrast to image classification, we observed in our specific application of text mining that the time-consuming process of deep learning does not outperform machine learning. At the contrary, in some cases, machine learning produces significantly better results. We believe that, in our experience, deep learning does not provide efficient results given the size of our database.

6 Conclusion

In this paper, we presented a comparative study of two different approaches of text classification using supervised machine learning classifiers. We started by identifying different methods of machine learning for text classification. Based on the literature review, we presented a survey on the machine learning techniques proposed for text classification. Through extensive experiments, we evaluated 6 methods based on our proposed dataset in the epidemiological domain. To the best of our knowledge, this is the first comparative study on scientific papers classification in the epidemiological domain. We proceeded with a careful selection of the different scientific papers, was made, based on a list of predefined classes according to the taxonomy of the epidemiological studies including: descriptive, analytical experimental and meta-analysis. Based on our experimental results, we emphasize that the learning done on the Abstract part (Introduction, Methods, Results, and Conclusion) is much more efficient than working with full paper because the divergence of the subject in question.

References

1. Aha, D.W.: Editorial. Artif. Intell. Rev. **11**(1–5), 7–10 (1997). https://doi.org/10.1023/A:1006538427943
2. Cohen, K., Hunter, L.: Getting started in text mining. PLoS Comput. Biol. **4**, e20 (2008). https://doi.org/10.1371/journal.pcbi.0040020
3. Cutler, A., Cutler, D.R., Stevens, J.R.: Random forests. In: Zhang, C., Ma, Y. (eds.) Ensemble Machine Learning, pp. 157–175. Springer, Boston (2012). https://doi.org/10.1007/978-1-4419-9326-7_5
4. Duong, H.T., Truong Hoang, V.: A survey on the multiple classifier for new benchmark dataset of Vietnamese news classification, pp. 23–28, January 2019. https://doi.org/10.1109/KST.2019.8687509
5. Mourya, A.K., ShafqatUlAhsaan, Kaur, H.: Performance and evaluation of different kernels in support vector machine for text mining. In: Mohanty, M.N., Das, S. (eds.) Advances in Intelligent Computing and Communication. LNNS, vol. 109, pp. 264–271. Springer, Singapore (2020). https://doi.org/10.1007/978-981-15-2774-6_33
6. Thanh Noi, P., Kappas, M.: Comparison of random forest, k-nearest neighbor, and support vector machine classifiers for land cover classification using sentinel-2 imagery. Sensors **18**(2), 18 (2017). https://doi.org/10.3390/s18010018

Evaluation of Stationary Wavelet Transforms in Reconstruction of Pure High Frequency Oscillations (HFOs)

Thouraya Guesmi[1,3(✉)], Abir Hadriche[1,2,3], Nawel Jmail[3,4], and Chokri Ben Amar[2]

[1] Institut Supérieur d'Informatique et de Multimédia, Gabes University, Teboulbou, Tunisia
Thouraya.guesmi@isimg.tn, abir.hadriche.tn@ieee.org
[2] Research Groups on Intelligent Machines Laboratory, REGIM, ENIS, Sfax University, Sfax, Tunisia
chokri.benamar@ieee.org
[3] Digital Research Centre of Sfax, Sfax University, Sfax, Tunisia
naweljmail@yahoo.fr
[4] Multimedia Information Systems and Advanced Computing Laboratory, MIRACL, Sfax University, Sfax, Tunisia

Abstract. High frequency oscillations (HFO) from, MEG (magnetoencephalography) and intracerebral EEG are considered as effective tools to identify cognitive status and several cortical disorders especially in epilepsy diagnosis.

The aim of our study is to evaluate stationary wavelet transform (SWT) technique performance in efficient reconstruction of pure epileptic high frequency oscillations, reputed as biomarkers of epileptogenic zones: generators of inter ictal epileptic discharges, and offhand seizures.

We applied SWT on simulated and real database to detect non-contaminated HFO by spiky element. For simulated data, we computed the GOF of reconstruction that reaches for all studied constraint (relative amplitude, frequency, SNR and overlap) a promising results. For real data we used time frequency domain to evaluate SWT robustness of HFO reconstruction. We proved that SWT is an efficient filtering technique for separation HFO from spiky events. Our results would have an important impact on the definition of epileptogenic zones.

Keywords: IEEG signal · Epilepsy · HFOs · SWT · GOF · SNR

1 Introduction

Over the past 15 years, researchers have shown usefulness of intra-cerebral activity above 70 Hz: High frequency oscillations (HFO) as efficient biomarkers for epileptogenicity. HFO has been considered as a clue of seizure build up and it appears especially, during ictal period. In fact HFO are exhibited as two sub band: ripples (80200) and fast ripples beyond 200 Hz [1].

© The Author(s) 2020
M. Jmaiel et al. (Eds.): ICOST 2020, LNCS 12157, pp. 357–363, 2020.
https://doi.org/10.1007/978-3-030-51517-1_32

HFOs can be detected visually by neurologist expert [2] or automatically: using automatic detectors developed on a preprocessing chain [3, 4].

To ensure the detection of HFOs, it is necessary to filter the used signal in HFO bands, however spiky component can disturb the detection stage due to induced false oscillations obtained by filter response [5]. Hence, it is necessary to choose accurate filtering technique within this framework.

Bénar et al. proved the efficiency of stationary wavelet transform in detection and separation between spikes and gamma oscillations.

Hence, we propose to study stationary wavelet transform performance in reconstruction of pure HFOs.

First, we tested SWT performance on filtered simulated data (in HFO frequency range) where we evaluated it for different constraints (SNR, overlap rate, relative amplitude and frequency range).

Second, our focus was to evaluate SWT robustness of HFO reconstruction on filtered real IEEG signal (in HFO frequency range) using time frequency analysis. These results would assist neurologist during diagnosis of pharmaco resistant patient by defining epileptogenic tissue that should be delineated through a surgical intervention.

In the first section, we depict our simulated and real data, the filtering technique and evaluation methods used. In the second section, we exhibit our obtained results and finally we conclude and discuss our results.

2 Materials and Methods

2.1 Materials

All signal-processing steps of our paper are executed using Matlab software (Mathworks, Natick, MA) with EEGLAB toolbox.

Simulated Data: Obtained by a combination of a spike, and HFO shapes as real IEEG signal, sampled at 1000 Hz. Through different tests, we created different sets of signal (composed of spikes and HFO) by varying different parameters: relative amplitudes, frequency of oscillations, signal to noise ratio (SNR) and overlapping rate: we obtained 4 sets of simulated data composed of spiky and HFO events. We increased the spiky amplitude by 2, 4, 6, 8 and 10 times compared to oscillatory one. We varied also oscillation's frequency in this range [80 150 100 200 250] Hz (ripples and fast ripples). Overlap between spike and HFO oscillations is changed with equal steps via the size of oscillations window: no overlap (spike and oscillation are completely separated) until we reached 100% overlap when spiky and oscillatory events are superimposed. The overlap step is equal to 25%. Finally, we ranged SNR ratio (Eq. 1) from −5 dB to 20 dB.

$$SNR = 10 * \log(S/N) \tag{1}$$

Where S is the simulated signal and N is the studied added noise.

Real Data: (IEEG) recordings for a pharmaco-resistant epileptic subject, where acquisition and pretreatment steps were assigned to clinical neurophysiology department of La Timone Hospital, Marseille [6] and validated by an expert neurologist. Our data is recorded on a Deltamed system, sampled at 1000 Hz with a low-pass filter. This particular IEEG signal is selected since it exhibits important epileptic HFOs patterns and regular spikes.

2.2 Methods

The Stationary Wavelet Transform SWT technique is a diversity of Dynamic Wavelet Transform with an advantage of overcoming decimation of DWT; which leads to a better maintain of signal characteristics. It performs even better than Continuous Wavelet Transform CWT by exceeding frequency-overlapping band.

In fact, SWT was used in various fields of application such as de-noising and detection [8], also, very useful in physiological signal analysis [7].

In [9] SWT was studied and implemented to reconstruct pre-ictal gamma oscillations in order to predict seizure build up. Hence, we proposed to study and evaluate SWT method performance in reconstruction of ripples and fast ripples: HFO. SWT decomposed a signal to be filtered into approximations and details coefficients, then, and through a thresholding steps (using masks), it allows to detect only desired parts by inverse of SWT method (iswt) [10]. Our thresholding step consists of creating a rectangle mask with a width equal to raw window studied and a length equal to 2 scales of decomposition (approximation and detail coefficients) [6]. SWT is a projection of scale $\theta_{j,k}$ function dilated and translated to obtain $cA_j(k)$ as approximations coefficients and $cD_j(k)$ as detail ones.

During implementation steps of SWT, we choose 6 levels of decomposition for a better detection of HFO [6]. We adopted the symlet wavelet family, since they are almost symmetrical to oscillation; moreover they are featured by their orthogonally which facilitate the reconstruction step.

Evaluation by Goodness of Fit (GOF) is used in different areas to evaluate performance of filtering technique [6, 11, 12]. After applying SWT we computed GOF between reconstructed simulated signals (reconstructed HFO) $s_r(t)$ and original simulated signals (original simulated HFO) s(t) by the following formula:

$$GOF = 1 - \left(\left(sum(s(t) - s_r(t))^2 \right) / sum(s(t))^2 \right) \tag{2}$$

To evaluate SWT filtering method robustness in recovering pure HFO, we calculated similarity rate of reconstructed HFO within original simulated HFO signals for different frequency range, relative amplitude, overlap rate and (SNR).

Time Frequency Representation: Obtained by a time-frequency transform that provides 2 dimensional domain of an original one dimensional signal. This card allows via visible inspection or thresholding step to define specific shape both in time and frequency plan in our case, we will define pure HFO from spiky events [13].

3   Results

3.1   Simulated Data

We depict in Fig. 1 three types of simulated data, where upper line is a temporal representation of a ripple, a spike and a spiky event with a ripple one. The lower line represent frequency plan of the studied events. Combining HFO and spiky event produces a complex shape in which it is difficult to distinguish basic elements.

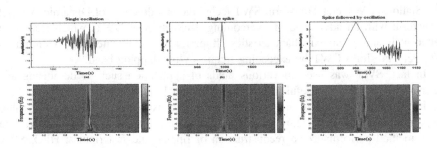

Fig. 1. Time representation of (a) single oscillation, (b) single spike, (c) spike followed by HFO, proceeded successively by their Time frequency plan.

In Fig. 2, we illustrated reconstruction of HFO by SWT technique for two frequency configurations; we studied different frequency effect on HFO reconstruction. SWT was able to reconstruct HFO with a minimum of spiky elements.

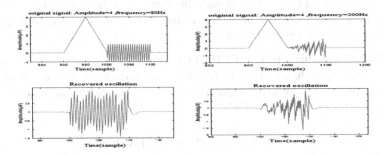

Fig. 2. Two sets of reconstruction of HFO (80 Hz and 200 Hz) by SWT, first line is original signal, second line is recovered HFO.

In Fig. 3(a), we gathered GOF values for HFO reconstruction after varying different relative amplitude between spiky and HFO events. We notice that for all relative amplitude, reconstruction result of HFO is beyond 78% for an amplitude of spiky event 8 times higher than HFO, and it reaches 97% for a relative amplitude equal to 4.

Hence, we can annotate that SWT have a good performance in reconstruction of HFO even for a low relative amplitude between spiky and HFO events.

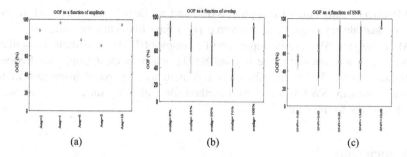

Fig. 3. GOF values for (a) different relative amplitudes of spiky and HFO events, (b) different temporal overlap and (c) different SNR rates.

We represent in Fig. 3(b) result of SWT reconstruction GOF for time overlaps constraint between spiky and HFO. We found that all configurations of overlap the GOF is beyond 80% for a low rate of overlap and total overlap, however the GOF rate declines for a rate of overlap >50% and <75%. We presented GOF as a box, where central mark is median, and 25th and 75th percentiles are edges of each box.

In Fig. 3(b), we displayed GOF result of HFO reconstruction as a function of SNR.

The best rate of GOF are obtained for SNR > 10 dB, which exceeds 85%, however GOF results are lower for low SNR with a median GOF around 58% and 75th percentiles above 82%.

3.2   Real Data

In Fig. 4, we depict time series of our real data (channel 26) and its representation in time frequency domain (upper line). Our choice (channel 26) was justified by high occurrence of HFO comparing to other channels (important activities: spiky events and different rhythms of oscillations and HFO in full overlap). We filtered our real data in

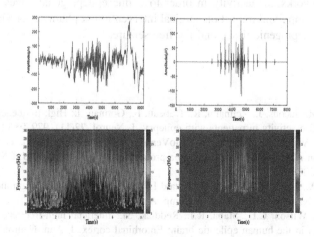

Fig. 4. Upper line: real data (channel 26), and pure recovered HFO by SWT, lower line time-frequency representation of raw, and pure HFO.

HFO frequency range than we applied SWT, and we depict pure recovered. In lower line we illustrate raw signal and recovered HFO time frequency domain.

After applying SWT, only ripples and fast ripples (HFO) are sustained, oscillatory activities with a frequency range beyond 80 Hz, which is clear from time frequency illustration. Hence, HFOs are efficiently reconstructed, by visual inspection of time frequency domain. SWT is a powerful method for separating such a range of oscillations frequency from spikes.

4   Conclusion

In our study, we tested performance of SWT filtering method, in reconstruction of pure HFO (HFO without spiky events) on simulated data and real signal. For simulated signal (inspired from IEEG recording), we evaluated robustness of SWT in HFOs reconstruction for several parameters that are proved very powerful in varying quality of obtained results. We studied effect of relative amplitude between HFO and spiky events, impact of frequency range (ripples and fast one), overlapping rate and finally signal-to-noise ratio. From our obtained results and for all studied constraint, SWT reconstruction of HFO reveal a good GOF rate. Hence, such study could be as a reference of SWT performance in reconstruction of HFO among 4 constraints (amplitude, frequency, SNR, overlap).

For real data, we evaluated performance of SWT reconstruction of HFO using time frequency representation and neurologist expert inspection.

SWT gives good results in reconstruction of non-contaminated HFO by spiky element even in bad environment (low SNR, different range of frequency, high overlap and low relative amplitude). These results predispose SWT for reconstruction and detection of all range of oscillatory frequency. Our obtained results are very promising in further study of HFO and its networks connectivity since we are dealing with pure HFO and hence non-contaminated cortical generators. Our perspectives are defining pure HFO networks connectivity in order to define epileptogenic zones. This result would have an important impact on surgical intervention of pharmaco- resistant patient to delineate epileptogenic tissue and get free seizure.

References

1. Zijlmans, M., Jacobs, J., Zelmann, R., Dubeau, F., Gotman, J.: High-frequency oscillations mirror disease activity in patients with epilepsy. J. Neurol. **72**(11), 979–986 (2009)
2. Hulsen, T., Vlieg, J.D., Alkema, W.: BioVenn- a web application for the comparison and visualization of biological lists using area-proportional Venn diagrams. J. BMC Genomics **9**(1), 488 (2008)
3. Hadriche, A., Jmail, N., Elleuch, R.: Pezard L: Different methods for partitioning the phase space of a dynamic system. Inter. J. Comp. Appl. **975**, 8887 (2014)
4. Bragin, A., Wilson, C.L., Staba, R.J., Reddick, M.: Interictal high-frequency oscillations (80–500 hz) in the human epileptic brain: Entorhinal cortex. J. Ann. Neurol. **52**, 407–415 (2002)

5. Birot, G., Kachenoura, A., Albera, L., Bénar, G.C., Wendling, F.: Automatic detection of fast ripples. J. Neurosc. Meth. **213**, 236–249 (2012)
6. Jmail, N., et al.: Integration of stationary wavelet transform on a dynamic partial reconfiguration for recognition of pre-ictal gamma oscillations. Heliyon **4**(2), e00530 (2018)
7. Tang, Z.P., Xu, S.L., Dai, X.Y., Hu, X.J., Liao, X.L., Cai, J.: S-wave tracing technique to investigate the damage and failure behavior of brittle materials subjected to shock loading. Int. J. Impact Eng **31**, 1172–1191 (2005)
8. Wang, X.H., Istepanian, R.S.H., Song, Y.H.: Microarray image de-noising using stationary wavelet transform. In: 4th International IEEE EMBS Special Topic Conference on Information Technology Applications in Biomedicine, pp. 15–18. IEEE press, Birmingham (2003)
9. Abdennour, N., Hadriche, A., Frikha, T., Jmail, N.: Extraction and localization of non-contaminated alpha and gamma oscillations from EEG signal using finite impulse response, stationary wavelet transform, and custom FIR. In: Kůrková, V., Manolopoulos, Y., Hammer, B., Iliadis, L., Maglogiannis, I. (eds.) ICANN 2018. LNCS, vol. 11140, pp. 511–520. Springer, Cham (2018). https://doi.org/10.1007/978-3-030-01421-6_49
10. Wang, S., et al.: Scalable social sensing of interdependent phenomena. In: 14th International Conference on Information Processing in Sensor Networks, pp. 202–213 (2015)
11. Frikha, T., et al.: Adaptive architecture for medical application case study: evoked Potential detection using matching poursuit consensus. In: 15th International Conference on Intelligent Systems Design and Applications (ISDA). IEEE press, Morocco (2015)
12. Hadriche A., et al.: The detection of Evoked Potential with variable latency and multiple trial using Consensus matching pursuit. In: 1st International Conference on Advanced Technologies for Signal and Image Processing (ATSIP). IEEE press, Sousse (2014)
13. Wang, S., et al.: Ripple classification helps to localize the seizure-onset zone in neocortical epilepsy. J. Epilepsia. **54**, 370–376 (2013)

Ensuring the Correctness and Well Modeling of Intelligent Healthcare Management Systems

Samir Ouchani[1(✉)] and Moez Krichen[2,3]

[1] LINEACT, École d'Ingénieur CESI, 13545 Aix-en-Provence, France
souchani@cesi.fr
[2] Faculty of CSIT, Al-Baha University, Al-Baha, Saudi Arabia
[3] ReDCAD Laboratory, University of Sfax, Sfax, Tunisia
moez.krichen@redcad.org

Abstract. Recent research focus more and more on IoT systems and their applications in order to make people life easier and controllable. The main aim is to expand IoT applications and services into various domains while ensuring communication and automated exchange between them. Recent research handles many issues related to IoT especially implementation, modeling, and deployment. However, many challenges need more deep and thorough analysis especially in terms of flexible modeling, extensible implementation, with respect to the privacy issue. This work focuses principally on modeling IoT systems dedicated to smart healthcare case. We attempt to address the emergency service by initiating a modeling mechanism for Healthcare Management System (HMS) by using UML diagrams, and propose an appropriate access control in order to reinforce it. Then, we ensure the correctness of the developed HMS by relying on the verification and validation based on a formal analysis that showed significant results by using Alloy tool.

Keywords: Healthcare Management Systems · IoT · UML · RBAC · Formal validation · Alloy

1 Introduction

Nowadays, unfortunately people are busy and neglect their little health issues such as low pulse rate, high blood pressure, etc. [6]. Among the most challenging objectives of our contemporary society is enhancing healthcare. The provision of quality care to patients while minimizing healthcare costs is a primary goal, while traditional patient evaluation, care, management and supervision practices are often performed manually by nurses [1]. Further, the emergency service is very sensitive for what the patient needs to care in real-time during the treatment period depending the case. Therefor, in order to support and improve healthcare processes we need a flexible system that make the health care services more robust [1, 16] by covering more special cases and respecting safety standards and users/patients privacy.

As evidence, one of the most important priorities of our society is to improve the performance of biomedical systems and healthcare infrastructures [1,11]. From a research perspective, Internet of Things (IoT) [9,10] innovations seek to build

© The Author(s) 2020
M. Jmaiel et al. (Eds.): ICOST 2020, LNCS 12157, pp. 364–372, 2020.
https://doi.org/10.1007/978-3-030-51517-1_33

intelligent systems that support and improve healthcare, by using smart sensors, which allow for automatic monitoring, tracking patients and collecting data from various sources in real-time. Nevertheless, IoT plays an important role in supplying patients and clinicians with convenience in the area of healthcare. This consists of a system which communicates via a network that links internal and external facilities, applications and devices that might support patients and doctors monitor, track and archive critical medical data. Some of the products include wearable health bands, smart meters, and smart video cameras, fitness shoes and smart watches. In this same direction, smartphones applications may contribute in sending medical records and in real time alerts to medical and emergency services [6, 15]. Such interconnected systems create a vast amount of data and information that should be managed effectively. That is already a hard and challenging task to achieve.

In the last few years, many substantial changes in the domain of IoT healthcare are happening. The way human beings and other devices connect and communicate is evolving and becoming better day after day. The ever-growing communication and information technologies [6] allow the control of healthcare outcomes and the decrease of healthcare costs. Consumers, patients and health experts need to think about some creative and more efficient approaches to enjoy the benefits of the revolutionizing IoT in healthcare. With the aid of the ability of IoT, they are now able to gather raw real-time data from very high numbers of patients via smart devices linked to an interconnected network during a continuous period of time. It will take a long time to completely realize the capabilities of these modern technologies. People will see medical experts achieving critical tasks in a much more reliable manner. These experts will not only produce reliable results but they will also save a lot of time, which should be of maximum gain. IoT's capabilities are really infinite and ever-growing [6].

The basic idea of the proposed solution is to provide patients with reliable and efficient health services by creating a networked knowledge infrastructure so that experts and physicians can make use of this data and make decisions quickly and efficiently. The suggested system will be equipped with apps by which a physician may examine patients anytime from anywhere. It will be also possible to work on emergency scenarios and give a warning to the doctor with the current status of the patient, and complete medical records. We model the whole system by relying on the standard modeling language UML including class, sequence, and use cases diagrams. Further to ensure the privacy of users (practitioners and patients) we develop a role based access control (RBAC) for the proposed health system. To fulfill the healthcare policies and the well correctness of the reinforcement as well as the functionality of the system, the proposed approach relies on Alloy analyzer in order to check automatically the requirements. Alloy [8] can express specifications of a system's structure and behavior as an abstract model to evolve and expand. Alloy language powered by Alloy Analyzer tool can be used to edit, build, and test its specifications. The analyzer simulates the specification and shows the system's flaws by checking the correctness and find the counter-examples that help to maintain the system. As well, it has the capabilities to present solutions in graphical format with customizing option. Depending on all these benefits, Alloy has been used for the analysis of many systems including security and software architectures. The proposed solution models first the health care system as well as the reinforcement mechanism using UML and express the related requirements in Alloy. It takes as input the system requirements as assertions and the reinforced model including UML diagrams and RBAC model. The results showed the effective correctness of the modeled system and its related reinforcement mechanism.

The next Sect. 2 describes the related work. Then, we present the modeling and the validation of the system. Finally, Sect. 5 concludes the paper and suggests the possible future research.

2 Related Work

In this section, we study the latest IoT contributions, its application in information services, and especially those targeting health care systems. We survey also the contributions dealing with IoT systems modeling, verification and validation.

- Ouchani [14] develops a formal framework to analyze the functional correctness of IoT systems. The proposed framework covers the main components of IoT systems and the approach is automatic. However, the framework suffers from the limitations inherited from PRISM and the security properties are not specified.
- Drira [2] discusses the challenges of modeling IoT in large scale systems called system-of-systems by focusing on interactions and real-time reconfigurations. This contribution presents an overview of architectural concepts without dealing with practical experiments.
- Rahman et al. [18] discuss the complexity of distributing services in many IoT devices as well as the challenges facing the system requirements for each level: devices, services, and applications. The proposed model assures a quality attributes such as update, interoperability, security, functional appropriateness, availability and adaptability. However, the verification process suffers from many limitations at the evaluation step.
- Gupta et al. [6] design an IoT-based health monitoring framework to reduce the neglect of healthcare. Their solution uses the second generation Intel Galileo board, an Arduino IDE that is explored to program the brain, and Xampp database. This solution provides support emergency medical services by collecting, integrating, and inter-operating of IoT data flexibly. However, they are limited in controlling the access and ensuring privacy.
- Madakam et al. [12] review IoT concepts that aim to unify everything into a common infrastructure using smart sensors. First, they focus on basic requirements, geneses, definitions, aliases and characteristics of IoT. Further, they present a various technologies and their usages in innumerable IoT applications into all the domains including medical, manufacturing, transportation, etc. Finally, they acknowledge the need to a standard definition and protocols as well as a universal architecture of IoT that allows for various technologies the ability to inter-operate.
- Gigli et al. [5] attempt services categorization provided by IoT systems, which aims to help building a service provider. They consider ubiquitous services which are collaborative aware. However, they require to overcome protocol distinctions among technologies and unify every aspect of the network.

- Mainak *et al.* [13] designs an agent based model which predict the response time of emergency service by taking into consideration the characteristics of road segments and driving behaviour of emergency vehicle drivers. First, they collecting real time driving data by Fire emergency service of Allahabad city using GPS logger HOLUX M1000C. Then, they analyze collected data in GIS along with road network, population density and land use data. Based on the analysis results, they model a fire emergency vehicle (FEV) service. For validation, they compare the theoretical response time with the measured one by simulating scenarios that have 80% matching segments.

- Hussein *et al.* [7] propose a coordination emergency responses framework using agent-based modeling. The main components of this model are Emergency Response Services, Coordination Unit, MCI, Command and Control Center, and Agent Based Simulation. In case of incident, the MCI sends an aid request to the command and control center which transfers all information needed to emergency response services. Next, all resource information are gathered and updated as necessary by this unit. Finally, the resulting plan from the coordination unit will be sent to the agent based simulation, which used to simulate emergency response tasks in real environments, and identify the best coordination mechanism plan to achieve the best response time.

- Catarinucci *et al.* [1] propose a "Smart Hospital System" (SHS) for automatic monitoring and tracking of patients, personnel, and biomedical devices. It composes of a "Hybrid Sensing Network" (HSN) that collects both environmental conditions and patients' physiological parameters as well as the IoT Smart Gateway that controls the overall SHS behavior. The user interfaces builtin RESTful services which allow user to communicate with the HSN through the 2-way Proxy.

- Molano *et al.* [17] propose an architecture of IoT applied to the industry. First, they present a metamodel that generates industrial cases by extending cyber physical systems to cover covers sensors and actuators to monitor manufacturing. However, safety of data and system accuracy, standardization of technology and interoperability of systems within actual deployments are not considered.

- Cristian *et al.* [4] review the artificial intelligence-IoT fusion with a focus on four important fields. They presents AI basics and the general concepts of computer vision and Fuzzy Logic, and their link with IoT. Besides, they present natural language processing to facilitate the humain-machine interaction.

- Espada [3] proposes a model for constructing and interpreting digital objects in IoT systems which can eliminate the management of pre-configuration and requirements. The model covers the integration and communication of digital objects, applications, devices and users.

Based on the discussed literature, few of them rely on the satisfiability analysis and the stand modeling language to ensure the robustness of the developed solution.

3   HMS Modeling

This section describes the structural and behavioral diagrams of **HMS** proposed system through UML use case, class, and sequence diagrams. Figure 1 shows the main actors and the possible use cases for **HMS**. The doctor can prescribe the status of a patient already registered by the IT Staff, and also can consult his medical reports. Each patient have a medical record, that can be filled or updated by a nurse, a doctor, or a smart object. These cases are only allowed for signed-in and authorized actors. A nurse and smart objects can fill or update the medical record whereas the doctor can consult, fill, update, and prescribe medicines to a patient.

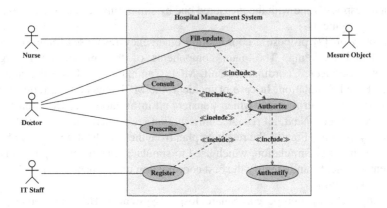

Fig. 1. Use case diagram for HMS.

Figure 2 shows the main classes that represent the structure of principle users and resources. Only the staff with the IoT can fill or update the patient's medical record if they have the authority to do that, also each update of the medical record will be saved automatically in the medical history. We consider also to a patient to have a holder regarding his treatments.

4   HMS Validation

In terms of system specification, Alloy is a modeling language including a formal syntax and semantics. A specified model in Alloy can be in ASCII format as well with a visual representation. Generally, Alloy targets the formal specification of object oriented data models that can be used generally in data modeling, that also can be displayed graphically. Also for systems analysis, Alloy is a verification tool that automatically analyze the properties (requirements) of alloy models. After checking the properties, Alloy might generate counterexamples in case of the property violation. Alloy consists of predicates, facts, relations and signatures. Signatures represent the different entities of the system. Relations specify the relations between them. Predicates and facts define constraints, which apply on relations and signatures.

Each Alloy model begins with the module declaration. The first step is to declare the signatures using the keyword sig. Then, we define the relations (fields) which associate atoms. To define a subset, we should use the keywords extends or in, also the multiplicity keywords such as one, lone, set, some, etc. Facts correspond to the constraints which must always hold. Finally, we define the predicate using the keyword pred and run it.

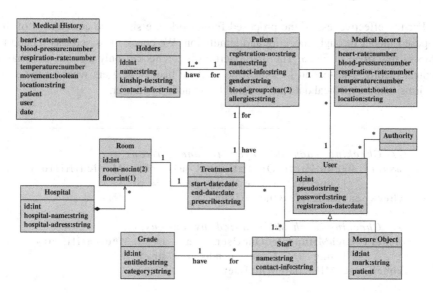

Fig. 2. Class diagram for HMS.

For the validation of **HMS**, we describe its classes and relations in Alloy specification respecting its syntax and logic. Listing 1.1 shows a fragment of the transformation of **HMS** into the input language of Alloy where sigs refer to classes, extends to associations, and the multiplicity to the class diagram relations.

Listing 1.1: HMS description in Alloy input language.

```
module hms  /* Model of hospital  management system. */

abstract sig User {}// Refer to user class

sig Staff extends User {// Refer to staff class
        g : one Grade}
sig MesureObject extends User{} // Refer to mesureObject class
sig Patient {// Refer to patient class
mr : MedicalRecord}
sig MedicalHistory { // Refer to medicalHistory class
        p : one Patient ,
        u : one User}
sig Holders {// Refer to holders class
        p : one Patient}
sig Treatment {// Refer to treatment class
        p : one Patient ,
        r : one Room,
        s : some Staff}
```

For the effectiveness of the proposed framework, we show the correctness of the proposed model through checking and simulation. We check the assertions related to HMS as described in Fig. 3. The first assertion is to check if only a single user has a medical record. The second looks for the medical history of users whereas the third confirms that the medical data are updated by an authorized user.

```
// Checking each MH refer to one patient
assert eachMHreferOnePatient { all mhs: MedicalHistory
       | one pt: Patient  | mhs.p = pt }
check eachMHreferOnePatient

// Checking each MH updated by one user
assert eachMHupdatedOneUser { all mhs: MedicalHistory
       | one ur: User  | mhs.u = ur }
check eachMHupdatedOneUser

// Checking single use of MR
assert singleUseMR { all ps: Patient  | one p: Patient
| ps.mr = p.mr }
check singleUseMR
```

Fig. 3. Checking HMS Assertions.

5 Conclusion

This contribution proposes a concrete model for healthcare system, especially for emergency service in order to facilitate the integration and communication of IoT measures, devices and management systems. First, we proposed UML modeling for the structural and behavioral description of the specific domain of emergency. Further, we proposed Alloy for ensuring the correctness of the model by expressing it safely into its input language. With respect to the obtained results we ensure the correctness of the proposed model. Regarding the obtained results, we target to extend the work in different directions. First, we generalize a meta model from where we can instantiate the model of different services rather than medical and health care. In addition, we have to automate the generation of Alloy code and prove its soundness. Also, we intend to provide, the network architecture including the web services for the different models. Then, we show the impact between them and how we can express and ensure the privacy when deployed. Our final target is to generate a mega system using micro-services architecture, with extensible secure services that can be deployed for different environments.

References

1. Catarinucci, L., et al.: An IoT-aware architecture for smart healthcare systems. IEEE IOT J. **2**(6), 515–526 (2015)
2. Drira, K.: Multiscale and multiobjective modelling: a perspective for mastering the design and operation complexity of IoT systems. In: 2017 40th International Convention on Information and Communication Technology, Electronics and Microelectronics (MIPRO), pp. 555–557 (2017)
3. Espada, J.: Service orchestration on the internet of things. IJIMAI **1**(7), 76–77 (2012)
4. García, C.G., Valdez, E.N., Díaz, V.G., García-Bustelo, B.P., Lovelle, J.C.: A review of artificial intelligence in the internet of things. IJIMAI **5**(4), 9–20 (2019)
5. Gigli, M., Koo, S.: Internet of things: services and applications categorization. Adv. Internet Things **1**(2), 27–31 (2011)
6. Gupta, P., Agrawal, D., Chhabra, J., Dhir, P.K.: IoT based smart healthcare kit. In: 2016 International Conference on Computational Techniques in Information and Communication Technologies (ICCTICT), pp. 237–242, March 2016
7. Dina, H., Maha, A., Dina, I.: Coordination emergency response framework-cerf- a proposed model. Int. J. Comput. Sci. Inf. Secur. **16**(11), 69–73 (2018)
8. Jackson, D.: Software Abstractions: Logic, Language, and Analysis. The MIT Press, Cambridge (2012)
9. Krichen, M.: Improving formal verification and testing techniques for internet of things and smart cities. Mob. Netw. Appl. 1–12 (2019)
10. Krichen, M., Cheikhrouhou, O., Lahami, M., Alroobaea, R., Jmal Maâlej, A.: Towards a model-based testing framework for the security of internet of things for smart city applications. In: Mehmood, R., Bhaduri, B., Katib, I., Chlamtac, I. (eds.) SCITA 2017. LNICST, vol. 224, pp. 360–365. Springer, Cham (2018). https://doi.org/10.1007/978-3-319-94180-6_34
11. Krichen, M., Maâlej, A.J., Lahami, M.: A model-based approach to combine conformance and load tests: an ehealth case study. Int. J. Crit. Comput.-Based Syst. **8**(3–4), 282–310 (2018)
12. Madakam, S., Ramaswamy, R., Tripathi, S.: Internet of things (IoT): a literature review. J. Comput. Commun. **3**(5), 124 (2015)
13. Mainak, B., Singh, V.: Development of agent based model for predicting emergency response time. Perspect. Sci. **8**, 04 (2016)
14. Ouchani, S.: Ensuring the functional correctness of IoT through formal modeling and verification. In: Abdelwahed, E.H., Bellatreche, L., Golfarelli, M., Méry, D., Ordonez, C. (eds.) MEDI 2018. LNCS, vol. 11163, pp. 401–417. Springer, Cham (2018). https://doi.org/10.1007/978-3-030-00856-7_27
15. Ouchani, S., Ait Mohamed, O., Debbabi, M.: Efficient probabilistic abstraction for SysML activity diagrams. In: Eleftherakis, G., Hinchey, M., Holcombe, M. (eds.) SEFM 2012. LNCS, vol. 7504, pp. 263–277. Springer, Heidelberg (2012). https://doi.org/10.1007/978-3-642-33826-7_18
16. Ouchani, S., Lenzini, G.: Attacks generation by detecting attack surfaces. Proc. Comput. Sci. **32**, 529–536 (2014)
17. Molano, J.R., Lovelle, J.C., Marín, C., Granados, J.J., Crespo, R.G.: Metamodel for integration of internet of things, social networks, the cloud and industry 4.0. J. Amb. Intel. Hum. Comput. **9**(6), 709–723 (2018)
18. Leila, R., Tanir, O., Johan, L.: Understanding iot systems: a life cycle approach. Proc. Comput. Sci. (PCS) **130**(1), 1057–1062 (2018)

Short Contributions: Wellbeing Technology

An Embedded ANN Raspberry PI for Inertial Sensor Based Human Activity Recognition

Achraf Jmal[1,2]([✉]), Rim Barioul[3], Amel Meddeb Makhlouf[1],
Ahmed Fakhfakh[1,2], and Olfa Kanoun[3]

[1] National School of Electronics and Telecommunications of Sfax,
University of Sfax, Sfax, Tunisia
Jmal.achraf@yahoo.com, {Amel.makhlouf,Ahmed.fakhfakh}@enetcom.usf.tn
[2] Centre de Recherche en Numérique de Sfax, Laboratoire des Technologies des
Systèmes Smart, LR16CRNS01, 3021 Sfax, Tunisia
[3] Professorship of Measurement and Sensor Technology, Technische Universität
Chemnitz, Chemnitz, Germany
{Rim.barioul,Olfa.kanoun}@etit.tu-chemnitz.de

Abstract. Human Activity Recognition (HAR) is one of the critical subjects of research in health and human machine interaction fields in recent years. Algorithms such as Support Vector Machine (SVM), K-Nearest Neighbors (K-NN), Decision Tree (DT) and many other algorithms were previously implemented to serve this common goal but most of the traditional Machine learning proposed solutions were not satisfying in term of accuracy and real time testing process. For that, a human activities analysis and recognition system with an embedded trained ANN model on Raspberry PI for an online testing process is proposed in this work. This paper includes a comparative study between the Artificial Neural Network (ANN) and the Recurrent Neural Network (RNN), using signals produced by the accelerometer and gyroscope, embedded within the BlueNRG-Tile sensor. After evaluate algorithms performance in terms of accuracy and precision which reached an accuracy of 82% for ANN and 99% for RNN, obtained ANN model was implemented in a Raspberry PI for real-time predictions. Results show that the system provides a real-time human activity recognition with an accuracy of 86%.

Keywords: Machine learning · Deep learning · HAR · Embedded ANN · LSTM-RNN · Raspberry PI · Python

1 Introduction

Human activity recognition (HAR) refers to the automatic detection of various physical activities performed by people in their daily lives [1]. Activity recognition can be achieved by exploiting information retrieved from sensors such as

Supported by German Academic Exchange Service, CRNS and ReDCAD.

M. Jmaiel et al. (Eds.): ICOST 2020, LNCS 12157, pp. 375–385, 2020.
https://doi.org/10.1007/978-3-030-51517-1_34

accelerometer, gyroscope etc., while the activity is being performed with the help
of Artificial Intelligence methods. In recent years, several machine learning and
deep learning algorithms for human activity recognition have been proposed.
Sukor et al. [2] used several methods of machine learning such as Support Vector Machine (SVM), Decision Tree (DT), and Multiple Layer Perception-Neural
Network (MLP-NN) to classify activities such as slow sitting, standing, upstairs,
downstairs and lying using the accelerometer sensor embedded in a smartphone.
The obtained results show that the use of Principal Component Analysis (PCA)
to reduce the dimensionality of features obtains higher recognition rate with the
rate of 96.85% for the DT algorithm and 100% for the MLP-NN algorithm which
may have over fitting problems. G. McCalmont et al. [3] also tested the activity
recognition performance. Three classifiers were used, including Artificial Neural
Network (ANN), K-Nearest Neighbor (KNN) and Random Forest (RF) to classify five exercises which are slow walking, normal walking, fast walking, upstairs
and down stairs using accelerometer, gyroscope and magnetometer. They found
that ANN models with many layers achieve an accuracy of 80% while RF and
KNN achieve an accuracy slightly above 70%. Song-Mi Lee et al. presented a
RF algorithm and achieve an accuracy of 89.1% [4]. Furthermore, three human
activity data, walking, running, and staying still, are gathered using smartphone
accelerometer sensor and classified with Convolutional Neural Network (CNN)
and had better performance 92.71% [4]. Furthermore Abdulmajid Murad et al.
[5] use a 3D accelerometer, 3D gyroscope and 3D magnetometer to classify six
activities. Four algorithms Extreme Learning Machine (ELM), SVM, CNN and
RNN are used to classify these activities. The best accuracy was achieved with
the RNN algorithms 96.7%. It could be considered that the ANN is one of the
best machine learning algorithm used for HAR and the RNN is reported to
overperform other deep learning algorithms in term of accuracy and precision
to recognize human activities. In addition, most of research in the field, validate their results with simulations, without comparing theses simulations with
results provided by real-time embedded and hardware based implementations.
So a lack of standalone, sensor based HAR systems, with embedded machine
learning and real-time response is remarked. This research aims is to compare
simulation results with results provided by a real-time implementation and to
judge performance gived by embedded ANN to recognize human activities. The
rest of this paper is arranged as follows: The second section introduces the ANN
architecture and process. In addition, an overview of the LSTM (Long Short
Term Memory) Recurrent Neural Network is presented in the third section. The
next section presents the data acquisition structure for HAR with the database
properties. Furthermore, an evaluation of ANN and LSTM-RNN using Receiver
Operating Characteristic (ROC) are presented. Moreover, to validate our simulations results, the developed ANN model is implemented in a Raspberry PI as
a real-time standalone HAR system.

2   Artificial Neural Networks/Feed Forward Neural Networks

Artificial Neural Networks, (ANNs), and their variants, are a class of Machine Learning (ML) techniques that have been proven, powerful throughout many applications such as machine translation [6], medical diagnosis [7] and many other fields [8]. ANNs were inspired by the neuroscience. Thus, the building block of an ANN is called a neuron. A basic neural network is shown in Fig. 1. It consists of an input layer, one or more hidden layers, and an output layer. Each layer consists of one or more neuron. Inputs are fed into the neurons that compute some output values based on the weights and biases associated with them. These outputs are summed and multiplied feed activation function to give to final output [9]. The activation function is a core logic of the neural networks. It defines the output of the neuron given an input or a set of inputs. There are several types of activation function like the "sigmoid function", the Hyperbolic Tangent function "Tanh", the Rectified Linear Unit function "ReLU" and the "softmax" activation function [10]. To boost model accuracy and precision, optimizers are added to the neural network. An optimizer update the weight parameters to minimize the loss function. There are several types of optimizers like "Adam" which is stands for adaptive moment estimation, "Adagrad", RmsProp and many other optimizers.

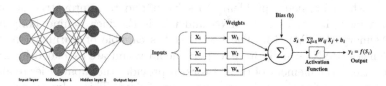

Fig. 1. Artificial Neural Network achitecture and process [11]

These steps are followed in order to train a neural network [9]:

Algorithm 1: Artificial Neural Network process

---

1. Initialize Network. Creates a new neural network ready for training. It accepts three parameters, the number of inputs, the number of neurons to have in the hidden layer and the number of outputs.

2. Randomly initialize weights w_i.. Each neuron has a set of weights that need to be maintained. One weight for each input connection and an additional weight for the bias.

3. Implement forward propagation to compute the output(s). Calculate and storage of intermediate variables (including outputs) for the neural network within the models in the order from input layer to output layer.

4. Implement the cost function. This is typically expressed as a difference or distance between the predicted value and the actual value.

5. Forward propagate input to a network output and calculate the derivative of an neuron output. All of the outputs from one layer become inputs to the neurons on the next layer.

---

3   Long Short Term Memory-RNN/Back Propagation Neural Networks

Recurrent Neural Networks are the only networks with internal memory, which makes them robust and powerful. In a RNN, Weights are applied to both the current input and the looping back output and are adjusted through gradient descent or back propagation [12]. The RNN work on this recursive formula (1) where X_t is the input at time step t, S_t is the state at time step t and F_w is the recursive function.

$$S_t = F_w * (S_{t-1}, X_t) \tag{1}$$

$$S_t = F_w(S_{t-1}, X_t) \tag{2}$$

$$S_t = \tanh(W_s * S_{t-1}, W_x * X_t) \tag{3}$$

$$Y_t = W_y * S_t \tag{4}$$

The recursive function is a tanh function (3), we multiply the input state with the weights of X mentioned as W_x and the previous state with W_s and then past it through a tanh activation to get the new state (3). To get the output vector, we multiply the new state S_t with W_y (4). RNN learn use back propagation through time. Therefore, we calculate the loss using the output, go back to each state, and update weights by multiplying gradients. The updating weights would be negligible and our network will not get any better. This problem is called vanishing gradients problem. To solve it and to improve the accuracy, we add a more interactions to RNN and this is the idea behind Long Short Term Memory (LSTM) [13]. The LSTM cell is capable of learning long-term dependencies. RNNs usually have a short memory and are extended by LSTM units to extend the memory of the network. It provides the capabilities to absorb more information from even longer sequences of data. This helps to boost the precision of the prediction by taking into account more data. The LSTM cell maintains three kinds of gates and one cell state: the input gate, the forget gate and the output gate. The architecture of an LSTM cell is shown in Fig. 2, where the input gate chooses what new information needs to be stored in the cell state. This is shown in Eq. 5 and 7, where i_t is the input gate layer output and C_t is the cell state update. The forget gate decides what existing information in cell state needs to be thrown away, this is shown in Eq. 8, where C_t is again the update of the cell state [12]. Finally, the output gate filters the output and determines the final cell output. This can be seen through Eqs. 9 and 10, where o_t is the output-gate layer output and h_t is the resulting hidden state for the given input. $\check{C}_t$ is called as intermediate cell state, used to calculate the C_t, which is the cell state using Eq. 6. The input gate and the intermediate cell state are added with the old cell state and the forget gate, and then this cell state is passed through tanh activation to be multiplied with the output gate [14]. The following steps are used to train a LSTM-RNN [14]:

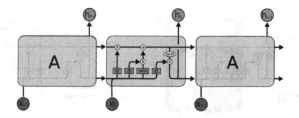

Fig. 2. Architecture of an LSTM cell

Algorithm 2: LSTM-RNN process

---

1. Calculate the input gate by passing the previous state and the input through sigmoid activation.

$$Input\ Gate : i_t = \sigma(W_i[h_{t-1}, X_t]) \tag{5}$$

2. Calculate the intermediate cell state by passing our input and the previous state through tanh activation.

$$Intermidate\ Cell\ State : \check{C}_t = \tanh(W_c[h_{t-1}, X_t]) \tag{6}$$

3. Perform element wise multiplication and calculate the forget gate and multiply it with the old state C_0.

$$Cell\ State : C_t = (i_t * \check{C}_t) + (f_t * \check{C}_t) \tag{7}$$

$$Forget\ Gate : f_t = \sigma(W_f[h_{t-1}, X_t]) \tag{8}$$

4. Add these to obtain a new cell state, which is C_1, and calculate the output gate and we multiply it with the cell state passed through the tanh activation.

$$Output\ Gate : o_t = \sigma(W_o[h_{t-1}, X_t]) \tag{9}$$

$$New\ State : h_t = o_t * \tanh(C_t) \tag{10}$$

---

4 Experimental Results

4.1 Activity Database Collection for HAR

The data acquisition system has a standard structure as shown in Fig. 3. The main component of the data acquisition phase is the sensors (BlueNRG-Tile), which measure the various attributes such as acceleration and velocity. The other components are the ST-BLE (BlueNRG-Tile) application, communication network, and a server to save data. The ST-BLE Sensor application is used for collecting and preprocessing the raw sensor signal [15]. Activity recognition component, which is built on the training and testing stages, relies mostly on machine learning and deep learning models. A large dataset of collected features for training the model is required for the training stage [16]. The data was collected from the Blue-NRG-Tile to measure the Acceleration from tri-axial accelerometer sensor and the Velocity from the tri-axial gyroscope. The dataset contains 3 human activities: sitting, walking and running. the dataset was recorded by 5 persons (2 boys and 3 girls) for 2 min each activity. Data recorded is along three dimensions of the X, Y and Z axis at 15 Hz frequency.

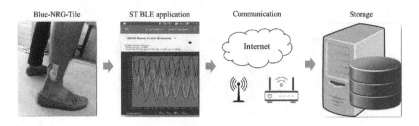

Fig. 3. Data acquisition structure for HAR system

Accelerometer and gyroscope of the BlueNRG-Tile placed on the right foot, are used to capture data. The dataset has a total of 219600 data samples and it was divided into 80% for training, 10% for the testing and 10% for the validation part.

4.2   ANN Evaluation

The ANN model is built using the Keras library. The model has one hidden layer with $N_{inputs+1}$ units which are used to extract features from the sequence of input data. The output layer provides the final predicted output. It is congured to utilize a 'Sigmoid' activation and the 'Adam' optimizer, used to boost accuracy. The model is compiled to run 50 epochs with a batch size of 1024 using 'Mean Squared Error' as its loss function and the accuracy as its performance metrics. Figure 4 shows the training session's progress over iterations and a confusion matrix to show how the model predicted versus true predictions. After training the model for 50 epochs, an accuracy above 82% with a loss of almost 10% are obtained. The confusion matrix shows that an overlap in the prediction of walking that is confused with running (22.18%). The addition of the gyroscope has the advantage of increasing the model accuracy (from 70% to 82%), decreasing the loss rate (from 15% to 10%) and subsequently increase the precision of prediction by class. The main difference between this model and the model trained with only accelerometer sensor data is the necessary number of iterations to achieve the highest accuracy or the lowest loss. The last model

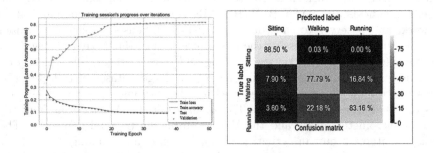

Fig. 4. ANN evaluation using accelerometer and gyroscope

requires 20 iterations to achieve an accuracy above 82%, whereas, this model needs only 7 iterations to achieve this value of accuracy with the minimum of loss rate (10%) which indicate the necessity of the gyroscope for inertial sensor based HAR system.

4.3 LSTM-RNN Evaluation

The LSTM-RNN model is built using the Keras library and Tensorflow as its backend. The model first has two hidden LSTM layers with ($N_{inputs+1}$) units each, which are used to extract features from the sequence of input data with the "ReLU" activation function for each neuron. The output layer was configured to utilize a 'Softmax activation and the 'Adam' optimizer was used to boost accuracy. The model was compiled to run 50 epochs with a batch size of 1024 using 'Mean Squared Error' as its loss function and the accuracy as its performance metrics. From Fig. 5, the accuracy reached about 99% for the first 10 iterations and the loss rate went down to about 10% with the first 50 iterations. The confusion matrix shows a slight overlap between walking and running activities (1.84%). The use of LSTM-RNN and the tri-axial accelerometer, the tri-axial gyroscope allows having good classification between walking and running activities and especially for sitting class. Human activities are recognized with high accuracy (about 99%) using a tri-axial accelerometer and gyroscope located at the right foot by using LSTM-RNN classifier. The LSTM-RNN using an accelerometer and gyroscope can be a reliable model to be implemented for real time human activity recognition, but the optimization metrics, such as the number of sensors used, the energy consumption, cost, the number of layers, units used and the complexity of the deep learning (LSTM-RNN) compared to the machine learning algorithm (ANN) needs to be taken into consideration [17]. The next section presents an implementation of ANN to validate our obtained simulations. To more understand the efficacy of these algorithms, our next focus research will be on the implementation of the LSTM-RNN for real-time recognition.

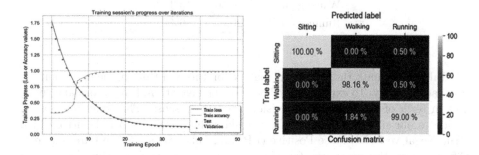

Fig. 5. LSTM-RNN evaluation using accelerometer and gyroscope

5   Real-Time HAR Implementation in Raspberry PI

After collecting data from the BlueNRG-Tile and building the ANN model using
an accelerometer and a gyroscope, this section presents an implementation of the
developed algorithm in a Raspberry PI using MPU6050 to capture data for real
time predictions as shown in Fig. 6. The prototype is tested to a boy of 16 years
old for 15 s. As shown in the Fig. 6, The MPU6050 is placed on the right foot
attached to the raspberry PI with jumper.

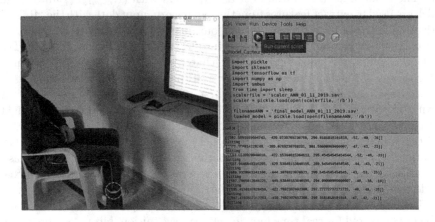

Fig. 6. Connecting the Raspberry PI with the MPU6050

Table 1. Confusion matrix for the real-time implementation

Actual	Predicted		
	Sitting	Walking	Running
Sitting	93.34%	6.66%	0%
Walking	0%	86.66%	13.34%
Running	0%	20%	80%

Table 1 presents the confusion matrix for the real-time implementation for
15 s each activity. To express the efficacy of the algorithm, the performance metrics in term of accuracy and precision needs to discuss. The confusion matrix
validates our simulation results. To calculate the accuracy, True Positive (TP),
True Negative (TN), False Positive (FP) and False Negative (FN) are required.
After testing the prototype for 15 s, an accuracy of 86% is achieved with an
average precision approximately 84%. Real-time simulation with the Raspberry
PI shows good results in term of prediction and differentiation between sitting,
walking and running activities. Obtained results from simulations and results

provided from the Raspberry, are very close, which rounds our prototype reliable and robust model. Moreover, to evaluate the performance of the considered approaches, we compare our models to other research works. We find that our trained models are more robust in term of accuracy compared to McCalmont, G. et al. [3] which achieve an accuracy above 80% for ANN and 70% for the KNN. Moreover, we compare our trained LSTM-RNN model which reached of an accuracy performance 99%, to Mi Lee, S. et al. [4] and Abdulmajid Murad et al. [5] which use a Convolutional Neural Network (CNN) algorithm and (Sequential ELM, SVM, CNN and RNN) respectively, the best accuracy was achieved with the RNN-LSTM algorithms (99%) The focus of next paper will be on a the implementation of LSTM-RNN in the Raspberry PI with a comparative study between ANN and LSTM-RNN for real-time HAR.

6   Conclusion

In this paper, a deep learning algorithm named Recurrent Neural Network (RNN) with LSTM memory units and keras was tested using accelerometer and gyroscope to classify and analyze human activities such as sitting, walking and running. This produced an overall accuracy of 99%. Furthermore, we have exported the ANN model using accelerometer and gyroscope to be implemented in a Raspberry PI. In addition, we have tested the model with data collected from the MPU6050 and we have successfully shown that the model provides good results in term of real-time prediction and classification with 86% of accuracy. For the future work direction, an IoT smart device of human activity recognition based on embedded deep learning will be developed. In addition, the deep learning algorithm in the medical fields to implement a real-time fall detection system and anomaly detection system for elderly monitoring, and disease prevention will be investigated.

References

1. Ramasamy, S.M., Roy, N.: Recent trends in machine learning for human activity recognition-a survey. Wiley Interdisc. Rev.: Data Mining Knowl. Discov. **8**(4), e1254 (2018)
2. Sukor, A.S.A., Zakaria, A., Rahim, N.A.: Activity recognition using accelerometer sensor and machine learning classifiers. In: IEEE 14th International Colloquium Signal Processing and its Application, CSPA 2018, no. March, pp. 233–238 (2018)
3. McCalmont, G., et al.: eZiGait: toward an AI gait analysis and sssistant system. In: 2018 IEEE International Conference on Bioinformatics and Biomedicine (BIBM), Madrid, Spain, pp. 2280–2286. IEEE (2019)
4. Lee, S.M., Yoon, S.M., Cho, H.: Human activity recognition from accelerometer data using convolutional neural network. In: 2017 IEEE International Conference on Big Data and Smart Computing (BigComp), Jeju, South Korea, pp. 131–134. IEEE (2017)
5. Murad, A., Pyun, J.Y.: Deep recurrent neural networks for human activity recognition. Sensors **17**(11), 2556 (2017). https://doi.org/10.3390/s17112556

6. Araújo, M., Pereira, A., Benevenuto, F.: A comparative study of machine translation for multilingual sentence-level sentiment analysis. Inf. Sci. **512**, 1078–1102 (2020). https://doi.org/10.1016/j.ins.2019.10.031

7. Mohamed, M.B., Makhlouf, A.M., Fakhfakh, A.: Intrusion cancellation for anomaly detection in healthcare applications. In: International Wireless Communications and Mobile Computing Conference (IWCMC) (2019). https://doi.org/10.1109/IWCMC.2019.8766592

8. Rashid, K.M., Joseph, L.: Times-series data augmentation and deep learning for construction equipment activity recognition. Adv. Eng. Inform. **42**, 100944 (2019). https://doi.org/10.1016/j.aei.2019.100944

9. Joselin, J., et al.: A review on neural networks. Int. J. Trend Sci. Res. Dev. (IJTSRD) **2**, 565–569 (2018). ISSN 2456-6470

10. Nwankpa, C.E., Ijomah, W., Gachagan, A., Marshall, S.: Activation Functions: Comparison of Trends in Practice and Research for Deep Learning. arXiv:1811.03378v1, pp. 1–20, 8 November 2018

11. Alkittawi, H.: A deep-learning-based fall-detection system to support aging-in-place. Texas A&M University-Corpus Christi Corpus Christi, Texas (2017)

12. Smagulova, K., James, A.P.: Overview of long short-term memory neural networks. In: James, A.P. (ed.) Deep Learning Classifiers with Memristive Networks. MOST, vol. 14, pp. 139–153. Springer, Cham (2020). https://doi.org/10.1007/978-3-030-14524-8_11

13. Pascanu, R., Mikolov, T., Bengio, Y.: On the difficulty of training recurrent neural networks. In: Proceedings of the 30th International Conference on Machine Learning, Atlanta, Georgia, USA, vol. 28, no. 2 (2013)

14. Pienaar, S.W., Malekian, R.: Human activity recognition using LSTM-RNN deep neural network architecture. In: IEEE 2nd Wireless Africa Conference (WAC), Pretoria, South Africa, 18–20 August 2019 (2019). https://doi.org/10.1109/AFRICA.2019.8843403

15. Jmal, A., Barioul, R., Makhlouf, A.M., Fakhfakh, A., Kanoun, O.: Human activity recognition from BlueNRG-tile sensor using recurrent neural network. In: 12th International Workshop on Impedance Spectroscopy (IWIS), Chemnitz, Germany, pp. 1–2. IEEE (2019)

16. Shoaib, M., Bosch, S., Incel, O.D., Scholten, H., Havinga, P.J.M.: Fusion of smartphone motion sensors for physical activity recognition. Sensors **14**, 10146–10176 (2014). https://doi.org/10.3390/s140610146

17. Oscar, D.L., Miguel, A.: Labrador: a survey on human activity recognition using wearable sensors. IEEE Commun. Surv. Tutor. **15**(3), 1192–1209 (2013). https://doi.org/10.1109/SURV.2012.110112.00192

Human Activities Recognition in Android Smartphone Using WSVM-HMM Classifier

M'hamed Bilal Abidine[✉] and Belkacem Fergani

Laboratoire d'Ingénierie des Systèmes Intelligents et Communicants,
LISIC Lab., Electronics and Computer Sciences Department,
University of Science and Technology Houari Boumediene (USTHB),
Algiers, Algeria
abidineb@hotmail.com

Abstract. Being able to recognize human activities is essential for several applications such as health monitoring, fall detection, context-aware mobile applications. In this work, we perform the recognition of the human activity based on the combined Weighted SVM and HMM by taking advantage of the relative strengths of these two classification paradigms. One significant advantage in WSVMs is that, they deal the problem of imbalanced data but his drawback is that, they are inherently static classifiers - they do not implicitly model temporal evolution of data. HMMs have the advantage of being able to handle dynamic data with certain assumptions about stationary and independence. The experiment results on real datasets show that the proposed method possess the better robustness and distinction.

Keywords: Activity recognition · Classification · Weighted SVM · HMM

1 Introduction

The advancement of technologies has facilitated the monitoring of human activities through the embedded sensors in a smartphone. Recently, smart phones, equipped with a rich set of sensors, are explored as alternative platforms for human activity recognition (HAR) [1, 2]. HAR technology aims at recognizing the behavior and activities of users through a series of observations, which has wide application [3, 4] in different areas, such as healthcare and military monitoring.

With smartphones becoming an integral part of daily human life [5], they are being preferred as the most usable appliances that could recognize human activities due to its powerful in terms of mobility, user-friendly interface, network capability, strong CPU, memory, and battery. They contain a large number of hardware sensors such as accelerometer, gyroscope, temperature, humidity, light sensor, and GPS receiver.

The human sensor based activity recognition is a combination of sensor networks hand-in-hand with the data mining and machine learning techniques [6]. The smartphones provide enormous amount of sensor data for one to understand the daily activity patterns of an individual.

The basic procedure for mobile activity recognition involves i) collection of labelled data, i.e., associated with a specific class or activity from users that perform sample activities to be recognized ii) classification model generation by using collected

M. Jmaiel et al. (Eds.): ICOST 2020, LNCS 12157, pp. 386–394, 2020.
https://doi.org/10.1007/978-3-030-51517-1_35

data to train and test classification algorithms iii) a model deployment stage where the learnt model is transferred to the mobile device for identifying new contiguous portions of sensor data streams that cover various activities of interest. Sensor data can be processed in real-time or logged for offline analysis and evaluation. The model generation is usually performed offline on a server system and later deployed to the phone to recognize the activity performed.

Recently, several authors [7, 8] have proposed many applications related to activity recognition on multiple body positions. Most of the work, like Ahmad [9], Tran [10], Awan [11], Shoaib [12], and Abidine [13], consider a single classifier approach to study activity recognition using smartphones. For the classification, SVMs are popular [8, 14]. It is also the case for HMMs [15] which they commonly used for time-series activity recognition. However, there is very limited number of publications in the literature that investigate the application of the WSVM classifier for smartphone data, and no one is found about applying the latter one on smartphone data or even on HAR system's datasets. Building a system with high precision to accurately identify these activities is a challenging task.

In this work, we adopted a new method for physical activity recognition using mobile phones that uses labels outputting WSVM in HMM. WSVM investigated the effect of overweighting the minority class on SVM modeling between the performed activities. HMM is a natural solution to address the activity complexity by — capturing and smoothing information during the transition between two activities (e.g. Walking and Standing). We also used the feature extraction approach that transforms the original high dimensional data to a lower dimensional feature space. The transformation can be linear or nonlinear. In this project, we employed the linear Principal Component Analysis (PCA) [16] to extract the feature vectors.

2 The Proposed HAR System by Combining WSVM-HMM Based PCA

2.1 Overview

Figure 1 shows the architecture of the proposed activity recognition system. Among the available labelled data, training and test subsets are chosen using the cross-validation mechanism. The constructed PCA space is then used for training and testing the Weighted SVM classifier. In the second step of the process is a pre-classification by 'WSVM', this phase is carried out by the 'cross-validation' will generate an estimate of the label vector.

The principal component features concatenated with the WSVM estimated label vector are employed as a new training data to train HMM classifier. The final classification is performed with the 'Viterbi' algorithm, by the use of a HMM model.

An estimated label vector is generated by the 'Viterbi' algorithm and the system will output the recognized activity (i.e., walking, running, and others).

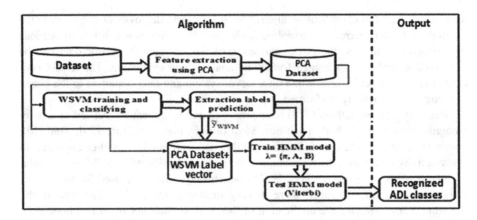

Fig. 1. Hybrid WSVM-HMM system based PCA approach.

2.2 Principal Component Analysis (PCA)

PCA [16] is an orthogonal projection-based technique such that the variance of the projected data is maximized. In our case, a large number of features are extracted by prepossessing the raw signals generated from different sensors. It is a widely used technique for dimensionality reduction, feature extraction, and data visualization through the construction of uncorrelated principal components that are a linear combination of the original variables. The PCA components can be counted by performing the eigenvector decomposition of the covariance matrix S:

$$S = \sum_{j=1}^{m} \left((\bar{x})_j - \mu \right) \left((\bar{x})_j - \mu \right)^T, \quad \mu = \frac{1}{m} \sum_{j=m}^{m} (\bar{x})_j. \tag{1}$$

This problem leads to solve the eigenvalue equation with λ *is the eigenvalue of S and V is the eigenvector corresponding to the* λ:

$$\lambda V = SV, ||V|| = 1. \tag{2}$$

Where $V = [v_1, v_2, ..., v_i]$, $(i = 1, ..., n)$ is the n × n matrix containing n eigenvectors and λ is an n × n diagonal matrix of eigenvalues of the covariance matrix. In Eq. (2), each n dimensional eigenvector v_i corresponds to the ith eigenvalue λ_i.

2.3 Weighted Support Vector Machines (WSVM)

Osuna et al. [17] proposed an extension of the SVM modeling, Weighted SVM algorithm to overcome the imbalance problem by introducing two different penalty parameter C_- and C_+ in the primal Lagrangian (Eq. 3) for the minority ($y_i = -1$) and majority classes ($y_i = +1$), as follow

$$\min_{s,b,\zeta} \frac{1}{2} w \bullet w + C_+ \sum_{i|y_i=1}^{m_+} \zeta_i + C_- \sum_{i|y_i=-1}^{m_-} \zeta_i \tag{3}$$

subject to $y_i(s \bullet \Phi(y_i) + b) \geq 1 - \zeta_i, \ \zeta_i \geq 0, \ i = 1, \ldots, m$.

m_+ *(resp. m_-)* the number of positive (resp. negative) instances in the initial database ($m_- + m_+ = m$). Solving the formulation dual of WSVM [17] gives a decision function for classifying a test point $y \in R^p$

$$f(x) = \text{sgn}\left(\sum_{i=m}^{m_{sv}} \alpha_i y_i K(x, x_i) + b\right). \tag{4}$$

We used the Gaussian kernel as follows: $K(x, y) = \exp\left(-\|x - y\|^2/2\sigma^2\right)$. Some authors [17–19] have proposed adjusting different cost parameters to solve the imbalanced problem. To extend Weighted SVM to the multi-class scenario in order to deal with N classes (daily activities), we have shown in [20] that the cost of mis-classifying a point from the small class should be heavier than the cost for errors on the large class. They used different misclassification C_i per class, use this conclusion can get a satisfactory result. By taking $C_- = C_i$ and $C_+ = C$, with m_+ and m_i be the number of samples of majority classes and number of samples in the ith class, the main ratio cost value C_i for each activity can be obtained by:

$$C_i = \text{round}(C \times [m_+/m_i]), \ i = 1, \ldots, N. \tag{5}$$

2.4   Hidden Markov Model (HMM)

HMM [21] comprises two parts: Markov chain and stochastic process. Markov chain, whose output is a sequence of state, can be described by the initial probability distri-bution for the states (π) and the state transition matrix (A), while stochastic process whose output is a sequence of observed values, is described by the observation probability matrix (B). Thus, a HMM can be described as:

$$A = a_{ij} = P(y_t = j|y_{t-1} = i) \text{ and } \sum_{j=1}^{N} a_{ij} = 1 \tag{6}$$

$$B = [b_j(O_t)] \tag{7}$$

$$b_j(O_t) = P(q_{k+1} = O_t/q_t = i) \tag{8}$$

$$\pi = [\pi_1, \pi_2 \ldots, \pi_N] \tag{9}$$

$$\pi_i = P(q_0 = i). \tag{10}$$

With: $i, j \in \{1, 2, ..., N\}$

O_t: Vector of observations

A standard HMM is a generative probabilistic model, which generates hidden states y_t from observable data x_t at each discrete time instant. In our case the hidden variable is the activities that the subject was performing at a given time step and the observable variable is the vector of sensor readings. HMM model mainly works on two basic principles as follows: the observable variable at time t, namely x_t, depends *only* on the hidden variable y_t. The hidden variable at time t, namely y_t, depends *only* on the previous hidden variable y_{t-1}.

Learning the parameters of these parameters corresponds to maximizing the joint probability p(x, y) between the sensor data and activities in the training data. The joint probability therefore factorizes as follows:

$$P(\mathrm{x}, \mathrm{y}) = \prod_{t=1}^{T} p(y_t|y_{t-1})p(x_t|y_t) . \tag{11}$$

The main aim of this model is to determine the best hidden state sequence from the observed output sequence that maximizes $p(\mathrm{x}, \mathrm{y})$.

3   Experimental Results and Analysis

3.1   Datasets

We validate our method on three public datasets whose information is summarized in Table 1. The first dataset used is from [22]: the Human Activity Dataset (HAR). The second dataset (HAPT) [23] with Postural Transitions is similar to previous dataset, further, it includes postural transitions in addition of the previous version of the dataset Records. The third dataset is from [24], titled Wireless Sensor Data Mining (WISDM). All datasets have been recorded by means of Android smartphone. For the annotation of the activities, the video-recorded is used to label the data manually. The HAR and

Table 1. Summary of datasets used in the evaluation

Houses	HAR	HAPT	WISDM
Nb of subjects	30	30	29
Annotation	Video	Video	Graphical user interface
$F_{Sampling}$ (Hz)	50	50	20
Features	561	561	6
Smartphone	Samsung Galaxy SII	Samsung Galaxy SII	Cell Phone
Position	Waist	Waist	Front leg pocket
Sensors	Accelerometer and gyroscope	Accelerometer and gyroscope	Accelerometer
Activities	6	12	6

HAPT datasets provide a large extracted features extracted by prepossessing the raw signals generated from sensors.

3.2 Results

These algorithms are tested under MATLAB environment and the WSVM algorithm is tested with implementation LibSVM [25] using Gaussian kernel is used for all the datasets. Each training dataset is normalized before classification within a range of $[-1, 1]$. We optimized the SVM hyper-parameters (σ, C) for all training sets in the range [0.1, 0.2, 0.5, 1] and {0.1, 1, 5, 10, 100}, respectively, to maximize the error rate of five fold- cross validation technique. The optimal parameters σ_{opt} = 0.9, 0.9, and 0.8 are found to be optimal the training dataset of HAR, HAPT, and WISDM, respectively. We show in the Table 2 that the fusion of principal component features with WSVM-HMM makes the model more robust, achieving better performance. One also notices for HAR dataset that the multi-class WSVM method improves the classification results over MC-SVM, MC-HF-SVM and HMM classifiers used alone. On the other hand, the results also show that WSVM outperforms HMM for recognizing activities for all datasets except for the HAPT dataset.

In terms of reducing the datasets, the feature reduction identifies the most relevant features for the learning process. We notice that PCA features can improve the discrimination between different activities than the original features. For WISDM the performances of activity recognition are low than HAR and HAPT datasets with 561 features. This is explained by the number of features (6) for WISDM is not sufficient when using PCA algorithm. Another reason to the lowest accuracy in WISDM dataset is attributed to the use only the accelerometer sensor comparatively to the HAR and HAPT that use the both accelerometer and gyroscope sensors.

Table 2. The micro-averaged measures: Recall, Precision, F-measure and Accuracy for all approaches in (%). Bold values are the results for our approach for each dataset.

Datasets	Approach	Recall	Precision	F-measure	Accuracy
HAR	MC-SVM [8]	89.6	89.9	89.7	89.3
	MC-HF-SVM [8]	89.3	89.2	89.2	89.0
	WSVM	92.4	91.6	91.9	93.9
	HMM	89.2	90.2	89.7	93.7
	Proposed	**94.0**	**96.7**	**95.3**	**94.9**
HAPT	WSVM	96.0	92.4	94.1	86.1
	HMM	98.3	97.1	97.7	96.5
	Proposed	**97.3**	**99.0**	**98.1**	**96.8**
WISDM	J48 [26]	81.7	–	–	85.1
	LogisticRegression [26]	68.4	–	–	78.1
	MultilayerPerceptron [26]	80.4	–	–	91.7
	WSVM	83.4	76.5	79.8	81.4
	HMM	79.4	80.0	79.7	84.9
	Proposed	**91.9**	**79.8**	**85.4**	**92.3**

Table 3. Confusion matrix of activities for the proposed method on the HAR dataset.

Activities	Walking	W. Upstairs	W. Downstairs	Sitting	Standing	Laying
Walking	**97.1**	2.1	0.7	0.0	0.0	0.1
Walking. Upstairs	1.2	**96.2**	2.4	0.1	0.1	0.0
Walking. Downstairs	0.7	2.2	**97.1**	0.0	0.0	0.0
Sitting	0.6	0.0	0.1	**83.5**	12.2	3.6
Standing	0.1	0.2	0.2	7.4	**91.4**	0.7
Laying	0.0	0.0	0.3	0.8	0.3	**98.6**

To get a detailed knowledge of the performances on each class corresponding to current activity for the HAR dataset with six different activities. We calculate the confusion matrix of the proposed method in Table 3. From these tables, we see that the best performances were obtained for the proposed method for all classes, in particular for the static activities (Sitting and Standing).

In the Table 3, 96.2% of 'W. Upstairs' activity instances are correctly recognized, while 2.4% goes into 'W. Downstairs' and 1.2% are confused with 'Walking' activity. The similar classes such as 'Walking', 'W. Upstairs', and 'W. Downstairs' show similar trend of sharing errors among each other. The reason is the similar status of smartphone when the user does these dynamic activities. We notice that the static activities share errors among each other. 12.2% of 'Standing' activity instances are confused with 'Sitting' activity and 7.4% of 'Sitting' activity instances are confused with 'Standing' activity. Intuitively, this can be explained by the fact that the patterns in the acceleration data between these activities are somewhat similar.

4   Conclusion and Future Work

Experimental results of the hybrid model presented demonstrate how it can be effectively employed for activity recognition of static and dynamic activities. It obtains a significant performance. Specifically, we show how the hybrid system obtained by using the WSVM label output a new feature added to the reduced data for training and testing HMM outperforms other well known supervised pattern recognition approaches. We consider that WSVM approach has great potential to deal the imbalance class in this human activity recognition problem. However, it must be noticed that hybridizing these schemes implies a more complex system. Fortunately, the training phase in a deployed activity recognizer is usually done offline, so we do not consider such growth of complexity a real problem in our domain.

References

1. Sarwar, M., Soomro, T.R.: Impact of smartphone's on society. Eur. J. Sci. Res. **98**(2), 216–226 (2013)
2. Abidine, M.B., Fergani, L., Fergani, B., Fleury, A.: Improving human activity recognition in smart homes. Int. J. E-Health Med. Commun. (IJEHMC) **6**(3), 19–37 (2015)

3. Klasnja, P., Pratt, W.: Healthcare in the pocket: mapping the space of mobile-phone health interventions. J. Biomed. Inf. **45**, 184–198 (2012)
4. Candás, J.L.C., Peláez, V., López, G., Fernández, M.Á., Álvarez, E., Díaz, G.: An automatic data mining method to detect abnormal human behaviour using physical activity measurements. Pervasive Mob. Comput. **15**, 228–241 (2014)
5. Shoaib, M., Bosch, S., Incel, D., Scholten, H., Havinga, P.J.M.: A survey of online activity recognition using mobile phones. J. Sens. (Basel, Switzerland) **15**(1), 2059–2085 (2015)
6. Fu, Y.: Human Activity Recognition and Prediction. Springer, Switzerland (2016). https://doi.org/10.1007/978-3-319-27004-3
7. Chetty, G., White, M., Akther, F.: Smart phone based data mining for human activity recognition, Elsevier Procedia Comput. Sci. – ICICT **46**(8), 1181–1187 (2015)
8. Anguita, D., Ghio, A., Oneto, L., Parra, X., Reyes-Ortiz, J.L.: Human activity recognition on smartphones using a multiclass hardware-friendly support vector machine. In: Bravo, J., Hervás, R., Rodríguez, M. (eds.) IWAAL 2012. LNCS, vol. 7657, pp. 216–223. Springer, Heidelberg (2012). https://doi.org/10.1007/978-3-642-35395-6_30
9. Ahmad, N., Han, L., Iqbal, K., Ahmad, R., Abid, M.A., Iqbal, N.: SARM: salah activities recognition model based on smartphone. Electronics **8**(8), 881 (2019)
10. Tran, D.N., Phan, D.D.: Human activities recognition in android smartphone using support vector machine. In: 2016 7th International Conference on Intelligent Systems, Modelling and Simulation (ISMS), pp. 64–68. IEEE (2016)
11. Awan, M.A., Guangbin, Z., Kim, H.C., Kim, S.D.: Subject-independent human activity recognition using smartphone accelerometer with cloud support. Int. J. Ad Hoc Ubiq. Comput. **20**(3), 172–185 (2015)
12. Shoaib, M., Scholten, H., Havinga, P.J.M.: Towards physical activity recognition using smartphone sensors. In: Proceedings of the 2013 IEEE 10th International Conference on Ubiquitous Intelligence and Computing and IEEE 10th International Conference on Autonomic and Trusted Computing, Italy 18–21, pp. 80–87 (2013)
13. Abidine, M.B., Yala, N., Fergani, B., Clavier, L.: Soft margin SVM modeling for handling imbalanced human activity datasets in multiple homes. In: 2014 International Conference on Multimedia Computing and Systems (ICMCS), pp. 421–426. IEEE (2014)
14. Alman, A., Lawi, A., Tahir, Z.: Pattern recognition of human activity based on smartphone data sensors using SVM multiclass. In: 1st International Conference on Science and Technology, ICOST 2019. European Alliance for Innovation (EAI) (2019)
15. Cheng, B.C., Tsai, Y.A., Liao, G.T., Byeon, E.S.: HMM machine learning and inference for Activities of Daily Living recognition. J. Supercomput. **54**(1), 29–42 (2010)
16. Jolliffe, I.T.: Principal Component Analysis, 2nd edn. Springer, NewYork (2010)
17. Osuna, E., Freund, R., Girosi, F.: Support vector machines: training and applications. Massachusetts Institute of Technology, Cambridge (1997)
18. Veropoulos, K., Campbell, C., Cristianini, N.: Controlling the sensitivity of support vector machines. In: Proceedings of the International Joint Conference on AI, pp. 55–60 (1999)
19. Huang, Y.M., Du, S.X.: Weighted support vector machine for classification with uneven training class sizes. In: Proceedings of the IEEE International Conference on Machine Learning and Cybernetics, vol. 7, pp. 4365–4369 (2005)
20. Abidine, B.M., Fergani, L., Fergani, B., Oussalah, M.: The joint use of sequence features combination and modified weighted SVM for improving daily activity recognition. Pattern Anal. Appl. **21**(1), 119–138 (2016). https://doi.org/10.1007/s10044-016-0570-y
21. Cheng, B.C., Tsai, Y.A., Liao, G.T., Byeon, E.S.: HMM machine learning and inference for activities of daily living recognition. J. Supercomput. **54**(1), 29–42 (2010). https://doi.org/10.1007/s11227-009-0335-0
22. https://archive.ics.uci.edu/ml/machine-learning-databases/00240/. Accessed Mar 2017

23. https://archive.ics.uci.edu/ml/datasets/SmartphoneBased+Recognition+of+Human
+Activities+and+Postural+Transitions Accessed 10 Mar 2016
24. http://www.cis.fordham.edu/wisdm/dataset.php. Accessed Mar 2017
25. Hsu, C.W., Chang, C.C., Lin, C.J.: A practical guide to support vector classification (2003). In: Chang, C.-C., Lin, C.-J.: 'LIBSVM: A library for support vector machines' ACM Transactions on Intelligent Systems and Technology, vol. 2, pp. 27:1–27:27 (2011). http://www.csie.ntuedu.tw/cjlin/libsvm
26. Kwapisz, J.R., Weiss, G.M., Moore, S.A.: Activity recognition using cell phone accelerometers. ACM SIGKDD Explor. Newslett. 12(2), 74–82 (2011)

Mobile Assistive Application for Blind People in Indoor Navigation

Hanen Jabnoun[1(✉)], Mohammad Abu Hashish[2], and Faouzi Benzarti[2]

[1] ESPRIT, School of Engineering, 2083 Tunis, Tunisia
hanene.jabnoun@esprit.tn
[2] LR-11-ES17 Signal, Images et Technologies de l'Information
(LR-SITI-ENIT), 1002 Tunis Le Belvédère, Tunisia
medabuhashish@yahoo.fr, benzartif@yahoo.fr

Abstract. Navigation is an important human task that needs the human sense of vision. In this context, recent technologies developments provide technical assistance to support the visually impaired in their daily tasks and improve their quality of life. In this paper, we present a mobile assistive application called "GuiderMoi" that retrieves information about directions using color targets and identifies the next orientation for the visually impaired. In order to avoid the failure in detection and the inaccurate tracking caused by the mobile camera, the proposed method based on the CamShift algorithm aims to introduce better location and identification of color targets. Tests were conduct in natural indoor scene. The results depending on the distance and the angle of view, defined the accurate values to have a highest rate of target recognition. This work has perspectives for this such as implicating the augmented reality and the intelligent navigation based on machine learning and real-time processing.

Keywords: Assistive application · Color targets · Camshift algorithm · Android application

1 Introduction

Vision is a vital human sense that plays a crucial role in the human perception of the environment. However, for the visually impaired, this information is not generally available through external intervention. In fact, to ensure safe and independent mobility, people are usually dependent on external information, planned experience, and existing technology to navigate in indoor environments or in unfamiliar outdoor. In this context, many researchers address the issue of how to enable these individuals to overcome the inability to navigate the environment independently and to understand the visual scene defined by a set of components and characteristics. In this work, we are considering to design a system that provides assistance for the visually impaired to better navigate in both indoor and outdoor environment.

M. Jmaiel et al. (Eds.): ICOST 2020, LNCS 12157, pp. 395–403, 2020.
https://doi.org/10.1007/978-3-030-51517-1_36

2 State of the Art

Recent technological developments provide technical assistance that helps to support visually impaired people in their daily tasks and improves their quality of life. In this context, sensory substitution systems [1–4] are devices that allow information normally acquired by a defective sensory organ and restored to another perceptive modality. For the visually impaired, it consists of transmitting visual information via the auditory or somatosensory system

First, the visuo-tactile substitution devices convert a visual image into tactile information. There are many devices such as the TVSS [5], TDU [6]. These tools are efficient in the recognition of simple forms, the possibility of reading and localization [7].

Moreover, the visuo-auditory substitution devices are based on the transformation of visual image into auditory information. Thanks to auditory system, visually impaired people use sounds for navigation that inform them about the environment and protect them from obstacles. There are many devices such as the Voice [7], PSVA [8], the Vibe [9], and See Colour [10].

These visual substitution systems are using the translation of visual information into another auditory sensory in order to assist visual impaired people. However, existing system needs hard equipment and sometimes the visual impaired should handle it in a backpack.

In addition, new technologies such as mobile phones or smartphones provide technical assistance to support the visually impaired in their daily tasks and aim to improve their quality of life. These devices are equipped with touch screens that ensure better user experience. In fact, they are more adaptable to the visually impaired people using a guiding system for way finding. So that, using a smartphone and its integrated camera, the system is able to detect objects such as the panels [11].

Another technology was presented in literature, which is the Near Field Communication (NFC). NFC is one of the newest technologies in the communication area. It has a rapid progress in mobile devices and an increase number of smartphones equipped with NFC readers. This technology combines identification and interconnection and enables secure communication between electronic devices [12]. In fact, the user has simply to touch the NFC tagged object in order to obtain detailed information.

Besides, there are other visual substitution applications based on voice and haptic replication. The user receives information when entering or sliding the finger on the screen using a screen reader that converts text to speech and ensure reading and navigating through the contents [13].

In addition, haptic is a technology that provides tactile feedback. For tactile-based interfaces [14], haptic can make the user feel and visualize the shape of an element without looking at the screen. It can also provide comments when the finger reaches the limit of an element or button.

The experiments results in literature [15] illustrate the ability of blind and visually impaired people to use assistive mobile application in order to locate the guide signs with an auditory feedback.

3   Proposed Method

In order to assist blind and visually impaired people in indoor navigation and facilitate the way finding, we propose a navigation system using mobile application that detects and reads colour targets retrieved through the integrated camera. The developed android application named "GuiderMoi" is mainly used to assist the blind person in indoor environment and buildings.

3.1   General Architecture

The general architecture of the proposed system based on mobile application is shown in Fig. 1.

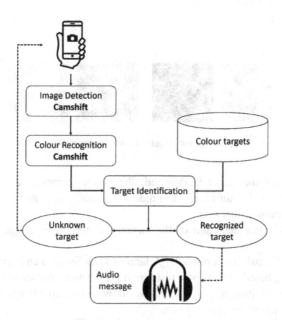

Fig. 1. General architecture

The colour targets are detected using the Camshift algorithm [16]. Once the colours are determined, a comparison is made with targets in database. If the target is unrecognized, we repeat the operation from the beginning. Otherwise, we continue processing to determine the direction. Finally, once the direction is determined, a vocal notification is launched to notify the user about his next direction.

3.2   Continually Adaptive MeanShift (Camshift) for Target Color Detection

Color targets are a tracking symbols designed to solve the problem of environmental labelling [17]. They are distinctive and difficult to confuse with a typical background clutter and are detectable by a robust algorithm that can work very quickly on a smartphone. Based on the idea of [18], we added the fourth color to detect the last direction.

In our proposed system, the colour targets are represented as four squares giving a particular orientation (Fig. 2):

- Red: turn left
- Black: turn right
- Blue: moving forward
- Green: back off

Fig. 2. Color targets (Color figure online)

Then, whenever the target is detected, the system provides a vocal directional orientation (for example "turn left") to guide the visually impaired to its desired destination from its current location.

In the step of color detection of the target, we use color recognition algorithms mainly Camshift.

Furthermore, Camshift (Continually Adaptive MeanShift) is an important algorithm for object tracking based on the color histogram [16]. The algorithm is based on finding the probability distribution map in a search window and iteratively updates the position and size of the window to convergence.

3.3   Camshift Algorithm

The Camshift algorithm uses the meanshift algorithm [16] in a loop varying the size of the window until convergence.

The window in the mean shift is applied with a given size. After convergence, the procedure is re-iterated with a new window, centred on the position found by the mean shift, but with a size depending on the zero order moment of the spatial distribution of the pixels probability previously calculated by the mean shift [16].

The different stages of Cam-shift are as follows:

- Initialize the window W: position and size.
- As long as W is moved with a certain threshold and the maximum number of iterations is not reached:

- Apply the mean shift; keep the center (x_c, y_c) and the zeo-order moment M_{oo}
- The window W will be centered on (x_c, y_c) with the width $w = 2\sqrt{\frac{M_{00}}{256}}$ and the height $h = 1.2\,w$

Cam-shift is mainly used in the image segmentation. In fact, after convergence of the mean shift, the height of the window is chosen 20% greater than its width, but this choice is arbitrary and can be changed according to the application.

4   Results and Discussion

In this section, we present the test conditions and the results of target detection and recognition depending on the distance, the angle of view and the luminosity. In addition, we worked on measuring variables (distance, angle, illumination) because of the sensitivity of mobile application in natural indoor environment conditions.

4.1   Target Detection

The tests are performed in real time in indoor scene. We used the mobile application (GuiderMoi) with variation on the distance, the angle of view and the illumination values (Fig. 3).

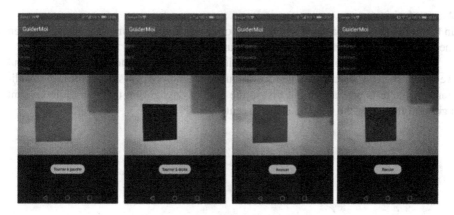

Fig. 3. The mobile application (GuiderMoi) detecting targets

Distances

First, we choose a reference angle of 90° and we change the distance between the target and the smartphone's camera calculated in centimetres.

Then, for each selected distance, we detect the target and we repeat the test ten times. Then we calculate the number of successful tests.

In addition, the tests are carried out first in the case of daylight in the case of fluorescent light and finally in the case of incandescent light.

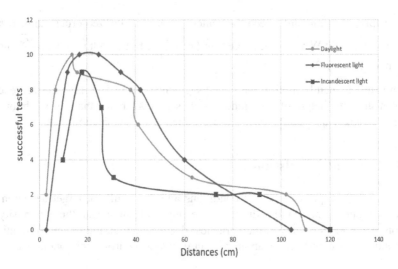

Fig. 4. Variation of successful tests by distance in the case of daylight, fluorescent light and incandescent light (Color figure online)

Furthermore, Fig. 4 shows that the target is well detected in the case of daylight but we notice that the detection range increases in the case of fluorescent light and decreases in the case of incandescent light.

Angle of vision

In this test, we choose a reference distance of 25 cm and we change the angle between the target and the smartphone camera calculated in degrees.

For each selected angle, we use the application (GuiderMoi) to detect the target and we repeat the test ten times. Then we calculate the number of successful tests. Additionally, the tests are carried out first in the case of daylight, in the case of fluorescent light and finally in the case of incandescent light (Fig. 5).

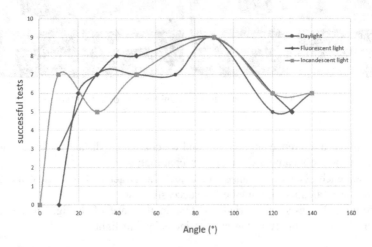

Fig. 5. Variation of successful tests by viewing angle case of daylight, fluorescent light and incandescent light (Color figure online)

We notice in Fig. 5 that the detection ranges with respect to daylight increases in the case of fluorescent light and decreases in the case of incandescent light.

4.2 Discussion

First, we tested the mobile application (GuiderMoi) under different conditions mainly distance, angle of view and illumination. We noticed that the colour of the targets was well chosen and their detection is robust especially for the red and the black targets. Then, in the case of illumination, the detection is better in the case of the fluorescent light since it is white and has no influence on the colours.

Moreover, for the distance between the target and the user, the detection is between 15 and 30 cm and the optimal distances are 25 cm. In addition, for the viewing angle, the best position is 90°.

Furthermore, for time processing, the mobile application (GuiderMoi) has the advantage of being in real time. Unfortunately, we have a loss of detection at distance greater than 1 m. In fact, the target becomes smaller and more difficult to identify. At a short distance, we get the reflection of the smartphone on the target that gives false colour detection. Besides, the user has to be exactly in front of the target in order to have a robust detection. We have a total loss of detection at the limits of the target that is to say at an angle of 0° and 180°. The navigation tests were successful in the case of fluorescent light, the user in front of the target with a distance equal to 25 cm.

There are some limitations to our approach. The first is that we are only using the Hue component of the HSV color space. This means that unless the object we are trying to track is not a single shade, then the results will likely be suboptimal.

To remedy this, we can simply extend the code to compute a 2D histogram using both the Hue and Saturation components. However, OpenCV currently does not support 3D histograms in the back projection calculation and Cam-Shift tracking.

The second limitation is tuning the number of bins in the color histogram. This will depend on many aspects, including the application conditions. We need to tune this parameter for our application.

Finally, if we are looking for a more robust tracking solution that can take into account texture and localized features, we should look into keypoints detection, local invariant descriptors (ex. DoG and SIFT), and matching between the sets of keypoints and their corresponding features.

5 Conclusion

In this paper, we propose a navigation system based on mobile application "GuiderMoi" to provide assistance for visually impaired in indoor environment. In fact, the mobile application provides information about directions and helps the visually impaired to navigate effectively and independently based on colour targets detection and identification. In future research, it would be interesting to study how we can improve mobile applications using augmented reality and intelligent navigation based on deep learning.

References

1. Ivanov, R.: Indoor navigation system for visually impaired. In: Proceedings of the 11th International Conference on Computer Systems and Technologies and Workshop for PhD Students in Computing on International Conference on Computer Systems and Technologies (2010)
2. Guerrero, L.A., Vasquez, F., Ochoa, S.F.: An indoor navigation system for the visually impaired. Sensors **12**(6), 8236–8258 (2012)
3. Cheraghi, S.A., Namboodiri, V., Walker, L.: GuideBeacon: beacon-based indoor wayfinding for the blind, visually impaired, and disoriented. In: IEEE International Conference on Pervasive Computing and Communications (PerCom). IEEE (2017)
4. Legge, G.E., et al.: Indoor navigation by people with visual impairment using a digital sign system. PloS one **8**(10), e76783 (2013)
5. Bach-y-Rita, P., Hughes, B.: Tactile vision substitution: some instrumentation and perceptual considerations. In: Warren, D.H., Strelow, E.R. (eds.) Electronic Spatial Sensing for the Blind, NATO ASI Series (Series E: Applied Sciences), vol. 99, pp. 171–186. Springer, Dordrecht (1985). https://doi.org/10.1007/978-94-017-1400-6_11
6. Kaczmarek, K.A.: The tongue display unit (TDU) for electro-tactile spatiotemporal pattern presentation. Scientia Iranica. Trans. D Comput. Sci. Eng. Electr. Eng. **18**(6), 1476–1485 (2011)
7. Meijer, P.B.L.: An experimental system for auditory image representations. IEEE Trans. Biomed. Eng. **39**, 112–121 (1992)
8. Capelle, C., Trullemans, C., Arno, P., Veraart, C.: A real-time experimental prototype for enhancement of vision rehabilitation using auditory substitution. IEEE Trans. Biomed. Eng. **45**, 1279–1293 (1998)
9. Durette, B., Louveton, N., Alleysson, D., Hérault, J.: Visuo-auditory sensory substitution for mobility assistance: testing TheVIBE (2008)
10. Bologna, G., Deville, B., Pun, T., Vinckenbosch, M.: Transforming 3D coloured pixels into musical instrument notes for vision substitution applications. EURASIP J. Image Video Process. **2007**, 14 (2007). https://doi.org/10.1155/2007/76204
11. Manduchi, R., Coughlan, J., Ivanchenko, V.: Search strategies of visually impaired persons using a camera phone wayfinding system. In: Miesenberger, K., Klaus, J., Zagler, W., Karshmer, A. (eds.) ICCHP 2008. LNCS, vol. 5105, pp. 1135–1140. Springer, Heidelberg (2008). https://doi.org/10.1007/978-3-540-70540-6_170
12. Alnfiai, M.: VirtualEyez: developing NFC technology to enable the visually impaired to shop independently. Dalhousie University Halifax, Nova Scotia (2014)
13. Rassmus-Gröhn, K.: Enabling Audio-Haptics. Department of Design Sciences, Lund University (2006)
14. Coughlan, J., Manduchi, R., Shen, H.: Cell phone-based wayfinding for the visually impaired. In: 1st International Workshop on Mobile Vision, Graz, Austria (2006)
15. Bradski, G., Kaehler, A.: Learning OpenCV: Computer Vision with the OpenCV Library. ACM Digital Library, New York (2008)
16. Jog, A., Halbe, S.: Object tracking using camshift algorithm in open CV. Int. J. Sci. Res. **1**(6), 37–39 (2012)

17. Comaniciu, D., Meer, P.: Mean shift: a robust approach toward feature space analysis. IEEE Trans. Pattern Anal. Mach. Intell. **24**, 603–619 (2002)
18. Coughlan, J., Manduchi, R.: A mobile phone wayfinding system for visually impaired users. Smith-Kettlewell Eye Research Institute San Francisco (2009)

Older People's Needs and Opportunities for Assistive Technologies

Jeffrey Soar, Lei Yu[⊠], and Latif Al-Hakim

University of Southern Queensland, Toowoomba, QLD 4350, Australia
{Jeffrey.Soar,Latif.Al-Hakim}@usq.edu.au,
Yulei19900803@gmail.com

Abstract. Older adults experience a disconnect between their needs and adoption of technologies that have potential to assist and to support more independent living. This paper reviewed research that links people's needs with opportunities for assistive technologies. It searched 13 databases identifying 923 papers with 34 papers finally included for detailed analysis. The research papers identified needs in the fields of health, leisure, living, safety, communication, family relationship and social involvement. Amongst these, support for activities of daily living category was of most interest. In specific sub-categories, the next most reported need was assistive technology to support walking and mobility followed by smart cooking/kitchen technology and assistive technology for social contacts with family member/other people. The research aimed to inform a program of research into improving the adoption of technologies where they can ameliorate identified needs of older people.

Keywords: Older people · Needs · Assistive technologies · Systematic review

1 Introduction

Global life expectancy rose from 64.2 years in 1990 to 72.6 years in 2019 [1]. There is increasing interest in and availability of support for people choosing to remain in their own homes and delay or avoid moving to institutional care, with an increasing need to improve access to services at home in health management, rehabilitation nursing and entertainment [2]. This research aimed to identify the state of matching needs with technologies focusing on support in the home environment to support independence in everyday activities. Important technology features include ease of use, security, safety, reliability and use independency as important factors in adoption of assistive technology [3]. There is a need for greater awareness of what smart home and assistive technologies are needed to guide technology developers as well as to increase the understanding of potential users of what is available and how it might benefit them.

"Assistive technology" is an umbrella term referring to a range of specialized technology used by people to support activities of daily living and specific tasks [4]. It is about the use of an array of electronic devices incorporated into everyday objects in order to monitoring the user's status and provide assistance as needed, including feedback, guidance, alerts or warnings [5]. Assistive technology has evolved with and emerged from information technology, passing from detecting and reporting problems, to assisting

M. Jmaiel et al. (Eds.): ICOST 2020, LNCS 12157, pp. 404–414, 2020.
https://doi.org/10.1007/978-3-030-51517-1_37

with prevention of ill-health and adverse events [6]. Smart home technologies refer to technology for clinical and wellness monitoring of people in their homes and/or promotes independence and quality of life [7]. The smart home and assistive technologies mentioned in this literature review covers use in both indoors and outdoors.

This paper aims to address three issues. First, to review the needs of older people for assistive technologies and smart home technologies by identifying relevant research. The methods involved searching bibliographic databases, to screen according to inclusion and exclusion criteria. Second, the paper aims to map needs with available smart home and assistive technologies according to the findings from identified papers. Third, to identify the knowledge gap of needs from older people and the gap of awareness of technologies available.

2 Method - Search Strategy and Eligibility of Study Selection

A search was undertaken of 13 bibliographic databases which included: A). Academic Search Ultimate; B). AHFS Consumer Medication Information; C). Anthropology Plus; D). Applied Science & Technology Source Ultimate; E). Business Source Ultimate; F). CINAHL with Full Text; G). Health Business Elite; H). Health Source - Consumer Edition; I). Health Source: Nursing/Academic Edition; J). Humanities Source Ultimate; K). Mental Measurements Yearbook with Tests in Print; L). Psychology and Behavioral Sciences Collection; and M). Sociology Source Ultimate.

Key words for the search were "Older people", "Elderly", "Old aged people", "Assistive technologies" and "Smart Home Technologies". There were some synonyms because there is a range of terms that authors may use as keywords. No doubt there will be other relevant research into this topic that has escaped our search which is a limitation of this review.

Before the study, we formulated the eligibility criteria which included: A). the result must focus on older people, while other groups can be involved such as younger people with disabilities, but the result towards other groups must be separately demonstrated in the conclusion of the research; B). The research should be based on empirical evidence, observed and calculated from data, questionnaire or interview, not be discussion papers without a data collection; C). The research should discuss older people's needs that are significantly beneficial to quality of life, including independent living skills, satisfaction of living, mental status, social involvement, selection of aged care mode, relationship with relatives, etc.; D). The factors discussed in the research positively link to and enhance with greater opportunities of assistive technologies which help older people with quality of life but not in other fields; E). The result should be published within 5 years; F); and the paper should be published in English. According to the assistive technologies mentioned and related to older people's quality of life, to researcher's introduction, to what researchers observed in sociology experiment, we classified older people's needs. The following result showed older people's needs in each type.

3   Results

By searching in 13 bibliographic databases we yielded 923 results. We excluded 386 papers due to duplication leaving 537 studies for screening. Based on the exclusion and inclusion criteria, we identified 34 papers for detailed analysis.

Though different researchers classified older people's needs in various ways, this paper, which looks into their broad types of needs, required a comprehensive way of classification. Our classifications were informed by Lee and Lim, who divided older people's need into health, leisure, living/safety and family relationship [8]. They included both indoor and outdoor activities, both physical and mental health, both independent living and interaction with others, both self-well-being conditions and objective environment improvement. We found this approach useful to distinguish different kinds of needs towards technologies, it made fewer overlaps and mixes when mapping to older people's needs. Based on their method, we refined categories, as a result, this review classified older people's needs towards smart home and assistive technologies into health, leisure, living, safety, communication, family relationship and social involvement – 6 categories in total. The clear summary of categories, subcategories with frequencies and identified papers is shown in Table 1.

Among the 6 categories of needs of older people related to smart home and assistive technologies, "Living" category was the highest priority, which represented 40% of the total concerns, followed by "Safety" (16%), "Health" (15%), "Family Relationship and Social Involvement" (11%), "Leisure" (10%) and "Communication" (8%). Looking into subcategories of specific needs, walking and mobility assistance was the most needed, which was mentioned 16 times by identified researchers, represented 6.7% of the entire spectrum of older people's needs, followed by social contacts with family member/other people and smart cooking/kitchen technology, which both were mentioned 12 times by identified researchers, represented 5.1% of the entire spectrum of older people's needs.

Relevant systematic reviews in the last 5 years used the keywords "Elderly", "Older people", "Smart Home Technologies" and "Assistive Technologies", our search found 26 relevant systematic reviews published. These were about older people's attitude to [9] or adoption of [10] technologies, as well as technology for specific disease [11–14], for social [15] and communication [16], for nursing or caregivers [17], for monitoring [18–20] and mental well-beings [21] - none of them were comprehensively about the whole spectrum of assistive technologies, at the same time, none of them comprehensively based on older people's broad spectrum of needs. here is a need for a review based on older people's needs that might be addressed by smart home and assistive technologies.

Table 1. The frequency of users' needs towards technologies

Category	Sub-category	References for articles mentioned	Frequency
Health	Sight/Vision Assistance Technology	[7, 9, 18, 21, 22, 26–28, 37]	9
	Long-term Pain Management	[12, 35]	2
	Rehabilitation Management	[16]	1
	Mood Recording/Management Technology	[6, 19, 24, 27, 30]	5
	Medication Reminder/Treatment	[6, 11, 17–19, 22, 27, 28]	8
	General Health Monitoring Technology	[6, 9, 21, 28, 31]	5
	Cognitive Ability Assistance Technology	[21, 26–28, 30]	5
	Nurse Call System	[6]	1
Leisure	General Recreational/Entertainment Technology	[7, 32]	2
	Tailored Games	[6, 7, 10, 16, 18–20, 34]	8
	Sports Assistive Technology	[7, 25, 28]	3
	Musical Instrument Playing Assistance	[6, 7, 16, 19, 34]	5
	Television and radio	[6, 9, 37]	3
	Travel Assistance	[30]	1
	Education Technology	[6, 32]	2
Living	Automatic Control Technology for Home Appliance	[6, 9, 11, 15, 17, 18, 22, 28, 31, 38]	10
	Gardening/Farming Assistance	[7, 27]	2
	Smart Cooking/Kitchen Technology	[7, 11, 13, 16–18, 21, 22, 24, 27–29]	12
	Toilet Use Assistance	[13, 17, 21, 22, 24, 27–29, 31]	9
	Cleaning and Laundry Assistance	[11, 17, 18, 21, 22, 24, 27–29, 35]	10
	Reaching and Grasping Technology	[9, 15, 16, 18, 21, 22, 24, 27, 29, 38]	10
	Showering Assistance	[13, 16, 18, 21, 22, 24, 27–29, 38]	10
	Dressing Assistance	[17, 18, 21, 22, 24, 27–29]	8
	Walking and Mobility Assistance	[9, 16–22, 24–27, 29, 31, 35, 38]	16
	Eating Reminder and Assistance	[17, 21, 24, 27, 28]	5
	Item Locating System	[11, 17, 28]	3

(*continued*)

Table 1. (*continued*)

Category	Sub-category	References for articles mentioned	Frequency
Safety	Overall Sense of Safety	[3, 6, 25, 32, 33]	5
	Falling Prevention	[17, 18, 23, 28, 31, 35, 38]	7
	Reminder for Declined Memory	[11, 15, 17, 22, 26, 34]	6
	Home/Location Finding Technology	[17, 21, 23, 28, 34, 35]	6
	Technology of Emergency Response/Warning about Potential Hazards	[13, 22–24, 30, 31, 34, 35]	8
	Gas Leakage Detector	[6, 13]	2
	Transportation Assistance	[9, 21, 22]	3
Family Relationship and Social Involvement	Finance Managing Assistance	[7, 17]	2
	Appointment/Issue Reminding Technology	[9, 17, 18, 28, 34]	5
	Shopping Assistance/Delivery	[17, 18, 22, 28, 30]	5
	Video Call System	[6]	1
	Assistance of Social Contacts with Family Member/Other People	[6, 10, 14, 17, 21, 26, 27, 29, 30, 32, 36, 37]	12
	Relative Recognizing Technology	[17]	1
Communication	Personal Communication Technology	[7, 9, 14, 18, 30, 34, 36]	7
	Smart Phone and Computer	[7, 9, 11, 23, 26, 34]	6
	Companionship Technology/Robots	[8, 14, 16, 18, 19, 36, 38]	7
Total			238

4   Discussion

There are three potential ways to link older people with assistive technologies or smart home technologies. The first one is to develop or innovate technologies as the initial activity and then promote the technology to older people and finally evaluate the result of impact. However, technologies that are acquired in ways that are not congruent with seniors' personal needs and circumstances run a higher risk of proving to be ineffective or inappropriate resulting in poor levels of adoption [22]. The second way is to focus on older people's attitude and adoption upon assistive technologies - to optimize user acceptance towards products by identifying and eliminating the barriers of adoption.

This includes research that looked at user attitude and acceptance and examined social factors which appropriately supports the relationship between users and service providers [23]. The third way is to listen to older people's needs and develop, optimize the technologies in specific orientation. Because some older adults experience a misfit between technology and needs, they must see the value of a device to use it [24]. The research reported on in this paper follows the third way, which looks into older people's detailed and specific needs at the beginning. the paper reviews the existed smart home and assistive technologies that cope with the needs, moreover, the direction of technologies' innovation.

To investigate older people's needs, much of the extant research reports on projects that chose the direct way, either by observing the phenomena or by analyzing data and transcript: 11 research reports tested the needs by enrolling older people into a clinical trial, project and intervention/control group to be observed and tested for the performance in real scenario; 20 research reports acquired the answer by questionnaire, survey, face-to-face or telephone interview, and derive the information from the data.

The existing literature reports on research that identified older people's needs of sight/vision assistance technology, long-term pain and rehabilitation management, mood recording/management technology, medication reminder/treatment, nurse call system, general health monitoring and cognitive ability assistance technology. We found the focus was mostly on the need for sight/vision assistance technology (represented 25% in this category), medication reminder/treatment (represented 22% in this category) and general health monitoring technology (represented 14% in this category). At this point, the highly recommended technologies were low vision assistive devices [25], health monitoring robots [26] and e-readers [27].

As for the needs for leisure, research results indicated that older people had the need for general recreational/entertainment technology, tailored games, sports assistive technology, musical instrument playing assistance, television and radio, travel assistance and education technology. We found that tailored games attracted 33% of research focus, which was the most needed by older people in this category. It was followed by 21% research results seeking for the technology for playing musical instrument. Game system, movie/music player [8], and entertainment console [28] were the most preferred.

The very significant category, living, represented of almost half of older people's needs towards smart home and assistive technologies. To be specific, walking and mobility assistance were the most focused (represented 25% in this category), followed by smart cooking/kitchen technology (represented 13% in this category). Older people had a rather broad range of needs in everyday living, including automatic control technology for home appliance, gardening/farming assistance, smart cooking/kitchen technology, toilet use assistance, cleaning and laundry assistance, reaching and grasping technology, shower assistance, dressing assistance, walking and mobility assistance, eating reminder and assistance and item locating system. Researchers found physical activity stimulation, home automation [27], smart power outlet, universal remote control [29] to be appropriate for older people.

Safety is a critical aspect for older people's both indoor and outdoor activities. according to identified papers, older people were concerned about overall sense of safety, falling prevention, reminder for declined memory, home/location finding technology, technology of emergency response/warning about potential hazards, gas leakage detector and transportation assistance. There was no doubt that technology of emergency response/warning about potential hazards was the most focused one (represented 22% in this category), followed by falling prevention (represented 19% in this category). Alarm system [30] was the most significant technology, together with gas/smoke sensor [29] and emergency call devices [31].

Communication, family relationship and social involvement played an important role in older people's mental health. Nine types of needs were identified, including finance managing assistance, appointment/issue reminding technology, shopping assistance/delivery, video call system, assistance of social contacts with family member/other people, relative recognizing technology, personal communication technology, companionship technology/robots, smart phone and computer. Among them, assistance of social contacts with family member and companionship technology/robots were pointed out by 45% of the researchers concentrating on this field. Video call system and social robots [32, 33] were the most recommended technologies.

Researchers looked into older people's target [25] and expectations [30, 34, 35] towards assistive technology, or just set the feature of a specific type assistive technologies [36] but did not include comprehensive view of assistive technologies. Some of the previous research focused on motivations [37, 38], barriers [39] and effectiveness [26] of smart home and assistive technologies – they focused more on adoption [8, 40, 41] than needs. Looking at the range of assistive technologies mentioned in the research, some research was broad enough but not specified, which just mentioned the whole range of assistive technology [42–45] or technology used in a very broad field [24, 46–50]. This is not useful enough to guide technology developers to map their detailed products to older people. On the other hand, some research provided very narrow view of assistive technologies [3, 28, 32, 33, 51–53], with only one or two specific technologies introduced.

There appears to be a need for an effective way to analyze and predict older people's needs that can be matched with the assistive technologies that are available.

5   Conclusion

There is existing literature into older people's needs in the field of health, leisure, living, safety, communication, family relationship and social involvement. Among them, living category was of most interest. To be more specific, assistive technology for walking and mobility were of the most interest by researchers. The information was gained mostly by interview, telephone talk, home visit or observation in a project. Though these methods were direct, liable, accurate, they were less efficient by directly interacting with older people, who might not be able to express their needs well because of inadequate awareness of technology or chronic disease that hinders the ability of communication. Another way to link older people's needs with technologies was to apply a technology push to older people and check the effectiveness and adoption, which may then cause misfit between older adults' needs and available technology. A better way may be needed to explore the opportunities for smart homes and assistive technologies neither by directly interviewing older people nor by technology push. One suggestion is that researchers can look into databases related to older people's health and quality of life – by analyzing the significant associating factors related to older people's independent living, smart home and assistive technologies contributing these factors, which can be referred as the future needed ones. The other solution might be seeking older people's needs in aged care service provision. To sum up, better method of exploring older people's needs and market demand of assistive technologies are required, broader types of older people's needs are to be discovered, at the same time, more types of assistive technologies are to be suggested by further research.

References

1. United Nations, World Population Prospects 2019, in Highlights, p. 2. United Nations, New York (2019)
2. Chen, F., Fang, C.: The functional weakening of family support for the aged and the outlet: the research on the elderly supporting model in the underdeveloped rural areas. Popul. Dev. **20**(1), 99–106 (2014)
3. Mattie, J., et al.: User perceptions of existing home access solutions and a novel home access device. Disabil. Rehabil. Assist. Technol. **11**(8), 668–677 (2016)
4. Blackman, S., et al.: Ambient assisted living technologies for aging well: a scoping review. J. Intell. Syst. **25**(1), 55–69 (2016)
5. Bruno, B., Sebastien, G., Bouchard, B. (eds.): Smart Technologies in Healthcare. Taylor & Francis Group, Abingdon (2017)
6. Alexandru, A., Ianculescu, M.: Enabling assistive technologies to shape the future of the intensive senior-centred care: a case study approach. Stud. Inf. Control **26**(3), 343–352 (2017)
7. Demiris, G., Hensel, B.K.: Technologies for an aging society: a systematic review of "smart home" applications. IMIA Yearb. Med. Inf. **2008**, 33–40 (2008)
8. Lee, S.-H.L., Lim, C.-H., Lee, S.: Needs and perceptions with smart technology usage in the elderly care facilities. Int. J. Contents **11**(4), 25–30 (2015)
9. Larsen, S.M., Mortensen, R.F., Kristensen, H.K., Hounsgaard, L.: Older adults' perspectives on the process of becoming users of assistive technology: a qualitative systematic review and meta-synthesis. Disabil. Rehabil. Assist. Technol. **14**(2), 182–193 (2019)
10. Yusif, S., Soar, J., Hafeez-Baig, A.: Older people, assistive technologies, and the barriers to adoption: a systematic review. Int. J. Med. Inform. **94**, 112–116 (2016)
11. Brims, L., Oliver, K.: Effectiveness of assistive technology in improving the safety of people with dementia: a systematic review and meta-analysis. Aging Ment. Health **23**(8), 942–951 (2019)
12. Klimova, B., Valis, M., Kuca, K.: Exploring assistive technology as a potential beneficial intervention tool for people with Alzheimer's disease – a systematic review. Neuropsych. Dis. Treat. **14**, 3151–3158 (2018)
13. Ienca, M., et al.: Intelligent assistive technology for Alzheimer's disease and other dementias: a systematic review. J. Alzheimer's Dis. **56**(4), 1301–1340 (2017)
14. Dias, B.: Older adults with Alzheimer's disease: a systematic review about the Occupational Therapy intervention in changes of performance skills. Braz. J. Occup. Ther./Cadernos Brasileiros de Terapia Ocupacional **26**(4), 926–942 (2018)

15. Góngora Alonso, S., Hamrioui, S., de la Torre Díez, I., Motta Cruz, E., López-Coronado, M., Franco, M.: Social robots for people with aging and dementia: a systematic review of literature. Telemed. e-Health **25**(7), 533–540 (2019)
16. Pedrozo Campos Antunes, T., et al.: Assistive technology for communication of older adults: a systematic review. Aging Ment. Health **23**(4), 417–427 (2019)
17. Madara Marasinghe, K.: Assistive technologies in reducing caregiver burden among informal caregivers of older adults: a systematic review. Disabil. Rehabil. Assist. Technol. **11**(5), 353–360 (2016)
18. Lussier, M., et al.: Early detection of mild cognitive impairment with in-home monitoring sensor technologies using functional measures: a systematic review. IEEE J. Biomed. Health Inform. **23**(2), 838–847 (2019)
19. Talal, M., et al.: Smart home-based iot for real-time and secure remote health monitoring of triage and priority system using body sensors: multi-driven systematic review. J. Med. Syst. **43**(3), 1 (2019)
20. Liu, L., Stroulia, E., Nikolaidis, I., Miguel-Cruz, A., Rios, Rincon A.: Smart homes and home health monitoring technologies for older adults: a systematic review. Int. J. Med. Inform. **91**, 44–59 (2016)
21. Scoglio, A.A., Reilly, E.D., Gorman, J.A., Drebing, C.E.: Use of social robots in mental health and well-being research: systematic review. J. Med. Internet Res. **21**(7), e13322 (2019)
22. Peek, S.T.M., et al.: Origins and consequences of technology acquirement by independent-living seniors: towards an integrative model. BMC Geriatr. **17**(1), 1–18 (2017). https://doi.org/10.1186/s12877-017-0582-5
23. Halloran, J.: The human element: social leveraging of user engagement with assisted living technology. Interact. Comput. **29**(3), 438–454 (2017)
24. Karlsen, C., Ludvigsen, M., Moe, C.E., Haraldstad, K., Thygesen, E.: Experiences of community-dwelling older adults with the use of telecare in home care services: a qualitative systematic review. JBI Database Syst. Rev. Implement. Rep. **15**(12), 2913–2980 (2017)
25. Casten, R., Rovner, B.W., Fontenot, J.L.: Targeted vision function goals and use of vision resources in ophthalmology patients with age-related macular degeneration and comorbid depressive symptoms. J. Vis. Impairment Blindness **110**(6), 413–424 (2016)
26. Shishehgar, M., Kerr, D., Blake, J.: The effectiveness of various robotic technologies in assisting older adults. Health Inform. J. **25**(3), 892–918 (2019)
27. Peek, S.T.M., Wouters, E.J., Luijkx, K.G., Vrijhoef, H.J.: What it takes to successfully implement technology for aging in place: focus groups with stakeholders. J. Med. Internet Res. **18**(5), e98 (2016)
28. Ku, A.: Fortune8: emotive family entertainment. In: International Conference Game & Entertainment Technologies, pp. 185–194 (2018)
29. Kamilaris, A., Kondepudi, S., Danial, N.: Understanding the activities and areas of concern of elderly population: the case of Singapore. Technol. Disabil. **27**(4), 141–153 (2016)
30. Burrows, A., Gooberman-Hill, R., Coyle, D.: Empirically derived user attributes for the design of home healthcare technologies. Pers. Ubiquit. Comput. **19**(8), 1233–1245 (2015). https://doi.org/10.1007/s00779-015-0889-1
31. Jännes, J., Hämäläinen, P., Hanski, J., Lanne, M.: Homelike living for elderly people: a needs-based selection of technological solutions. Home Health Care Manage. Pract. **27**(2), 64–72 (2015)
32. Chu, M.T., Khosla, R., Khaksar, S.M., Nguyen, K.: Service innovation through social robot engagement to improve dementia care quality. Assist. Technol. **29**(1), 8–18 (2017)

33. Bedaf, S., Marti, P., Amirabdollahian, F., de Witte, L.: A multi-perspective evaluation of a service robot for seniors: the voice of different stakeholders. Disabil. Rehabil. Assist. Technol. **13**(6), 592–599 (2018)

34. Nasr, N., et al.: The experience of living with stroke and using technology: opportunities to engage and co-design with end users. Disabil. Rehabil. Assis. Technol. **11**(8), 653–660 (2016)

35. Thoma-Lürken, T., Bleijlevens, M.H.C., Lexis, M.A.S., de Witte, L.P., Hamers, J.P.H.: Facilitating aging in place: a qualitative study of practical problems preventing people with dementia from living at home. Geriatr. Nurs. **39**(1), 29–38 (2018)

36. García-Soler, Á., et al.: Inclusion of service robots in the daily lives of frail older users: a step-by-step definition procedure on users' requirements. Arch. Gerontol. Geriatr. **74**, 191–196 (2018)

37. Andrews, J.A., Brown, L.J., Hawley, M.S., Astell, A.J.: Older adults' perspectives on using digital technology to maintain good mental health: interactive group study. J. Med. Internet Res. **21**(2), e11694 (2019)

38. Smaerup, M., Grönvall, E., Larsen, S.B., Laessoe, U., Henriksen, J.J., Damsgaard, E.M.: Exercise gaming – a motivational approach for older adults with vestibular dysfunction. Disabil. Rehabil. Assist. Technol. **12**(2), 137–144 (2017)

39. Egan, K.J., Pot, A.M.: Encouraging innovation for assistive health technologies in dementia: barriers, enablers and next steps to be taken. J. Am. Med. Dir. Assoc. **17**(4), 357–363 (2016)

40. Orellano-Colón, E.M., Rivero-Méndez, M., Lizama, M., Jutai, J.W.: Assistive technology unmet needs of independent living older Hispanics with functional limitations. Disabil. Rehabil. Assist. Technol. **13**(2), 194–200 (2018)

41. Doughty, K., Williams, G.: New models of assessment and prescription of smart assisted living technologies for personalised support of older and disabled people. J. Assist. Technol. **10**(1), 39–50 (2016)

42. Jiancaro, T., Jaglal, S.B., Mihailidis, A.: Technology, design and dementia: an exploratory survey of developers. Disabil. Rehabil. Assist. Technol. **12**(6), 573–584 (2017)

43. Orellano-Colón, E.M., Rivero-Méndez, M., Lizama, M., Jutai, J.W.: Development of an assistive technology intervention for community older adults. Phys. Occup. Ther. Geriatr. **35**(2), 49–66 (2017)

44. Meristö, T., Laitinen, J.: Digital innovations_opportunity to elderly people. In: Proceedings of ISPIM Conferences, pp. 1–6 (2018)

45. O'Connell, M., et al.: Anticipated needs and worries about maintaining independence of rural/remote older adults: opportunities for technology development in the context of the double digital divide. Gerontechnology **17**(3), 126–138 (2018)

46. Boman, I.-L., Persson, A.-C., Bartfai, A.: First steps in designing an all-in-one ICTbased device for persons with cognitive impairment: evaluation of the first mockup. J. Indian Acad. Geriatr. **12**(1), 28 (2016)

47. Löfqvist, C., Slaug, B., Ekström, H., Kylberg, M., Haak, M.: Use, non-use and perceived unmet needs of assistive technology among Swedish people in the third age. Disabil. Rehabil. Assist. Technol. **11**(3), 195–201 (2016)

48. D'Onofrio, G., et al.: Assistive robots for socialization in elderly people: results pertaining to the needs of the users. Aging Clin. Exp. Res. **31**(9), 1313–1329 (2019)

49. Mayer, P., Güldenpfennig, F., Panek, P.: Towards smart adaptive care toilets. Stud. Health Technol. Inf. **260**, 9–16 (2019)

50. Nguyen, T., Irizarry, C., Garrett, R., Downing, A.: Access to mobile communications by older people. Australas. J. Ageing **34**(2), E7–E12 (2015)

51. Saracchini, R., Catalina, C., Bordoni, L.: A mobile augmented reality assistive technology for the elderly. Tecnología asistencial móvil, con realidad aumentada, para las personas mayores. **23**(45), 65–73 (2015)
52. Callari, T.C., Moody, L., Magee, P., Yang, D.: 'Smart – not only intelligent!' co-creating priorities and design direction for 'smart' footwear to support independent ageing. Int. J. Fashion Des. Technol. Educ. **12**(3), 313–324 (2019)
53. Chang, R.C.-S., Lu, H.-P., Yang, P.: Stereotypes or golden rules? Exploring likable voice traits of social robots as active aging companions for tech-savvy baby boomers in Taiwan. Comput. Hum. Behav. **84**, 194–210 (2018)

Towards a Formal Context-Aware Workflow Model for Ambient Environment

Roumeissa Khennaoui[✉] and Nabil Belala[✉]

MISC Laboratory,University of Constantine 2 Abdelhamid Mehri,
Constantine, Algeria
{roumeissa.khennaoui,nabil.belala}@univ-constantine2.dz

Abstract. Ambient systems owns some particular characteristics that makes their context awareness a sincere problem; they are composed of heterogeneous distributed devices, some of these devices may appear and disappear during operations. In addition, users interacting in these systems are themselves dynamic. Therefore, context-aware workflow management allows workflows to adapt dynamically according to the environment changes. Context information are complex and diverse which makes the modeling the key issue. This paper presents an approach to model context-aware workflows. First, we describe the workflow using Ag-LOTOS. Then, based on this description, we build the contextual planning system *CPSw* that allows the presentation of the context at each activity state.

Keywords: Modeling of physical and conceptual information in smart environments · Context awareness · Ambient intelligence · Formal description · Workflow

1 Introduction

In order to meet the needs of everyday life, systems are becoming more and more complex, which leads to seek to give more atomicity and initiative to the different software modules. To respond to this technological evolution, ambient intelligence [1] is a new paradigm of distributed systems where the environment is aware of the user's needs and find a way to fulfill that need to improve the quality of people's life.

Due to the extreme mobility of users, ubiquitous software [2] run in a highly dynamic and varying environment. Therefore, context awareness [3] and context adaptation [4] are some important aspects for pervasive software that have to be aware of the context's changes, and dynamically adjust their execution [4]. Context-aware workflow [5] is an interesting field that allows workflows to adapt dynamically to the context changes in ubiquitous environment.

To achieve this goal, no many results have been accomplished in workflow's context modelling. [6] proposes a context-aware workflow management system

© The Author(s) 2020
M. Jmaiel et al. (Eds.): ICOST 2020, LNCS 12157, pp. 415–422, 2020.
https://doi.org/10.1007/978-3-030-51517-1_38

(WFMS) for navigation applications in ubiquitous computing. In [7], a dynamic context-aware access control for pervasive computing in enterprise environment is proposed. However, [8,9] allow users to model their daily activities in the form of workflow adaptable to context information. [10] proposes an approach to build a flexible model to adapt business process based on context. In [11], both the conceptual model and the workflow model are defined based on OWL.

Considering that the ambient systems manage our daily life such as smart hospital, smart home, robots, etc., errors are critical regarding human life. Many WFMS tools [12,13] exist and allow the modelling and verification of workflows. However, mathematical approaches are proved to be more effective [14]. [15] describes the workflow patterns in the formal specification language LOTOS [16]. In addition, [17] proposes an approach to specify and verify the service composition using LOTOS.

In this paper, we describe at first the workflow using Ag-LOTOS [18], a formal specification model based on LOTOS. Ag-LOTOS is a formal technique based on process algebra that allows to formally describe the workflow and to verify properties on the model. Then, the contextual planning system of the workflow (CPSw) [19] is built based on the semantics of Ag-LOTOS constrained by contextual information. Unlike the previous work, our approach allows a formal description of the context as *pre*- and *post*-condition in each state of all the possible traces and adjust the changes dynamically. The proposed model can be used in the verification process to check some contextual properties.

2 The Context-Aware Workflow Model

2.1 Ag-LOTOS for Workflows

Business Process Management (BPM) has been defined by van der Alast as "a way to support business processes using methods, technique and software to model, execute, control and analyze operational processes involving humans, organizations, applications, documents or any other source of information" [20]. However, a workflow can be defined as "business process automation during which documents, information or tasks are passed from one participant to another according to a set of process rules" [20]. A workflow pattern [21] represents the abstraction of most frequent activities sequence, and are composed when specifying new workflows.

In this section, we aim to use Ag-LOTOS [18] to improve workflow specification by including contextual information to each state of the workflow model, and by modeling the ambient characteristics such as communication and mobility that cause the dynamic changes of the context.

Similar to LOTOS [16], Ag-LOTOS concurrency allows the modeling of parallel activities. The Ag-LOTOS subsystem support allows the composition of workflow elements. Since Ag LOTOS is derived from LOTOS, we follow the procedure of mapping of the workflow patterns to LOTOS notation applied in [14] and citecite6 to give the suitable definition of each operator in the workflow context. To specify activities in details, we can simply model them with Ag-LOTOS sub-processes (hierarchy of processes). Note that Ag-LOTOS processes are used to model activities in the workflow. However, the process in the workflow context indicates a set of activities.

Ag-LOTOS expressions are written by composing actions through the LOTOS operators.

The syntax is defined as follows [18]:

$$P ::= E$$

$$E ::= exit|stop$$

$$a; E|E \odot E \quad (a \in \partial)$$

$$|hide\, L\, in\, E$$

$$\mathcal{H} ::= move(l) \quad (\mathcal{H} \subset \partial, l \in \ominus)$$

$$|x!(v)|x?(v) \quad (x \in \mathcal{U}, v \in \mathcal{M})$$

$$\odot ::= \{|[L]|, |||, \gg, [], \|, [>\}$$

Where ∂ is a finite set of observable actions, L is a subset of ∂ and $\mathcal{H} \subset \partial$ is the set of ambient intelligence primitives, which represent the mobility and the communication. $\ominus$ is the finite set of spatial localities of the pervasive environment, $\mathcal{U}$ is a finite or infinite set of users, with which the user can communicate, and $\mathcal{M}$ is the set of messages that can be sent or received.

An essential component of a process definition is its behavior expression E. A behavior expression is built by applying an operator, e.g., $\gg$, to other behavior expressions. A behavior expression may also include instantiations of other processes.

Termination. In Ag-LOTOS, the termination is represented via the operator *stop* witch indicates the inaction while the *exit* operator expresses the successful termination.

Fail. In $A = fail$, *fail* represents the fact that the execution of an activity A fails because of the dynamic context of the workflow.

Prefix. The operator ';' is used to prefix a behavior expression with an action to produce a new one. Note that actions are the elementary units executed by activities.

Hiding. *hide* is used to express the discriminator pattern (similar to LOTOS). An external gate is used to invoke the subprocess that enables the activity. This gate is hidden inside the discriminator to avoid any external synchronization (see [14, 15] for further details).

Respectively, the set $\odot$ represents the standard LOTOS operators.

Sequence. The sequential composition operator $\gg$ is used to represent the sequence pattern.

Cycle. A loop in a process allows the repetitive execution of activities, $P ::= E \gg P$.

Choice. $A[\,]B$, activity A or B will be chosen.

Disabling. During the activity execution, it is possible to indicate its failure with the disabling operator $[>$. $A\,[> B$ means activity A may be disabled by activity B which interrupts the main flow and uses *stop* instead of *exit*.

Parallelism (general case). $A\,||[L]|\,B$ means if the process (activity A) is ready to execute some action at one of the synchronization gates, it is forced, in the absence of alternative actions, to wait until the process (activity B) offers the same action.

Full Synchronization. $A\,||\,B$ means that if $L = \partial$, the two composed activities are forced to execute in complete synchronicity.

Pure Interleaving. If $L = \emptyset$, the absence of synchronization leads to the absence of interaction points among processes, this is achieved through the interleaving operator '$|||$'.

2.2 Contextual Planning System of the Workflow

In order to illustrate the concept of the formal design of workflows with the contextual information, the contextual planning system is built from an Ag-LOTOS specification using the rules in Table 1.

Table 1. The semantic rules.

Action:
$$\frac{ws \xrightarrow{a} ws' \quad a \in Act}{(ws, l) \xrightarrow{a} (ws', l)}$$

Mobility:
$$\frac{ws \xrightarrow{move(l')} ws' \quad (l \neq l')}{(ws, l) \xrightarrow{move(l')} (ws', l')}$$

Communication:
$(a)\dfrac{ws \xrightarrow{x!(u)} ws' \quad (u \in \mathcal{U})}{(ws, l) \xrightarrow{x!(u)} (ws', l)}$
$(b)\dfrac{ws \xrightarrow{x?(u)} ws' \quad (u \in \mathcal{U})}{(ws, l) \xrightarrow{x?(u)} (ws', l)}$

The Contextual Planning System of the Workflow (CPSw) based on CPS [22] takes into account two types of information: workflow planning state ws and locality l. Table 1 shows the operational semantic rules that define the possible planning state changes for the workflow. From an initial planning state (ws_0, l), we apply these rules to produce the CPSw. The contextual planning system CPSw is a labeled Kripke structure (S, s_0, Tr, L) where S is the set of contextual planning workflow states, $s_0 = (ws_0, l) \in S$ is the initial planning state of the workflow, $Tr \subseteq S \times \partial \cup \{T\} \times S$ is the set of transitions which are denoted $s \xrightarrow{a} s'$, and $L : S \to \ominus$ is the location labeling function.

3   Case Study

In this paper, we target on context-aware workflow models for ubiquitous company. Let there be an enterprise with several helpdesk employees associated with smart badges that provide the system with spatial information at each moment.

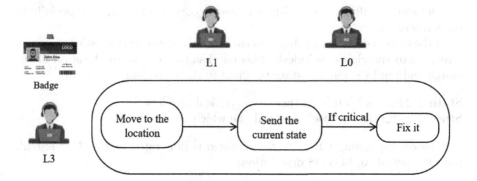

Fig. 1. The scenario that illustrate the case study.

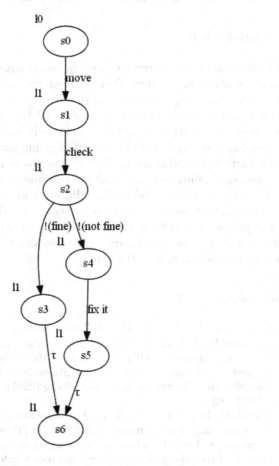

Fig. 2. The CPSw corresponding tot the case study.

The scenario illustrated in Fig. 1 is highly context dependent, especially in the following way:

If the system detects a problem on the switch in datacenter location, he sends a request to the closest helpdesk. This one has to move to the location of the switch and send the current state by email to the management system:

State 1 `fine`, indicate that there is no critical problem.
State 2 `not_fine`, in case of critical one which need to be fixed.

The corresponding CPSw to the scenario is illustrated in Fig. 2. It is built from the initial Ag-LOTOS description:

```
move(11); check;
    (x!(fine); exit [] x!(not_fine); fix_it(11); exit
```

4   Conclusion

Workflow systems are currently used by many organizations including health care, automation and finance. Context awareness is the ability for workflows to react to the changing situations. In this paper, we introduced a context-aware workflow model, the CPSw, that presents all the possible evolutions of workflow's activities constrained by the contextual information. CPSw is constructed formally based on Ag-LOTOS description giving the set of activities.

We learned that using Ag-LOTOS to describe workflow activities is a promising approach. Mainly, because it allows a formal description of the current context in each state as *pre*- and *post*-conditions, and dynamically adjusts the modifications. Furthermore, it allows the verification and validation of the model.

The proposed model can be used in the verification process to verify certain contextual properties. For future works, we aim to consider different types of context information such as the time.

References

1. Remagnino, P., Foresti, G.: Ambient intelligence: a new multidisciplinary paradigm. IEEE Trans. Syst. Man Cybern. - Part A: Syst. Hum. **35**(1), 1–6 (2004)
2. Ramos, C.: Ambient intelligence a state of the art from artificial intelligence perspective. In: Neves, J., Santos, M.F., Machado, J.M. (eds.) EPIA 2007. LNCS, vol. 4874, pp. 285–295. Springer, Heidelberg (2007). https://doi.org/10.1007/978-3-540-77002-2_24
3. Abowd, D., Dey, A.K., Orr, R., et al.: Context-awareness in wearable and ubiquitous computing. Virtual Reality **3**(3), 200–211 (1998)
4. Smanchat, S., Ling, S., Indrawan, M.: A survey on context-aware workflow adaptations. In: Proceedings of the 6th International Conference on Advances in Mobile Computing and Multimedia, pp. 414–417 (2008)
5. Wieland, M., Kopp, O., Nicklas, D., Leymann, F.: Towards context-aware workflows. In: CAiSE07 Proceedings of the Workshops and Doctoral Consortium, vol. 2, no. S25, p. 15 (2007)

6. Tang, F., Guo, M., Dong, M., Li, M., Guan, H.: Towards context-aware work-flow management for ubiquitous computing. In: 2008 International Conference on Embedded Software and Systems, pp. 221–228. IEEE (2008)
7. Zhu, Z., Xu, R.: A context-aware access control model for pervasive computing in enterprise environments. In: 2008 4th International Conference on Wireless Communications, Networking and Mobile Computing, pp. 1–6. IEEE (2008)
8. Avenoglu, B., Eren, P.E.: A context-aware and workflow-based framework for pervasive environments. J. Amb. Intell. Hum. Comput. 10(1), 215–237 (2019)
9. Carolis, B.D., Ferilli, S., Redavid, D.: Incremental learning of daily routines as workflows in a smart home environment. ACM Trans. Interact. Intell. Syst. (TiiS) 4(4), 1–23 (2015)
10. Da Cunha Mattos, T., Santoro, F.M., Revoredo, K., et al.: A formal representation for context-aware business processes. Comput. Ind. 65(8), 1193–1214 (2014)
11. Wang, P., Li, H., Zhang, B.: Context-aware workflow modeling approach using OWL. In: The 26th Chinese Control and Decision Conference (2014 CCDC), pp. 4161–4165. IEEE (2014)
12. Salimifard, K., Wright, M.: Petri net-based modelling of workflow systems: an overview. Eur. J. Oper. Res. 134(3), 664–676 (2001)
13. Sadiq, S., Orlowska, M., Sadiq, W., et al.: Data flow and validation in workflow modelling. In: Proceedings of the 15th Australasian Database Conference, vol. 27, pp. 207–214 (2004)
14. Carchiolo, V., Longheu, A., Malgeri, M.: Using LOTOS in workflow specification. In: ICEIS, no. 3, pp. 364–369 (2003)
15. Takecian, P. L., Ferreira, J. E., Malkowski, S., Pu, C.: Using LOTOS for rigorous specifications of workflow patterns. In: 6th International Conference on Collaborative Computing: Networking, Applications and Worksharing (CollaborateCom 2010), pp. 1–7. IEEE (2010)
16. Bolognesi, T., Brinksma, E.: Introduction to the ISO specification language LOTOS. Comput. Netw. ISDN Syst. 14(1), 25–59 (1987)
17. Dumez, C., Bakhouya, M., Gaber, J., Wack, M.: Formal specification and verification of service composition using LOTOS. In: Proceedings of the 7th ACM International Conference on Pervasive Services (2010)
18. Chaouche, A.C., Seghrouchni, A.E.F., Ilié, J.M.: A formal approach for contextual planning management: application to smart campus environment. In: Bazzan, A., Pichara, K. (eds.) IBERAMIA 2014. LNCS, vol. 8864, pp. 791–803. Springer, Cham (2014). https://doi.org/10.1007/978-3-319-12027-0_64
19. Chaouche, A.C., Seghrouchni, A.E.F., Ilié, J.-M., et al.: A higher-order agent model with contextual planning management for ambient systems. In: Kowalczyk, R., Nguyen, N. (eds.) Transactions on Computational Collective Intelligence XVI, pp 146–169. LNCS, vol. 8780. Springer, Heidelberg (2014). https://doi.org/10.1007/978-3-662-44871-7_6
20. van der Aalst, W., Ter Hofstede, A., Weske, M.: Business process management: A survey. In: van der Aalst, W.M.P., Weske, M. (eds.) BPM 2003. LNCS, vol. 2678, pp. 1–12. Springer, Heidelberg (2003). https://doi.org/10.1007/3-540-44895-0_1
21. van der Aalst, W., Ter Hofstede, A., Kiepuszewski, B., et al.: Workflow patterns. Distrib. Parallel Databases 14(1), 5–51 (2003)
22. Chaouche, A.C., Seghrouchni, A.E.F., Ilié, J.-M., et al.: From intentions to plans: a contextual planning guidance. In: Camacho, D., Braubach, L., Venticinque, S., Badica, C. (eds.) Intelligent Distributed Computing VIII. Studies in Computational Intelligence, vol. 570, pp. 403–413. Springer, Cham (2015). https://doi.org/10.1007/978-3-319-10422-5_42

The PULSE Project: A Case of Use of Big Data Uses Toward a Cohomprensive Health Vision of City Well Being

Domenico Vito[1]([⊠]), Manuel Ottaviano[2], Riccardo Bellazzi[1], Cristiana Larizza[1], Vittorio Casella[3], Daniele Pala[3], and Marica Franzini[3]

[1] Centre of Health Technologies, Università degli studi Pavia, Via Adolfo Ferrata 5, 27100 Pavia, Italy
dvito.pulse@gmail.com, {riccardo.bellazzi, cristiana.larizza}@unipv.it
[2] E.T.S.I. de Telecomunicació, Universidad Politécnica de Madrid, Madrid Av. Complutense, 30, 28040 Madrid, Spain
mottaviano@lst.tfo.upm.es
[3] Department of Civil Engineering and Architecture, Università degli studi Pavia, Via Adolfo Ferrata 5, 27100 Pavia, PV, Italy
{vittorio.casella, daniele.pala, marica.franzini}@unipv.it

Abstract. Despite the silent effects sometimes hidden to the major audience, air pollution is becoming one of the most impactful threat to global health. Cities are the places where deaths due to air pollution are concentrated most.

In order to correctly address intervention and prevention thus is essential to assest the risk and the impacts of air pollution spatially and temporally inside the urban spaces. PULSE aims to design and build a large-scale data management system enabling real time analytics of health, behaviour and environmental data on air quality. The objective is to reduce the environmental and behavioral risk of chronic disease incidence to allow timely and evidence-driven management of epidemiological episodes linked in particular to two pathologies; asthma and type 2 diabetes in adult populations. developing a policy-making across the domains of health, environment, transport, planning in the PULSE test bed cities.

Keywords: Air pollution · Health · Data platform · Participation

1 Introduction

Air pollution has become silently and hiddendly one of the most impactful menace to global health.

The European Environmental agency [1] estimates that premature deaths attributable to exposure to air pollution of fine matter particles reach are about 412 000 in over 41 EU countries. The exposure to NO2 and O3 concentrations on the same countries in 2016 has been around 71000 and 15000 respectively.

© The Author(s) 2020
M. Jmaiel et al. (Eds.): ICOST 2020, LNCS 12157, pp. 423–431, 2020.
https://doi.org/10.1007/978-3-030-51517-1_39

The health threat of air pollution remain located mostly in cities. But the effects does not only limitate on wellbeing, but are also econonomical. The most vulnerable to the risks are lower income socio-economic groups that nowadays are also the most exposed to environmental hazards.

Air pollution indeed does not represent only a sanitary issue: it's burden reflects also in increasing medical costs.

Air pollution thus, is a problem can be only addressed with a strategic vision can only be addressed with long term targeted policies, majorly in urban environments.

In the year 2015 ITU and the United Nations Economic Commission for Europe (UNECE) gave the definition of smart and sustainable city as "an innovative city that uses information and communication technologies (ICTs) and other means to improve quality of life, efficiency of urban operation and services, and competitiveness, while ensuring that it meets the needs of present and future generations with respect to economic, social, environmental as well as cultural aspects". This definition led also in 2016, in the United for Smart Sustainable Cities initiative (U4SSC). This open global platform responded to United Nations Sustainable Development Goal 11: "Make cities and human settlements inclusive, safe, resilient and sustainable.", offering an enabling environment to spread knowledge and innovation globally [2]. Also the health sector has been contaminated by this vision: the increase of social networking, cloud-based platforms, and smartphone apps that support data collection has enhance opportunities to collect data outside of the traditional clinical environment. Such informative explosion allowed patients to collect and share data among each other, their families and clinicians.

Patient-generated health data (PGHD) is defined as health-related data generated and recorded by or from patients outside of the clinical areas. This data could be an important resource available for patient, clinicians and decision makers to be used by to address a current or emerging health issue, and most of it is globally wide, also if they are integrated by information coming from diffuse sensory/IoT devices and Manually input voluntary data reported by the patients, caregivers, or generic citizen participation bring to shared decision-making. The definitions above helps to understand the context of PULSE project. PULSE aims to design and build a large-scale data management system enabling real time analytics of flows of personal data.

The objective is to reduce the environmental and behavioral risk of chronic disease incidence to allow timely and evidence-driven management of epidemiological episodes linked in particular to two pathologies; asthma and type 2 diabetes in adult populations. Developing a policy-making across the domains of health, environment, transport, planning in the PULSE test bed cities.

The project is currently active in eight pilot cities, Barcelona, Birmingham, New York, Paris, Singapore, Pavia, Keelung and Taiwan, following a participatory approach where citizen provide data through personal devices and the PulsAIR app, that are integrated with information from heterogeneous sources: open city data, health systems, urban sensors and satellites. PULSE foster long-term sustainability goal of establishing an integrated data ecosystem based on continuous large-scale collection of all stated heterogeneous data available within the smart city environment.

2 The PULSE Project

PULSE project is goaled on build a set of extensible models and technologies to predict, mitigate and manage health problems in cities and promote population health.

Currently PULSE is working in eight global cities. It harvest a multivariate data platform feed by open city data, data from health systems, urban and remote sensors and personal devices to minimize environmental and behavioral risk of chronic disease incidence and prevalence and enable evidence-driven and timely management of public health events and processes. The clinical is on asthma and Type 2 Diabetes in adult populations: the project has been pioneer in the development of dynamic spatio-temporal health impact assessments through exposure-risk simulation model with the support of WebGis for geolocated population-based data.

PULSE gives finally a more wide vision of wellbeing were it is intended also in the relationship with environmental conditions.

2.1 Data Collection Principles

Acquisition, systematization and correlation of large volumes of heterogeneous health, social, personal and environmental data is among the core and primary activities in the PULSE project.

The overall goal of the deployments involves deriving additional values from the acquired data, through: developing more comprehensive benchmarking and under-standing of the impact of social and environmental factors on health and wellbeing in urban communities, thereby broadening the scope of public health.

On this sake PULSE has developed tools for end-users (primarily citizens and patients, public health institutions and city services) that leverage open, crowd-sourced and remote sensing data, through integration, enrichment and improved accuracy/reliability of risk models, to guide actions and deliver interventions aiming to mitigate asthma and T2D risk and improve healthy habits and quality of life.

Figure 1 shows the conceptual schema of the relationships among dataflows.

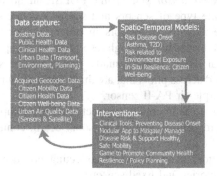

Fig. 1. PULSE data flow conceptual structure. The figure shows the collected data clustered on the basis of macro pourpouses

2.2 Clinical Focus

PULSE project focuses on the link between air pollution and the respiratory disease of Asthma, and between physical inactivity and the metabolic disease of Type 2 Diabetes. The risk assessment for this two pathologies comprises the evaluation respectively of:

- *for type 2 diabetes:* behavioural risks associated (i.e. reduced exercise/physical activity at home or in public places). This is associated with higher risk of T2D onset in a dose-response relationship. The assessment use unobtrusive sensing/data collection and volunteered data to collect baseline measures of health and wellbeing, and tracking and model mobility at home and across the city (including time, frequency and route of mode of transit and/or movement).
- *for asthma:* Environmental/exposure risks (i.e. exposure to air pollution, especially with regard to near roadway air pollution). Poor air quality is associated with higher risk of Asthma onset and exacerbation.

Risks of diseases onset are evaluated thorough risk assessment models, that in PULSE are biometric simulation models that predict the risk of the onset of the ashtma and diabetes in relationship to air quality.

The models has been developed by chosen ones from a literature review of the prediction models of type 2 diabetes (T2D) onset and asthma adult-onse. Some of them were selected to be implemented and recalibrated on the datasets available on PULSE repository and adding new variables [12].

2.3 Data Architecture

PULSE architecture is composed by 5 main structures [15]: PULSEAir, App Server, AIR Quality distributed sensor system, GisDB, WebGIS and Personal DB.

- *PULSE App:* is the personal App provided to the participants in charge of collecting sensors data and interacting with the users to propose interventions and gamification. PulsAIR is available both for iOS and Android and can be connected to FitBit, Garmin and Asus health tracker devices.
- *AIR Quality distributed sensor system:* the PULSE air quality sensor's system is composed of multiple type of sensors and sensor's datasets: it combines mobile sensors and mobile network of sensors in order monitor the variable trends in emission within urban areas with an high resolution and to appropriately address the temporal and spatial scales where usually pollutants are spread. Two types of sensors has been used across pilots that are the AQ10x of DunavNet (20+, deployed in all pilots) and PurpleAir PA-II sensor.
- *App Server:* This structure internally connects PULSE components.
- *Personal DB:* This repository contains personal detail, connectivity, activity logs, pilot sites structured data, etc....
- *GISDB:* This repository is in charge of collecting non-personal sources of data: satellite, open repositories and fixed sensors.
- *WebGIS:* This data engine is in charge of aggregating and exploiting all the collected data to build front-end visualizations through maps.

3 Well Being Model and Urban Wellbeing

The WHO definition of health includes reference to wellbeing: health is "a state of complete physical, mental and social wellbeing and not merely the absence of disease or infirmity" [4]. Wellbeing is a dynamic construct comprised of several dimensions. In a cohomprensive view of wellness can be defined 3 main domain of wellness: the psycological health, the physical health and the subjective wellbeing. Subjective wellbeing (SWB) is often measured via validated psychometric scales, and individual and community surveys. Subjective wellbeing is linked to Health-Related Quality of Life (HRQoL) but is not synonymous with it. The factors identified as the most important for subjective wellbeing vary across space, time and cultural context (Fig. 2).

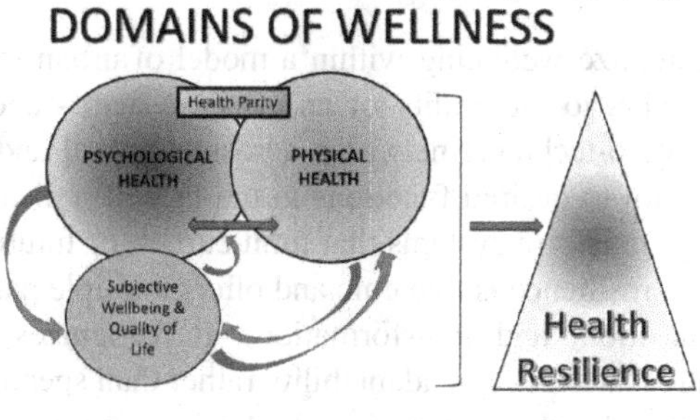

Fig. 2. Model of the domains of wellness

Wellness entails contemporary also the simultaneous fulfillment of the three types of needs. Personal needs (e.g., health, self-determination, meaning, spirituality, and opportunities for growth), are intimately tied to the satisfaction of collective needs such as adequate health care, environmental protection, welfare policies, and a measure of economic equality; for citizens require public resources to pursue private aspirations and maintain their health. Wellness also concerns relational needs. Two sets of needs are primordial in pursuing healthy relationships among individuals and groups: respect for diversity and collaboration and democratic participation.

Most approaches to community wellbeing (or its associated terms) follow a components approach: the majority of them have, at their core, an emphasis on individual wellbeing. PULSE has focused on defining and developing a new concept of Urban Wellbeing tied to the broader concept of Urban Health Resilience. This recognizes the connections between the physical characteristics of the urban environment (including assets and deficits) and human health (including both physical and psychological health). The PULSE concept of Urban Wellbeing refers to the interaction between the positive and negative experiences within cities (whether objective or subjective), and the individual and community practices of mobility and placemaking. This novel interpretation of Wellbeing focuses on the dynamic interplay between individual psychological characteristics and strengths, neighborhoods in which people live and work, and the capacity of individuals to respond to environmental and interpersonal stressors [6]. Within our population urban health model, the physical and social environments are understood as key drivers of Wellbeing. This prioritizes an integrated, or relational, approach to urban places and health equity, including population differences in Wellbeing. Central to this relational approach is the idea that place matters – that our health and wellbeing are shaped by the characteristics of the settings where we live and work, and these environments are in turn shaped by our health-related actions and behaviours. Several recent studies have highlighted this important dynamic. Using data from the English Longitudinal Study of Aging, Hamer and Shankar [7] found that individuals who hold more negative perceptions of their neighbourhood report less positive Wellbeing, and experience a greater decline in Wellbeing over time.

Of course, place itself can have a profound impact on our Wellbeing.

3.1 Urban Resilience and Wellbeing

In PULSE, we contextualize wellbeing within a model of urban resilience:

Urban resilience refers to the ability of an urban system - and all its constituent socio-ecological and socio-technical networks across temporal and spatial scales – to maintain or rapidly return to desired functions in the face of a disturbance, to adapt to change, and to quickly transform systems that limit current or future adaptive capacity. In this definition, urban resilience is dynamic and offers multiple pathways to resilience (e.g., persistence, transition, and transformation). It recognizes the importance of temporal scale, and advocates general adaptability rather than specific adaptedness. The urban system is conceptualized as complex and adaptive, and it is composed of socio-ecological and socio-technical networks that extend across multiple spatial scales. Resilience is framed as an explicitly desirable state and, therefore, should be negotiated among those who enact it empirically.

Resilient urban neighborhoods can be broadly defined as those that have lower than expected premature mortality (measured via the Urban Health Indicators).

In PULSE, we define Urban Wellbeing as an integral component of Urban Resilience. Urban Wellbeing, in this context, refers to the individual traits and capacities to prepare for, respond to, and recover from the personal and interpersonal challenges encountered in cities. These challenges could include experiences of bias and exclusion, on the one hand, and exposure to under-resourced or polluted environments, on the other. Each of these challenges is associated with physiological and psychological stress at the individual and community level. Stress is, of course, antithetical to Wellbeing. Translating this concepts into data constructs two main instruments are available into PULSE architecture: the risk assessment models, previously described and the urban maps.

3.2 Urban Maps

The physical environment, socio-economic and cultural conditions, urban planning, available public or private services and leisure facilities are some of the factors that can have an effect on a person's health. Hence, an interest in the study of geographical patterns of health-related phenomena has increased in recent years. Within this context, maps have been demonstrated to be a useful tool for showing the spatial distribution of many types of data used in public health in a visual and concise manner [13, 14]. For example, it permits the study of general geographical patterns in health data and identifying specific high-risk locations. An example of these maps in PULSE are the personal exposure maps. Personal exposure is a concept from the epidemiological science to quantify the amount of pollution that each individual is exposed to, as a consequence of the living environment, habits etc.

Personal exposure has been obtained matching the data from the dense network of low-cost sensors and the informations on habits coming from the PulsAIR app. Following the sampling rate of the sensors the data has been calculated.

Figure 3 shows a map for the personal exposure to PM10 with an hourly frequency.

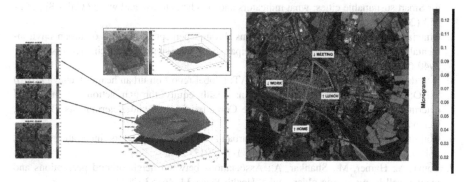

Fig. 3. Personal exposure map to PM10

Furthermore using the GPS tracks from the PulsAIR app, FitBit and the personal exposure, an estimate of inhaled pollutant has been obtain in association to three classes of movement by the speed of body translation; standing, walking and running, considering the breaths per minute and the air volume per breath [15].

Personal exposure result has been also traced into exposure paths as in Fig. 3: a time-lapse of 1 min correspond to a dot movement line.

4   Conclusions

The multivariate data driven approach of PULSE gives an example of a new conception of health and wellness, not only focused on individual health status, but also on the relationship between individual and environment. Such vision can be also directed toward the definition of "planetary health" provided by "The Lancet Contdown" [16]. The data driven approach pursuited in PULSE has surely given a great opportunity to implement such a vision, that maybe would not so immediatiate without possibility to integrate different sources of data.

Acknowledgments. This research was funded by the European Union's research and innovation program H2020 and is documented in grant No 727816. In particular, PULSE was funded under the call H2020-EU-3.1.5 in the topic SCI-PM-18-2016 - Big Data Supporting Public Health Policies.

More information on: www.project-pulse.eu.

References

1. EEA (European Environment Agency): Air Quality in Europe 2019 EEA Report No 10/2019, Copenhagen (2019)
2. Aapo, H., Peter Bosch, P., Airaksinen, M.: Comparative analysis of standardized indicators for Smart sustainable cities: what indicators and standards to use and when? Cities **89**, 141–153 (2019)
3. Ottaviano, M., et al.: Empowering citizens through perceptual sensing of urban environmental and health data following a participative citizen science approach. Sensors **19**(13), 2940 (2019)
4. World Health Organization - UN HABITAT: Global report on urban health. Geneva (2016)
5. WHO: Closing the gap in a generation: health equity through action on the social determinants of health. Final report of the Commission on Social Determinants of Health, Geneva (2008)
6. Corburn, J., Cohen, A.K.: Why we need urban health equity indicators: integrating science, policy, and community. PLoS Med. **9**(8), 1–6 (2012)
7. Toma, A., Hamer, M., Shankar, A.: Associations between neighborhood perceptions and mental well-being among older adults. Health Place **34**, 46–53 (2015)
8. Fisher, G.G., Lindsay, H.R.: Overview of the health and retirement study and introduction to the special issue. Work Aging Retire. **4**(1), 1–9 (2018)
9. Jenny, N.S., et al.: Biomarkers of key biological pathways in CVD. Global Heart **11**(3), 327–336 (2016)
10. Stern, M.P., Williams, K., Haffner, S.M.: Identification of persons at high risk for type 2 diabetes mellitus: do we need the oral glucose tolerance test? Ann. Intern Med. **136**(8), 575–581 (2002)
11. Kahn, H.S., Cheng, Y.J., Thompson, T.J., Imperatore, G., Gregg, E.W.: Two risk-scoring systems for predicting incident diabetes mellitus in U.S. adults aged 45 to 64 years. Ann. Intern Med. **150**(11), 741–751 (2009)
12. Di Camillo, B., et al.: HAPT2D: high accuracy of prediction of T2D with a model combining basic and advanced data depending on availability. Eur. J. Endocrinol. **178**(4), 331–341 (2018)
13. Waller, L.A., Gotway, C.A.: Applied Spatial Statistics for Public Health Data. Wiley, Great Britain (2004)
14. Esnaola, S., Montoya, I., Calvo, M., Aldasoro, E., Audícana, C., Ruiz, R., et al.: Atlas de mortalidad en áreas pequeñas de la CAPV (1996–2003). Donostia-San Sebastián. Servicio Central de Publicaciones del Gobierno Vasco (2010)

15. Vito, D., et al.: Dynamic spatio-temporal health impact assessments using geolocated population-based data: the PULSE project. In: Proceeding of World Clean Air Conference 2019, pp. 654–673. Turkish National Committee for Air Pollution Research, Istanbul (2019)

16. Watts, N., et al.: The lancet countdown on health and climate change: from 25 years of inaction to a global transformation for public health. The Lancet **391**(10120), 581–630 (2018)

ForeSight - An AI-driven Smart Living Platform, Approach to Add Access Control to openHAB

Jochen Bauer[1]([✉]) [ID], Michael Hechtel[1], Christoph Konrad[1][ID],
Martin Holzwarth[1], Hilko Hoffmann[2], Thomas Feld[3], Sven Schneider[1][ID],
Ingo Zinnikus[2], Andreas Mayr[1][ID], and Jörg Franke[1]

[1] Institute for Factory Automation and Production Systems,
Friedrich-Alexander-University Erlangen-Nürnberg,
Egerlandstraße 7-9, 91058 Erlangen, Germany
jochen.bauer@faps.fau.de
[2] Deutsches Forschungszentrum für Künstliche Intelligenz GmbH,
Stuhlsatzenhausweg 3, 66123 Saarbrücken, Germany
[3] Strategion GmbH, Albert-Einstein-Straße 1, 49076 Osnabrück, Germany

Abstract. We created an approach for a smart living platform called ForeSight which consists of different modules: a service engineering module, a Web of Things (WoT)-based Internet of Things (IoT) module and an artificial intelligence (AI) component. This paper describes how openHAB, a smart home middleware, is extended to fulfill platform requirements related to a successful interaction with the IoT module of ForeSight, more precisely, to add identity and access management (IAM) to openHAB and comply with European privacy laws.

Keywords: Architecture · Artificial intelligence · openHAB · Platform · Privacy · Smart home · Smart living

1 Motivation

In recent years, the smart home market has proven its relevance [1,2]. If all 43 million households in Germany were equipped with smart home technology by 2030 with an average value of 3,000 EUR, this would result in a market potential of 129 billion EUR [3]. For other European countries, the situation seems to be similar [4]. Beyond smart homes, the term "smart living" ranges over various areas that are separated today concerning energy management, health and home automation [5]. The smart home is a core element in a connected world, as well as smart city and smart grid [6]. This will lead to more comfort, better assistance and increased safety and security as well as improved resource efficiency and reduced overall costs. The base for such advanced opportunities is the intense usage of AI.

Supported by German Federal Ministry for Economic Affairs and Energy.

M. Jmaiel et al. (Eds.): ICOST 2020, LNCS 12157, pp. 432–440, 2020.
https://doi.org/10.1007/978-3-030-51517-1_40

The ForeSight project follows the approach of an open platform which integrates AI-based solutions, interoperability, context-awareness and established building automation technologies into a flexible multi-domain and multi-component system ranging across different manufacturers and industries [6]. Furthermore, ForeSight will provide the flexibility to add new services and offers corresponding tools for service providers. In Europe, privacy and security issues play an important role [7]. Data needs to be handled carefully. To ensure this, ForeSight will create an adequate IAM mechanism and be as restrictive as possible to ensure privacy concerns, i.e. we will try to keep data stored locally, whenever it is possible.

2   State of the Art

These days, systems for energy management, classic smart home use cases like lighting as well as health applications exist. To optimize residents' benefits it is useful to combine these three domains and make them controllable by one single platform, which allows domain and vendor independence. In other areas like manufacturing industry reference architecture models have been established to visualize needs to improve interoperability in general. We adapted these models like RAMI 4.0 [8] to the smart living domain (see Fig. 1). Accordingly, we strive to enable an interoperability level on the business model layer.

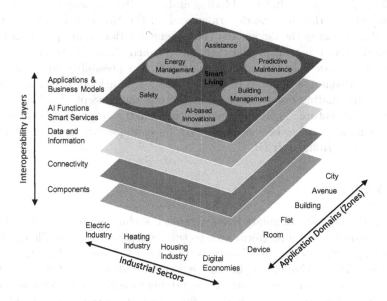

Fig. 1. Proposed reference architectural model of smart living.

After describing necessities of interoperability, privacy and security, we need to introduce the concepts of IAM to ensure a solid base for reaching our goals.

There are four topics when it comes to IAM, which need to be considered. In a first step, the user who wants to access the system needs to identify himself (Identification). This claim needs to be verified (Authentication) by the system. Subsequently, it is necessary to grant appropriate rights to the user (Authorisation). For many systems and domains, it is mandatory to log different system events for ensuring auditing, monitoring or tracing (Accountability) [9].

To carry out a target group-oriented authorization, four basic concepts are considered. The first is identity-based access control (IBAC), which provides an access control list for each object, which in turn contains all subjects that are allowed to access the corresponding object [10]. The second concept, role-based access control (RBAC), provides different read and write permissions (generally: transactions) for different user groups [11]. Attribute-based access control (ABAC) defines a similar approach to RBAC, except that users are granted rights based on certain attributes of subjects and objects and environmental conditions [12]. The last type, capability-based access control (CapBAC) turns the rights management the other way around and grants rights based on the token that the user hands over at login [13]. This token then contains an indication of the possibilities a user has on the platform.

openHAB is a smart home middleware, so it is possible to control different systems in one single graphical user interface (GUI) or app. The software uses specific components to offer an abstraction layer for all of its subsystems. To connect to a third-party system like Homematic [14], it is necessary to create a binding. After activating the binding it is possible to search for accessible objects, here for the Homematic bridge and all the Homematic devices, e.g. a switch. The signal of the device and the triggered action from openHAB to the Homematic device is transported through so-called channels. To create a GUI a sitemap is needed. In the sitemap file there is a possibility to name items. An item is a concrete instance of a thing and a channel can be mapped to an item. For automating event-driven tasks there is the concept of rules, a script-like openHAB feature. There are several other smart living middleware systems or promising approaches besides openHAB, for example, universAAL, HomeKit and Connected Home over IP.

3   Challenges

To fulfill the idea of our smart living reference architectural model (see Fig. 1) it is necessary to offer a platform architecture which is able to handle upcoming requests as flexible as possible. The corresponding IAM needs to be considered in all systems. This is challenging because existing middleware systems need to be used to connect to different smart home systems to achieve an adequate market penetration. Moreover, as mentioned before, security interferes with comfort, so new concepts need to be evaluated in regard to user acceptance.

openHAB does not yet provide access rights for different user groups and thus does not offer authentication for end-users, besides developer-addressed possibilities. Therefore, openHAB needs to be extended. In addition, there are three variants that allow access from outside on the basis of an encrypted connection. The most secure option is to set up virtual private networks (VPN) to access your system via the router. The second option is to use the specially designed myopenHAB cloud, which can be accessed like various other cloud platforms via a tunnel connection. The third option is to set up a reverse proxy before openHAB, which in turn uses authentication and security certificates to ensure that the smart living system is protected from unauthorized external access. Such remote access strategies are important for several use cases like predictive maintenance scenarios in smart buildings.

4   Approach

ForeSight offers a flexible mechanism to handle requests, i.e. it is possible that requests are handled in the local network or, if necessary, will be forwarded to cloud services to increase performance. The core of ForeSight's architecture approach is the thinking object (TO) - a device or group of devices which offers a specific service to the user or other TOs (see Fig. 2). There are three main modules, which are interacting to fulfill the system needs, here a service engineering module for service providers, e.g. a company of the housing industry, and an AI module to handle requests for computationally intensive operations, e.g. visually based object identification, and an IoT module to connect to different smart home middleware systems, e.g. openHAB, which will be able to connect to many different vendor-specific systems. Summing up, ForeSight is connecting to openHAB to ensure interoperability on a syntactic level. Besides, ForeSight will enable the usage of different smart home middleware systems like universAAL as well.

It will be necessary and helpful for TOs if attributes like context sensitiveness, interoperability, semantic information, data management capabilities, rights management, security and privacy are available. In addition, it is helpful to create a digital twin of the corresponding building and another digital twin of the user to predict their specific behavior. As mentioned before it needs to be considered to handle requests exclusively in the local network. Therefore, we create strategies to adapt cloud-based approaches to edge computing as well, especially methods like preprocessing and device performance enhancements. To verify our concepts different use cases, e.g. smart door and smart kitchen, will be implemented. To prove that our approaches are independent of one technology we are using a minimum of two different technology stacks for each use case, e.g. a common router-based stack (internet router and a smart home middleware), and a smart meter gateway based technology stack (see Fig. 2). First, the use cases will be implemented in laboratories and afterwards in real-world environments like Future Living Berlin [15].

To describe our approach more precisely we want to follow a request through our ForeSight platform. The service provider is a company in the housing industry. When a new tenant rents a flat, a picture and fingerprints of the tenant are captured and this data is stored in a database and transferred to the IoT and

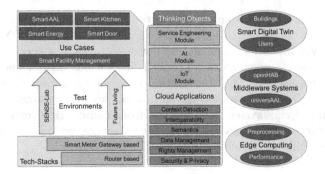

Fig. 2. Simplified architecture of the ForeSight Cloud Platform with its three main modules (service engineering, AI module and IoT module).

AI module, so that the available smart door can be updated with new data. The tenant wants to enter the door and uses his fingerprints and the camera at the door captures a small video sequence. This video is sent to the AI module and the IoT module will receive a reply if the person is verified. To ensure interoperability there is a WoT-based data model available in the IoT module and a corresponding openHAB connection that both systems can communicate with each other to transfer semantic information. Each time there is a data transfer from one module to another module, a privacy and security filter will be applied to ensure that only authorized actions will occur.

This paper focuses on the IoT module, so the AI module and service engineering module will not be described in detail. The AI module of ForeSight offers so-called base services which are important for common AI use cases like object identification. Otherwise, there are complex use cases of the housing industry like a tenant change process. Such use cases benefit enormously by intense AI support. To simplify service engineering for service providers we will offer GUI-driven configuration tools, that companies are able to describe their digital business models easily. The service provider does neither need to consider technical details of the AI module nor the IoT module or the complexity of different smart home middleware systems like openHAB.

As stated before, openHAB needs to be extended to fulfill an adequate IAM mechanism. In doing so, we decided to use a sidecar approach (see Fig. 3). That means, openHAB is handling its core functions and as a sidecar, we use a proxy server and the tool Auth-router, so common logging functions and configuration options will be available for the system by using these third party tools. The sidecar approach will simplify the consideration of existing systems, for example, logging and tracing.

Besides adequate logging functionality, user and group management need to be addressed as well. We decided to use RBAC as a strategy to add IAM to openHAB. RBAC is minimizing configuration effort during the system's maintenance because necessary changes can be done by changing one specific role or group. This mechanism can be understood by tenants, which is important

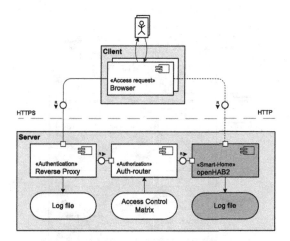

Fig. 3. Sidecar approach: Two external tools, here Proxy Server and Auth Router will extend the openHAB environment by enabling relevant services, for example, logging and tracing.

for accepting such safety-relevant systems in their own home. Furthermore, it is possible to combine this strategy with the sidecar approach. Additionally, RBAC does not need to change openHAB's core data model, so it is possible to extend openHAB by developing such a binding. We created this binding, which offers Auth-router functionality to the user openHAB's backend. The procedure for creating a user is shown below (see Fig. 4). For openHAB it is then possible to generate one specific sitemap for each role and so IAM of systems' resources are ensured. The routing ensures that no user can access sitemaps which are generated for different roles. Our openHAB binding considers user management as well.

ForeSight considers the concept of TOs that combine aspects of three research areas: smart environments (i.e. the physical infrastructure such as sensors, actuators and networks), ambient intelligence (an intelligent network of sensors, radio modules, and computers to proactively but sensibly support people in their lives [16]), AI (agent systems, machine learning techniques). TOs represent physical as well as virtual objects. They aggregate and abstract sensor data of devices to deduce value-added services to users. Several TOs such as sensors, actuators, and lighting in a building can be combined to execute a coordinated activity, e.g. to guide residents through a building.

5   Implementation

We developed an openHAB extension to connect to the WoT-based IoT module of ForeSight [17]. This extension will be continuously improved and maintained. Beside the WoT binding we added user management support for openHAB by generating and calling exact one sitemap for each role and restricting the access

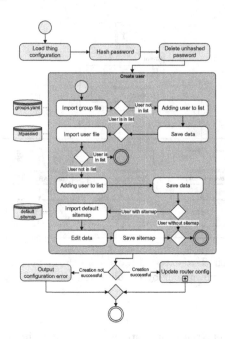

Fig. 4. openHAB Auth Binding - create user procedure.

for non-authorized users. The ForeSight platform with all of its submodules is currently being developed until the end of 2022.

6 Discussion

Challenges of semantics and interoperability have long been known in the era of the IoT, especially if different subsystems should work together flawlessly without an overlying de-facto standard. Our approach of trying to offer a WoT-based cloud application, where an AI module and different smart home middleware systems are allowed to connect seems promising for us: We are confident to fulfill all requirements European laws are demanding. Furthermore, we think that it is possible to create a holistic IAM from cloud-driven systems which are often offering CapBAC strategies to smart home middleware systems, that need to be extended in relation to their specific software architectural patterns. Therefore, we need to create strategies to integrate other smart home middleware systems besides openHAB as well, either advanced approaches like universAAL or existing systems like HomeKit or Z-Wave. It is important for ForeSight that lots of existing smart home middleware systems are becoming part of ForeSight, so that ForeSight can achieve its goal to play an important role in the smart living domain.

Extending openHAB by RBAC was helpful to improve access control for tenants in that chosen scenario for a first proof of concept. Hopefully, we will be able to switch from the sidecar approach to a native openHAB solution. Currently, the openHAB developer community seems to work on such strategic ideas for the upcoming major update (version 3.0).

References

1. IDC Worldwide: Quarterly Smart Home Device Tracker (2019). https://www.idc. com/getdoc.jsp?containerId=prUS44971219. Accessed 18 Feb 2020
2. MarketsandMarkets: Smart Home Market by Product (Lighting Control, Security & Access Control, HVAC, Entertainment, Smart Speaker, Home Healthcare, Smart Kitchen, Home Appliances, and Smart Furniture), Software & Services, and Region - Global Forecast to 2024 (2019). https://www.marketsandmarkets. com/Market-Reports/smart-homes-and-assisted-living-advanced-technologie- and-global-market-121.html. Accessed 18 Feb 2020
3. ZVEI: Zukunftsmarkt Smart Living. Smart Home Haushalte in Deutschland (2019)
4. Statista: Smart Home - Deutschland (2019). https://de.statista.com/outlook/279/ 137/smart-home/deutschland. Accessed 18 Feb 2020
5. Bauer, J., Kettschau, A., Michl, M., Bürner, J., Franke, J.: Die intelligente Wohnung als Baustein im Internet der Dinge. In: Weidner, R., Redlich, T. (eds.) Erste Transdiziplinäre Konferenz zum Thema Technische Unterstützungssysteme, die die Menschen wirklich wollen., Hamburg, pp. 298–307 (2014)
6. Bauer, J., et al.: ForeSight - platform approach for enabling ai-based services for smart living. In: Pagán, J., Mokhtari, M., Aloulou, H., Abdulrazak, B., Cabrera, M.F. (eds.) ICOST 2019. LNCS, vol. 11862, pp. 204–211. Springer, Cham (2019). https://doi.org/10.1007/978-3-030-32785-9_19
7. Zibuschka, J., Nofer, M., Zimmermann, C., Hinz, O.: Users' preferences concerning privacy properties of assistant systems on the internet of things. In: American Conference on Information Systems (AMCIS 2019) (2019, forthcoming)
8. Deutsches Institut für Normung e.V. (DIN): DIN SPEC 91345:2016–04: Referenzarchitekturmodell Industrie 4.0 (RAMI4.0). Beuth (2016)
9. Eckert, C.: IT-Sicherheit: Konzepte-Verfahren-Protokolle. Walter de Gruyter (2013)
10. Hu, V.C., Ferraiolo, D., Kuhn, R., Schnitzer, A., et al.: Guide to Attribute Based Access Control (ABAC) Definition and Considerations: National Institute of Standards and Technology (2014)
11. Ferraiolo, D., Kuhn, D.R., Chandramouli, R.: Role-Based Access Control. Artech House, Boston (2003)
12. Hu, V.C., Kuhn, D.R., Ferraiolo, D.F.: Attribute-based access control. Computer 48(2), 85–88 (2015)
13. Rotondi, D., Piccione, S.: Managing access control for things: a capability based approach. In: Proceedings of the 7th International Conference on Body Area Networks, pp. 263–268 (2012)
14. Heinle, S.: Heimautomation mit KNX, DALI, 1-Wire und Co. Rheinwerk Computing, Bonn (2016)
15. Eberhard, B.: Future Living Berlin Website (2020). https://future-living-berlin. com/. Accessed 20 Feb 2020

16. Augusto, J.C.: Ambient intelligence: the confluence of ubiquitous/pervasive computing and artificial intelligence. In: Schuster, A.J. (ed.) Intelligent Computing Everywhere, pp. 213–234. Springer, London (2007). https://doi.org/10.1007/978-1-84628-943-9_11

17. Schneider, S.: Mozilla WebThing Binding openHAB Developer Community Webpage (2020). https://community.openhab.org/t/mozilla-webthings-binding/92782. Accessed 20 Feb 2020

Author Index

Printed in the United States
By Bookmasters